The Ziggurat Model

A Framework for Designing Comprehensive Strategies and Supports for Autistic Individuals

Updated and expanded with the Underlying Characteristics Checklist for Early Intervention (UCC-EI) – backed by a comprehensive case study. The Ziggurat Model, for individuals across the spectrum and across the lifespan, is now even more fine-tuned for early intervention.

Release 2.1

Ruth Aspy, Ph.D., and Barry G. Grossman, Ph.D.

Foreword by Gary B. Mesibov, Ph.D.

The Ziggurat Group
www.zigguratgroup.com

The Ziggurat Group

© 2022 Ziggurat Group

www.zigguratgroup.com

Publisher's Cataloging-in-Publication

Aspy, Ruth.
Grossman, Barry G.

The ziggurat model : a framework for designing comprehensive strategies and supports for autistic individuals / Ruth Aspy and Barry G. Grossman; foreword by Gary B. Mesibov. -- Rel. 2.1 [4th ed.] -- Dallas, Texas: Ziggurat Group, ©2022.

p. ; cm.

ISBN: 979-8-9858045-0-8
Revision of the 3rd ed. (2011) with updated references and expansion of forms and case studies to include early childhood.
Includes bibliographical references.

1. Autistic people--Rehabilitation. 2. Autism--Treatment.

3. Asperger's syndrome--Patients--Rehabilitation. 4. Asperger's syndrome--Treatment. 5. Autism spectrum disorders--Patients--Rehabilitation. 6. Behavioral assessment. I. Grossman, Barry G. II. Title.

RC553.A88 A87 2022
616.85/882--dc22

Disclaimer: Content in this book is provided for informational purposes only and is not intended to serve as professional, mental health, or medical advice. You acknowledge that this information is provided "as is" for general information only. It should not relied upon as a substitute for consulting with qualified professionals.

This book is designed in Papyrus and Stone Serif.

Printed in the United States of America.

Dedication

For our families – for your love – and especially for putting up with us

**For those on the autism spectrum – with appreciation
for all that you offer and all that you endure**

Acknowledgments

When the Ziggurat Model was created, Ruth was the first to say, "Do you know what we have here? We've got a book." We could never have anticipated what those few words would set in motion, however this book could not have come about without the support of our family, friends, and colleagues.

Beginning to put our ideas on paper was a daunting task. We greatly appreciate the assistance of Lissa Cone, Michael Goldman, and Charlie Ornstein, who served as our early editors and helped to clarify our thoughts and develop our voice. As our book proposal was nearing completion, we had the good fortune of meeting Brenda Smith Myles. Brenda was enthusiastic from the moment she learned about the project. She encouraged us to stop obsessing and submit the proposal. We have been members of Brenda's fan club for some time. Through this process, we have become even more impressed by her brilliance, kindness, and energy. We are honored to have Brenda as a mentor and a friend.

Moving from the book proposal to completed manuscript has been a long endeavor. We appreciate the patience and guidance of our skilled editor and advisor, Kirsten McBride. Vivian Strand has taken our sketches and crude illustrations and turned them into art.

As we developed the Ziggurat Model, we found Eric Schopler's iceberg analogy to be an eloquent way of illustrating the importance of the autism that underlies behavioral concerns. We built on this analogy to develop the ABC-I. We had the good fortune to briefly correspond with Dr. Schopler. He was encouraging and kind. Eric Schopler was a pioneer in the field, and his passing in 2006 was a great loss. Gary Mesibov, who has provided leadership alongside of Dr. Schopler, graciously agreed to write the foreword to the book.

Writing this book coincided with a rare opportunity to experience a bond of trust and support with coworkers who shared our passion for helping those with special needs and who in the process became like extended family. Joanie Cassity, Karen Fischer, Susan Jamieson, and Ann McKeever provided leadership and set the tone of kindness. Ann also generously shared the sanctuary of her home and friendly, wagging tails to provide comic relief. It seemed that each time we met a milestone in this process, we were in Ann's home. Through sharing knowledge in their specialty areas, Nicole Brin, Kim Davis, Angela Medrano, Sherri Millington, Sarah Welbourne, and Penny Woods helped to refine the Underlying Characteristics Checklist.

We are fortunate to have friends who also happen to be experts in the field of autism spectrum disorders. Each has contributed at unique points along the way. Debra Gomez helped to make the explanation of the levels of the Ziggurat more consistent and understandable. Amy Bixler Coffin was the first to read the manuscript in its entirety and the first professional to apply the model based on the written text. Her feedback was both encouraging and enlightening. Throughout, Ashley De Ville's expertise in interventions for children with autism enhanced our ideas. She showed endless patience to two crazed writers. Ashley is a treasured friend. Kristi Sakai offered us a new perspective on our lives. She saw an importance to this work and encouraged us to persevere. She is an inspiration to us.

The Ziggurat illustrates the importance of a solid foundation. Family is our foundation, without which this work could never have been possible. We greatly appreciate their patience and love. Angie, Kevin, William, Beth, Sarah, and Bekah provided musical interludes that gave us something special to look forward to. They, along with Lissa, Daniel, and Lauren, supported us by keeping us in their hearts and thoughts. Virgie has been a touchstone – providing us with perspective, comic relief, and moral support. She is wise in areas in which we are clueless and patiently coached us. Jan and Fred (aka Mom and Dad), Shari, Charlie, Miles, David, Kimberly, Rosie, Ashley, and Joshua helped to re-center us. They nurtured, cheered, advised, asked for constant updates, and pushed us towards the finish line – yes, we are finally done!

As we now transition into version 2.1, it amazing how much can change. We would like to thank some additional special people in our lives including Stephanie, Bobby, and Benji for their patience and kindness along with Kevin Miller who helped to make this possible.

Our thanks to those who have made this project a reality.

Notes on Release 2.1

Since the first edition of the Ziggurat Model was published in 2007, we have seen some amazing outcomes. Parents and professionals have written to tell us how the Ziggurat has made a difference in the lives of autistic individuals. Moreover, we are seeing systems change through the use of the model. The Ziggurat Model has been adopted district-wide, agency-wide, and across states and provinces. Universities are using the Ziggurat Model to prepare future educators, speech-language pathologists, and other professionals. Professionals currently in practice have been equipped to use the model through professional development programs. The Ziggurat Model has been helpful in our own work. We are pleased that others are now "Zigging" and learning of its many benefits. While a seemingly simple concept, the framework of the Ziggurat Model helps to ensure comprehensive program design and to move away from an ineffective piecemeal approach.

We have learned much about the Ziggurat Model through our own work and through teaching others to use the model. The field has also evolved since the first edition of this book with an increased awareness of the power of early intervention as well as increased understanding of the impact of autism spectrum disorder (ASD) on individuals who are higher functioning.

Release 2.1 reflects these changes. One of the newest features is the addition of the Underlying Characteristics Checklist – Early Intervention. While the Ziggurat Model has always been appropriate for use with individuals across the lifespan, we saw a growing need to develop a tool that reflects the unique needs of the 3-month to 72-month age group. The UCC-EI offers a necessary alternative to the traditional approach of identifying very young children who are in need of services based on the use of developmental checklists alone – too many children have been missed; furthermore, use of this tool will assist in identifying targets for intervention beyond the strictly developmental. Release 2.1 includes an early childhood case study in Chapter 3.

The field is always changing. A few short years ago, we saw the merging of diagnostic subtypes into a single autism spectrum. Females with autism, a group near and dear to our hearts, are under-identified and misunderstood. At last, there is a growing understanding of their unique needs but much work remains. We have worked to include autistic people across gender and across the spectrum. Additionally, the increased awareness of the overlap between autism and catatonia is reflected herein. Last, terminology has changed as the important voices of people on the spectrum are being heard. We have done our best to respect these voices.

We hope that the group of people who are "Zigging" will continue to grow for the benefit of individuals across the spectrum.

Kindly,

Ruth Aspy and Barry G. Grossman

Table of Contents

Foreword

It is a pleasure for me to introduce this impressive work by Ruth Aspy and Barry Grossman. The authors present their Ziggurat Model as unique, a claim made by many authors about their work, but not usually fully realized. In this case, however, I think the authors do not overstate their case, having created something original, thoughtful, practical, and, indeed, unique.

I don't think I have ever written a foreword for a book before without personally knowing the authors, but I was drawn to this work for several reasons. First, when you read this book, you are quickly convinced that the authors really know children and how they think and learn, especially children with disabilities. Second, the authors have clearly broadened their clinical knowledge by reading a lot of relevant literature and assimilating it impressively. Third, the authors have a creative way of integrating what they know, what they have read, and what others have done in presenting a genuinely creative and unique synthesis. Finally, the authors have the practitioner in mind and offer ideas that will be readily applicable and very helpful.

In addition to these many assets, I like the way the authors understand that the ultimate skill in working with children with disabilities is in the process of developing the interventions. They neither oversimplify by suggesting that cookbook strategies or simple techniques will work, nor do they make the process of teaching students with autism spectrum disorder so complicated that few readers will be able to trudge through their book and find anything that they can understand well enough to apply. Instead, they have dealt with ASD in all of its complexity but have generated a process that is neither too simple-minded to work nor too complex to apply. Their excellent balance is a great asset, along with their thorough understanding of their subject matter and their creativity in assimilating a variety of approaches.

Although I have not personally met Ruth Aspy or Barry Grossman, I have developed great respect for their knowledge and clinical instincts for educating students with ASD. Reading their book makes me really want to meet them because they obviously understand this field and have some unique and creative ideas for developing successful intervention programs. I think that a wide range of parents and professionals will also want to meet these talented authors after reading this book to share more of their knowledge and to express their appreciation for this excellent contribution to the field.

> – Gary B. Mesibov, Ph.D.
> Professor and Director of Division TEACCH

Introduction

The Ziggurat Model is unique. While it is easy to find volumes of information describing specific interventions, it is difficult to find information on how to develop an intervention plan. This book presents a process and framework for designing comprehensive intervention plans for autistic individuals of all ages.

As psychologists, we are often asked questions such as, "How can I get my child to stop interrupting conversations?" or "How do I know which intervention to use?" These questions imply that there is a single response that could resolve a specific concern and that a given strategy is appropriate for all autistic people. It is no surprise that parents and professionals feel confused when tried-and-true behavior techniques do not work. Further, they become frustrated because well-established interventions do not result in long-term gains.

We believe that it is shortsighted to assume that a pervasive disorder can be effectively treated with any single approach. We have discovered that even evidence-based interventions may fail if the stage is not properly set through the use of multiple interventions targeted specifically at an individual. Thus, a "piecemeal" approach will, at best, provide temporary or partial improvement. Furthermore, interventions must *address characteristics that underlie autism itself.*

The Ziggurat Model is unique. It is designed to address true needs or underlying deficits that result in social, emotional, and behavioral concerns. As such, the model is designed to help parents, teachers, speech pathologists, psychologists, occupational therapists, counselors, school administrators, autism consultants, and others to design in-depth, individualized interventions that work with this population.

This book is intended for readers of all skill levels. Novices to the field will learn the characteristics of autism and be introduced to a variety of research-based approaches to addressing the needs of this population. More advanced readers will gain a deeper understanding of the complex behavioral manifestations of this condition and expand their knowledge of intervention tools.

COMPONENTS OF THE ZIGGURAT MODEL

The Intervention Ziggurat is the centerpiece of the Ziggurat Model. It contains five levels in a hierarchical structure. Each level represents an area that must be addressed in order for an intervention plan to be comprehensive. Further, each level contributes to the effectiveness of the other levels. Building from the foundation of the Ziggurat, these levels are:

- Sensory and Biological
- Reinforcement
- Structure and Visual/Tactile Supports
- Task Demands and Positive Environment
- Skills to Teach

If needs on each level of the Ziggurat are not addressed, the intervention will not be as effective, and skills will not develop. As skills increase, less intensive interventions will be required on the lower levels of the Ziggurat because the teaching of new skills allows for growth and makes a permanent difference for the person on the spectrum.

The underlying needs and characteristics related to autism must be addressed – this is a key premise of the Ziggurat Model. The Ziggurat Model includes three assessment tools – the Underlying Characteristics Checklist (UCC), the Individual Strengths and Skills Inventory (ISSI), and the ABC-Iceberg (ABC-I) – designed to identify these underlying factors. The UCC is a descriptive instrument that can be completed by multiple respondents and that provides a "snapshot" of how autism is expressed for an individual in the following areas: Social; Restricted Patterns of Behavior, Interests and Activities; Communication; Sensory Differences; Cognitive Differences; Motor Differences; Emotional Vulnerability; and Medical or Biological Factors. The ISSI builds from the UCC to identify an individual's strengths in each UCC area. The ABC-I incorporates a traditional functional behavior assessment and helps to illustrate patterns of behavior.

The Ziggurat Worksheet, a guide for the intervention planning process, is also detailed throughout the book. Use of the Ziggurat Worksheet ensures that an intervention is comprehensive. In brief, a complete intervention plan addresses all five levels of the Ziggurat, the underlying needs identified through the use of the UCC, and provides for intervention at three points – antecedent, behavior, and consequence.

STRENGTHS OF THE ZIGGURAT MODEL

The Ziggurat Model was designed to simplify a complex process. Parents and professionals will find the framework of the Ziggurat Model to be a guide in developing more thorough and effective interventions.

The Ziggurat Model is a valuable resource for public school professionals who must remain in compliance with federal and state guidelines. Specifically, recent trends in special education law emphasize the use of scientifically based research approaches along with a focus on response to intervention (RTI). Additionally, there is a strong push for incorporating positive behavioral interventions and supports (PBIS) based on a functional behavioral assessment. The Ziggurat Model is consistent with these practices.

The Ziggurat Model may be used alone or in combination with another model – the Comprehensive Autism Planning System (CAPS; Henry & Myles, 2007). Each of these models is strong, but together they are even stronger.

CAPS is a unique method of developing and implementing a meaningful program for an autistic individual. Its structure fosters consistent use of supports to ensure success as well as data collection to measure that success. Compatible with current trends in education, including NCLB, RTI, and SWPBS (school-wide positive behavioral support), CAPS is simple and easy to use (Henry & Myles, 2007).

First, this book outlines evidence-based interventions on each of the five levels of the Ziggurat. Additionally, the ABC-I tool incorporates a functional behavioral assessment that facilitates development of an individually designed intervention. The Ziggurat Model also emphasizes a proactive, positive approach by requiring reinforcement and antecedent-based interventions. Ongoing assessment allows for changes to the intervention plan at each level gauged on progress.

Finally, the Ziggurat Model promotes collaboration and communication among parents and professionals. The assessment tools are designed to incorporate the perspectives of multiple team members while ensuring that they work from the same reference point – the individual's underlying characteristics of autism. The Ziggurat Worksheet promotes collaboration by helping parents and professionals to understand their part in the larger intervention picture. Thus, through the use of the Ziggurat Model, the whole truly is greater than the sum of its parts.

This capacity to facilitate collaboration lends the Ziggurat Model to be an effective consultation tool. The model may be used throughout the consultation process (e.g., identification of concerns, assessment, development of intervention, monitoring and assessing progress) and can also be used to help evaluate an existing evaluation plan.

While the Ziggurat Model is designed to address the needs of all all autistic individuals, this book emphasizes the higher functioning population.

CHAPTER HIGHLIGHTS

- *The Ziggurat Model provides a process and framework for designing individualized, comprehensive intervention plans for individuals on the spectrum of all ages.*

- *The Intervention Ziggurat is the centerpiece of the Ziggurat Model and contains five levels in a hierarchical structure: (a) Sensory and Biological, (b) Reinforcement, (c) Structure and Visual/Tactile Supports, (d) Task Demands and Positive Environment, and (e) Skills to Teach.*

- *Each level of the Intervention Ziggurat impacts the others, and all levels must be addressed in order for an intervention plan to be comprehensive.*

- *A key premise of the Ziggurat Model is that the underlying needs and characteristics related to autism must be addressed.*

- *The Ziggurat Model includes three assessment tools to aid in identifying the underlying needs and characteristics related to autism: (a) the Underlying Characteristics Checklist (UCC), (b) the Individual Strengths and Skills Inventory (ISSI), and (c) the ABC-Iceberg (ABC-I).*

- *The Ziggurat Worksheet may be used to help ensure that an intervention plan is comprehensive.*

- *The Ziggurat Model helps to meet federal and state guidelines that focus on use of evidence-based practices, response to intervention, and positive behavioral interventions and supports based on functional behavior assessments.*

- *The Ziggurat Model promotes collaboration and communication among team members throughout all stages of the intervention process. The companion system, CAPS, facilitates implementation of intervention plans developed using the Ziggurat Model.*

---

[1] *The numerous case scenarios were created for the purpose of illustration and education. All individuals described in the scenarios are fictitious and based on our experience and imagination. Any similarity to real individuals is coincidental.*

1 The Context of Autism

*"I have learned you are never too
small to make a difference."*

– Greta Thunberg

Autism is a form of neurodiversity. Greta Thunberg, a woman on the spectrum, climate change activist, and Time magazine's person of the year 2019, notes that autism makes her different. She says her autism leads to her "superpower" and describes challenges based on the same neurology. The neurodiversity of autism is expressed differently in each individual. Understanding autism is essential. Too often, the needs of autistic people are addressed with the same approaches that are used with their neurotypical peers. Seeing each individual's autism – their challenges and strengths or superpowers – is the first step to improving the lives of individuals on the spectrum.

The chapter begins with a discussion of characteristics of autism followed by a few vignettes of individuals on the spectrum. It closes with a review of three theories used to explain behaviors observed in individuals on the autism spectrum: executive dysfunction, impaired theory of mind, and weak central coherence.

CHARACTERISTICS OF AUTISM

Autism is a complex neurodevelopmental condition that manifests differently in each individual; however, a pattern of characteristics is used to define this condition. While autism is often evident in early childhood, it may not be recognized until much later when the social and communication demands exceed current skills or coping ability. It is not uncommon for autism to first be recognized in adolescence as social-communication and other demands increase. A description of many of the characteristics and associated features of autism is provided below.

Social

One of the most common myths about autism is that individuals on the spectrum do not want to socialize with others. In reality, it is not uncommon to hear these children or adults express the desire to have friends. Nevertheless, they are often uncomfortable in social settings and tend to have difficulty making friends. Unwritten social codes, readily understood by others, often seem indecipherable to them. For example, while other children learn through experience that certain behaviors are seen as "gross" or "babyish" by their peers, autistic children may miss these lessons and persist in behaviors such as picking their noses, carrying cartoon character lunch boxes, or wanting to sit on their teachers' laps beyond an age where such behaviors are typical. This leads to a high risk of being taken advantage of or bullied and difficulty knowing if they are being teased.

Those who do not understand the social challenges often conclude that individuals on the spectrum are rude or "spoiled." This is especially true of those who are academically strong. It is assumed that if they are bright and talented in other areas, their social differences are by choice. A brief summary of common social differences is listed below.

Common Social Differences

- Appears unresponsive to others
- Has difficulty imitating simple movements and sounds
- Interacts with others as if they were objects (e.g., cause and effect)
- Has difficulty recognizing the feelings and thoughts of others (mindblindness)
- Uses poor eye contact or fails to orient to others
- Has difficulty maintaining personal space; physically intrudes on others
- Lacks tact or appears rude
- Has difficulty making or keeping friends
- Has difficulty joining an activity
- Is naïve, easily taken advantage of, or bullied
- Has difficulty understanding others' nonverbal communication
- Has difficulty understanding jokes

Restricted Patterns of Behavior, Interests, and Activities

There is a wide range of repetitive behaviors across the spectrum. Behaviors may include clapping, finger flicking, rocking, or fascination with movement or parts of objects or intense interests. For some on the spectrum, interests may appear different when compared with others the same age (e.g., playing with toddler toys or Barney at age 12), or may be unusual at any age (e.g., washing machines, traffic lights, construction equipment). Some may know countless details about their unusual interests and spend much time immersed in them. These preoccupations sometimes take precedence over social interaction or may become the dominant topic of conversation.

Repetitive behavior may also take the form of a strong need for sameness or, as Oliver Sacks put it, a "rage for order" (BBC, 1996). Autistic individuals tend to prefer things to be the same and function best in a predictable environment. Therefore, change from one activity or setting to another – transition – may cause distress. The distress caused by changes or transitions may be expressed through repetitive questions that may persist even though it is apparent that the questioner already knows the answer. Even changes that would seem to be positive, such as earning extra time on the computer or a surprise trip to get ice cream, may result in distress. Faced with unpredictable events, individuals with ASD often feel overwhelmed, and may engage in behaviors such as meltdowns, social withdrawal, self-injury or increased scripting. A brief summary of common differences in this area is listed below.

Common Behavioral Differences

- Stares intensely and for long periods of time at objects that move
- Seeks repetition of certain sounds, words, phrases, or music
- Expresses strong need for routine or "sameness"
- Expresses desire for repetition
- Has eccentric or intense preoccupations/absorption in own unique interests
- Asks repetitive questions
- Seems to be unmotivated by customary rewards
- Displays repetitive motor movements
- Has problems handling transition and change
- Has strong need for closure or difficulty stopping a task before it is completed

Communication

Communication differences have great impact on individuals on the spectrum. Limited ability to use and understand nonverbal forms of communication (facial expressions or body language) may have a devastating impact on daily interactions. Some may lack verbal expressive language while others, who have age-typical communication skills, may temporarily lose their ability to speak under stress. Additionally, deficits in the social aspects of language – pragmatics – can result in social blunders, such as interrupting others, persisting in talking after the listener has clearly become bored, or failing to distinguish if they are being laughed at or laughed with.

Common Communication Differences

- Has difficulty or makes no attempt to make clear requests
- Displays absence of a social smile or displays a "vacant" smile
- Has little or no speech
- Has difficulty expressing wants and needs
- Makes sounds or states words or phrases repeatedly [non-echolalic] (e.g., humming, "well actually")
- Displays immediate or delayed echolalia (reciting lines from movies, repeating an-other person's question or statements, repeating sounds, etc.)
- Interprets words or conversations literally/has difficulty understanding figurative language

- Has difficulty with rules of conversation (e.g., interrupting others, asking inappropriate questions, poor eye contact, difficulty maintaining conversation)
- Fails to initiate or respond to social greetings
- Has difficulty using gestures and facial expressions
- Has difficulty starting, joining, and/or ending a conversation
- Has difficulty asking for help
- Makes irrelevant comments
- Has difficulty expressing thoughts and feelings
- Speaks in an overly formal way
- Gives false impression of understanding more than actually does
- Talks incessantly
- Uses an advanced vocabulary
- Uses mechanical, "singsong" voice, or speech sounds that are unusual in other ways (e.g., prosody, cadence, tone)
- Has difficulty following instructions
- Has difficulty understanding language with multiple meanings, humor, sarcasm, synonyms
- Has difficulty talking about others' interests

Figurative Language

Individuals on the spectrum often have difficulty recognizing the use of figurative language. This was evident in a fifth-grade class when the teacher was showing her students several methods for solving the same math problem. She commented, "There is more than one way to skin a cat." Lissa, a girl on the spectrum in the class, shouted in an appalled and surprised voice, "Why would anyone want to skin a cat?"

This may be illustrated somewhat less delicately by the example of a third grader, Kevin, who hesitated while his teacher repeated several times a request for him to "flip off the overhead." Kevin eventually, and with reluctance, went to the overhead and shocked his teacher and classmates with his interpretation of her request.

ASSOCIATED FEATURES

Associated features are characteristics that are not necessary for a diagnosis but are often present in individuals diagnosed with ASD. The associated features discussed here include sensory, cognitive, and motor differences; and emotional vulnerability.

Sensory Differences

Abnormalities in processing incoming sensations such as sight, smell, sound, touch, taste, pain, and temperature are experienced by 70 to 80% of the ASD population (Harrison & Hare, 2004; Klintwall et al., 2011; Myles, Cook, Miller, Rinner, & Robbins, 2000; Volkmar, Cohen, & Paul, 1986). In some, the differences affect only one sensory area. In others, multiple senses are impacted. The differences may be expressed through hypersensitivity or hyposensitivity; distortions of perceptions; general sensory overload; difficulties using more than one sense at a time; or confusion of channels (such as visual responses to sounds) (Harrison & Hare; Klintwall et al.).

Sensory differences may make even routine daily experiences especially challenging. For those who are hypersensitive to sound, for example, the hum of an air conditioner or the chatting of peers may be distracting or even painful experiences. Hypersensitivity to touch may result in resistance to wearing shoes or perceiving an accidental tap from a peer as an intentional punch. Similarly, aversion to, or preoccupation with, smells may result in difficulty participating in routine activities. For example, the smell of chemicals in a department store may be so aversive that shopping becomes a miserable experience or the smell of perfume may lead to reluctance to interact with the person wearing it. Because of hypersensitivities, crowded or loud places are often especially stressful. Undersensitivity or hyposensitivity, may also be problematic. For example, failure to perceive pain may lead to lack of treatment for serious illness or injuries. Sensory abnormalities may result in an increase in the expression of social, communicative, and repetitive symptoms. A brief summary of common sensory differences is listed below.

Common Sensory Differences

- Often responds in a developmentally unusual/rigid manner to eating (e.g., avoids many textures, foods, and flavors)
- Frequently preoccupied with sensory exploration of objects (e.g., mouths, licks, chews, sniffs, holds close to eyes, rubs, squeezes, or uses object to make sounds)
- Responds in an unusual manner to pain (e.g., overreacts or seems unaware of an illness or injury)

- Responds in an unusual manner to light or color (e.g., focuses on shiny items, shadows, reflections, shows preference or strong dislike for certain colors)
- Responds in an unusual manner to temperature
- Responds in an unusual manner to smells (e.g., may comment on smells that others do not detect)
- Seeks activities that provide touch, pressure, or movement (e.g., swinging, hugging, pacing)
- Avoids activities that provide touch, pressure, or movement (e.g., resists wearing certain types of clothing, strongly dislikes to be dirty, resists hugs)
- Makes noises such as humming or singing frequently

Cognitive Differences

Many of the common characteristics of cognitive functioning in autism are outcomes of weak central coherence or deficits in executive function, which in turn are the result of physiological differences in the brain. These factors are discussed later in this chapter.

Most individuals diagnosed with autism show some unevenness in their cognitive abilities. It is estimated that savant characteristics (i.e., extraordinary skill in narrow area) occur in as many as one third of individuals on the spectrum (Hill & Frith, 2003; Howlin, Goode, Hatton, & Rutter, 2010), with many having IQs in the gifted range. However, those diagnosed with ASD often have some cognitive area in which skills have not developed to the expected level contrasted with other areas of their cognitive functioning at or above age level. This uneven cognitive profile often results in academic difficulties.

Children diagnosed with AS have a higher than normal rate of specific learning disabilities in math and reading (Reitzel & Szatmari, 2003). However, regardless of the presence or absence of a specific learning disability, most autistic students exhibit characteristics that make functioning in an academic setting challenging. For example, weaknesses in comprehension skills are often noted. Thus, the ability to recount facts and details tends to come with much greater facility than the ability to use those facts in abstract reasoning tasks. Generalization of skills – the ability to apply concepts in real-life contexts – is also a common challenge.

Further, the tendency to have narrow and intense areas of interest may impact academic performance in diverse ways. For example, it is possible for the range of interests to be so narrow that students do not engage in learning activities unless they pertain to their special preoccupations. In the most extreme cases, autistic individuals seem to escape into a private world of preoccupation and obsession. They may be so focused on their favorite subject that it is seemingly impossible to divert their attention to something else. Conversely, these intense interests may become an area of specialization and result in academic excellence.

Individuals on the spectrum often exhibit characteristics similar to those seen in Attention-Deficit/Hyperactivity Disorder (ADHD), such as inconsistent memory retrieval, poor problem-solving and organizational skills, and distractibility. Difficulty completing homework is an additional challenge often reported by the parents of children from both diagnostic groups. In fact, ADHD is often the first diagnosis received by individuals who eventually are diagnosed with ASD. In a study of children with an ASD and at least normal intelligence levels, 95% demonstrated significant symptoms of inattention and 75% met the criteria for a clinical diagnosis of ADHD (Sturm, Fernell, & Gillberg, 2004). A brief summary of common cognitive differences is listed below.

Common Cognitive Differences

- Does not generalize learned skills to new settings or demonstrate those skills consistently upon request
- Has difficulty maintaining engagement in meaningful self-directed activities (e.g., persists with activities but only within preferred interests)
- Has excellent memory for details (e.g., facts, stories, movies, songs)
- Displays extensive knowledge in narrow areas of interest
- Displays poor problem-solving skills
- Demonstrates poor organizational skills
- Withdraws into complex inner worlds/fantasizes often
- Is easily distracted by unrelated details – has difficulty knowing what is relevant or makes off-topic comments
- Displays weakness in reading comprehension despite strong word recognition ability
- Knows many facts and details but has difficulty with abstract reasoning (weak central coherence)
- Has difficulty applying learned skills in new settings
- Has academic skills deficits
- Has attention problems
- Displays very literal understanding of concepts
- Has difficulty understanding the connection between behavior and resulting consequences

Motor Differences

Most, if not all, individuals diagnosed with an ASD have significant differences in motor functioning (Ghaziuddin & Butler, 1998; Mari, Castiello, Marks, Marraffa, & Prior, 2003; Page & Boucher, 1998; Rapin, 1996; Staple & Reed, 2010). Historically, motor differences have been considered to be associated with, but not central features of, autism. The role of motor differences is beginning to take more of a center stage. For example, Nayate, Bradshaw, and Rinehart (2005) note that studies have established that motor differences emerge during the first 12 months – before social and communication differences appear – leading some to suggest that developmental motor milestones may soon be used as early diagnostic indicators of ASD (Mari, Marks, Marraffa, Prior, & Castiello, 2003). Some researchers assert that motor differences may actually underlie characteristics of autism such as repetitive movements and difficulties with imitation.

Others have highlighted the importance of motor differences in autism. Catatonia, a movement disorder characterized by slowness in movements and verbal responses, difficulty in initiating and completing actions, and increased need for prompting, is seen in a higher frequency in people diagnosed with ASD than in the general population (Wing & Shah, 2006). Wing and Shah estimate that 6 to 17% of those with ASD who are over the age of 15 experience a serious "catatonia like deterioration" (p. 37).

Since social and academic skills are often learned through movement, motor skill deficits may have a pervasive impact on development (Baranek, 2002; Cummins, Piek, & Dyck, 2005). The diagnostic and developmental aspects of motor development underscore the central role of motor functioning in understanding and treating autism.

Difficulty with handwriting, including reluctance to complete tasks that require writing, is one of the most evident outcomes of these motor differences in school settings. Handwriting tasks often result in frustration, not only for the child, but for teachers and parents as well. Similar frustration is often seen with athletic activities. (It should be noted that the social and sensory demands of many athletic activities often compound motor skill impediments.) A brief summary of common motor differences is listed below.

Common Motor Differences

- Demonstrates awkward motor movements (e.g., head flops backwards when placed into sitting position, crawls, walks or runs atypically for age, walks on toes)
- Has difficult maintaining hold or actively resists grasping objects or a tool (e.g., chalk, crayon, marker, pencil, paintbrush) for purposeful activities

- Displays unusual facial expressions or grimaces
- Has balance difficulties
- Resists handwriting or does not attempt without encouragement
- Has poor handwriting
- Has poor motor coordination or is accident prone
- Writes slowly
- Has deficits in athletic skills
- Walks with an awkward gait
- Displays unusual body postures and movements or facial expressions (e.g., odd postures, stiffness, freezing, facial grimacing)
- Has difficulty starting or completing actions (e.g., may rely on physical or verbal prompting by others)

Emotional Vulnerability

The world of emotions is particularly challenging for individuals on the autism spectrum. Not only are they less able to understand verbal and nonverbal expressions in others, they also have difficulty understanding and managing their own emotions. When faced with stress, children with high-functioning ASD are at greater risk for rages or tantrums, also described as "neurological storms" (Myles & Southwick, 2005). Increased risk for depression and suicide, as well as frequent tantrums or rage, provides further evidence of emotional vulnerability.

Depression is one of the most common emotional or psychiatric disorders among individuals with ASD (Ghaziuddin, Ghaziuddin, & Greden, 2002; Kim, Szatmari, Bryson, Streiner, & Wilson, 2000; Lynn, 2007; McPheeter, Davis, Navarre, & Scott, 2011). Typical symptoms of depression such as irritability, sadness, crying spells, and sleep and appetite disturbance are often present. The risk for suicidal behaviors and completed suicides is especially high. In addition to these typical symptoms, depression may be accompanied by an increase in preoccupations and rituals and greater frequency of aggressive outbursts (Ghaziuddin, Ghaziuddin, & Greden). A brief summary of common differences in this area is listed below.

- Exhibits more extreme emotional responses in duration and/or intensity than other children of the same age

- Emotional responses are not related to the situation (e.g., laughs for no apparent reason)

- Is anxious or easily stressed

- Appears to be depressed or sad

- Becomes stressed when presented with new task or novel situation

- Exhibits rage reactions, panic attacks, or or "meltdowns" - sometimes in response to apparently minor events

- Injures self (e.g., bangs head, picks skin, bites nails until they bleed, cuts self)

- Makes suicidal comments or has attempted suicide

- Has difficulty tolerating mistakes

- Has low frustration tolerance

- Has low self-esteem, makes negative comments about self

- Has difficulty identifying, quantifying, expressing, and/or controlling emotions (e.g., can only recognize and express emotions in extremes)

- Has a limited understanding of own and others' emotional responses

- Has difficulty managing stress and/or anxiety

VIGNETTES

Latisha

Latisha is a fourteen-year-old teenager on the spectrum. She is on the advanced track at school. She had friends in elementary school but most of those relationships slowly drifted apart when she entered middle school. She has a few online friends with whom she plays video games. Latisha's parents say that she talks excessively on her own topics (e.g., hawks and other birds of prey) and struggles to talk about others' topics of interest. Latisha told her mother, "I am confused by how everyone else feels. I think I'm supposed to have feelings that I don't have." Latisha tends to keep to herself at school. She avoids eating in the cafeteria with her peers. Latisha says she cannot tolerate the smells and sounds. The school librarian allows her to eat in the library office where she volunteers. Latisha spends her lunchtime writing novels that she shares with the librarian. The librarian and Latisha's English teacher submitted Latisha's work where it won top awards at the district and state levels.

In the classroom, Latisha will not raise her hand to participate. One teacher observed Latisha deeply scratching her skin after giving an incorrect answer. Parents say that Latisha is easily embarrassed and she worries about others thinking that she is "stupid." Parents are concerned that Latisha spends a great deal of time developing "masks" that she uses in order to blend in. Sometimes Latisha stands in front of the mirror and practices scenes from television shows. She takes notes on these scenes and memorizes lines to use later in conversation. Most of her teachers comment on how smart and polite she is. The following are some characteristics and associated features of autism observed by Latisha (self-report):

Social
- Have difficulty understanding what others may be thinking
- Find it difficult to make or keep friends
- Feel that I have to "play a part" or pretend to be someone else in order to fit in
- Have difficulty using eye contact or facial expressions

Restricted Patterns
- Need routines for most day-to-day activities or find change distressing
- Prefer to spend as much time as possible engaged in one activity or interest

Communication
- Find it difficult to know what to talk about in social situations
- Have difficulty keeping a conversation going
- Have difficulty talking about others' interests

Sensory
- Avoid certain clothes because of their texture or fit
- Become emotionally overwhelmed by certain places, events, music, or people

Emotional Vulnerability
- Replay events and conversations over and over in my mind to analyze what I could have said or done differently
- Injure self (e.g., cut self, pick at skin)
- Feel that others expect me to have feelings that I don't have

Kiran

Kiran is a three-year-old autistic boy who loves animals and is gentle with the family dog. When he was twelve months old, his parents were concerned that he could not hear because he did not consistently respond to sounds or attempts to interact. An audiologist concluded that Kiran hears well. He was delayed in learning to walk and struggles to hold objects such as eating utensils and crayons. Kiran has difficulty eating solid foods and is underweight for his age. He sleeps well and has mastered daytime toileting skills.

Kiran has a seven-word vocabulary and does not yet speak in phrases. He points to desired objects but becomes frustrated when others do not understand him. He is drawn to looking at moving objects and will stare at the ceiling fan. Kiran becomes easily distressed and it is difficult to comfort him. When his parents hold him, Kiran pushes away. He does not initiate hugs or cuddling. Mother feels that Kiran sees her as an object. She says that he does not respond to or treat her differently than a stranger. Kiran loves music. He imitates movements and will dance with others. Some of Kiran's characteristics and associated features of autism are listed below.

Social

- Appears to be unresponsive to others (e.g., unaware of the presence of others)
- Does not calm or quiet in response to a familiar adult's face or voice
- Responds in an unusual manner to affection (e.g., resists hugs or overreacts when others offer comfort)
- Treats others as if they were objects solely to gain assistance or a desired object (e.g., pulls parent to door)

Restricted Patterns

- Stares intensely and for long periods of time at objects that move (e.g., stares at fan or rolling credits of television show/movie)

Communication

- Has current speech delay
- Does not respond or shows delayed response when name is called
- Has difficulty or makes no attempt to make clear request (e.g., does not lift arms to be picked up, only labels objects - does not request by name)
- Fails to respond to verbal or nonverbal greetings by giving a verbal response (e.g., by saying "hi" and "bye")

Sensory

- Often shows an extreme overreaction to activities that provide touch or pressure
- Often responds in a developmentally unusual/rigid manner to eating (e.g., avoids many textures, foods, and flavors)

Motor

- Has difficulty using hands for fine-motor tasks (e.g., holding a crayon, using eating utensils, turning a single page, fastening, buttoning, and zipping)

Emotional Vulnerability

- Does not find pleasure in activities and interactions similarly to children the same age; seems withdrawn

OTHER CONDITIONS ASSOCIATED WITH AUTISM

High rates of co-occurring mental and physical health conditions are common (see Figure 1.1). One study found that 74% of autistic children had one or more co-occurring condition while 47% had two or more (Rast, et al., 2021). According to Fombonne (2003), approximately 6% of autistic individuals have a coexisting medical condition. Co-occurring mental health conditions are more prevalent in those with autism compared to the general population (Lai et al., 2019). The exact reason why autism co-occurs with other conditions is unknown, but it may be related to complex underlying neurological and genetic factors.

Co-occurring mental health conditions, such as anxiety and depression, may result from challenges associated with having autism, including severe social impairments, sensory differences, fewer meaningful age-appropriate relationships, and the increased potential of being victimized by others. Further, studies have found evidence that camouflaging (actively suppressing autistic traits in order to "blend in") is associated with more significant mental health concerns (Beck, et al., 2020; Hull et al., 2021).

Another reason for co-occurring mental health conditions may be the the lack of availability of well-trained providers. Zebro et al. (2015) surveyed adult providers and found that the majority rated their knowledge of autism as poor or fair. Not surprisingly, when autistic people are surveyed, they report concern with the lack of appropriate mental health services (Cam-Crosbie et al., 2019; Raja, 2014). Barriers to obtaining support can lead to chronic mental health concerns.

It is important to note that risk is not always the same across the spectrum. For example, studies find that depression and anxiety are more common among higher functioning individuals (Kim et al., 2000). In addition, approximately 30% of children with classic autism have epilepsy whereas risk is decreased for children with Asperger Syndrome (Gillberg, 1991). The risk of epilepsy is even higher for those with both autism and intellectual disability (Gillberg & Billstedt, 2000).

Condition	Source(s)
Medical Conditions	
Epilepsy	American Psychiatric Association, 2013; Hrdlicka et al., 2004; Mouridsen, Rich, & Isager, 2011
Psychiatric Conditions	
Mood Disorders (e.g., depression, bipolar disorder, dysthymia)	American Psychiatric Association, 2013; Kim, Szatmari, Bryson, Streiner, & Wilson, 2000; Ghaziuddin, Ghaziuddin, & Greden, 2002; Green, Gilchrist, Burton, & Cox, 2000; Simonoff et al., 2008
Anxiety Disorders	Green et al., 2000; Kim et al., 2000; Simonoff et al., 2008; White, Oswald, Ollendick, & Scahill, 2009
Attention-Deficit/Hyperactivity Disorder (ADHD)	American Psychiatric Association, 2013; Gadow, DeVincent, Pomeroy, & Azizian, 2004; Kim et al., 2000; McPheeters et al., 2011
Obsessive-Compulsive Disorder (OCD)	Gadow et al., 2004; Green et al., 2000
Tourette Syndrome/Tic Disorders	Gadow et al., 2004; Kadesjo & Gilberg, 2000; Simonoff et al., 2008
Oppositional Defiant Disorder (ODD)	Green et al., 2000; Simonoff et al., 2008
Learning Differences	
Learning Disabilities	Fombonne, 1999; Klin, Sparrow, Marans, Carter, & Volkmar, 2000; Mayes & Calhoun, 2003; Morgan et al., 2002; Reitzel & Szatmari, 2003
Poor Reading Comprehension	American Psychiatric Association, 2013; Chiang & Linn, 2007; Norbury & Nation, 2011
Specific Learning Disability in Written Expression	Mayes & Calhoun, 2003

Figure 1.1. Selected list of high rate coexisting conditions with autism.

Catatonia

Catatonia is a disorder commonly associated with autism; however, it often goes unrecognized and undiagnosed. Some have described it as "hidden in plain sight" (Dhossche & Wachtel 2010). Catatonia is a disorder that is experienced by 12 to 20% of individuals with autism spectrum disorder (Shah, 2019). Onset is typically between 10 and 19 years; however, it may occur in younger children (Wing & Shah, 2000).

Like autism, catatonia impacts posture/movement, speech, mood, and behavior making it challenging to distinguish from autism itself. Further confounding is the fact that catatonia manifests in opposing ways. One set of characteristics of catatonia falls under the category of immobility – "stuckness" (e.g., mutism, stupor, difficulty starting movements required to eat or drink, difficulty crossing thresholds, slow movement). In contrast, catatonia also causes symptoms of excitability (e.g., agitation, hyperactivity, unintentional destructive behaviors). In autism, symptoms tend to come and go within the course of a day (Ohta, Kano, & Nagai, 2006). The fluctuating nature of this condition can be confusing to others. For example, adults may find it hard to understand when they observe a child, who was unable to talk or move earlier in the day, riding a bike in the afternoon. The nature of catatonia may leave the impression that the stuckness and agitation (catatonia) are purposeful or willful.

While the co-occurrence of catatonia and other conditions, such as depression or schizophrenia, has been widely known for years, the relationship between catatonia and autism has remained obscure. The inclusion of catatonia in the fifth edition of the Diagnostic and Statistical Manual (DSM-5) as a specifier for autism (APA, 2013) was a step towards recognizing catatonia in individuals with autism and providing necessary interventions. Unfortunately, awareness of catatonia has not increased significantly; thus, catatonia remains in the shadows.

When catatonia goes unrecognized, it goes untreated. In autism, early catatonia related symptoms can become more severe. When that happens, it can be terribly incapacitating and even life-threatening/fatal. The longer catatonia is left untreated, the harder it is to reverse. It is time for those involved in the autism community to recognize and gain an understanding of catatonia to prevent unnecessary suffering.

Common Symptoms of Catatonia in Autism

- Immobility or slowness in walking
- Inability to eat or drink or slowness in eating or drinking
- Tics
- Pacing
- Freezing during actions
- Difficulty crossing lines or thresholds
- Fixed eye gaze
- Odd facial expressions or grimacing
- Slowed speech or mutism
- Self-injurious behaviors
- Incontinence
- Echolalia
- Unusual body postures
- Increased repetitive or ritualistic behavior
- Increased reliance on verbal or physical prompts
- Agitated or seemingly hostile behaviors
- Alternating between being still and excessively active
- Difficulty initiating and completing actions
- Is unresponsive to the environment
- Displays autonomic changes (e.g., slowed breathing or pulse irregularities, or increased sweating)

THEORETICAL PERSPECTIVES ON AUTISM

While knowledge of the common characteristics of autism provides a basis for understanding those who have the disorder and for designing appropriate interventions, we are left with the question, "What differences or causes underlie or explain these characteristics?" The search for the underlying differences has led to three overlapping areas of investigation: executive functioning, theory of mind, and central coherence. An answer to this question will allow for fine-tuning intervention strategies.

Theory of Executive Dysfunction

The theory of executive functioning is the first area of investigation used to explain some of the behaviors observed in individuals with autism. While the term "executive functioning" or EF is somewhat ill defined, it is considered to encompass a broad group of mental processes, including working memory, behavior inhibition, planning, mental flexibility (shifting sets), task initiation and performance monitoring, and self-regulation. Researchers have found that the prefrontal cortex of the brain, also known as the frontal lobes, is responsible for these functions. One author describes the frontal lobes as a chief executive officer in charge of coordinating and commanding other brain structures for a common purpose (Goldberg, 2001).

Relationship Between Executive Functioning and "Autistic" Behaviors

It is believed that executive skills deficits cause "autistic" behaviors. For example, we know how difficult it is for individuals on the spectrum to handle changes. According to the theory, this rigidity is attributed to poor mental flexibility. Restricted or narrow interests and repetitive behaviors can also be explained by deficits in this area. Further, many children and adolescents on the spectrum have intense temper outbursts or meltdowns. From an executive deficit perspective, we would say that they cannot self-regulate, meaning that they do not have the skill to calm themselves. One of the core features of autism, lack of social reciprocity – the natural back-and-forth we use in conversing with one another – can be explained by poor performance monitoring (Clawson et al., 2010). In order to hold a conversation, we tune in to cues from our listeners and adjust so that they understand us. For example, cues help us know when to pause, when to ask questions, and even when to change the topic. An example can help to illustrate the relationship between EF and characteristics of autism.

John

John is a boy on the spectrum. Socially, John struggles with his peers. He talks endlessly about his interests and does not seem to pick up on the not-so-subtle "I'm bored" cues his peers give him. Lately, he has been having a hard time finding a peer willing to play with him. Further, even though he is working above grade level, he cannot seem to complete his work at school. He does not start an assignment without being asked several times. John's ability to tolerate frustration is poor. He prefers routine and quickly becomes angry over things such as small changes in his schedule and his brother not playing what he likes. To his parents and teachers, his anger seems unpredictable and extreme.

According to the theory, John displays several executive skills deficits, including poor performance monitoring, task initiation, self-regulation, and mental flexibility.

Executive Dysfunction and the Brain

If the theory of executive dysfunction is accurate, individuals on the spectrum should have differences in how their brains look and work, and they should have specific deficits with executive skills. Researchers have found that the brains of many with autism are actually bigger and heavier than others' (Lainhart et al., 1997; Redcay & Courchesne, 2005).

Specifically, studies have shown that autistic children display accelerated brain growth during the first two to four years of life. Following this period, growth stops abruptly (Redcay & Courchesne). This abnormal growth pattern is believed to result in poor neural connections across the brain (Courchesne & Pierce, 2005) as well as increased brain size (C. D. Frith, 2003; Redcay & Courchesne). One area of overgrowth is the frontal cortex where executive functioning is believed to reside (Carper, Moses, Tigue, & Courchesne, 2002). While the reason for this finding is unknown, Hill and Frith (2003) note that during periods of brain development "faulty connections" are usually eliminated or "pruned" (p. 283). C. D. Frith speculates that individuals on the spectrum may fail to undergo this pruning process, resulting in increased brain size. Together, increased size and poor neural connections across the brain are believed to result in symptoms of autism, including executive skill deficits as well as mindblindness and weak central coherence, to be discussed later.

Research Support for Theory of Executive Dysfunction

The theory of executive dysfunction has been partially supported by research. Studies have consistently found that autistic children do poorly on problem-solving tests that tap planning skills (Bennetto et al., 1996; Russo et al.; Rutter). Also, researchers have found that autistic children often have problems with working memory (Bennetto et al.; Russo et al., 2007; Rutter, 2011) and perseveration or set-shifting (Bennetto et al.; Ozonoff, 1997; Pennington & Ozonoff, 1996; Russo et al.).

Some studies have found that autistic children did poorly when they had to inhibit a natural response (Geurts, Verté, Oosterlaan, Roeyers, & Sergeant, 2004). For example, Hughes and Russell (1993) used a task that required inhibition of a natural response. In this study, participants could only remove a marble from a box by turning a knob or maneuvering a switch first rather than reaching in and removing the marble. Results showed that autistic children had more difficulty inhibiting their natural response than did the comparison group. Other studies have found that individuals with autism did poorly on tasks that required more than one EF skill, such as working memory and response inhibition (Russo et al., 2007) and set-shifting and response inhibition (Russo et al.; Rutter, 2011).

While understanding the impact of EF deficits on task performance is important, it would be more meaningful if these skills could be directly linked to specific "autistic" behaviors. Unfortunately, there is little evidence of such a connection in the literature. There are several other criticisms of the executive dysfunction theory.

First, Hill and Frith (2003) point out that the results of studies on EF are not consistent. In fact, some individuals on the spectrum do not show any problems with EF. Another problem with the theory is the fact that executive skill deficits are not exclusive to autism. Other disorders that share deficits in EF include ADHD, Obsessive-Compulsive Disorder, and Tourette's Syndrome. As such, the use of EF as a diagnostic indicator for autism would be impossible. Regardless of these issues, Hill and Frith note that the theory is helpful because strategies that target these deficits can be of great benefit for individuals with ASD.

Impaired Theory of Mind

As mentioned, social difficulties are central to the challenges faced by those with autism. From infancy, they struggle with social situations that their typically developing peers handle with ease. Impairment in the ability to think about and understand thoughts and feelings is widely hypothesized as underlying the challenges faced in social interaction. The term "theory of mind" (ToM) is used to describe this ability to understand mental states, including beliefs, thoughts, desires, perceptions, intentions, and feelings, and to apply this understanding to predict the actions of others.

Development of Theory of Mind

Typically developing infants learn that the face is a critical source of information about the thoughts and feelings of others. Thus, they learn to follow the gaze of another person in order to share an interest or to predict his or her behavior. By the age of 14 months, development of joint attention, the awareness of the focus of another's attention, is completed (Baron-Cohen & Swettenham, 1997). With this awareness, children begin to point at a desired object in order to encourage another person to look at it. In contrast, children with ASD show an early lack of interest in the human face and deficits in the ability to share eye-to-eye gaze. They have difficulty learning to interpret facial expressions (Pelphrey et al., 2002).

Samuel

Samuel, a boy in elementary school, expressed amazement after a girl in gym class told his teacher that he was being mean to her during a basketball game. Samuel explained that he had only been "cheering her on" by shouting, "You can do better than that!" each time she missed a basket. Due to his weak ToM skills, he was unable to see hurt and frustration register on her face each time he cheered. As a result, Samuel was surprised by the reprimand for being a "bad sport."

Individuals who are high functioning often gain an ability to consciously or systematically use ToM skills; however, even the most able individuals on the autism spectrum continue to be limited in their ability to use these skills intuitively in demanding social situations (Hill & Frith, 2003). Thus, even in adulthood, people with the diagnosis of ASD tend to use erratic and random patterns when scanning a face, and they often fail to focus on the facial features that reveal emotions (Pelphrey et al., 2002). These delays in the development of skills for interpreting facial expressions and establishing joint attention are a likely foundation for the delayed development of ToM (Baron-Cohen & Swettenham, 1997).

False-Belief Studies

Researchers have found that by the age of 4, typically developing children are able to infer the beliefs of others. A series of studies using "false-belief" tasks provided early evidence that ToM is impaired in individuals with ASD (Klin et al., 2002). In false-belief experiments, an object, such as a doll, is put in a location in front of a child and a second person. The second person is then asked to leave the room. While the second person is out of the room, the child observes as the doll is hidden in a new location. The child is then asked where he believes that the second person will look to find the doll.

Studies show that by the age of 4, most children are able to infer that the absent individual would look in the wrong place for the object because of a false belief about its location (Wimmer & Perner, 1983). Similar experiments with children diagnosed with ASD have found that their ability to make inferences about the beliefs of others is delayed, thus providing support for the impaired ToM hypothesis. Baron-Cohen and Swettenham also use the term "mentalizing failure" to describe this weakness in individuals with ASD (1997).

Mindblindness

Disruption in the development of ToM results in what is called "mindblindness;" that is, difficulty in recognizing the feelings and thoughts of others. Knowledge of mindblindness is essential for those who wish to understand and help individuals with on the spectrum. This is true, because while a number of underlying differences likely exist in ASD, "Nothing captures the essence of autism so precisely as the idea of "mindblindness" (Happé, 1997, p. 25).

Baron-Cohen and Swettenham (1997) suggest that mindblindness may explain a wide range of social differences in individuals with ASD. For example, mindblindness limits the ability to explain and predict the behavior of others, thus making it difficult to distinguish between accidental and intentional behavior. Mindblindness may also partially explain the difficulty with recognizing words that describe mental states (e.g., sad, frustrated, remorseful, and pensive) and in using words to describe one's own feelings (Baron-Cohen & Swettenham). Further, confusion may result when implied meanings or non-literal language, such as irony, sarcasm, or analogy, is used, as illustrated in the following example.

Miles

At the beginning of the school year, a teacher reviewed the rules for behavior in the library. In an effort to impress upon the children the seriousness of the rules, she said, "You are not to talk. You are not to fidget. Don't even breathe." Miles, a fourth-grader in her class, threw his hand up in the air and asked, "When you say don't breathe in the library, is that a joke?"

A teacher unfamiliar with the confusion over figurative speech often experienced by children who are high functioning in other ways might have concluded that Miles was being rude or insubordinate. However, because his teacher was trained in the characteristics of autism, she realized that due to mindblindness, Miles might not have understood her sarcasm, and she recognized that he was genuinely concerned that he would have to risk his life in order to check out a book.

Because deception requires an awareness of the beliefs of others and the ability to manipulate those beliefs, mindblindness may also play a role in the delay in telling lies seen among many autistic children. We have often met with parents who are confused when we reassure them that their child's first apparent lie may have a silver lining. That is, while honesty is a virtue for all children, their child's efforts to change another person's beliefs by means of a "lie" is a positive sign of a developing ToM.

Finally, the challenges in social use of language for starting and maintaining a conversation may also have a basis in mindblindness. The ability to read a person's interest level, emotional expressions, and nonverbal messages is critical to success in interacting with others (Klin et al., 2002).

Janice

Janice is fascinated by horses. She introduces herself by describing her favorite breed and inquiring about the listener's favorite horses. She then recounts the plot of a movie about horses and proceeds by reciting an exhaustive list of horse facts. Adults initially find Janice charming and are impressed by how bright she is, but after a while they begin to tire of the one-sided conversation. They begin to look away and try to subtly redirect her. Eventually, they have to interrupt her and direct her to another task.

Janice's third-grade peers are less tolerant of her endless speeches about horses than the adults in her life. While Janice occasionally encounters a "new friend" who will listen for a while, none of her peers shares her level of fascination, and soon they start to avoid her. Janice misses critical information provided when others check their watches, look away, or roll their eyes. Other children her age are able to see these behaviors as signs that they are losing the interest of their audience. According to the theory of mind, Janice has mindblindness and is unable to receive and interpret these signals; she is feeling confused by the behavior of others and is experiencing social rejection.

Theory of Weak Central Coherence

In 1989, Uta Frith proposed that cognitive differences seen in autism might be explained by a concept known as "central coherence." As problem solvers, we generally put together the pieces of a puzzle in order to "get the big picture." Central coherence describes the general tendency to integrate information into a meaningful whole. Researchers have studied the theory of central coherence extensively and have found substantial support for Frith's idea (Booth, Charlton, Hughes, & Happé, 2003; Booth & Happé, 2010; Burnette et al., 2005; Happé & Frith, 2006; Pellicano, Maybery, & Durkin, 2005; Plaisted, Saksida, Alcántra, & Weisblatt, 2003).

The theory that individuals on the autism spectrum exhibit weak central coherence (WCC) has been explored through the use of homographs. Homographs, words with one spelling but two meanings such as "tear" and "read," are pronounced differently depending on their meaning in a sentence. Individuals diagnosed with an ASD mispronounce homographs more often than their typically developing peers due to failure to take the context of the sentence into consideration (Hill & Frith, 2003).

Advantages of Weak Central Coherence

WCC is sometimes described as a style of processing information (Booth et al., 2003) that has advantages as well as disadvantages. For example, those with WCC have an advantage on tasks that require processing parts over wholes, or a focus on the details (Adams & Jarrold, 2011; Baron-Cohen & Swettenham, 1997; Happé, 1997). One such task is the embedded-figures task that requires the ability to find hidden objects incorporated into a larger picture. Another task in which WCC provides an advantage is block design. Block design tasks require using colored blocks to recreate a design from a picture. Both the embedded-figure and the block design tasks are visuo-spatial, in which seeing the big picture interferes with performance (Hill & Frith, 2003; Pellicano et al., 2005). Those with weak central coherence, who tend to focus on details and miss the global picture, usually perform well on this type of task.

A nonholistic style of perception is also an advantage on a task requiring the identification of a familiar face given parts of the face. Children with ASD do as well with photographs of facial segments as they do with pictures of the whole face. By comparison, their typically developing peers tend to recognize faces more easily when presented with photographs of the whole face (Baron-Cohen & Swettenham, 1997). This difference indicates that autistic children are processing faces based on separate features rather than on the composite.

While strong discrimination skills seen in WCC may explain performance on specific tasks, WCC may also explain some of the hallmark characteristics of individuals with ASD. Thus, Hill and Frith (2003) speculate that encyclopedic knowledge in a specific area may result from the strong interest in and ability to discriminate details in some area of obsessive interest.

Disadvantages of Weak Central Coherence

Despite advantages such as those presented above, WCC leads to a disadvantage on tasks that require the interpretation of information based on context, or drawing conclusions based on the big picture (Baron-Cohen & Swettenham 1997; Booth & Happé, 2010; Happé, 1997; O'Loughlin & Thagard, 2000). Because social and academic settings place constant demands on these abilities, they are especially challenging for individuals with ASD. For example, starting early in elementary school, children are asked to determine the theme of a story. They are routinely expected to determine the meaning or pronunciation of a word based on context in a sentence. Tests of reading comprehension and tasks that require students to compare and contrast concepts also demand the ability to use context.

Disadvantages of WCC go beyond the academic world to impact social functioning. Happé (1997) suggests that WCC may explain why even individuals on the autism spectrum with stronger ToM abilities struggle socially in real-world settings. According to Happé, social success requires the ability to understand the social context; therefore, even individuals who have developed the skills to read and interpret nonverbal cues and have gained some understanding of the emotions and thoughts of others (ToM) struggle to apply these skills in daily life. As Happé (1997, p. 24) states, "It may be that a theory of mind mechanism which is not fed by rich and integrated contextual information is of little use in every day life."

The Interrelationships Among the Three Theoretical Perspectives

The three theories reviewed above are not necessarily mutually exclusive. For example, researchers believe that certain executive skills are required to have a theory of mind (Carlson, Mandell, & Williams, 2004; Carlson, Moses, & Breton, 2001; Carlson, Moses, & Claxton, 2004; Joseph & Tager-Flusberg, 2004; Moses, 2001; Pellicano, 2010). Additionally, some researchers believe that executive dysfunction can explain weak central coherence (Pellicano et al., 2005; Rinehart, Bradshaw, Moss, Brereton, & Tonge, 2000), whereas others argue that the two concepts are independent of one another (Booth et al., 2003). Findings are also mixed with regard to the relationship between theory of mind and weak central coherence (Baron-Cohen & Hammer, 1997; Fisher & Happé, 2006; Frith & Happé, 1994; Jarrold, Butler, Cottington, & Jiminez, 2000; Morgan, Maybery, & Durkin, 2003; Pellicano et al.).

To illustrate, we encounter parents who report that their child knows when she is happy or sad and responds appropriately to these feelings in others at home. They are, therefore, confused by the child's difficulty in using these same skills on the playground or at lunch with peers. It is possible that the skill of recognizing the feelings of others (ToM) can be used in familiar and routine situations at home but not in more complex or chaotic contexts. In other words, while ToM skills are in place, the ability to use them may be overtaxed in complex, real-world environments due to WCC.

Regardless of the degree to which these concepts are interrelated, knowledge of these theories helps us to better understand the behaviors of individuals on the spectrum and is crucial in developing successful interventions.

SUMMARY

People on the autism spectrum share common characteristics including – social differences, communication differences, and repetitive behaviors or obsessive interests. Further, features include sensory, cognitive, and motor differences as well as emotional vulnerability. Autism frequently co-occurs with mental and physical health conditions. One common but under-recognized condition is catatonia. Our understanding of autism has been furthered through the development of three theories: executive functioning, theory of mind, and central coherence. Knowledge of the characteristics of ASD and the theories regarding underlying differences reflected in ASD is essential to the development of effective intervention plans.

CHAPTER HIGHLIGHTS

- *In order to develop effective interventions, one needs to understand the context of autism.*

- *Autism is a complex neurodevelopmental condition often evident in early childhood but sometimes not recognized until later.*

- *Autism is marked by impairments in – social functioning, repetitive behaviors, and communication in addition to sensory, cognitive and motor differences, and emotional vulnerability.*

- *Autism often co-occurs with other medical and psychiatric conditions.*

- *Co-occuring mental health conditions are more prevalent in those autism compared to the general population.*

- *While the reason for the co-occurence of autism and mental and physical health conditions is unknown, neurological and genetic factors are implicated. Additionally, some disorders (e.g., depression and anxiety) are believed to result from the experience of living with autism.*

- *Camouflaging (actively suppressing autistic traits) is associated with more significant mental health concerns.*

- *A lack of well-trained providers contributes to the chronicity of co-occurring conditions.*

- *Catatonia is a disorder commonly associated with autism. It impacts posture/movement, speech, mood, and behavior.*

- *Catatonia often goes unrecognized, in part, because characteristics of autism and catatonia overlap.*

- *The longer catatonia is left untreated, the harder it is to reverse.*

- *Three main theories attempt to explain the common characteristics of autism: executive functioning, theory of mind, and central coherence. Some argue that the three concepts are interrelated while others assert that they are independent.*

- *Deficits in executive functioning (EF) are believed to result in behaviors commonly seen in those with ASD. Executive functioning refers to a broad group of mental processes, including working memory, inhibition, planning, flexibility, task initiation and performance monitoring, and self-regulation.*

- *Theory of Mind (ToM) is used to describe the ability to understand the mental states of others (e.g., beliefs, thoughts, desires, perceptions, intentions, and feelings) and apply this understanding to predict the actions of others.*

- *Disruption in the development of ToM results in "mindblindness," and is believed to explain a wide range of social differences displayed by those with ASD.*

- *Central coherence describes the ability to integrate information into a meaningful whole. Autistic individuals with ASD are believed to display a style of processing known as weak central coherence (WCC). That is, they tend to focus on details (parts) while losing sight of the whole.*

- *Individuals with weak central coherence demonstrate an advantage when memorizing facts and details and a disadvantage when having to interpret information based on context.*

2 Assessment

*"You got to be careful if you
don't know where you're going,
because you might not get there."*

– Yogi Berra

In response to the complexities of autism and the pervasive needs of individuals on the spectrum described in Chapter 1, the current chapter introduces the Ziggurat Model, an innovative approach to designing interventions. The Ziggurat Model (ZM) is a research-centered system for designing comprehensive treatments and resolving challenging behaviors. The model capitalizes on strengths in order to address underlying deficits. It is assessment driven and provides a framework for ensuring that complex needs are fully addressed.

We have chosen the ziggurat, a pyramid-like structure consisting of discrete levels, to represent a framework for developing well-founded and thorough interventions. The ZM consists of two main components: assessment and intervention design. The assessment portion of the model will be discussed here. The process of developing interventions based on the levels of the Intervention Ziggurat will be discussed in Chapter 3.

Assessment is essential to the development of individualized programs that capitalize on strengths and address challenges. In this chapter we review two traditional approaches to conceptualizing behavior – one focuses on observable behaviors (functional assessment) and the other focuses on underlying traits or characteristics (TEACCH approach). A new conceptual model developed by the authors, the ABC-Iceberg (ABC-I), incorporating an informal descriptive assessment, is also introduced. The ABC-I builds on the strengths of both traditional approaches while overcoming their limitations.

FUNCTIONAL BEHAVIORAL ASSESSMENT

Behavior assessment is the fundamental element in designing interventions. One form of behavior assessment is known as a functional behavior assessment or FBA. "Functional assessment is the process of identifying the variables that reliably predict and maintain problem behaviors" (Horner & Carr, 1997, p. 85). Research has shown that interventions based on functional assessment are more likely to reduce problem behaviors (Carr et al., 1999; Ellingson, Miltenberger, Stricker, Galensky, & Garlinghouse, 2000).

The creation of an FBA is a complex process consisting of fundamental elements: the ABCs (antecedent, behavior, and consequences) that essentially describe a behavior and the events that occur before and after. Before discussing the steps of conducting an FBA, it is important to understand the nature of reinforcement and punishment. Fred's behavior in the following example will help to illustrate these concepts.

Fred

Fred is a 10-year-old boy on the spectrum. He is having difficulty in music class and P.E. In both environments, he screams while covering his ears, which is disrupting the rest of the class. On a few occasions, he has torn out pages of his music book and he has pushed students during games in the gymnasium. Each time he acts out, Fred is removed from class. His behavior is not getting any better; in fact, he seems to melt down more quickly now than he did at the start of the year.

The fact that Fred misbehaved again more quickly after being removed from class suggests that he was inadvertently being rewarded for the target behavior. By definition, reinforcement should result in an *increase* in behavior. In contrast, consequences that are punishing always result in a *decrease* in behavior. In this scenario, Fred's teachers may have thought that removing him would be an effective form of punishment but as we just witnessed, it was not.

Figure 2.1 depicts a tool for better understanding the terms "reinforcement" and "punishment." In this scenario, removal of something dreaded (being in music and P.E.) is considered negative reinforcement for Fred. The terms "negative" and "positive" as used in Figure 2.1 may appear confusing. They simply mean that something has been removed/avoided or added. From a behavioral perspective, we would say that Fred was being negatively reinforced or rewarded for acting out. Fred's teachers were also being negatively reinforced for removing him from class because, from the teachers' perspective, removing a disruptive student could be viewed as desirable.

The teachers worked with the school psychologist to identify ways to make P.E. and music class less stressful for Fred. The team then developed a plan to teach him new coping and social skills and to reinforce him for using these new skills in P.E. and music. When Fred showed early signs of frustration, rather than removing him from class as they used to, the teachers coached him to use his new skills. They gave him something he liked, a reinforcer, each time he practiced the new skills. Fred began receiving reinforcement for appropriate behaviors instead of for aggressive and disruptive behaviors. As predicted, he started using more coping and social skills and fewer inappropriate behaviors. This improvement in behavior occurred because of careful attention to the role of reinforcement.

Reinforcement and Punishment Grid		
	Desired	**Dreaded**
Apply	Positive Reinforcement	Punishment
Remove	Negative Punishment	Negative Reinforcement

Note. The grid illustrates that application or removal of an item or event can be rewarding or punishing depending on whether it is desired or aversive to an individual.

Figure 2.1. Grid for determining whether a consequence is reinforcing or punishing.

While the FBA examines events that occur in the environment before and after a behavior occurs, it is important to note that the behavioral perspective essentially ignores other non-observable, within-child factors such as communication deficits or sensory differences that may have been underlying reasons why these two environments were aversive to Fred.

Assumptions About FBA

According to Scheuermann and Webber (2002), functional assessment is based on five assumptions that have been established in the literature (Foster-Johnson & Dunlap, 1993; O'Neill et al., 1997).

1. Behavior serves a function.
2. Behavior is related to antecedents and consequences.
3. Behavior may be impacted by factors outside of immediate antecedents and consequences.
4. Behavior may result from biological factors.
5. Behavior may result from skill deficits.

We will look briefly at each of these in turn.

Behavior Serves a Function

Understanding the function of a behavior is important for designing effective interventions. It is best accomplished through completion of an FBA. Fred's behavior served a purpose – to escape from being in music and P.E. Thus, his behaviors could be viewed as a solution to his problem. That is, his actions (screaming, pushing peers, etc.) resulted in a temporary solution (being removed from class). The intervention developed for Fred was effective because he was taught to use coping skills as an alternative to his former escape-motivated behaviors (e.g., screaming, tearing papers).

But escape is just one possible function of behavior. The most common functions identified through functional assessment in addition to escape/avoidance include the attainment of adult and/or peer attention, a tangible item, access to a preferred activity, and sensory stimulation. As we saw in the example above, the desire to escape or avoid unpleasant demands or activities can be highly motivating. Sometimes behavior is an attempt to gain the attention of adults and/or peers. What we may consider negative attention, such as being stared at for saying something rude to the teacher, may not be interpreted as such by autistic individuals. Behavior may also result in acquiring something desirable such as an activity, food, or object. Sensory reinforcement would include behaviors that are self-stimulating, such as rocking back and forth, humming, or pacing.

Behavior Is Related to Antecedents and Consequences

"Behaviorism maintains that all behavior is a function of the interaction between environmental events and behavior rather than being controlled by hypothetical entities (e.g., 'mind,' 'will,' and 'self')" (Gresham, Watson, & Skinner, 2001, p. 157). These environmental events are referred to as antecedents and consequences.

Antecedents may broadly be defined as events that occur prior to a behavior. For example, a parent's request to clean up or a teacher giving a student an assignment could be "triggers" for behavior problems. (These will be discussed in more detail below.) While the term "consequence" may sound negative, it simply refers to an event that occurs *after* a behavior. For example, redirecting a student who is off task, providing praise for following directions correctly, isolation from peers for hitting, private conversations with the teacher after disrupting the class, and sending a child to his room for arguing are all examples of consequences.

Understanding events that occur before and after a behavior helps to identify patterns and informs the intervention planning process.

Behavior May Be Impacted by Factors Outside of Immediate Antecedents and Consequences

While it is believed that behaviors result from immediate antecedents and consequences, other factors, known as *setting events*, may increase the probability of behaviors occurring. Setting events include factors such as illness, having an argument with Mom on the way to school, hunger, and family changes such as divorce or death. Understanding the impact of these factors is an important part of designing effective behavioral interventions.

Behavior May Result from Biological Factors

The importance of considering biological factors when interpreting behavior cannot be overstated. If an individual is in pain, tired, or has recently changed prescriptive medications, for example, she may behave differently and become less responsive to other interventions. Thus, biological factors set the stage for interventions to succeed or fail.

Amy

Amy's behavior in class changed recently. She stopped working independently and became disruptive. Her teacher found that rewards did not seem to make a difference any more. When her teacher phoned Amy's parents, she discovered that Amy had been experiencing severe migraine headaches. Amy's teacher struggled to find strategies that were effective. She reduced the amount of work Amy had to do, made visuals to remind her to raise her hand, and tried different rewards, all to no avail. After a week, Amy's doctor was able to find a medication to stop her migraines and her behavior rapidly improved.

This demonstrates the impact of biological factors on behavior and highlights the need to address them in all interventions.

Behavior May Result from Skills Deficits

Due to the nature of a pervasive developmental disorder such as autism, individuals on the spectrum have many gaps in skills that cut across domains (e.g., social, communication, cognitive, sensory). Often, needs are communicated through behavior. A "meltdown," for example, can be viewed as a strong indicator of emotional vulnerability and a need to learn coping skills. Similarly, dominating conversations by talking exclusively about obsessions may indicate an inability to understand others' perspectives and a lack of skills for keeping a conversation going (by asking the listener questions).

Skill deficits can be a major source of behavioral concerns and are a key area to address in all interventions.

Components of a Functional Behavioral Assessment

Completion of an FBA is essential to designing interventions from a behaviorist's perspective. The FBA process is also a good source of data for measuring progress later on. The process begins by looking at a behavior and the contingencies that increase or decrease the likelihood of its occurrence.

Behavior

An FBA begins with identifying a behavior of concern and defining it in a way that is observable and clear. This objective description is known as an *operational definition*. For example, "acts badly" is too vague and would be difficult to measure. Observers might define "bad" differently. The operational definition, on the other hand, describes what it looks like when a child acts "bad" – interrupts teacher by shouting, throws papers on floor, and runs out of the classroom.

Behaviors that are operationally defined meet two criteria:

1. Behaviors are observable and measurable.
2. Using the definition, two people are able to identify the same behavior when it occurs.

Examples of operational definitions are provided in Figure 2.2. Note that ill-defined descriptions can be clarified using observable and measurable terms by objectively describing what the behavior looks like when it occurs.

Vague		Operationally Defined
She's lazy	⟶	Does not put homework assignments in bin
	⟶	Puts head on desk during math
He does not listen	⟶	Looks away when mother talks to him
	⟶	Interrupts the conversation of others with comments about ceiling fan manufacturers
She's mean	⟶	Makes derogatory comments about other people's appearance
	⟶	Walks away from friend if a third person joins the group
He's oppositional	⟶	Shouts no! when asked a "wh" question (who, what, when, etc.)
	⟶	Does not comply when instructed to turn off the TV

Figure 2.2. **Examples of operational definitions for vague descriptions of behavior.**

Once a behavior is operationally defined, it is possible to collect data about its frequency, duration, and/or severity. After implementation of an intervention plan, data can again be collected in order to measure the effectiveness of the intervention.

Antecedents

The next step in the FBA process consists of describing antecedents or "triggers." These are environmental factors that occur before the problem behavior, such as starting a new activity, working in a group of peers, or having a substitute teacher. Figure 2.3 lists some common antecedents.

As discussed earlier, some antecedents – setting events – are less immediate to the situation but still impact behavior. Other antecedents are readily identified by observation. In other situations, careful data collection is necessary to determine the related antecedents. That is, the trigger is not always apparent. Remember to consider biological factors, sensory differences, skill deficits, performance deficits, and environmental changes or circumstances in determining the pattern as illustrated in the following vignette.

Mark

Mark seemed more off task at school the day after a three-day weekend. He continuously asked his teacher if the class was going to art today. After asking for the fifth time, his teacher said, "No more questions." During the days and weeks that followed, Mark cried in class every time his peers raised their hand to ask a question.

In this scenario, there was one obvious antecedent – the schedule change (a three-day weekend). While this initially helped to explain Mark's agitation and repetitive questioning, his teacher was confused because there had been several three-day weekends, and even a week-long break, since school started. Mark had never taken this long to adjust. His teacher was mystified why this break caused more difficulties for him. It was not until she heard him crying and repeatedly mumbling, "No questions," that she was able to piece together his concern. She realized that the actual antecedent was her initial comment, "No more questions." Because of Mark's concrete interpretation of language, he believed that asking questions was now against the rules in school.

Common Antecedents

- Time of day
- Presence of specific peers
- Specific classroom subject
- Transition from more preferred to less preferred activity (e.g., playing video game to homework)
- Change in routine
- Settings with decreased/increased structure (e.g., hallways, classroom, grocery store)
- Request to stop a behavior
- Punishment
- Medication changes
- Family circumstances (e.g., new baby, parental divorce, parent's new job, financial stress)
- Environmental changes (e.g., new paint at home, different classroom desk arrangement, weather)

Figure 2.3. Common antecedents to behavior.

Consequences

The final component in identifying the function of behavior is to consider the consequences. This refers to both positive and negative events that occur after the behavior. Examples include private conversation with the teacher, isolation from peers, loss of recess, earning stickers, shortening a task, delay of task, and receiving additional help.

Another example of an FBA is depicted in Figure 2.4. In this case, the *behavior*, "loner" on playground, was operationally defined as wandering the perimeter, flapping hands, shaking sticks in front of his eyes, and talking to himself. The *antecedent* was being on the playground at recess and all related environmental factors – noises, reduced structure, and so on. The most obvious *consequence* of this behavior was isolation from peers.

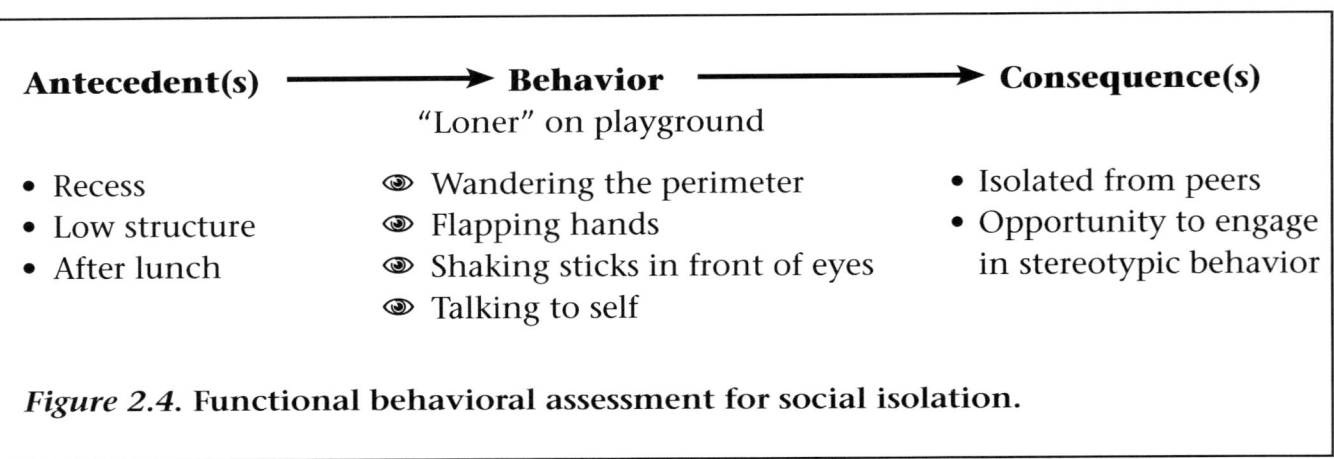

Antecedent(s) ⟶ Behavior ⟶ Consequence(s)

"Loner" on playground

- Recess
- Low structure
- After lunch

- 👁 Wandering the perimeter
- 👁 Flapping hands
- 👁 Shaking sticks in front of eyes
- 👁 Talking to self

- Isolated from peers
- Opportunity to engage in stereotypic behavior

Figure 2.4. **Functional behavioral assessment for social isolation.**

This boy's teacher decided that the function of his behavior was to escape something overwhelming to him (interaction with peers on the playground). She decided to assign him a peer buddy for recess and to allow him to work in the library for the first half of recess to decrease the length of time he was exposed to the stresses of the playground setting.

Figure 2.5 depicts an FBA for a student who had behavior problems in school. The antecedent was a request to complete a written task. His teacher said that he displayed "meltdowns," which were operationally defined as episodes where he hit the teacher, yelled, cried, and/or put his head on the table. Consequences for the behavior were missing recess and completing the work in a specialized setting.

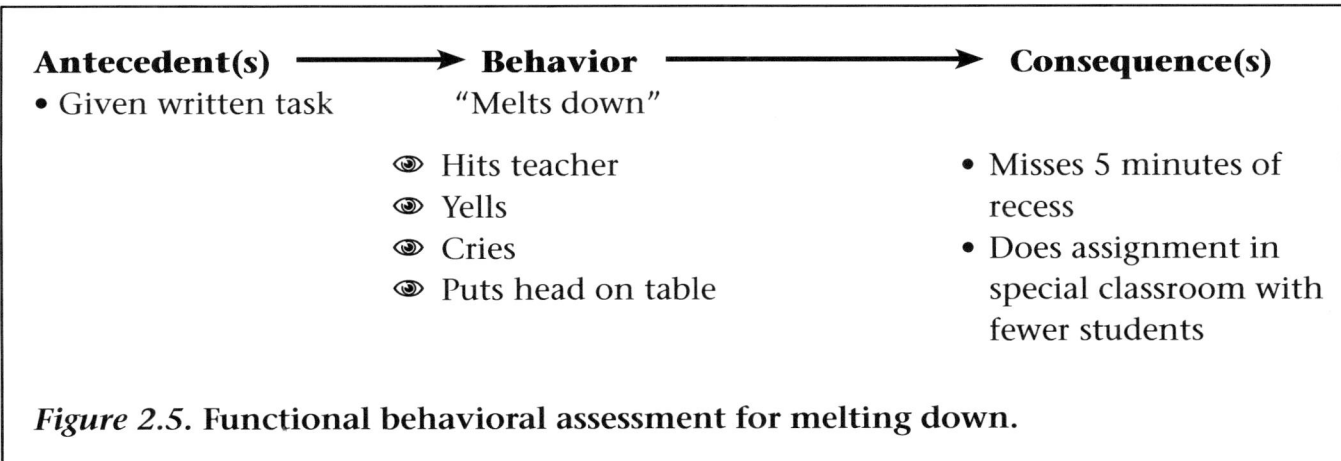

Antecedent(s) ⟶	Behavior ⟶	Consequence(s)

Antecedent(s) ⟶ **Behavior** ⟶ **Consequence(s)**

• Given written task   "Melts down"

            👁 Hits teacher
            👁 Yells
            👁 Cries
            👁 Puts head on table

• Misses 5 minutes of recess
• Does assignment in special classroom with fewer students

Figure 2.5. Functional behavioral assessment for melting down.

In looking at the patterns, the teacher determined that the function of the behavior was to escape or avoid written work. Based on this information, she developed an intervention to maintain the demands while rewarding the student for time spent working.

Interventions Based on Functional Behavioral Assessment

After identifying the function of behavior, interventions can be developed. Interventions based on the FBA can be designed to make changes at three different points – the antecedent, behavior, or consequence.

- *Antecedent interventions* are best described as preventive. They prevent problem behaviors by changing environmental factors that precede them.

- *Interventions at the point of behavior* take the form of teaching skills sometimes called replacement behaviors. For example, rather than interrupting a lesson, one can teach a student to raise her hand. Or instead of yelling and hitting others, one can teach an individual to ask for help or take deep breaths to calm down.

- *Consequence interventions* change the factors that follow and sustain behavior. Ideally, this type of intervention consists of designing rewards or reinforcement for replacement or productive behaviors. Rewards are an essential component in teaching skills. *It is not possible for learning to occur without reinforcement.*

ABC Framework

Understanding of antecedents, behaviors, and consequences provides three points of intervention – antecedent interventions (preventive), behavior interventions (teaching a skill), and consequence interventions (reinforcement of new skills). For example, knowing that an individual has difficulty with writing, one can reduce the work (antecedent strategy), teach him to use a word processor (behavior strategy), and reward him for completing written tasks (consequence strategy). Use of all three points of the ABC framework ensures more thorough and effective interventions.

The FBA focuses on observable behaviors, while invisible biological factors and specific diagnoses are treated as irrelevant for intervention planning. Indeed, some argue that biological factors, such as hunger or anxiety (Carr, 1994), and diagnostic characteristics and genetic conditions (Reese, Richman, Zarcone, & Zarcone, 2003) should be considered when examining behavior. "An evaluation of the interaction between diagnostic characteristics and environmental events may lead to a more individualized functional assessment of challenging behavior displayed by young children with autism" (Reese et al., p. 88). In summary, Schopler (1994) and the current authors assert that a strict behavioral approach fails to take into account the underlying characteristics considered to be critical to understanding behaviors and designing interventions. In other words, *interventions based only on an FBA are created without consideration of the autism context.*

THE ICEBERG ANALOGY

The iceberg is a universal analogy for describing critical aspects of objects or circumstances that are not apparent without careful observation. The creators of the Treatment and Education of Autistic and Communication handicapped Children (TEACCH) approach applied this analogy to aid in understanding the behaviors of individuals on the spectrum. The Ziggurat Model expands this analogy.

The TEACCH Iceberg

In contrast to the behavioral approach that focuses mainly on observable behaviors, TEACCH emphasizes the importance of identifying underlying strengths and needs related to the disor-

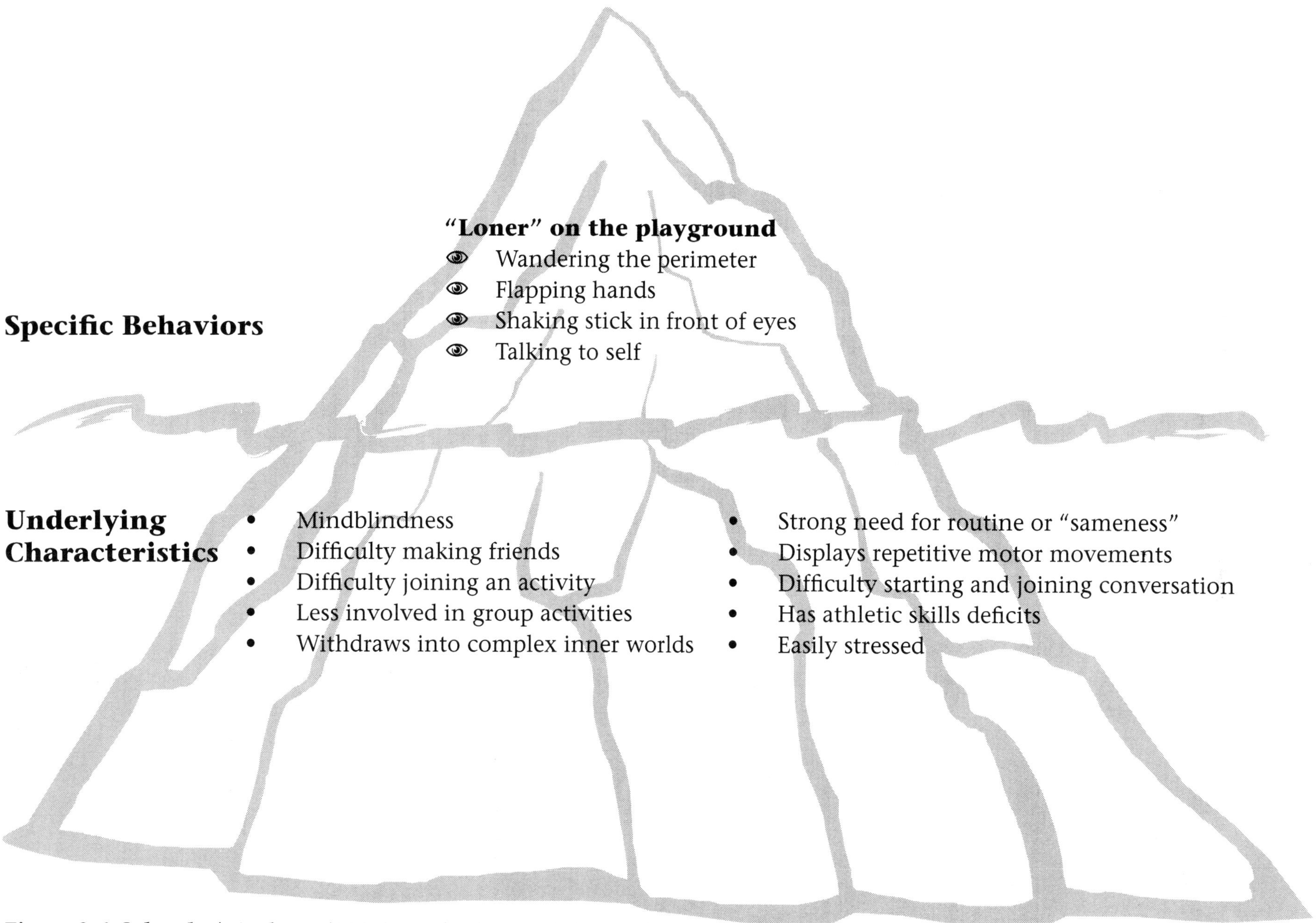

Specific Behaviors

"Loner" on the playground
- Wandering the perimeter
- Flapping hands
- Shaking stick in front of eyes
- Talking to self

Underlying Characteristics
- Mindblindness
- Difficulty making friends
- Difficulty joining an activity
- Less involved in group activities
- Withdraws into complex inner worlds

- Strong need for routine or "sameness"
- Displays repetitive motor movements
- Difficulty starting and joining conversation
- Has athletic skills deficits
- Easily stressed

Figure 2.6. Schopler's iceberg (1994) applied to social isolation.

Adapted from *Behavioral priorities for autism and related developmental disorders,* by E. Schopler, 1994. In E. Schopler & G.B. Mesibov (Eds.), *Behavioral Issues in Autism* (p. 73), New York: Plenum Press. Copyright 1994. With kind permission of Springer Science and Business Media.

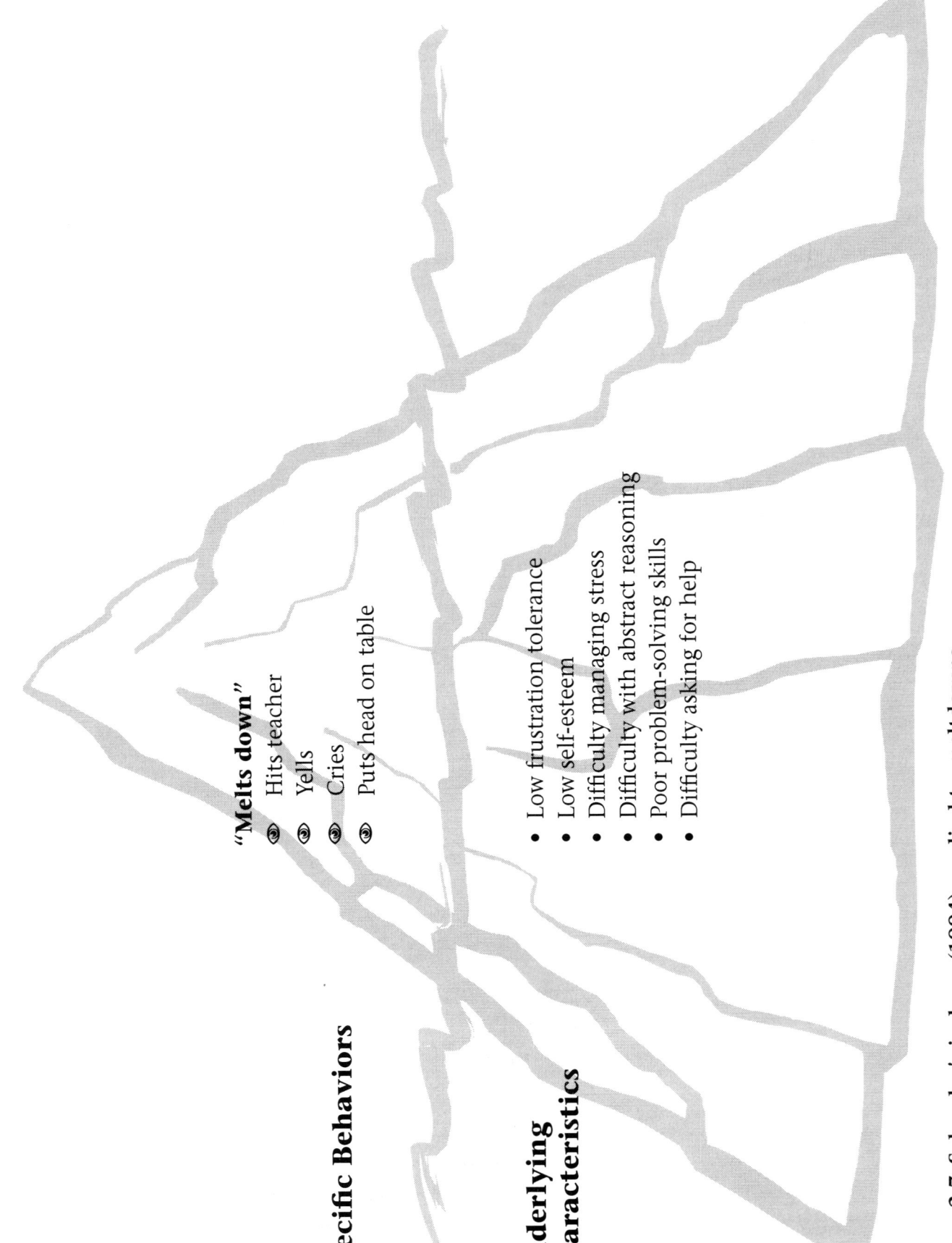

"Melts down"
- Hits teacher
- Yells
- Cries
- Puts head on table

Specific Behaviors

- Low frustration tolerance
- Low self-esteem
- Difficulty managing stress
- Difficulty with abstract reasoning
- Poor problem-solving skills
- Difficulty asking for help

Underlying Characteristics

Figure 2.7. Schopler's iceberg (1994) applied to meltdowns.

Adapted from *Behavioral priorities for autism and related developmental disorders*, by E. Schopler, 1994. In E. Schopler & G.B. Mesibov (Eds.), *Behavioral Issues in Autism* (p. 73), New York: Plenum Press. Copyright 1994. With kind permission of Springer Science and Business Media.

der itself. Schopler's (1994) use of an iceberg, in which the observed behaviors are represented by the tip of the iceberg while the unseen causes lie beneath the surface of the water, best depicts this approach. Thus, interventions based on the iceberg concept are designed to address underlying deficits or characteristics associated with autism (see Figures 2.6 and 2.7).

There are several routes to determining the underlying factors of a behavior. Knowledge of underlying factors comes from formal and informal assessment and awareness of the characteristics of autism. With experience and training, it is often possible to begin to theorize about underlying factors without in-depth assessment. For example, if a child is socially isolated on the playground, we immediately begin to consider possible underlying causes such as sensory factors – heat; noise; weak theory of mind – difficulty knowing what other children enjoy doing; obsessions – interests not shared by peers; and poor communication skills – not knowing how to ask to join a game. The iceberg analogy, while emphasizing the underlying characteristics of ASD, fails to include an analysis of patterns of behavior; therefore, it is limited in its usefulness for addressing specific behavior concerns.

A more structured assessment will help to identify additional underlying factors. The Ziggurat Model incorporates a special assessment – the Underlying Characteristics Checklist (UCC) – to accomplish this task (see sample on page 58).

Consideration of patterns of behavior in addition to underlying characteristics will lead to a better understanding of specific behavioral concerns and their unseen causes. The next section will describe one of the three assessment tools of the Ziggurat Model – the ABC-I. While overcoming limitations of both the FBA and the iceberg analogy, the ABC-I benefits from the strengths of each.

The ABC-Iceberg

The traditional iceberg analogy (Schopler, 1994) examines the relationship between the underlying characteristics of ASD and a given behavior. The combined ABC-Iceberg (ABC-I) has the added benefit of looking at events that occur before and after a behavior (antecedent and consequences). As depicted in Figures 2.8 and 2.9, the ABCs have been added to the iceberg. Examination of these patterns indicates additional aspects of the underlying disorder that may be involved. Compare the example in Figure 2.6 depicting the analysis of social isolation, which includes only the description of the behavior, to the example in Figure 2.8, which includes descriptions of both the antecedents and the consequences along with the behavior. The inclusion of the before and after events brings more aspects of the

Antecedent(s) ⟶ Behavior ⟶ Consequence(s)

Antecedent(s)
3
- Recess
- Low structure
- After lunch

Behavior
1 "Loner" on the playground
2
- Wandering the perimeter
- Flapping hands
- Looking at bugs
- Talking to self

Consequence(s)
4
- Isolated from peers
- Opportunity to engage in stereotypic behavior

Specific Behaviors

5
- Abnormal sensitivity to sound and visual stimuli
- Seeking activities that provide movement
- Difficulties with starting/joining/ending a conversation
- Mindblindness
- Easily stressed
- Unique interests/intense preoccupations
- Difficulty understanding nonverbal communication
- Poor problem-solving skills
- Poor motor coordination

Underlying Characteristics
- Difficulty joining an activity
- Difficulty making friends
- Difficulty joining an activity
- Less involved in group activities
- Withdraws into complex inner worlds
- Strong need for routine or "sameness"
- Displays repetitive motor movements
- Has athletic skills deficits

Figure 2.8. ABC-I model applied to social isolation.

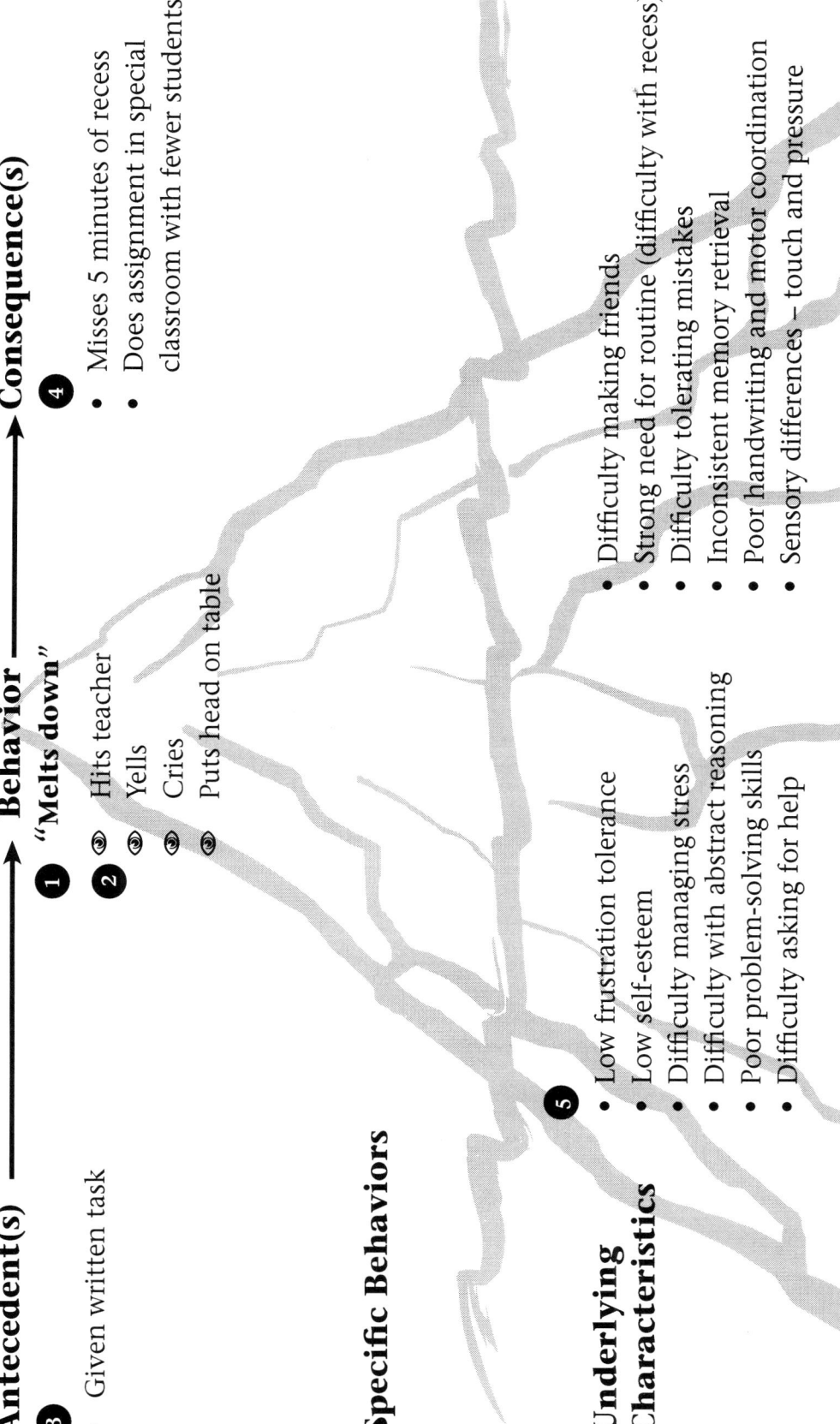

Antecedent(s) ➝ **Behavior** ➝ **Consequence(s)**

3
- Given written task

1 "Melts down"

2
- ② Hits teacher
- ② Yells
- ② Cries
- ② Puts head on table

4
- Misses 5 minutes of recess
- Does assignment in special classroom with fewer students

Specific Behaviors

Underlying Characteristics

5
- Low frustration tolerance
- Low self-esteem
- Difficulty managing stress
- Difficulty with abstract reasoning
- Poor problem-solving skills
- Difficulty asking for help

- Difficulty making friends
- Strong need for routine (difficulty with recess)
- Difficulty tolerating mistakes
- Inconsistent memory retrieval
- Poor handwriting and motor coordination
- Sensory differences – touch and pressure

Figure 2.9. ABC-I model applied to meltdowns.

ASD to light. Consequently, with the additional information – that low structure was an antecedent and isolation from peers was a consequence – it becomes apparent that difficulties with problem solving and understanding nonverbal communication are additional factors that intervention must address. A comparison of Figures 2.7 and 2.9 provides an additional example of the benefits of including the ABCs. Recognizing that written work is an antecedent is an important step in understanding that difficulties with handwriting, sensory differences, and perfectionism should also be considered to be underlying factors.

It is important to note that this child has repeatedly received the consequence of missing recess but to no avail. This suggests that this consequence is not an effective form of punishment because it has failed to result in a decrease in the meltdown behaviors in the way that would be expected for typically developing children. The social impairments of autism – difficulties in unstructured social settings – are then added to the factors that must be considered in the intervention. For example, we may need to provide the child with a card listing recess activities to select from, train peers to engage the child in recess activities, and so on. Without looking at the patterns and underlying characteristics, this type of intervention may appear unusual for addressing meltdowns. It is likely, though, that increasing social success could decrease meltdowns in a number of ways. For example, the student could be calmer in class, self-esteem could be increased, there would be more motivation to cope without meltdowns in order to keep the privilege of recess, skills to communicate successfully at recess could be generalized to communicate needs in an academic setting, and so on.

In short, the relationship between the behavior and the characteristics of the disorder becomes more evident when the antecedents and consequences are included in the assessment.

The ABC-I also helps to overcome limitations of the FBA. As mentioned earlier, interventions based solely on an FBA do not address underlying factors or the impact of ASD on behavior. That is, without understanding the behavior in the context of the disorder, interventions are designed as if the ASD is not a factor. For example, the "meltdown" scenario depicted in Figure 2.9 (ABC portion) leads to the conclusion that the function of the behavior is to escape written tasks (or at least to avoid doing them independently). Several interventions could be designed based on this hypothesis without considering the underlying autism. They might be effective; however, without considering the disorder, they might cause more harm than good or be merely "band aids" by ignoring critical underlying areas for intervention.

An intervention strategy for a child who cries and hits when asked to write might be to double the amount of recess missed from 5 minutes to 10 minutes for each incident of "melting down." Such an intervention may be effective for the typical child who enjoys recess; however, for the child with autism, it might be negatively reinforcing. In other words, because removal from recess provides escape from the overwhelming social and sensory demands of the playground, it may be highly rewarding for a child on the spectrum and would, therefore, result in an *increase* in meltdowns. This example demonstrates how failing to take the underlying characteristics into consideration might lead to unanticipated, harmful results.

Again, consider the student who melts down when given written tasks. An intervention based strictly on the antecedents and consequences might be to strongly reinforce each 2 minutes of writing without yelling and crying, and so on. While it is possible that this intervention would result in increased time writing without meltdowns, similar to the proverb of "teaching a man to fish," addressing underlying factors, such as low frustration tolerance, social skills deficits, and sensory differences, would have a more lasting impact. Further, these skills are more likely to transfer (generalize) outside of the specific classroom setting (e.g., playground) to other situations that may be frustrating (e.g., math and spelling). As a result, interventions based solely on the FBA model may simply be "band aids" that temporarily alter the behavior, without any true change or growth.

One of the greatest challenges in designing interventions is the ability to "see the autism." That is, one must have a strong enough grasp of the characteristics of ASD to be able to see past the surface behavior – recognizing the importance of what lies beneath. In this manner, it becomes apparent that an intense need for routine and sameness may explain what appears to be oppositional and defiant behavior. This shift in perspective is crucial. Without an accurate perception, we are more likely to punish behaviors than to work to prevent them and teach missing skills. This is not to say that all behaviors are related to ASD; however, *when uncertain, it is always better to intervene as if the behavior is related to the disability.*

The ABC-I is an essential tool that builds on the strengths of the FBA model and iceberg analogy. Assessing the patterns of behavior with an understanding of the characteristics of ASD provides the information necessary to develop comprehensive interventions that target the behaviors in addition to the core features of the disorder. The following section discusses how to assess the underlying disorder using the Underlying Characteristics Checklist.

THE UNDERLYING CHARACTERISTICS CHECKLIST AND THE INDIVIDUAL STRENGTHS AND SKILLS INVENTORY

The Underlying Characteristics Checklist (UCC) is an informal assessment tool designed by the authors specifically to identify characteristics across a number of domains associated with ASD for the purpose of intervention (see Figure 2.14). There are five versions of the UCC. The UCC-EI (Early Intervention) is for children aged 3 to 72 months across all levels of functioning. The UCC-CL was designed for individuals 6+ years with below average cognitive skills. The UCC-HF is for individuals 6+ years with average or above cognitive skills. Two self-report measures, the UCC-SR-Adolescent (12-18 years) and UCC-SR-Adult (18+ years) – not illustrated in this book – provide invaluable insights for a variety of uses including program planning, developing counseling goals, and improving personal understanding.

The UCC is not designed for diagnosis; however, it is a helpful component of a comprehensive autism evaluation. The results are used to develop a comprehensive intervention incorporating each of the five levels of the Ziggurat to be discussed in the following chapters: (a) Sensory and Biological, (b) Reinforcement, (c) Structure and Visual/ Tactile Supports, (d) Task Demands and Positive Environment, and (e) Skills to Teach.

The UCC and ISSI may be completed by parents, teachers, or other service providers, such as occupational therapists, speech pathologists, or psychologists. In practice, it is best to have multiple respondents complete the UCC/ISSI because this provides additional perspectives. Furthermore, because the UCC/ISSI requires respondents to review a list of behaviors exhibited by individuals with ASD, their understanding of the underlying autism becomes strengthened. *Thus, the process of completing the UCC/ISSI becomes an intervention in itself.* Increased awareness of the impact of autism and decreased frustration with the individual on the spectrum often result; therefore, the UCC/ISSI is also a helpful tool for professionals who provide consultation services to those working with individuals with ASD.

When specific behavioral difficulties are present, the results of the UCC provide a source for identifying the underlying characteristics on the ABC-I. At times, the focus of an intervention plan is not to address particular behavioral concerns, but to plan a general or global intervention program. In these cases, the checked items from the UCC may be used as the basis for designing the intervention using the Ziggurat Model. Figure 2.10 depicts this process.

For *general* intervention plans, complete the UCC and ISSI and design a program using the Intervention Ziggurat. Refer to Global Intervention Plan: Guide to Establishing Priorities.

In order to address *specific behavioral concerns*, complete the ABC-I using information gathered through observation and the UCC and ISSI. Design a comprehensive, targeted behavior plan using the Intervention Ziggurat. Refer to Specific Intervention Plan: Guide to Establishing Priorities.

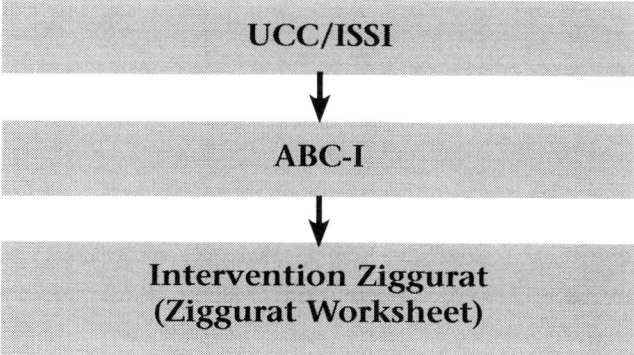

Figure 2.10. **Pathways to intervention using the Ziggurat Model.**

The UCC (see Figure 2.14) is comprised of eight areas. The first three represent the autism spectrum triad, Social; Restricted Patterns of Behavior, Interests, and Activities; and Communication. Characteristics that are often associated with ASD are addressed in the remaining four areas: Sensory Differences; Cognitive Differences; Motor Differences; and Emotional Vulnerability. An eighth underlying factor is included on the UCC – Known Medical and Other Biological Factors. When using the form, the rater simply places a check mark next to each item that describes the characteristics or behaviors of an individual on the spectrum.

The *Notes* column provides a space to describe how a given characteristic is expressed in an individual. Information in this column may include specific examples, frequency of behavior, common antecedents or triggers, and so on. The UCC provides a snapshot of the autism in an individual. The Notes section helps to bring clarity to this picture. Further, this information aids in communicating with others involved in intervention and becomes a basis of comparison for follow-up. These items are then addressed through interventions based on the Intervention Ziggurat to be described in Chapter 3.

An additional column, *Description of Mastered or Developing Skills*, is included on the UCC-EI. This column is used to describe skills related to the corresponding checked items that are demonstrated by the child. Mastered and developing skills are included to guide the respondent/team to design more individualized and appropriate interventions based on the child's abilities and strengths.

The UCC-HF and UCC-CL also include a column labeled *Follow-Up*. This column is completed after interventions have been implemented and allows for an informal evaluation of intervention outcomes to be used for intervention adjustment and planning. The UCC-EI does not have a follow-up column. Because the early years are a period of rapid development, the follow-up is done by completing a new UCC-EI form. The ISSI (Individual Strengths and Skills Inventory) was designed to accompany the UCC (see Figure 2.15). It consists of eight areas that parallel the eight areas of the UCC. The purpose of this tool is to ensure that underlying strengths and skills are considered by the team in the intervention design process. The ISSI is embedded in the UCC-EI. It is completed as a separate form when using the UCC-HF or UCC-CL. The ISSI form is located in Appendix B.

Case Example

Jonathan is a 10th-grade student on the autism spectrum. Although he is a bright, well-behaved student, he is failing science. His teacher, Ms. Gordesky, thinks that Jonathan does not care about school. He does not write his assignments in his planner. As a result, he often fails to turn in his homework. He does not participate in class or group activities. She has found him sneaking his personal copy of The Lord of the Rings *inside his science book. On a recent unit test, Jonathan did not complete an entire section. When she asked him what happened, Jona-than politely replied, "I already answered those for the test review." Ms. Gordesky has also ob-served that Jonathan reads in the hallways, during lunch, and before class. During free time, he reads at his desk while his classmates socialize. When people greet him, he often ignores them. At times, he "traps" students in lengthy conversations about the appendices of the book. Jona-than is most animated and able to make eye contact when discussing* The Lord of the Rings. *At other times, his mood seems "flat" and eye contact is fleeting.*

The ABC-I may be used to examine the function of Jonathan's behavior in light of ASD. The following section reviews each step of Jonathan's assessment using the ABC-I and the UCC. Assessment is the foundation for developing his intervention using the Ziggurat Model.

Using the ABC-Iceberg and the UCC

Jonathan's behavior was described by Ms. Gordesky as "Not caring about school." In order to more closely analyze Jonathan's behavior, Ms. Gordesky's description must be operationalized. The specific observable behaviors are: not writing down assignments or turning in homework, reading during class, and lack of participation during classroom and group activities. After careful observation of these specific behaviors, antecedents and consequences were identified. Figure 2.11 depicts the completed top portion of the ABC-Iceberg.

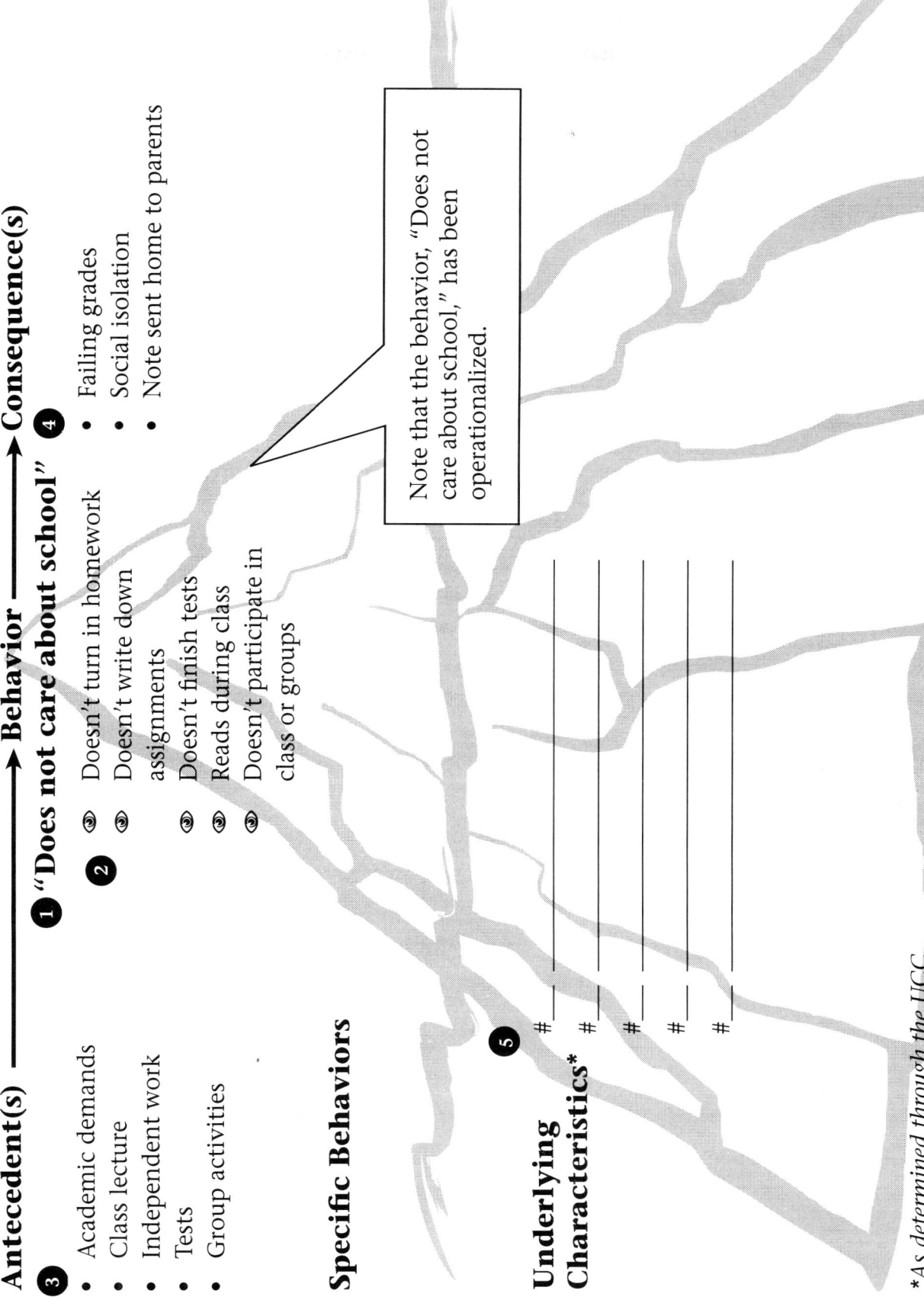

Antecedent(s) ⟶ **Behavior** ⟶ **Consequence(s)**

① "Does not care about school" **④**

③
- Academic demands
- Class lecture
- Independent work
- Tests
- Group activities

②
- Doesn't turn in homework
- Doesn't write down assignments
- Doesn't finish tests
- Reads during class
- Doesn't participate in class or groups

- Failing grades
- Social isolation
- Note sent home to parents

Note that the behavior, "Does not care about school," has been operationalized.

Specific Behaviors

Underlying Characteristics*

⑤
- # _____
- # _____
- # _____
- # _____
- # _____

*As determined through the UCC.

Figure 2.11. ABC-I model applied to off-task behaviors.

Figure 2.12 depicts Ms. Gordesky's impression of the consequences (positive and negative). If her hypothesis is correct, then Jonathan's failure to complete work and participate in class should decrease because it is being punished by failing grades and negative notes sent to his parents. (By definition, punishment always leads to a decrease in behavior.) Ms. Gordesky's perceptions would be accurate for most of Jonathan's neurotypical peers, who are motivated by social interaction and grades. However, the fact that this behavior has persisted suggests that what is reinforcing and punishing for Jonathan is different. Figure 2.13 depicts the consequences from Jonathan's perception.

The ABC portion of Figure 2.11 includes only observable aspects of the situation. A UCC may be used to discern how Jonathan's autism may contribute to his behavior by identifying behaviors related to autism that may become *targets for intervention*. Figure 2.14 and 2.15 summarize possible responses about Jonathan that Ms. Gordesky might provide on the UCC and ISSI. Only Ms. Gordesky's responses are shown here; however, it is best practice to have multiple responders complete the UCC and ISSI.

The process of completing the UCC may lead to a change in perspective regarding Jonathan's behavior and needs because it illuminates the link between autism and behavior. Thus, the initial impression of Jonathan as an indifferent, defiant, and rude student changes to seeing him as overwhelmed by the school environment and unprepared to deal with the social demands. Without recognizing that mindblindness is a factor, Jonathan's failure to complete the entire test may be bewildering at best. From Jonathan's perspective, he has answered these questions before, and he believes that his teacher is thinking the same thing. The thought that all students are expected to complete the whole test – whether or not they did the review – is not part of his world view. Moreover, the thought that not finishing something as crucial as a unit test could be considered oppositional never occurred to him. Understanding that Jonathan's withdrawal and failure to complete his test are signs of poor coping skills and mindblindness – rather than an "attitude problem" – is crucial to effective and humane, intervention.

Reinforcement and Punishment Grid

	Desired	Dreaded
Apply	**Positive Reinforcement**	**Punishment** • Failing grades • Note home to parents
Remove	**Negative Punishment** • Immersion in books results in a loss of opportunity for peer interaction	**Negative Reinforcement**

Note. Ms. Gordesky believes that peer interaction and good grades are desired by Jonathan and that, therefore, negative notes, failing grades, and lack of participation are punishing.

Figure 2.12. Reinforcement and punishment grid from teacher's perspective.

Reinforcement and Punishment Grid

	Desired	Dreaded
Apply	**Positive Reinforcement** • Attains more time to read *The Lord of the Rings* by avoiding work and class participation	**Punishment**
Remove	**Negative Punishment**	**Negative Reinforcement** • Decreases social stress by avoiding group work and class participation

Note. Jonathan sees increased time to read and avoidance of stress as reinforcing.

Figure 2.13. Reinforcement and punishment grid from Jonathan's perspective.

UNDERLYING CHARACTERISTICS CHECKLIST-HF

Ruth Aspy, Ph.D., and Barry G. Grossman, Ph.D.

NAME: *Jonathan*   COMPLETED BY: *Mrs. Gordesky*

DATE: *5-15-*   FOLLOW-UP DATE:

DIRECTIONS: Place check beside all items that apply and describe behaviors observed.

Area	Item	✔	Notes	Follow-Up
SOCIAL	1. Has difficulty recognizing the feelings and thoughts of others (mindblindness)	✔	*Keeps talking when people are tired of listening. Thinks that teacher is thinking what he thinks.*	
	2. Uses poor eye contact	✔	*With adults and peers.*	
	3. Has difficulty maintaining personal space, physically intrudes on others			
	4. Lacks tact or appears rude	✔	*Ignores others' attempts at engaging him in conversations. Criticizes what others read.*	
	5. Has difficulty making or keeping friends	✔	*He's a loner. No real friends at school.*	
	6. Has difficulty joining an activity			
	7. Is naïve, easily taken advantage of, or bullied			
	8. Tends to be less involved in group activities than most same-age individuals	✔	• *Avoids group work.* • *Chooses independent assignments when given option.* • *Alone during lunch.*	
	9. Has difficulty understanding others' nonverbal communication (e.g., facial expressions, body language, tone of voice)			
	10. Has difficulty understanding jokes	✔	*He has a delayed response to jokes. Seems like he looks to peers to see if they are laughing and then imitates them when jokes are told.*	
	11. Other			
RESTRICTED PATTERNS OF BEHAVIOR, INTERESTS, AND ACTIVITIES	12. Expresses strong need for routine or "sameness"	✔	*Reads the same books over and over.*	
	13. Expresses desire for repetition			
	14. Has eccentric or intense preoccupations/absorption in own unique interests	✔	• *The* Lord of the Rings *series* • *Swords* • *Medieval history*	
	15. Asks repetitive questions			
	16. Seems to be unmotivated by customary rewards			
	17. Displays repetitive motor movements (e.g., flaps hands, paces, flicks fingers in front of eyes)			
	18. Has problems handling transition and change			
	19. Has strong need for closure or difficulty stopping a task before it is completed	✔	*He needs reassurance that he can work on science lab tomorrow if he does not finish in one day.*	
	20. Other	✔	*Repeats phrases from books and movies.*	

Figure 2.14. UCC for Jonathan.

Area	Item	✔	Notes	Follow-Up
COMMUNICATION	21. Makes sounds or states words or phrases repeatedly [non-echolalic] (e.g., humming, "well actually")			
	22. Makes up new words or creates alternate meanings for words or phrases			
	23. Displays immediate or delayed echolalia (e.g., recites lines from movies, repeats another person's questions or statements, repeats sounds)			
	24. Interprets words or conversations literally/has difficulty understanding figurative language			
	25. Has difficulty with rules of conversation (e.g., interrupts others, asks inappropriate questions, makes poor eye contact, has difficulty maintaining conversation)	✔	*He walks away without saying anything.*	
	26. Fails to initiate or respond to social greetings			
	27. Has difficulty using gestures and facial expressions			
	28. Has difficulty starting, joining, and/or ending a conversation	✔	*Jonathan will not join in others' conversations.*	
	29. Has difficulty asking for help			
	30. Makes irrelevant comments			
	31. Has difficulty expressing thoughts and feelings			
	32. Speaks in an overly formal way	✔	*Frequently says, "hither with" and "doubtlessly."*	
	33. Gives false impression of understanding more than he/she actually does			
	34. Talks incessantly, little back-and-forth			
	35. Uses an advanced vocabulary	✔	*Uses vocabulary words I would not expect for a 10th-grade student.*	
	36. Uses mechanical, "singsong" voice or speech sounds unusual in other ways (e.g., prosody, cadence, tone)			
	37. Has difficulty following instructions			
	38. Has difficulty understanding language with multiple meanings, humor, sarcasm, or synonyms			
	39. Has difficulty talking about others' interests	✔	*Talks only about his interests.*	
	40. Other			

Figure 2.14. UCC for Jonathan (continued).

Area	Item	✔	Notes	Follow-Up
SENSORY DIFFERENCES	41. Responds in an unusual manner to sounds (e.g., ignores sounds or over-reacts to sudden, unexpected noises, high-pitched continuous sounds, or complex/multiple noises)			
	42. Responds in an unusual manner to pain (e.g., overreacts or seems unaware of an illness or injury)			
	43. Responds in an unusual manner to taste (e.g., resists certain textures, flavors, brands)			
	44. Responds in an unusual manner to light or color (e.g., focuses on shiny items, shadows, reflections, shows preference or strong dislike for certain colors)			
	45. Responds in an unusual manner to temperature			
	46. Responds in an unusual manner to smells (e.g., may comment on smells that others do not detect)	✔	*Often complains about the smell in the lab.*	
	47. Seeks activities that provide touch, pressure, or movement (e.g., swinging, hugging, pacing)	✔	*Jonathan leans from side to side while standing in the hallway or talking.*	
	48. Avoids activities that provide touch, pressure, or movement (e.g., resists wearing certain types of clothing, strongly dislikes to be dirty, resists hugs)			
	49. Makes noises such as humming or singing frequently			
	50. Other			
COGNITIVE DIFFERENCES	51. Displays extensive knowledge in narrow areas of interest	✔	*Fantasy, history.*	
	52. Displays poor problem-solving skills			
	53. Has poor organizational skills			
	54. Withdraws into complex inner worlds/fantasizes often			
	55. Is easily distracted by unrelated details – has difficulty knowing what is relevant or makes off-topic comments			
	56. Displays weakness in reading comprehension with strong word recognition	✔	*Fails chapter tests.*	
	57. Knows many facts and details but has difficulty with abstract reasoning (i.e., weak central coherence)	✔	*Able to memorize the periodic table but cannot balance formulas.*	

Figure 2.14. UCC for Jonathan (continued).

Area	Item	✓	Notes	Follow-Up
COGNITIVE DIFFERENCES	58. Has difficulty applying learned skills in new settings			
	59. Has academic skills deficits			
	60. Has attention problems	✓	*Except when he is reading his book.*	
	61. Displays very literal understanding of concepts			
	62. Recalls information inconsistently (i.e., seems to forget previously learned information)	✓	*Jonathan is able to show skills on test reviews but fails the unit tests.*	
	63. Has difficulty understanding the connection between behavior and resulting consequences			
	64. Other			
MOTOR DIFFERENCES	65. Has balance difficulties			
	66. Resists or refuses handwriting tasks			
	67. Has poor handwriting			
	68. Has poor motor coordination (e.g., accident prone, difficulty using fasteners)			
	69. Writes slowly			
	70. Displays atypical activity level (e.g., over-active/hyperactive, under-active/hypoactive)			
	71. Has athletic skills deficits			
	72. Displays an awkward gait			
	73. Displays unusual body postures and movements or facial expressions (e.g., odd postures, stiffness, "freezing," facial grimacing)			
	74. Has difficulty starting or completing actions (e.g., may rely on physical or verbal prompting by others)			
	75. Other			

Figure 2.14. UCC for Jonathan (continued).

Area	Item	✔	Notes	Follow-Up
EMOTIONAL VULNERABILITY	76. Is easily stressed – worries obsessively			
	77. Appears to be depressed or sad			
	78. Has unusual fear response (e.g., lacks appropriate fears or awareness of danger or is overly fearful)			
	79. Appears anxious			
	80. Exhibits rage reactions or "meltdowns"			
	81. Injures self (e.g., bangs head, picks skin, bites nails until they bleed, bites self)			
	82. Makes suicidal comments or gestures			
	83. Displays inconsistent behaviors			
	84. Has difficulty tolerating mistakes			
	85. Has low frustration tolerance			
	86. Has low self-esteem, makes negative comments about self			
	87. Has difficulty identifying, quantifying, expressing, and/or controlling emotions (e.g., can only recognize and express emotions in extremes or fails to express emotions – "emotionally flat")			
	88. Has a limited understanding of own and others' emotional responses	✔	*He thinks that I'm mad at him when I ask him to stop working and finish it tomorrow.*	
	89. Has difficulty managing stress and/or anxiety	✔	*Poor coping skills.*	
	90. Other			

Area	Description	Notes	Follow-Up
KNOWN MEDICAL OR OTHER BIOLOGICAL FACTORS			

Figure 2.14. UCC for Jonathan (continued).

Individual Strengths and Skills Inventory

Ruth Aspy, Ph.D., and Barry G. Grossman, Ph.D.

When designing an effective intervention plan, it is important to consider individual strengths. Please describe strengths in the following areas:

Social

- Polite student
- Enjoys talking to peers about his interests
- Makes eye contact when discussing his interests
- Shows desire to "fit in"

Behavior, Interests, and Activities

- Loves to read – reads above grade level
- Handles transition and change well
- Diligent in pursuit of interests

Communication

- Able to communicate effectively on preferred topics
- Able to vary tone of voice when discussing topics of interest

Sensory

- Eats a variety of foods
- Able to tolerate noise well

Cognitive

- Bright student
- Able to complete assignments independently
- Reads above grade level

Motor

- Writes legibly
- Good gross- and fine-motor skills
- Performs well in individual sports

Emotional

- Mood brightens when discussing interests
- Does not become upset with grades/mistakes
- Responds calmly to conflict

Biological

- Passed hearing and vision screening

Figure 2.15. ISSI for Jonathan.

The final portion of the ABC-I may be completed by using information gathered from the UCC. Items from the UCC that are most directly related to antecedents, behavior, and consequences are listed on the bottom portion of the ABC-I (see Figure 2.16). In determining the items to include on the bottom of the ABC-I, *each item endorsed* on the entire UCC is reviewed. If uncertain regarding the relatedness of a particular item to a behavior, it is important to err on the side of including the underlying characteristic. In other words, it is better to address a need that does not apply than not to address one that does. This process is dynamic. Identifying the antecedents, behaviors, and consequences often results in the realization that additional underlying characteristics exist. Additional UCC items should then be endorsed and reflected on the ABC-I. Instructions for completion and a copy of the ABC-I form are included in Appendix D.

This case demonstrates the importance of assessment in the process of conceptualizing behavior and designing interventions. In this case example, we looked at the antecedents and consequences to better understand the behavior pattern. We also looked at the underlying factors using the UCC. This information was combined on the ABC-Iceberg – facilitating the analysis of the observable in relation to factors that lie beneath the surface. This important step sets the stage for purposeful, thoughtful intervention design.

FOLLOW-UP

After an intervention plan has been implemented, the UCC again plays an important role as a tool for tracking progress and determining if changes are necessary. During the planning of the intervention, the team should discuss an appropriate interval of time for implementation of the intervention prior to evaluating its effectiveness. Follow-up data may be qualitative and/or quantitative. Either or both types of data can be recorded on the UCC in the Follow-Up column.

Qualitative. Conduct informal observations of behavior in settings similar to the original observation settings in order to evaluate outcomes.

Quantitative. Conduct more formal observations in settings similar to the original settings by taking frequency, duration, etc., data on the operationally defined behaviors.

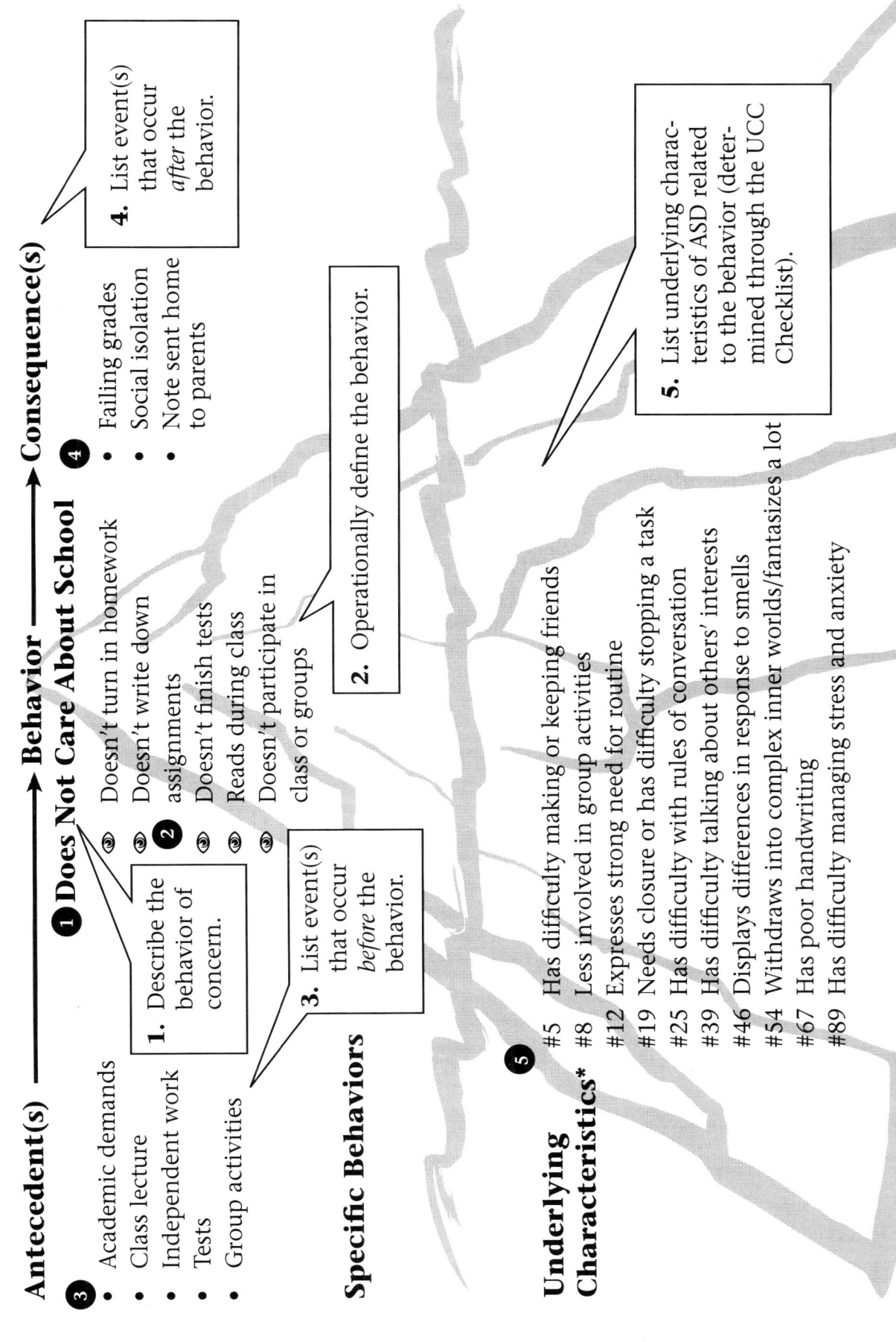

Antecedent(s) ──────➤ **Behavior** ──────➤ **Consequence(s)**

❶ Does Not Care About School

❸
• Academic demands
• Class lecture
• Independent work
• Tests
• Group activities

3. List event(s) that occur *before* the behavior.

❷
ⓐ Doesn't turn in homework
ⓐ Doesn't write down assignments
ⓐ Doesn't finish tests
ⓐ Reads during class
ⓐ Doesn't participate in class or groups

1. Describe the behavior of concern.

2. Operationally define the behavior.

❹
• Failing grades
• Social isolation
• Note sent home to parents

4. List event(s) that occur *after* the behavior.

5. List underlying characteristics of ASD related to the behavior (determined through the UCC Checklist).

Specific Behaviors

Underlying Characteristics*

❺
#5   Has difficulty making or keeping friends
#8   Less involved in group activities
#12 Expresses strong need for routine
#19 Needs closure or has difficulty stopping a task
#25 Has difficulty with rules of conversation
#39 Has difficulty talking about others' interests
#46 Displays differences in response to smells
#54 Withdraws into complex inner worlds/fantasizes a lot
#67 Has poor handwriting
#89 Has difficulty managing stress and anxiety

As determined through the UCC.

Figure 2.16. Completed ABC-I for Jonathan.

At follow-up, three outcomes may occur:

Outcome	Response
1. No improvement has occurred	Revise interventions
2. Behavioral difficulties have increased	Revise interventions
3. Behavioral improvements have occurred	Revise goal behaviors

Any of these outcomes requires a new/revised intervention plan. Based on the information recorded in the Follow-Up column, a new Ziggurat Worksheet should be completed to help design a new comprehensive intervention plan. (Chapter 9 contains information that is helpful for this kind of troubleshooting.)

SUMMARY

Assessment guides intervention. The Ziggurat Model incorporates three assessment tools that have been discussed in this chapter. The first, the ABC-I, combines FBA with the iceberg analogy, allowing for an analysis of patterns of behavior within the context of ASD. The second, the UCC, examines behavior across eight areas. The information gathered through use of the ABC-I and the UCC sets the stage for targeted and individualized intervention plans. The UCC also serves as a tool for monitoring the outcomes of the intervention plan and revising the plan as needed.

CHAPTER HIGHLIGHTS

- *Functional behavioral assessments are used to examine events that occur before and after a behavior and help to identify patterns.*

- *Antecedents are environmental factors that occur before a behavior.*

- *Consequences refer to both positive and negative events that occur after a behavior.*

- *By definition, reinforcement must result in an increase in behavior. In contrast, consequences that are punishing always result in a decrease in behavior.*

- *Interventions based on the FBA can be designed to make changes at three different points – antecedent, behavior, or consequence.*

- *The FBA focuses exclusively on observable behaviors, treating knowledge of specific diagnoses, such as ASD, as irrelevant for intervention planning.*

- *The iceberg metaphor is used to address underlying deficits or characteristics associated with autism.*

- *One of the greatest challenges in designing interventions is the ability to "see the autism."*

- *The ABC-Iceberg (ABC-I) is a tool for assessing the patterns of behavior with an understanding of the characteristics of ASD.*

- *The Underlying Characteristics Checklists (UCC-HF, UCC-CL, and UCC-EI) are informal assessment tools designed specifically to identify characteristics across a number of domains associated with ASD.*

- *The Individual Strengths and Skills Inventory (ISSI) was designed to ensure that underlying strengths and skills are considered in the intervention design process. It parallels the first eight areas of the UCC.*

3 The Intervention Ziggurat: Framework for Change

"There is nothing so stable as change."
– Bob Dylan

With assessment information in hand, the actual process of planning intervention begins. An overwhelming array of interventions for ASD are available on the Internet and in books and articles. They are described as treatments or sometimes even "cures." In reality, the complexity and pervasive nature of autism suggest that there are no simple solutions. Furthermore, autism presents so differently within and across individuals that a one-size-fits-all approach to intervention is not possible. *Interventions must be specifically designed for an individual.*

Unfortunately, up until now, there has been no road map to guide this process. The Ziggurat Model (ZM) facilitates the development of an individualized comprehensive intervention plan based on treatments supported by scientific research. Rather than haphazardly selecting and implementing single strategies that address only surface concerns, the ZM guides the development of a series of approaches designed to target the behavioral concerns, as well as the core features of the disorder.

This chapter presents the Intervention Ziggurat (IZ), the core of the ZM, to guide this process. Use of the ZM for addressing specific behavioral needs (targeted intervention planning) and for global or general program design is described. The chapter concludes with a discussion of the advantages of the model.

INTERVENTION ZIGGURAT

The IZ facilitates the development of targeted, comprehensive positive interventions. It incorporates five critical levels, structured in a hierarchy: Sensory and Biological, Reinforcement, Structure and Visual/Tactile Supports, Task Demands and Positive Environment, and Skills to Teach (see Figure 3.1).

Starting at the base or foundation, the first three levels of the Ziggurat depict internal and environmental factors. More specifically, Level 1, Sensory and Biological, addresses basic internal factors that impact all functioning. The second level addresses motivational needs prerequisite to skill development. Level 3 draws on the strength of visual processing and addresses the need for order and routine that is fundamental to autistic individuals. The final two levels of the IZ focus on understanding expectations in light of the characteristics of autistic individuals and targeting appropriate skills to develop.

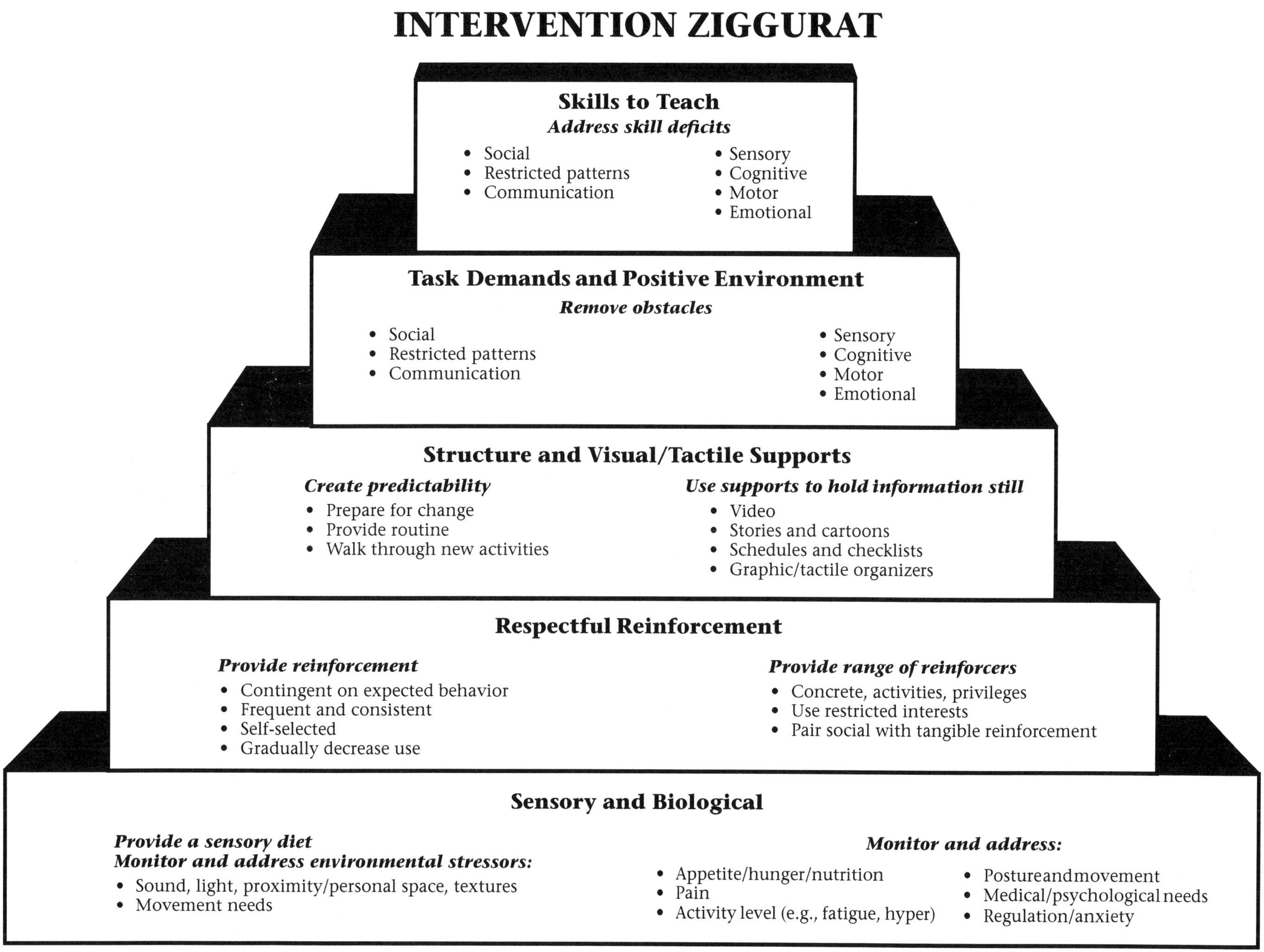

INTERVENTION ZIGGURAT

Skills to Teach
Address skill deficits

- Social
- Restricted patterns
- Communication
- Sensory
- Cognitive
- Motor
- Emotional

Task Demands and Positive Environment
Remove obstacles

- Social
- Restricted patterns
- Communication
- Sensory
- Cognitive
- Motor
- Emotional

Structure and Visual/Tactile Supports

Create predictability

- Prepare for change
- Provide routine
- Walk through new activities

Use supports to hold information still

- Video
- Stories and cartoons
- Schedules and checklists
- Graphic/tactile organizers

Respectful Reinforcement

Provide reinforcement

- Contingent on expected behavior
- Frequent and consistent
- Self-selected
- Gradually decrease use

Provide range of reinforcers

- Concrete, activities, privileges
- Use restricted interests
- Pair social with tangible reinforcement

Sensory and Biological

Provide a sensory diet
Monitor and address environmental stressors:

- Sound, light, proximity/personal space, textures
- Movement needs

Monitor and address:

- Appetite/hunger/nutrition
- Pain
- Activity level (e.g., fatigue, hyper)
- Posture and movement
- Medical/psychological needs
- Regulation/anxiety

Figure 3.1. Intervention Ziggurat.

Sensory and Biological

The base of the Ziggurat represents what is, in one sense, the basis of all behavior – biology. This is especially important in the case of autism – a disorder that has strong genetic and neurological underpinnings. Multiple interacting genes are involved in the development of ASD. In fact, twin studies indicate that across the spectrum, the heritability rate exceeds 90%. This is higher than any other heritable disorder, including schizophrenia and bipolar disorder (Nicolson & Szatmari, 2003; Rutter, 2000; Santangelo & Tsatsanis, 2005). Significant differences in the structure and development of the brain (size, volume, and mass) have been identified (Nicolson & Szatmari). These differences result in sensory and biological needs that often differ from those of neurotypical individuals. Unmet sensory and biological needs result in changes in behavior. For this reason, the development of effective behavior intervention programs requires consideration of biological factors and inclusion of interventions to address needs at this level. With individuals on the autism spectrum, this consideration must be informed by an understanding of biological and sensory differences fundamental to the disorder itself.

Motor and Sensory Functioning

Motor clumsiness, awkward gait, and fine- and gross-motor deficits have been noted at a higher rate in individuals with ASD than in the general population (Rinehart, Bradshaw, Brereton, & Tonge, 2002). Further, in individuals with ASD, atypical patterns of sensory functioning are present as early as 9 months of age (Baranek, 2002). Sensory "preoccupations," the tendency to repeat behaviors that stimulate one sense, are consistent symptoms of ASD, present in as many as 90% of the population (Baranek). Significant differences in sensory processing are evident in the majority of individuals with ASD (Baranek; Dunn, Myles, & Orr, 2002). Finally, abnormalities have been noted in all of the senses – sight, sound, smell, touch, and taste (Baranek). These differences impact awareness of the environment as well as ability to use and understand information gathered through the senses (Dunn et al.; Huebner, 2001; Myles et al., 2004).

Sleep

Differences in the biological process of sleep are also important considerations. Increased rates of sleep difficulties among individuals with ASD are well documented (Hoffman et al., 2005; Honomichl, Goodlin-Jones, Burnham, Gaylor, & Anders, 2002; Polemini, Richdale, & Francis, 2005), and are associated with increased symptom expression (Hoffman et al.; Schreck, Mulick, & Smith, 2004). Sleep differences include atypical bedtime routines, behavior difficulties at bedtime, waking during the night, waking early in the morning, and difficulty going to sleep.

Current research indicates that individuals with AS exhibit more sleep disturbances than those with the diagnosis of autism or typically developing individuals. Disturbed patterns of sleep frequently experienced by children with the diagnosis of AS include less REM sleep, increased waking during the night, poor sleep quality, and more disoriented waking (Polemini et al.).

Implications for Intervention

Research findings indicating genetic differences and structural anomalies of the brain confirm the pervasive and fundamental role of biology in ASD. The sleep disturbances, language deficits, anxiety, attention deficits, and sensory and motor difficulties seen so often in individuals on the autism spectrum likely result from these underlying factors. Biological functioning may also impact behavior in a more typical fashion. For example, hunger, pain, fatigue, illness, nutrition, and general health influence the behavior of everyone. The best potential for constructive or positive behavior occurs with health and physical equilibrium.

> *Note.* An analysis of the impact of biological and sensory factors is a necessary part of planning an intervention. Genetic makeup and the structure of the brain will not be changed by nonmedical interventions; however, interventions may be changed to adjust for attention and language deficits, clumsiness, sleep disturbances, and so on. Modifying the environment to ensure physical health and comfort and optimal sensory arousal level may be critical to the success of an intervention program.

Reinforcement

The second level of the Ziggurat represents another fundamental need – reinforcement. It is defined as "a situation or event that follows a particular behavior, resulting in an increased likelihood that a behavior will recur in the future" (Bregman & Gerdtz, 1997, p. 611). Students learn to raise their hand because they want to be called on. Children learn that when they complete their chores, they earn their allowance. Adults go to work because they want a paycheck. Further, provided that the consequence is desirable, the behavior will be displayed more in the future. Individuals most often make choices that result in the greatest payoff.

Sometimes avoidance of an activity carries a greater incentive than does participation. For example, a person who struggles with understanding social interactions may find browsing the Internet more rewarding than interacting with family members. A student who finds heat and noise aversive may be more motivated to leave his work incomplete to avoid recess and stay in the air-conditioned classroom for study hall. These examples highlight the fact that there may be important differences in what individuals on the spectrum find reinforcing compared to their neurotypical peers.

The ultimate goal of comprehensive interventions is to help individuals develop skills that will increase their chance of lifelong success. Reinforcement is essential to the process of acquiring new skills. Over time, as a skill is mastered, reinforcement is still required to maintain behavior. Individuals on the spectrum may lack skills that their age-mates have acquired. Therefore, they will require instruction and reinforcement for specific behaviors that are generally assumed to have been mastered by those in their age group. This mistaken assumption may lead to punitive approaches to addressing failure to display a skill that has actually never been acquired.

Angie

Angie, a sixth-grade autistic student, needed help from her teacher to complete her math assignment. Although four other students were standing in line at the teacher's desk waiting for assistance, Angie walked directly to her teacher's side and began asking her question. The teacher reprimanded Angie for being "inconsiderate" of her peers and sent her to the hall to think about what she had just done.

Angie, who had been encouraged in the past to ask for help when she needed it, sat in the hall wondering why asking the teacher a question was inconsiderate to her peers. The teacher, for her part, assumed that all sixth-graders knew how and why to take turns. Because Angie was so bright, the teacher never imagined that this was a skill Angie had not yet mastered.

For many, the natural consequences of displaying a skill are sufficient to support its occurrence. However, these consequences may not be as reinforcing for those on the spectrum; therefore, additional incentives are required. For example, the natural consequence of greeting others may be a nonverbal response (e.g., smile, wave). The value of this may be missed by many on the spectrum. This raises an additional point to consider – *autistic individuals may need additional reinforcers for behaviors that others learn naturally.*

Certain aspects inherent in ASD make reinforcement more challenging; specifically, attention problems, narrow and unusual interests, and decreased interest in social praise. An example will help to illustrate some of these difficulties.

Michael

Michael is a 6-year-old boy on the autism spectrum. He enjoys puzzles, blocks, and cars. He does not play with his peers. Michael has good language skills; however, he typically only converses to request one of his preferred activities. He has difficulty focusing during class activities and does not participate during calendar time on the floor. At times, he leaves the circle in an attempt to play with blocks. When redirected, he will sometimes hit his teacher.

Shortening the time delay between behavior and the consequence by increasing the rate of reinforcement is central to effective intervention design for individuals showing symptoms of inattention. Providing consequences more rapidly is one way of changing the demands of a task to increase success. The appropriate rate of reinforcement may be two hours or two weeks depending on the individual and the task. However, because most individuals on the spectrum experience attention difficulties, they need more rapid reinforcement to be successful. For Michael in the above example, this means that in order for him to participate in calendar time, meaningful reinforcers must be provided more rapidly than for his peers.

Most autistic individuals have narrow and unusual interests that can make it challenging to find salient reinforcers. While most children are reinforced by watching a Disney film, for example, a child on the spectrum may be more motivated by an opportunity to watch an episode of *This Old House* due to an intense interest in construction. Similarly, in school, stickers, points, or privileges such as being the line leader may be effective consequences for most children; however, an autistic child in this environment might not share an interest in these kinds of reinforcers. *It is important to think outside of the box in order to find effective incentives*.

Siegel (2003) notes that, for individuals with ASD, pursuing their own wishes is often more valuable than the risk of displeasing others. In other words, social motivation may not be meaningful to them. While Michael's classmates enjoyed the opportunity to please their teacher and receive her praise during calendar time, he did not. Instead, the opportunity to play with blocks was more rewarding to Michael, and his aggression was motivated by the desire to attain his goal (blocks). Michael was seemingly unaffected by his teacher's less-than-happy facial expressions and tone of voice in response to being hit. Loss of her approval did not register with him.

Siegel (2003) points out that much of our world is built upon the assumption that we want to please others and receive approval. For instance, students participate in class discussions to receive approval from their classmates and praise from their teacher. When the teacher praises a few students for sitting correctly, she expects that others will quickly follow suit because they also want to be praised. Similarly, children follow their parents' directions in order to please them, hear their praise, and avoid their disapproval.

These incentives are like gold to most children but not necessarily to those on the spectrum, who may be more interested in pleasing themselves even if this means ignoring or doing the opposite of what adults tell them. In short, individuals on the spectrum may lack the motivation to participate and attend to activities based on social reinforcement. This is especially problematic in settings, such as schools, that are based on this premise. According to Siegel (2003), these environments must be restructured such that meaningful rewards are available for children with ASD. Further, eventually, these children must be taught to respond to social incentives by pairing them with salient reinforcers.

Returning to Michael, his teacher quickly learned that he was not motivated by the social reinforcers that were available. So she decided to use puzzles, blocks, and cars to reward him for specific behaviors such as participation during calendar time and appropriate play with a peer during centers. She paired her social praise with presentation of his reinforcers in order to increase the value of her comments. Over time, her praise should become more meaningful.

Note on Punishment

When developing the IZ, we first considered naming this level consequences in recognition of the fact that many interventions include reinforcement as well as different forms of punishment. Ultimately, however, we decided to minimize the role of punishment by an exclusive focus on reinforcement in the Ziggurat Model.

This decision was made for two primary reasons. First, one of the greatest challenges in designing interventions for autistic individuals is the ability to "see the autism." It is often difficult to recognize when behavior difficulties are directly related to ASD. When uncertain, it is always better to intervene as if the behavior is related to the autism. It is never acceptable to punish an individual for his or her disability. It is preferable to address the underlying skill deficits through instruction and reinforcement. Next, punishment is a stressor. Given that simply participating in daily activities is often highly stressful for those on the spectrum, additional stress caused by punitive approaches should be avoided. This is not to say that consequences may not appropriately include punishment at times; however, a system of checks and balances must be in place before considering a punitive approach. In contrast, reinforcement should always be a major emphasis of all intervention plans.

Structure and Visual/Tactile Supports

The third level of the Ziggurat, Structure and Visual/Tactile Supports, is based on core characteristics of ASD, including deficits in verbal communication and a need for routine and order. Verbal communication deficits are primary characteristics of ASD, leading to a disadvantage in school, family, and work settings, where most communication is accomplished through talking and listening. Weaknesses in processing auditory information compound this disadvantage.

Additionally, individuals on the spectrum often have an intense drive to find order and make sense of their world. They have difficulty predicting what will happen or what others are likely to do in a given situation; therefore, they tend to continually need direction and input. This again leaves them at a disadvantage at home, school, and work, where expectations for independence rise throughout childhood, adolescence, and young adulthood. In each environment, high levels of structure and routine may be built into the daily schedule in order to increase success and independence.

People on the spectrum tend to conceptualize ideas and experiences in a visual way. For example, many develop visual images or pictures to represent memories that most others would store in words. Because of this strong tendency, visual supports are critical aspects of an intervention program. In comparison to other forms of input, visual supports may be referred to as needed, thereby placing less demand on memory.

Visual information such as pictures, written schedules, or even cartoon strips is used to address a variety of needs, including increased predictability and explanation of social situations. Visual supports have been shown to improve communication skills in children on the spectrum who have some verbal abilities (Thieman & Goldstein, 2004). Furthermore, visual supports can serve to break down a task into a series of steps (task analysis) to be followed one at a time. This facilitates independence in areas such as adaptive and social skills and academic tasks.

Oliver Sacks (BBC, 1996) describes a "rage for order," the need for routine and predictability often expressed by autistic individuals. The lack of predictability is a frequent trigger of behavioral difficulties. Unpredicted changes – rainy days, new menus in the cafeteria, TV schedules, hairstyles – might lead to confusion and anxiety, and even rage. Provision of high levels of structure and routine decreases problem behaviors. The predictability provided through increased structure also results in increased independence because the ability to predict and understand events in the day decreases the need to rely on others.

Structure and visual/tactile supports are interrelated concepts. Both increase the ability of individuals on the spectrum to predict and understand the world.

Structure and visual/tactile supports may be introduced into the intervention design at multiple points. In other words, they may be antecedent, behavior, or consequence interventions. For example, an intervention for a young adult preparing for a job interview addresses the need for structure and visual supports at each point. Introducing a written schedule of the steps of a job interview a week prior to the meeting is an example of using a visual support as an antecedent intervention. This intervention would increase the predictability and, therefore, the structure of the new situation. Providing a video of a peer modeling the skills and traits that the employer is seeking is an example of using an intervention at the point of behavior. The video is a visual support designed to teach new behaviors or interview skills. Finally, following a role play of interview skills, a written list of the skills successfully demonstrated could be provided as a visual support at the point of consequences.

The TEACCH program pioneered the use of structure and visual supports (Mesibov, Shea, & Schopler, 2004). Many of these methods will be highlighted in Chapter 6 where specific visual interventions and approaches for increasing structure are discussed.

Task Demands and Positive Environment

In designing interventions, it is important to consider the task demands by asking questions such as:

- Is it appropriate to expect John to be able to sit in a classroom for 45 minutes?
- What are the social demands for Maria at work?
- Can Marty copy information from the board?
- Does Larry have the skills to handle a field trip to the art museum?

For the purpose of designing quality interventions, expectations must be reasonable; that is, an individual must be capable of succeeding either independently or with assistance. Task difficulty is the focus of the fourth level of the Ziggurat. A case example helps illustrate the importance of this level.

Nathan

Nathan is an 18-year-old college student on the spectrum. With the assistance of a job coach, he works at a local drug store to help pay for school. His latest obsessive interest is learning about the drugs that the customers take. Nathan quickly memorizes common medications and can easily recall which customers take them. Although the pharmacist admires his ability to learn these complex facts, Nathan was recently reprimanded for divulging confidential information. A regular customer came to pick up her medication. Nathan smiled as he quickly told her, in a loud voice, that her prescription was an antidepressant. He proceeded to recite the names of other customers who take the same medication. The customer was visibly upset and complained to the pharmacist and store manager. Nathan could not understand why she was angry.

The continuum of task demands, from easy to difficult, is depicted in Figure 3.2. Demands are easiest for tasks that can be accomplished independently. For example, Nathan was adept at working the cash register and computer without assistance. He also remembered information about medications. These would be considered easy tasks for Nathan. This level of task demand is appropriate when the goal is to have an individual function independently and successfully and to build self-esteem.

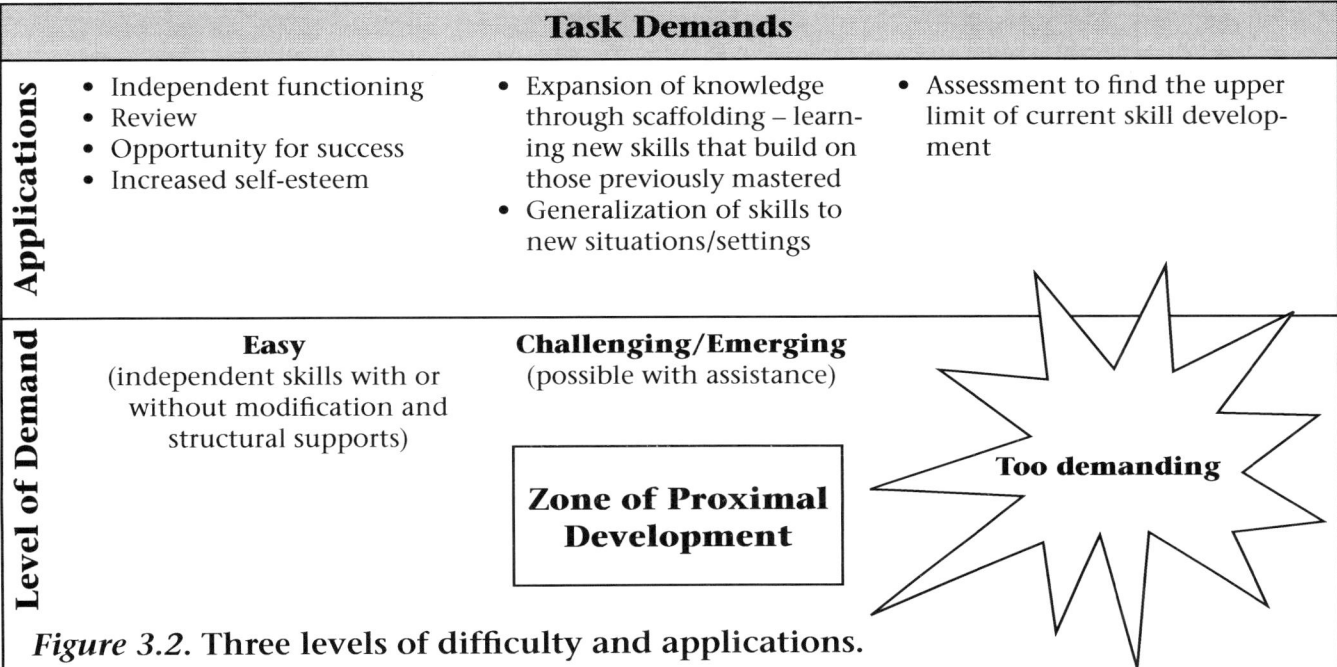

Figure 3.2. Three levels of difficulty and applications.

The Challenging/Emerging section of Figure 3.2 is perhaps best summarized by Vygotsky's concept of the zone of proximal development (ZPD) (1978, as cited in Miller, 1993, pp. 380-381):

> The zone of proximal development defines those functions that have not yet matured but are in the process of maturation, functions that will mature tomorrow but are currently in an embryonic state. The functions could be termed the "buds" or "flowers" of development rather than the "fruits" of development.

Essentially, the ZPD refers to skills that can currently only be accomplished with assistance. Presenting tasks within the ZPD is appropriate when trying to teach new concepts that build on known skills and when seeking to generalize previously mastered skills to new settings. Returning to Nathan, while he had some fundamental skills for successful customer interaction, some demands were too challenging for him to accomplish independently. Had Nathan's pharmacist understood that his skills in this area were emerging, she could either have provided additional support or reduced the demands of the task so that he could accomplish it independently (e.g., provide a visual reminder not to discuss medicine or other customers) or allow Nathan to work in the pharmacy instead of out on the floor with customers.

Even with support, some tasks can be too demanding, as depicted in the final portion of Figure 3.2. Because academically successful individuals on the spectrum often appear very capable, it is easy to assume that their skills are equally developed across areas (e.g., cognitive, social, emotional, communication). Due to the misperception that the requisite skills are present, others may conclude that the autistic person is being defiant, stubborn, or rude. For example, Nathan's boss likely thought that he was being rude or insensitive. That is, given his advanced ability to grasp difficult information, it never occurred to the pharmacist that Nathan lacked some fundamental social skills and an age-appropriate understanding of privacy, confidentiality, and personal boundaries.

It is rarely appropriate to present a task that is too difficult. Tasks that are too difficult may result in emotional and behavioral problems – meltdowns, failure, disruption to self and others, increased isolation and rejection, and so on. When difficulties persist, it is important to consider the possibility that task demands have been set too high. In order to gain an understanding of a person's abilities, it may be necessary to test the boundaries of skills. This is often done as part of educational or occupational assessment.

This level of the Ziggurat provides another avenue for behavior intervention and is a crucial piece of a well-designed plan. By acknowledging and carefully adjusting task demands, we can often prevent problems. The goal of many interventions is to instill skills so that an individual can independently accomplish a task. Identification of skills to teach is subsumed in this level; therefore, consideration of task demands helps to set the stage for essential skill development. If a task is too demanding, the individual will fail or become overwhelmed and quit. If the task is too easy, skills will not expand. The ZPD represents an optimal level for new learning (challenging with assistance). Adjusting task demands so that they are appropriate provides an optimal level for functioning and new learning.

Skills to Teach

The first four levels of intervention set the stage for new skill development. Revisiting the example of Nathan helps to illustrate this process.

Nathan *(continued)*

Nathan's job coach worked with the pharmacist and store manager to develop a comprehensive intervention using all levels of the Ziggurat. They made sure that he had adequate breaks during his shift, during which he often read the Physician Desk Reference Guide to Medications. *His job coach was aware that Nathan's job was rewarding to him because he was earning money to buy a computer and because he was fascinated with learning about drugs. At home, his parents had posted visual reminders so that he could independently remember to brush his teeth, wash his hair, and wear deodorant – especially on days he worked.*

Together, the job coach and the pharmacist made a plan for Nathan's daily job assignment. On days when the coach could not be present, Nathan did not spend time with customers. Instead, he worked on the computer in the pharmacy helping to prepare prescriptions. On days when the job coach could be present, Nathan worked behind the register. The coach modeled appropriate interactions with the customers. He employed a visual strategy (card) to remind Nathan about the rules for conversing with customers (e.g., Don't talk about other customers, ask the pharmacist to answer questions about the medicines, use low, quiet volume to discuss customer business).

The key diagnostic characteristics of ASD – social and communicative functioning, repetitive behavior and preoccupations, and associated features such as sensory, cognitive, motor, and emotional vulnerability – may be thought of as areas of skills deficits to be addressed on this level of the Ziggurat. For Nathan, his job functioning was most impacted by his social skills deficits; therefore, the job coach and the pharmacist decided that Nathan had to learn some social skills before he could work independently with customers. Specifically, he had to understand the concept of privacy. They used a visual aid, called a privacy circle, to illustrate appropriate topics for discussion with specific people – pharmacist, customers, parents, job coach, and so on. Using modeling, role play, and visual strategies, Nathan learned the skills necessary for him to be successful at his job.

Nathan's plan demonstrates the importance of skill building in a thorough intervention. Had only the first four levels of the Ziggurat been addressed, Nathan might have been successful in only limited aspects of his job. As a result, he might have been permanently assigned to the stock room or a computer tasks; however; through recognizing and addressing skills deficits related to autism (communication, preoccupations, social), he was eventually able to develop the skills to do his job independently.

Autism is a lifelong condition that requires intervention throughout the lifespan. Only when a basic level of health and comfort is established, reinforcement is available, the environment is made predictable through structure and visual/tactile supports, and task demands are carefully designed can skills be effectively taught and demonstrated.

The foundation levels decrease the impact of autism in any given situation and set the stage that permits a lesson to occur and learning to be demonstrated. As skills increase, less intensive interventions will be required on the lower levels of the Ziggurat because it is the teaching of new skills that allows for growth and makes a permanent difference for the person on the spectrum.

INTERDISCIPLINARY APPROACH

Because interventions developed using the Ziggurat Model are comprehensive, implementation may require the expertise or participation of a number of people. Thus, it is anticipated that parents, family members, teachers, speech pathologists, psychologists, physicians, occupational therapists, job coaches, and others are active in implementing portions of the plan. This is one of the many benefits of using the Ziggurat Model – providing a big picture and bringing service providers together so they are all working towards a common goal. The model also helps all players to see how they are contributing to the overall process.

Juan

Juan is a fifth-grade student who is diagnosed with "high-functioning ASD." His most difficult class is P.E. The noise level is high during games, and Juan sometimes covers his ears and complains. When the class plays team sports, Juan becomes upset when his team is behind and displays anger toward teammates who are not playing as well as he would like them to. He sometimes stomps his feet, walks away, and shouts at anyone who is nearby. Even when he is not angry, Juan makes off-putting comments such as, "You can do better." He has heard coaches say this before and does not realize that it can be interpreted differently when coming from a peer. When his teammate retaliates, an argument ensues. In talking with Juan, it becomes clear that he believes that his peers are making mistakes on purpose. He thinks that saying, "You can do better" will encourage them to play better.

Juan receives services through special education. An interdisciplinary team developed a plan to address his needs. He receives speech therapy services to address communication needs, occupational therapy to assist him with sensory differences, and psychological services to assist teachers with behavioral concerns. Juan receives special assistance in the classroom and his teachers make accommodations to facilitate his learning. Juan's parents play an integral role. They help teach social skills, provide opportunities to interact with his peers and maintain communication with school staff.

UNDERLYING CHARACTERISTICS CHECKLIST-HF
Ruth Aspy, Ph.D., and Barry G. Grossman, Ph.D.

NAME: *Juan*　　　　　　　　　　　　　COMPLETED BY: *Team*

　　　　　　　　　　　　　　　　　　DATE:　*10-24*　　　　　　FOLLOW-UP DATE:

DIRECTIONS: Place check beside all items that apply and describe behaviors observed.

Area	Item	✔	Notes	Follow-Up
SOCIAL	1. Has difficulty recognizing the feelings and thoughts of others (mindblindness)	✔	*Juan can't understand that his comments hurt his clasmates' feelings.*	
	2. Uses poor eye contact			
	3. Has difficulty maintaining personal space, physically intrudes on others			
	4. Lacks tact or appears rude	✔	*Sometimes makes rude comments in the classroom, cafeteria, and gymnasium.*	
	5. Has difficulty making or keeping friends			
	6. Has difficulty joining an activity			
	7. Is naïve, easily taken advantage of, or bullied			
	8. Tends to be less involved in group activities than most same-age individuals			
	9. Has difficulty understanding others' nonverbal communication (e.g., facial expressions, body language, tone of voice)	✔	*Can't read facial expressions of others.*	
	10. Has difficulty understanding jokes			
	11. Other			
RESTRICTED PATTERNS OF BEHAVIOR, INTERESTS, AND ACTIVITIES	12. Expresses strong need for routine or "sameness"			
	13. Expresses desire for repetition			
	14. Has eccentric or intense preoccupations/absorption in own unique interests			
	15. Asks repetitive questions			
	16. Seems to be unmotivated by customary rewards			
	17. Displays repetitive motor movements (e.g., flaps hands, paces, flicks fingers in front of eyes)			
	18. Has problems handling transition and change	✔	*Becomes upset with major changes in routine.*	
	19. Has strong need for closure or difficulty stopping a task before it is completed			
	20. Other			

Figure 3.3. UCC and ISSI for Juan.

Area	Item	✔	Notes	Follow-Up
COMMUNICATION	21. Makes sounds or states words or phrases repeatedly [non-echolalic] (e.g., humming, "well actually")			
	22. Makes up new words or creates alternate meanings for words or phrases			
	23. Displays immediate or delayed echolalia (e.g., recites lines from movies, repeats another person's questions or statements, repeats sounds)			
	24. Interprets words or conversations literally/has difficulty understanding figurative language			
	25. Has difficulty with rules of conversation (e.g., interrupts others, asks inappropriate questions, makes poor eye contact, has difficulty maintaining conversation)	✔	*Interrupts in class and has difficulty allowing others to talk when working with groups.*	
	26. Fails to initiate or respond to social greetings			
	27. Has difficulty using gestures and facial expressions			
	28. Has difficulty starting, joining, and/or ending a conversation			
	29. Has difficulty asking for help			
	30. Makes irrelevant comments			
	31. Has difficulty expressing thoughts and feelings	✔	*Difficulty talking about what upsets him.*	
	32. Speaks in an overly formal way			
	33. Gives false impression of understanding more than he/she actually does	✔	*Always nods head and says he understands even when it is apparent that he does not.*	
	34. Talks incessantly, little back-and-forth			
	35. Uses an advanced vocabulary			
	36. Uses mechanical, "singsong" voice or speech sounds unusual in other ways (e.g., prosody, cadence, tone)			
	37. Has difficulty following instructions			
	38. Has difficulty understanding language with multiple meanings, humor, sarcasm, or synonyms			
	39. Has difficulty talking about others' interests			
	40. Other			

Figure 3.3. UCC and ISSI for Juan (continued).

Area	Item	✔	Notes	Follow-Up
SENSORY DIFFERENCES	41. Responds in an unusual manner to sounds (e.g., ignores sounds or over-reacts to sudden, unexpected noises, high-pitched continuous sounds, or complex/multiple noises)	✔	*Becomes upset in P.E. due to loud noises. Covers ears at recess and in the cafeteria.*	
	42. Responds in an unusual manner to pain (e.g., overreacts or seems unaware of an illness or injury)			
	43. Responds in an unusual manner to taste (e.g., resists certain textures, flavors, brands)			
	44. Responds in an unusual manner to light or color (e.g., focuses on shiny items, shadows, reflections, shows preference or strong dislike for certain colors)			
	45. Responds in an unusual manner to temperature			
	46. Responds in an unusual manner to smells (e.g., may comment on smells that others do not detect)			
	47. Seeks activities that provide touch, pressure, or movement (e.g., swinging, hugging, pacing)			
	48. Avoids activities that provide touch, pressure, or movement (e.g., resists wearing certain types of clothing, strongly dislikes to be dirty, resists hugs)			
	49. Makes noises such as humming or singing frequently			
	50. Other			
COGNITIVE DIFFERENCES	51. Displays extensive knowledge in narrow areas of interest			
	52. Displays poor problem-solving skills			
	53. Has poor organizational skills	✔	*Loses papers and required materials (e.g., pencil, scissors).*	
	54. Withdraws into complex inner worlds/fantasizes often			
	55. Is easily distracted by unrelated details – has difficulty knowing what is relevant or makes off-topic comments			
	56. Displays weakness in reading comprehension with strong word recognition			
	57. Knows many facts and details but has difficulty with abstract reasoning (i.e., weak central coherence)	✔	*Seems to recall small facts but misses the "big picture."*	

Figure 3.3. UCC and ISSI for Juan (continued).

Area	Item	✔	Notes	Follow-Up
COGNITIVE DIFFERENCES	58. Has difficulty applying learned skills in new settings			
	59. Has academic skills deficits			
	60. Has attention problems			
	61. Displays very literal understanding of concepts	✔	*Doesn't recognize that the statement "You could do better" can be interpreted in more than one way.*	
	62. Recalls information inconsistently (i.e., seems to forget previously learned information)			
	63. Has difficulty understanding the connection between behavior and resulting consequences			
	64. Other			
MOTOR DIFFERENCES	65. Has balance difficulties			
	66. Resists or refuses handwriting tasks	✔	*Doesn't complete assignments that require extensive writing.*	
	67. Has poor handwriting			
	68. Has poor motor coordination (e.g., accident prone, difficulty using fasteners)			
	69. Writes slowly			
	70. Displays atypical activity level (e.g., over-active/ hyperactive, under-active/hypoactive)			
	71. Has athletic skills deficits	✔	*Less skilled than most boys his age.*	
	72. Displays an awkward gait			
	73. Displays unusual body postures and movements or facial expressions (e.g., odd postures, stiffness, "freezing," facial grimacing)			
	74. Has difficulty starting or completing actions (e.g., may rely on physical or verbal prompting by others)			
	75. Other			

Figure 3.3. UCC and ISSI for Juan (continued).

Area	Item	✔	Notes:	Follow-Up:
EMOTIONAL VULNERABILITY	76. Is easily stressed – worries obsessively			
	77. Appears to be depressed or sad			
	78. Has unusual fear response (e.g., lacks appropriate fears or awareness of danger or is overly fearful)			
	79. Appears anxious			
	80. Exhibits rage reactions or "meltdowns"	✔	*Occurs in P.E. and sometimes during group activities in the classroom.*	
	81. Injures self (e.g., bangs head, picks skin, bites nails until they bleed, bites self)			
	82. Makes suicidal comments or gestures			
	83. Displays inconsistent behaviors			
	84. Has difficulty tolerating mistakes	✔	*In self and others. Comments to peers and hurts their feelings.*	
	85. Has low frustration tolerance	✔	*Small things upset Juan.*	
	86. Has low self-esteem, makes negative comments about self			
	87. Has difficulty identifying, quantifying, expressing, and/or controlling emotions (e.g., can only recognize and express emotions in extremes or fails to express emotions "emotionally flat")	✔	*Cannot tell when he hurts his peers' feelings.*	
	88. Has a limited understanding of own and others' emotional responses			
	89. Has difficulty managing stress and/or anxiety			
	90. Other			

Area	Description	Notes	Follow-Up
KNOWN MEDICAL OR OTHER BIOLOGICAL FACTORS			

Figure 3.3. UCC and ISSI for Juan (continued).

Individual Strengths and Skills Inventory

Ruth Aspy, Ph.D., and Barry G. Grossman, Ph.D.

When designing an effective intervention plan, it is important to consider individual strengths. Please describe strengths in the following areas:

Social

- Desires friends
- Helpful to peers and adults
- Willingly participates in group activities

Behavior, Interests, and Activities

- Responds well to rewards

Communication

- Accurately displays emotions with facial expressions
- Communication improves with the aid of visual supports (e.g., cartooning)

Sensory

- Works well in quiet settings

Cognitive

- Reads on grade level

Motor

- Skilled using a keyboard

Emotional

- Enthusiastic about sports
- Generally, a happy and optimistic child

Biological

- Energetic
- Sleeps well

Figure 3.3. UCC and ISSI for Juan (continued).

After assessing strengths and challenges using the UCC and ISSI (Figure 3.3) and conducting an FBA using the ABC-I, Juan's team determined patterns as well as several characteristics of ASD underlying Juan's behavior (see Figure 3.4).

Referring to the IZ, Juan's parents, teachers, occupational therapist, psychologist, and speech pathologist developed two comprehensive intervention plans based on all five levels of the Ziggurat – Global and Specific. The two types of plans will be discussed later in the chapter. The specific plan is discussed here. The plan included giving Juan soft earplugs to wear before he entered the gymnasium. Juan's teacher also developed a reward system with Juan's help. Juan earned points during the day that were traded for the following privileges:

- Extra computer time
- Small toys
- Triple points for "keeping his cool" in P.E.
- Bonus points at home based on his performance at school during the day

To help him remember what to do if he felt angry, Juan was given a small "coping" card with three calming strategies.

- Take deep breaths
- Go to quiet place (this was a predetermined quiet location where he could be alone)
- Ask teacher for help

Juan's teacher wrote some therapeutic stories with the assistance of the district psychologist to help him to learn that it is okay to lose a game. She also sat down with Juan. Together they developed a Comic Strip Conversation™ (Gray, 1994). This helped him to understand the perspective of his teammates when he told them they could "do better." Finally, Juan's speech pathologist taught him how to give compliments, and she wrote several "scripts" on the back of his coping card. After practicing and mastering this skill, it was added to his P.E. reward system.

Several of these interventions had been tried unsuccessfully in isolation in the past. Assessing patterns and identifying underlying characteristics became the foundation for designing a more comprehensive intervention plan individualized to meet Juan's needs. Using the Ziggurat Model helped all members of Juan's team to work together instead of individually. Because all the levels of the Ziggurat were addressed by an interdisciplinary team, the intervention was effective.

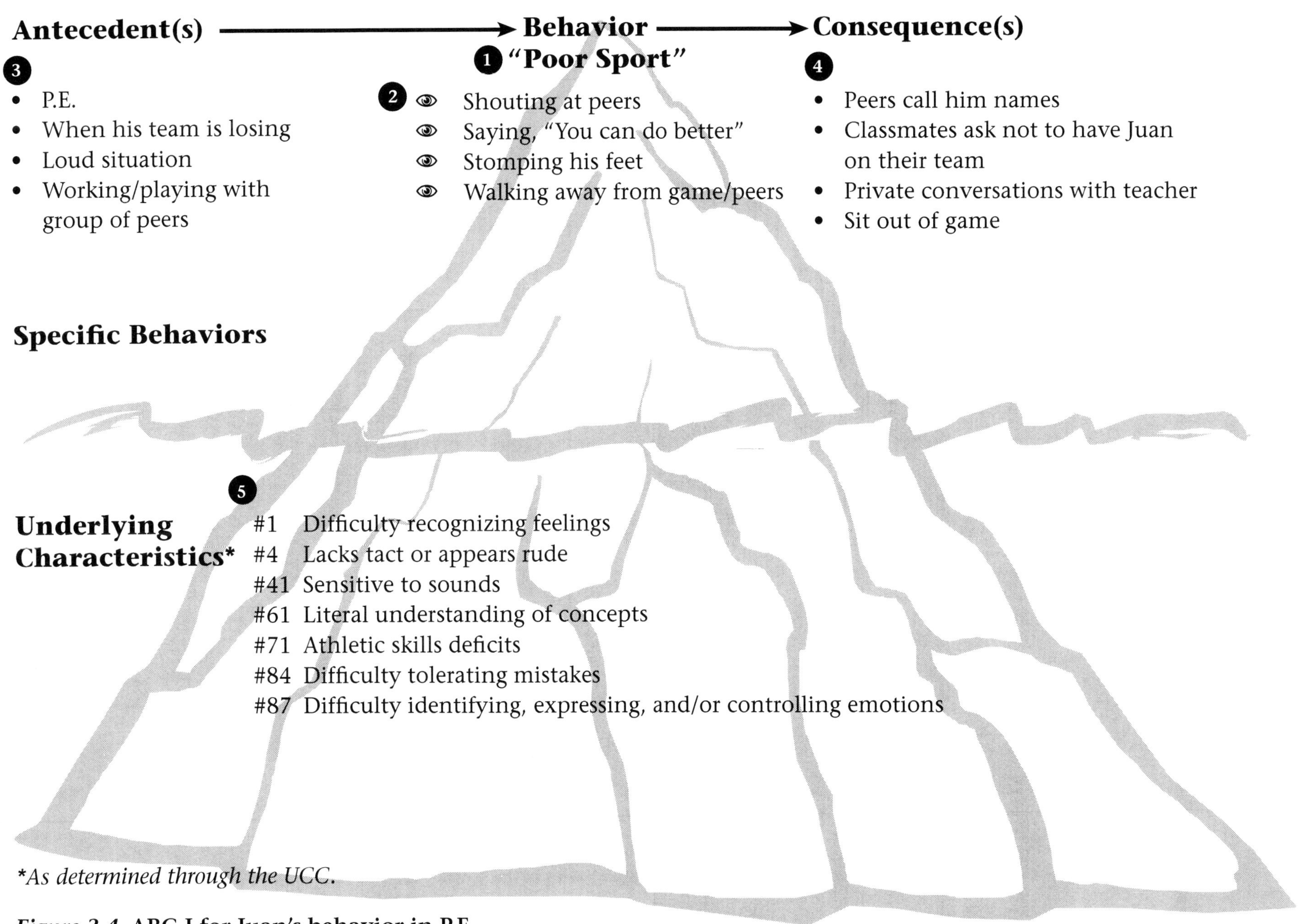

Antecedent(s) → Behavior → Consequence(s)

③ Antecedent(s)
- P.E.
- When his team is losing
- Loud situation
- Working/playing with group of peers

① Behavior "Poor Sport"

②
- Shouting at peers
- Saying, "You can do better"
- Stomping his feet
- Walking away from game/peers

④ Consequence(s)
- Peers call him names
- Classmates ask not to have Juan on their team
- Private conversations with teacher
- Sit out of game

Specific Behaviors

Underlying Characteristics*

⑤
- #1 Difficulty recognizing feelings
- #4 Lacks tact or appears rude
- #41 Sensitive to sounds
- #61 Literal understanding of concepts
- #71 Athletic skills deficits
- #84 Difficulty tolerating mistakes
- #87 Difficulty identifying, expressing, and/or controlling emotions

*As determined through the UCC.

Figure 3.4. ABC-I for Juan's behavior in P.E.

MOVING FROM ASSESSMENT TO INTERVENTION DESIGN

The components of the Ziggurat Model guide the intervention process (see Figure 3.5). The assessment tools, the UCC, ISSI, and the ABC-I, were discussed earlier. Use of an additional component, the Ziggurat Worksheet (ZW), ensures that critical elements are considered and that the intervention plan is complete. These components may be used to develop an intervention plan to address (a) global needs or (b) specific behavioral concerns – the two paths of intervention. The ZW and the two paths of intervention are described below.

Assessment Tools
Underlying Characteristics Checklist (UCC)
Individual Strengths and Skills Inventory (ISSI)
ABC-Iceberg (ABC-I)

Comprehensive Intervention Planning
Ziggurat Worksheet (ZW)
- Incorporates the five levels of the Intervention Ziggurat
- Addresses underlying needs identified with the UCC
- Includes three points of intervention (A-B-C)

Implementation
Implement intervention
Evaluate outcomes

Figure 3.5. Components of the Ziggurat Model.

Ziggurat Worksheet

The specially designed Ziggurat Worksheet is used to create a comprehensive intervention. (A copy of the Ziggurat Worksheet is included in Appendix E.) As illustrated in Figure 3.6, several checks and balances have been incorporated. First, all five levels of the Ziggurat are represented. Interventions should occur on all levels in order to be "complete." Next, each level of the Ziggurat contains space for documenting which underlying characteristics are being addressed. All interventions should "hit" on at least one underlying need. If an intervention does not address an underlying factor, it should not be included. Third, given that interventions can occur at three points – before (antecedents – prevention), during (behavior – teaching skills), and after (consequences) – the ABC column on the right-hand side of the worksheet is used to check at which point the intervention occurs (antecedent,

Ziggurat Worksheet

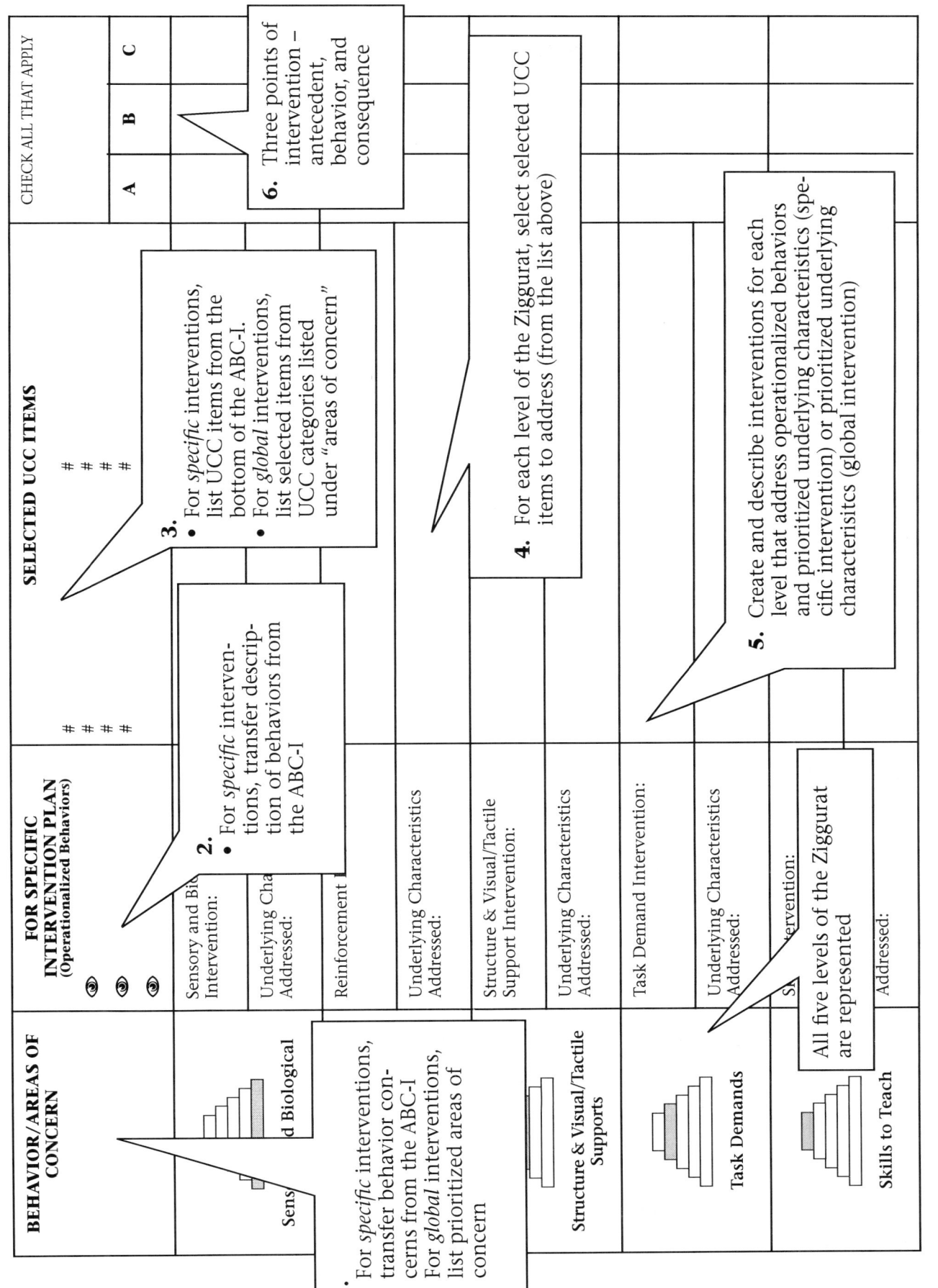

Figure 3.6. Ziggurat Worksheet. This form is used to ensure that interventions are comprehensive. Note that all five levels are represented, underlying characteristics are addressed, and intervention occurs at three points.

behavior, or consequence). A mark is placed by *each* item that applies. While A, B, and C may not be all be checked for a single level, a quick scan across the completed page should reveal that all are represented. This kind of check and balance ensures that the intervention plan incorporates prevention, strategies for skill development, and reinforcement.

Completing the Ziggurat Worksheet is not a linear process; it is more fluid. One cannot simply work from the top of the page to the bottom because decisions about interventions on one level often impact decisions on other levels. For example, it is impossible to think about the Skills to Teach level without considering interventions at the Reinforcement and Task Demands levels.

There are three main points of entry to the intervention design process (see box below summarizing the entry points). Sometimes it is helpful to begin by considering effective interventions that are already in place and then determining if they address any of the selected underlying characteristics. If so, the appropriate level(s) should be determined, and these interventions should be included on the worksheet. When designing a new intervention, some prefer to begin by selecting a specific prioritized underlying characteristic. Once a characteristic has been selected, interventions are developed to address the need, and the level(s) on which the interventions belong are determined.

It is also possible to design interventions by first considering the Ziggurat level. This is often done when troubleshooting an existing intervention plan (see Chapter 9). The approach may also be helpful when a team believes that interventions on a specific level are not adequate. Regardless of the entry point, the plan is developed based on consideration of behaviors of concern. This is why the Ziggurat Worksheet contains boxes for summarizing behaviors. These boxes are an additional way to ensure that the comprehensive plan addresses the concerns that set the team in motion.

Approaches to Completing the Ziggurat Worksheet	
Entry Points	**Process**
Intervention	1. Determine if the intervention addresses identified underlying needs 2. Determine which level(s) the intervention addresses 3. Write the specific need and intervention on the appropriate level(s)
UCC Item	1. Develop intervention to address the identified underlying need(s) 2. Determine which level(s) the intervention addresses 3. Write the specific need and intervention on the appropriate level(s)
Ziggurat Level	1. Select the UCC item(s) to address 2. Develop intervention to address the identified underlying need(s) 3. Write the specific need and intervention on the appropriate level(s)
All interventions must be linked to identified underlying need(s).	

Ziggurat Worksheet

BEHAVIOR/AREAS OF CONCERN	FOR SPECIFIC INTERVENTION PLAN (Operationalized Behaviors)	SELECTED UCC ITEMS	CHECK ALL THAT APPLY A	B	C
"Poor Sport" ① Shouting at peers ② Saying "You can do better" ③ Stomping his feet ④ Walking away		#1 Difficulty recognizing feelings #84 Difficulty tolerating mistakes #4 Lacks tact or appears rude #87 Difficulty identifying, expressing, and/or controlling emotions #41 Sensitive to sounds #61 Literal understanding of concepts #71 Athletic skills deficits			
Sensory and Biological	Sensory and Biological Intervention:	• Allow Juan to use soft earplugs in P.E.	✓		
	Underlying Characteristics Addressed:	#41 Sensitive to sounds			
Respectful Reinforcement	Reinforcement Intervention:	• Use a positive reward system for keeping his "cool" in P.E. Can earn bonus points at home.			✓
	Underlying Characteristics Addressed:	#87 Difficulty identifying, expressing, and/or controlling emotions			
Structure & Visual/Tactile Supports	Structure & Visual/Tacto;e Support Intervention:	• Use "coping card" with calming strategies. • Use Comic Strip Conversation and therapeutic stories.		✓	
	Underlying Characteristics Addressed:	#1 Difficulty recognizing feelings #4 Lacks tact or appears rude #84 Difficulty tolerating mistakes #87 Difficulty identifying, expressing, and/or controlling emotions			
Task Demands	Task Demand Intervention:	• Provide earplugs and "scripts" to make gym class less demanding for Juan. • P.E. teacher will modify challenging physical activities.	✓		
	Underlying Characteristics Addressed:	#41 Sensitive to sounds #71 Athletic skills deficits			
Skills to Teach	Skill Intervention:	• Use "coping card" with calming strategies (take deep breaths, go to quiet place, and ask for help). • Teach Juan that it is okay to lose a game. • Help Juan learn alternate meanings of the same phrase, "You can do better." • Teach Juan how to give compliments.	✓	✓	
	Underlying Characteristics Addressed:	#4 Lacks tact or appears rude #61 Literal understanding of concepts #84 Difficulty tolerating mistakes #87 Difficulty identifying, expressing, and/or controlling emotions			

Figure 3.7. Ziggurat Worksheet for Juan.

In sum, a complete intervention meets the following requirements:

1. All five levels of the Ziggurat are addressed.
2. Several core, underlying characteristics are included.
3. Intervention occurs at three points (ABC – antecedent, behavior, and consequence strategies).

Let's return to Juan's intervention plan detailed on Figure 3.7. This plan is considered comprehensive because it meets all three conditions. First, all five levels of the Ziggurat are represented.

- His plan includes strategies to address his *sensory needs*. Juan is given earplugs to help with the noise level in P.E. Meeting this need will help him to be more calm and increase the likelihood that other interventions will be successful. It would be difficult for Juan to learn and demonstrate any new skills if he was in a constant state of distress.

- Establishing *positive contingencies* for behavior is a crucial piece in any intervention. Because Juan is able to select from a list of reinforcers he helped to develop, he should be more motivated to earn points by demonstrating the expected behaviors and skills. Having points carry over into the home setting adds to his level of motivation.

- Some of the demands in P.E. may be overwhelming to Juan. For example, successfully participating on a team requires mastery of certain social skills as well as strategies to deal with frustration. Using *visual strategies* such as a "coping card" builds upon a known strength for many individuals on the spectrum.

- Juan's plan reduces the social demands to be consistent with his skill level. Giving him a "coping card" means that he will not have to generate strategies when he is upset.

- Juan lacks some social skills necessary to be successful in P.E. His teacher will use therapeutic stories to help him to understand how others feel when he "encourages" them, and he will be taught how to give compliments to make classmates feel good. Stories also can help Juan understand that it is okay to lose a game.

Juan's plan meets the second criterion of a comprehensive plan by addressing several characteristics of autism underlying his behavior in P.E. Strategies on the five levels address his sensory differences, mindblindness, difficulty expressing emotions, low frustration tolerance, and difficulty tolerating mistakes.

Last, Juan's plan addresses the third component required for a comprehensive plan because interventions occur at all three points. First, several prevention strategies are used, including use of earplugs and a coping card. Second, Juan will be taught replacement skills such as how to give a compliment and cope with frustration by taking a short break or asking for help. Finally, the positive point system will provide him with incentives for displaying skills and managing his behavior in P.E.

When designing an effective intervention plan, it is important to consider individual strengths. This is accomplished through completion of the Individual Strengths and Skills Inventory (ISSI). Completing the ISSI focused the team on Juan's strengths, enabling them to build on his strengths when designing an intervention plan for him. The interventions developed on the Ziggurat Worksheet reflect this focus. For example, knowing that Juan learns best with visual supports, the team used cartoon drawings to help him to better understand the thoughts and feelings of others. Juan enjoys sports. This enthusiasm will increase his involvement in interventions focused on success in P.E.

Two Paths for Intervention

As established in Chapter 2, assessment is the initial step in designing effective interventions. The Ziggurat Model employs two tools: the UCC/ISSI and the ABC-I. Which tools are used depends on the purpose of intervention design – general program or specific behavior concerns (see Figure 2.10). For a general program, UCC/ISSI is all that is required. For the specific plan, the ABC-I is also required. In either case, the assessment tools are used in conjunction with the Intervention Ziggurat (see Figure 3.1), and the overall intervention plan is documented on a worksheet (see Figure 3.6).

There is a tendency to identify and address specific needs as they emerge. For example, if a child is not speaking, parents seek out speech services; if social skill difficulties arise, group counseling may be provided. Such an approach is problem focused – a specific plan. A global or general program, on the other hand, involves stepping back and looking at the characteristics and impact of ASD on the individual. This helps to facilitate broader program design. The preventive, "big picture" approach is often overlooked when creating interventions. By addressing essential core features, subsequent problems may be avoided. Inevitably, however, specific behavioral concerns arise and more targeted interventions will be required.

As mentioned, the ZM may be used for both purposes. The model ensures that difficulties are addressed comprehensively. All individuals *must* have a global plan. Not all will have a specific plan. When implementing a specific intervention plan, the global program remains in place and is compatible with the specific plan.

Over time, it will be necessary to update the UCC and ISSI and review progress in order to identify any emerging areas of need. Ideally, this process is completed by an interdisciplinary team. Based on the information gathered, changes may be made to the intervention programs and new, problem-focused interventions may be developed, as needed.

Now, let's look at the two intervention paths.

Designing a General Program

All interventions based on the ZM begin with completion of the UCC and ISSI. In order to develop a general program, users first select key concerns from several areas identified on the UCC. These are transferred to the ZW (see item #1 on Figure 3.6). From the list of UCC concerns, users select UCC items from selected areas to address. The selected items are transferred to the ZW (see item #3 on Figure 3.6). To accomplish this, parents and professionals take a "big picture" perspective and think about their long- and short-term vision for the individual (see Figure 3.8). For example, parents often voice the hope that their child will be able to function independently as an adult or that their child will develop the skills necessary to have healthy, loving relationships. These kinds of "big picture" goals may be used to set priorities.

After key UCC areas are identified, UCC items are selected from each area. Parents and professionals are advised to focus on essential and pivotal skills. The Global Intervention Plan: Guide to Establishing Priorities form, which explains and expands on this process, is provided in Appendix C.

After prioritized items are selected from the UCC, the ZW is used to complete the remaining steps of intervention development. Ashley's case example helps to illustrate this process.

Developing a Meaningful Global Intervention Plan
Staying on target

Vision: Think Big Picture

Begin with the end in mind – Stephen R. Covey

- What is the long- and short-term vision?
- Which UCC areas would have the greatest impact on achieving this vision?

Other Important Factors to Consider

- **Settings** – Which UCC areas have the greatest impact on the individual's ability to function in multiple settings?
- **Quality of Life** – Which UCC areas have the greatest impact on the individual's quality of life?

Choose UCC Items from Key UCC Areas

- Choose items that are essential (necessary for progress) and developmentally appropriate. Emphasize items that are more pivotal (building blocks for additional skills). Avoid selecting redundant items.

Figure 3.8. Developing a meaningful Global Intervention Plan.

Ashley

Ashley is a seventh-grade student who moved to a new school. The teacher asked her parents to complete a UCC and ISSI to help design a general program for her. Staff added their comments to the UCC/ISSI. (The UCC and ISSI are summarized in Figure 3.9.) Based on this informal assessment, an interdisciplinary team (including Ashley's parents) met and developed Ashley's program together.

Team members completed the Global Intervention Plan Guide (Figure 3.10) as the first step of developing a meaningful intervention plan for Ashley. They decided that the key UCC areas were Social, Cognitive Differences, and Emotional Vulnerability and, therefore, determined that Ashley's general program would focus on these areas (see top-left corner, Areas of Concern, Figure 3.11). From the key areas of the UCC (Social, Cognitive Differences, and Emotional Vulnerability), they selected essential items to address and transferred these to the Ziggurat Worksheet (see Figure 3.11).

With the targets for a meaningful intervention identified, it was time to begin to create intervention strategies for each level of the Ziggurat. Keeping in mind Ashley's strengths and skills identified on the ISSI, the team developed several intervention strategies to address selected UCC items. To ensure that these needs were addressed, they indicated which underlying characteristics the strategies targeted. In the ABC column on the right, they placed a check by all that applied.

The team continued through all the levels until the ZW was complete. The resulting document represents a general program that can be implemented by all of those involved with Ashley (see Figure 3.11).

During the process of developing intervention strategies, it is important to ensure that the interventions address *at least one* of the selected UCC items. If an underlying UCC item cannot be identified, do not include the intervention. This guideline also applies when considering interventions that are currently being implemented. Strategies that do not link to at least one of the selected UCC items are off target and should not be included in the global intervention plan. *Energy should be put into implementing intervention strategies that address underlying needs and, therefore, have a greater impact.*

As teams go through the design process, they may also reevaluate selected UCC areas and items. When this occurs, make the appropriate changes to the Ziggurat Worksheet to reflect the new perspective. Note that Ashley's intervention is comprehensive. Interventions were designed for each level of the Ziggurat and contain core features from the UCC. Lastly, interventions occurred at all three points (antecedent, behavior, and consequence).

UNDERLYING CHARACTERISTICS CHECKLIST-HF
Ruth Aspy, Ph.D., and Barry G. Grossman, Ph.D.

NAME: *Ashley* COMPLETED BY: *Parents and staff*

DATE: *9-21* FOLLOW-UP DATE:

DIRECTIONS: Place check beside all items that apply and describe behaviors observed.

Area	Item	✔	Notes	Follow-Up
SOCIAL	1. Has difficulty recognizing the feelings and thoughts of others (mindblindness)	✔	*Can't tell how parents, siblings, and friends are feeling.*	
	2. Uses poor eye contact			
	3. Has difficulty maintaining personal space, physically intrudes on others			
	4. Lacks tact or appears rude	✔	*Makes comments that hurt others' feelings.*	
	5. Has difficulty making or keeping friends	✔	*Ashley relates best with adults. There are only one or two peers who will spend time with her.*	
	6. Has difficulty joining an activity			
	7. Is naïve, easily taken advantage of, or bullied			
	8. Tends to be less involved in group activities than most same-age individuals	✔	• *Does not enjoy group activities (youth groups, sports, etc.).* • *Often does not participate in class activities.*	
	9. Has difficulty understanding others' nonverbal communication (e.g., facial expressions, body language, tone of voice)			
	10. Has difficulty understanding jokes			
	11. Other			
RESTRICTED PATTERNS OF BEHAVIOR, INTERESTS, AND ACTIVITIES	12. Expresses strong need for routine or "sameness"			
	13. Expresses desire for repetition			
	14. Has eccentric or intense preoccupations/absorption in own unique interests	✔	*Interested in animals, especially horses.*	
	15. Asks repetitive questions	✔	*At home and at school.*	
	16. Seems to be unmotivated by customary rewards	✔	*Unaffected by praise and time with peers.*	
	17. Displays repetitive motor movements (e.g., flaps hands, paces, flicks fingers in front of eyes)			
	18. Has problems handling transition and change			
	19. Has strong need for closure or difficulty stopping a task before it is completed			
	20. Other			

Figure 3.9. Ashley's UCC and ISSI completed by her parents and staff.

Area	Item	✔	Notes	Follow-Up
COMMUNICATION	21. Makes sounds or states words or phrases repeatedly [non-echolalic] (e.g., humming, "well actually")			
	22. Makes up new words or creates alternate meanings for words or phrases			
	23. Displays immediate or delayed echolalia (e.g., recites lines from movies, repeats another person's questions or statements, repeats sounds)			
	24. Interprets words or conversations literally/has difficulty understanding figurative language			
	25. Has difficulty with rules of conversation (e.g., interrupts others, asks inappropriate questions, makes poor eye contact, has difficulty maintaining conversation)	✔	*Receives speech therapy services to address this concern.*	
	26. Fails to initiate or respond to social greetings			
	27. Has difficulty using gestures and facial expressions			
	28. Has difficulty starting, joining, and/or ending a conversation	✔	*Diagnosed with speech impairment in pragmatic language.*	
	29. Has difficulty asking for help			
	30. Makes irrelevant comments	✔	• *Asks peers what type of pet they have. She talks excessively about animal facts.* • *Asks off-topic questions and makes off-topic comments in class.*	
	31. Has difficulty expressing thoughts and feelings			
	32. Speaks in an overly formal way	✔	*Seems to "lecture" when she talks about animals.*	
	33. Gives false impression of understanding more than he/she actually does			
	34. Talks incessantly, little back-and-forth			
	35. Uses an advanced vocabulary	✔	*Uses advanced terminology such as "indigenous" and Latin terms.*	
	36. Uses mechanical, "singsong" voice or speech sounds unusual in other ways (e.g., prosody, cadence, tone)			
	37. Has difficulty following instructions			
	38. Has difficulty understanding language with multiple meanings, humor, sarcasm, or synonyms			
	39. Has difficulty talking about others' interests			
	40. Other			

Figure 3.9. Ashley's UCC and ISSI completed by her parents and staff (continued).

Area	Item	✔	Notes	Follow-Up
SENSORY DIFFERENCES	41. Responds in an unusual manner to sounds (e.g., ignores sounds or over-reacts to sudden, unexpected noises, high-pitched continuous sounds, or complex/multiple noises)			
	42. Responds in an unusual manner to pain (e.g., overreacts or seems unaware of an illness or injury)			
	43. Responds in an unusual manner to taste (e.g., resists certain textures, flavors, brands)			
	44. Responds in an unusual manner to light or color (e.g., focuses on shiny items, shadows, reflections, shows preference or strong dislike for certain colors)			
	45. Responds in an unusual manner to temperature			
	46. Responds in an unusual manner to smells (e.g., may comment on smells that others do not detect)			
	47. Seeks activities that provide touch, pressure, or movement (e.g., swinging, hugging, pacing)	✔	*Ashley does not like tags in her clothing.*	
	48. Avoids activities that provide touch, pressure, or movement (e.g., resists wearing certain types of clothing, strongly dislikes to be dirty, resists hugs)			
	49. Makes noises such as humming or singing frequently			
	50. Other			
COGNITIVE DIFFERENCES	51. Displays extensive knowledge in narrow areas of interest	✔	*Animals and insects.*	
	52. Displays poor problem-solving skills	✔		
	53. Has poor organizational skills			
	54. Withdraws into complex inner worlds/fantasizes often	✔	*Categorizes people in her life as different animals. For example, she describes one classmate as a "rattlesnake."*	
	55. Is easily distracted by unrelated details – has difficulty knowing what is relevant or makes off-topic comments			
	56. Displays weakness in reading comprehension with strong word recognition			
	57. Knows many facts and details but has difficulty with abstract reasoning (i.e., weak central coherence)	✔		

Figure 3.9. Ashley's UCC and ISSI completed by her parents and staff (continued).

Area	Item	✔	Notes	Follow-Up
COGNITIVE DIFFERENCES	58. Has difficulty applying learned skills in new settings			
	59. Has academic skills deficits	✔	• *Difficulty with reading comprehension and writing.* • *Grades are declining across subject areas.*	
	60. Has attention problems	✔		
	61. Displays very literal understanding of concepts			
	62. Recalls information inconsistently (i.e., seems to forget previously learned information)			
	63. Has difficulty understanding the connection between behavior and resulting consequences			
	64. Other			
MOTOR DIFFERENCES	65. Has balance difficulties			
	66. Resists or refuses handwriting tasks			
	67. Has poor handwriting	✔		
	68. Has poor motor coordination (e.g., accident prone, difficulty using fasteners)			
	69. Writes slowly	✔		
	70. Displays atypical activity level (e.g., over-active/hyperactive, under-active/hypoactive)			
	71. Has athletic skills deficits			
	72. Displays an awkward gait			
	73. Displays unusual body postures and movements or facial expressions (e.g., odd postures, stiffness, "freezing," facial grimacing)			
	74. Has difficulty starting or completing actions (e.g., may rely on physical or verbal prompting by others)			
	75. Other			

Figure 3.9. Ashley's UCC and ISSI completed by her parents and staff (continued).

Area	Item	✔	Notes	Follow-Up
EMOTIONAL VULNERABILITY	76. Is easily stressed – worries obsessively	✔	• Worries about looking "different" when pulled out of class for speech therapy. • Stresses over schoolwork and grades.	
	77. Appears to be depressed or sad			
	78. Has unusual fear response (e.g., lacks appropriate fears or awareness of danger or is overly fearful)			
	79. Appears anxious			
	80. Exhibits rage reactions or "meltdowns"			
	81. Injures self (e.g., bangs head, picks skin, bites nails until they bleed, bites self)			
	82. Makes suicidal comments or gestures			
	83. Displays inconsistent behaviors			
	84. Has difficulty tolerating mistakes			
	85. Has low frustration tolerance			
	86. Has low self-esteem, makes negative comments about self			
	87. Has difficulty identifying, quantifying, expressing, and/or controlling emotions (e.g., can only recognize and express emotions in extremes or fails to express emotions – "emotionally flat")			
	88. Has a limited understanding of own and others' emotional responses			
	89. Has difficulty managing stress and/or anxiety	✔	Ashley is not sleeping well. She complains about stomach pains.	
	90. Other			

Area	Description	Notes	Follow-Up
KNOWN MEDICAL OR OTHER BIOLOGICAL FACTORS	• Sleep • Pain in stomach	• Ashley is not sleeping well. She wakes up frequently during the night. • Ashley complains about stomach pains.	

Figure 3.9. Ashley's UCC and ISSI completed by her parents and staff (continued).

Individual Strengths and Skills Inventory

Ruth Aspy, Ph.D., and Barry G. Grossman, Ph.D.

When designing an effective intervention plan, it is important to consider individual strengths. Please describe strengths in the following areas:

Social

- Interacts best with adults
- Ashley enjoys talking to peers about animals
- Able to make eye contact when talking about her interests

Behavior, Interests, and Activities

- Has strong interests and extensive knowledge about animals, especially horses
- Handles transition and change well

Communication

- Has good vocabulary
- Speech appears more skilled when talking about her interests

Sensory

- Eats a variety of foods
- Tolerates noises well

Cognitive

- Demonstrates strong attention span
- Has good rote memory
- Expresses desire to do well academically

Motor

- Demonstrates good balance – able to ride horses
- No longer makes repetitive hand movements

Emotional

- Ashley copes best when she is well rested
- Able to identify her own basic emotions

Biological

- Eats well
- Is generally healthy

Figure 3.9. Ashley's UCC and ISSI completed by her parents and staff (continued).

Global Intervention Plan: Guide to Establishing Priorities

Ruth Aspy, Ph.D., and Barry G. Grossman, Ph.D.

Directions: Following completion of the UCC and ISSI, the next step is to identify UCC **areas** and **items** that will result in a *meaningful* Global Intervention Plan. Consideration of priorities and strengths for an individual facilitates selection of UCC areas and items. The following questions are provided as a guide.

Selecting UCC Areas

Vision   "Begin with the end in mind" – Stephen R. Covey

• What is the long- and short-term vision of/for the individual?
  Note that "long-term" and "short-term" may be defined differently in order to be meaningful.

Long term - Ashley will have friends and will go to college.
Short term - Ashley will successfully participate in one group activity with peers each week. (e.g., soccer, choir, youth group, equestrian club). Ashley will complete tasks on grade level.

⊙ Which UCC **areas** would have the greatest impact on achieving this vision?

Social, Emotional Vulnerability, Cognitive Differences, Motor Differences

Settings

• In what settings does the individual participate?

School, church, neighborhood

⊙ Which UCC **areas** have the greatest impact on the individual's ability to function in multiple settings?

Social, Cognitive Differences, Emotional Vulnerability

Quality of Life

• What is most important to the individual? What provides a sense of well-being?
  Consider independence, relationships, play/leisure activities, safety, health, etc.

Animals, especially horses, insects. Facts

⊙ Which UCC **areas** have the greatest impact on the individual's quality of life?

Social, Emotional Vulnerability

Key UCC Areas

Based on your answers to the questions above, place an X next to the key UCC **areas**.

*Transfer to the **Areas of Concern** section of the Ziggurat Worksheet.*

☒ Social
☐ Restricted Patterns of Behavior Interests, and Activities
☐ Communication
☐ Sensory Differences

☒ Cognitive Differences
☒ Motor Differences
☒ Emotional Vulnerability
☐ Known Medical or Other Biological Factors

Selecting UCC Items

Key UCC Items

Select key UCC **items** for *each* of the UCC **areas** listed above. Choose items that are essential (necessary for progress) and developmentally appropriate. Emphasize items that are pivotal (building blocks for additional skills). Avoid selecting redundant items.

Write key item numbers and descriptions below. These items will be used to develop interventions, keeping strengths and skills (identified on the ISSI) in mind.

*Transfer items to the **Selected UCC Item** section of the Ziggurat Worksheet and develop interventions.*

#1 Mindblindness
#8 Tends to be less involved in group activities
#54 Withdraws into complex inner worlds
#59 Has academic skills deficits

#60 Has attention problems
#67 Has poor handwriting
#69 Writes slowly
#89 Has difficulty managing stress and/or anxiety

Figure 3.10. Global Intervention Plan Guide completed by Ashley's team.

Ziggurat Worksheet

BEHAVIOR/AREAS OF CONCERN Social, Emotional Vulnerability, Cognitive Differences, Motor Differences	FOR SPECIFIC INTERVENTION PLAN (Operationalized Behaviors)	SELECTED UCC ITEMS	CHECK ALL THAT APPLY		
			A	B	C
		#1 Has difficulty recognizing the feelings and thoughts of others (mindblindness) #8 Tends to be less involved in group activities #54 Withdraws into complex inner worlds/fantasizes often #59 Has academic skills deficits #60 Has attention problems #67 Has poor handwriting #69 Writes slowly #89 Has difficulty managing stress and/or anxiety			
(ziggurat image) **Sensory and Biological**	Sensory and Biological Intervention:	• Parents will take Ashley to a psychiatrist for consultation regarding anti-anxiety medication. • Provide activities that incorporate movement throughout her school day. • Request evaluation of motor skills and sensory functioning to be completed by an occupational therapist.	✓		
	Underlying Characteristics Addressed:	#60 Has attention problems #67 Has poor handwriting #69 Writes slowly #89 Has difficulty managing stress and/or anxiety			
(ziggurat image) **Respectful Reinforcement**	Reinforcement Intervention:	• Provide a strong reinforcer for any required pull-out activity (e.g., speech therapy). • When possible, make reinforcers a shared activity with a peer. • Reinforce Ashley by providing her with a brief period of time to talk or draw about animals and her fantasy world for participating in group activities.			✓
	Underlying Characteristics Addressed:	#8 Tends to be less involved in group activities #54 Withdraws into complex inner worlds/fantasizes often			
(ziggurat image) **Structure & Visual/Tactile Supports**	Structure & Visual/Tactile Support Intervention:	• Use video. Provide Ashley with a social skills group that uses video-tape to model social behaviors and review Ashley's performance in role play. Reinforce for demonstrating skills. • Allow Ashley to highlight or underline main ideas of passages in order to promote comprehension. • Provide Ashley with starter sentences and graphic organizer for written tasks. • Give Ashley a "coping card" or list of strategies to use to address stress and anxiety. Reinforce her for demonstrating the use of skills. • Give Ashley a card with a list of the steps to start a conversation, including noteworthy conversational manners.	✓	✓	✓
	Underlying Characteristics Addressed:	#8 Tends to be less involved in #59 Has academic skills deficits #89 Has difficulty managing stress and/or anxiety			

Figure 3.11. Ziggurat worksheet for Ashley's global intervention.

Ziggurat Worksheet

Task Demands	Task Demand Intervention:	• Provide Ashley with starter sentences and graphic organizer for written tasks. • Allow Ashley to work in a smaller group of peers. Assign her a role in which she would have the highest chance of success. • Give Ashley a peer "buddy" in class to assist her with focus and participation. • Reduce the amount of writing required or allow for oral response. • Allow Ashley to type work if possible.	✓
	Underlying Characteristics Addressed:	#8 Tends to be less involved in group activities #59 Has academic skills deficits #60 Has attention problems #67 Has poor handwriting #69 Writes slowly	✓
Skills to Teach	Skill Intervention:	• Provide Ashley with social skills instruction in order for her to learn to read facial expressions and interact more successfully with peers and adults. Reinforce for accurate identification of feelings based on pictures, videos, and real life. • Provide speech therapy services to address pragmatic language concerns. • Teach Ashley how to use a graphic organizer. Reinforce use of new skills. • Provide Ashley with academic skills intervention (writing and reading). Reinforce new skills. • Teach Ashley different ways to cope with stress and anxiety. Reinforce use of skills.	✓
	Underlying Characteristics Addressed:	#1 Has difficulty recognizing the feelings and thoughts of others (mindblindness) #59 Has academic skills deficits #67 Has poor handwriting #69 Writes slowly #89 Has difficulty managing stress and/or anxiety	✓

Figure 3.11. Ziggurat worksheet for Ashley's global intervention (continued).

The Ziggurat Model is appropriate for individuals across the spectrum and across the lifespan. While Ashley's case study illustrated the model's use for a teenager on the spectrum, the case that follows describes a 4-year-old child on the spectrum and the Ziggurat plan that was developed to address her needs.

Leigh Ann

When Leigh Ann was 22 months old, her parents noticed that she was not interacting with other children at daycare and that she was often distressed by loud sounds. Leigh Ann's parents were worried that her language appeared limited compared to the other children in her class. Also, she did not seem to enjoy games like peek-a-boo and spent most of her time playing alone. Leigh Ann is now 4 years old and attends a public school early childhood program. The school evaluation team identified her with ASD and speech impairment.

Leigh Ann's evaluation report describes many characteristics related to ASD. She communicates using 4- to 5-word sentences. She does not seem interested in others and often withdraws from group activities. When she plays near peers, she often takes their toys from them and does not seem to notice that they begin to cry as a result. Eye contact is fleeting. At home, Leigh Ann prefers solitary activities. When she does initiate social interactions with adults and peers, it is usually in order to have her needs met (e.g., requesting preferred objects or food), to point out sparkly objects, or to get others to join her as she recites the names of the Disney Princesses. Leigh Ann requires prompting to engage in play and extended social interactions that are not related to her interests.

Leigh Ann's parents say that she has some repetitive and narrow interests. For example, she watches the same Disney Princess movies for hours and recites lines or acts out scenes from the films. She occasionally asks her parents or sisters to join her in reciting lines; however, she becomes upset if they do not recite them exactly as they are in the movie. Leigh Ann has a princess backpack that she insists on carrying with her when she leaves home. It is filled with princess dolls, dress-up clothing, and princess activity books. She often lines up her princess figures according to clothing color and height.

Leigh Ann spends extended periods of time engaged in repetitive motor behaviors such as wiggling her fingers in her peripheral vision. She also appears to seek movement by shaking objects close to her eyes, spinning, and jumping. Leigh Ann displays some sensory differences. For example, her parents say that it is a "struggle" to brush her teeth and to get her to keep her shoes and socks on her feet. She is startled by unexpected movement and appears distressed by loud or unexpected sounds. She has difficulty participating in activities in a loud setting, such as school assemblies or eating in a crowded restaurant. She appears visually distracted and captivated by straight lines, such as table edges, corners of books, DVD cases, and the keys on her grandparents' piano. Leigh Ann's parents and teachers are concerned that she does not join her peers in play and often wanders away from the morning circle.

According to Leigh Ann's parents, previous interventions used at home (e.g., therapeutic listening and time-out, which she does not seem to mind) have not been effective. At school, she is provided with a picture schedule, princess floor square (for circle time), and weighted vest and lap pad. She receives speech therapy at school and attends private occupational therapy three times weekly.

Leigh Ann's multidisciplinary team, including her parents and teachers, met to develop a new program for her. The team began by completing the Underlying Characteristics Checklist-Early Intervention (UCC-EI) and Individual Strengths and Skills Inventory (see Figure 3.12). The team then discussed priorities for Leigh Ann using the Global Intervention Plan: Guide to Establishing Priorities worksheet (see Figure 3.13). After discussing the key questions – vision, settings, and quality of life – they determined that the following areas of ASD should be the focus of the intervention plan: Social; Restricted Patterns of Behavior, Interests, and Activities; Communication; and Sensory Differences. The team selected items from each of these areas to develop a meaningful plan for Leigh Ann.

Once priorities were established, Leigh Ann's team developed interventions using the Ziggurat Worksheet (see Figure 3.14). They began by reviewing interventions currently in place – those that addressed *Selected UCC Items* were included on the worksheet. Other strategies were considered to be off target and, therefore, were not included in Leigh Ann's comprehensive plan. Next, they created new interventions, making sure that each UCC item was well addressed and that sufficient strategies were developed for each level.

UNDERLYING CHARACTERISTICS CHECKLIST-EI

Ruth Aspy, Ph.D., Barry G. Grossman, Ph.D., with Kathleen Ann Quill, Ed.D.

CHILD'S NAME: *Leigh Ann* AGE: 52 months COMPLETED BY: *Mr. and Ms. Johnson and Ms. Swanson*

DATE: *9/12* RELATION TO CHILD: Parents and teacher

DIRECTIONS: Place check beside all items that apply and describe behaviors observed.

Area	Item	Age of Concern (refer to developmental norms)	✔	Notes (Describe behavior/characteristic in more detail)	Description of Mastered or Developing Skills
SOCIAL	1. Appears to be unresponsive to others (e.g., unaware of presence of others)	**4 months** Mark only if child is **at least** this age.	✔	• *Does not understand when she intrudes on others' space.* • *Tunes everyone out when focused on princess toys –difficult to distract her.*	• *Tells others about her princess dolls.* • *Prompts others to get them to recite movie lines with her – appears to enjoy this interaction.*
	2. Does not use sustained and purposeful eye contact or watch faces intensely	**4 months** Mark only if child is **at least** this age.	✔	*Eye contact is fleeting.*	
	3. Does not respond to others' attempts to share attention through eye gaze or pointing	**4 months** Mark only if child is **at least** this age.			
	4. Shows little curiosity about or interest in the immediate environment – appears to be in "own world"	**4 months** Mark only if child is **at least** this age.	✔	*At school, she does not participate in activities and prefers to play alone.*	*Leigh Ann will point out "sparkly" objects to others, and she tries to get others to join her as she recites the names of the Disney princesses.*
	5. Shows little interest in or response to positive social communication/initiations (e.g., cheerful/ playful voice or baby-talk)	**4 months** Mark only if child is **at least** this age.	✔	*Plays alone.*	
	6. Does not calm or quiet in response to a familiar adult's face or voice	**5 months** Mark only if child is **at least** this age.			
	7. Does not respond to the emotional expressions of familiar others	**6 months** Mark only if child is **at least** this age.	✔	*Does not seem to notice when her peers cry after she takes away their toys.*	*Able to identify happy and sad expressions of favorite characters in movies.*
	8. Has difficulty imitating simple movements and sounds	**6 months** Mark only if child is **at least** this age.			
	9. Does not use movement, sound, or gestures to gain attention of caregivers	**7 months** Mark only if child is **at least** this age.			
	10. Responds in an unusual manner to affection (e.g., resists hugs, or overreacts when others offer comfort)	**7 months** Mark only if child is **at least** this age.	✔	*Did not like to be held when she was an infant.*	*Will initiate short hugs.*
	11. Has difficulty using and perceiving nonverbal communication (e.g., tone of voice, gestures, facial expressions)	**8 months** Mark only if child is **at least** this age.	✔	*Doesn't notice when her peers are crying.* *Has limited facial expressions.*	
	12. Treats others as if they were objects/solely to gain assistance or a desired object (e.g., pulls parent to door)	**8 months** Mark only if child is **at least** this age.	✔	*Wants others to recite names of Disney princesses and lines from her favorite movies.*	

Figure 3.12. Leigh Ann's UCC and ISSI completed by her parents and staff.

Area	Item	Age of Concern (refer to developmental norms)	✔	Notes (Describe behavior/characteristic in more detail)	Description of Mastered or Developing Skills
SOCIAL	13. Has difficulty taking turns in play or social activities – social reciprocity (e.g., peek-a-boo, pat-a-cake)	**9 months** Mark only if child is **at least** this age.	✔	*Plays alone.*	*With prompting and assistance, Leigh Ann will play with others.*
	14. Isolates self from others or chooses solitary play consistently and across settings	**9 months** Mark only if child is **at least** this age.	✔	*Prefers to play alone with preferred toys and activities.*	*Attempts to engage others to join her as she recites names of the Disney princesses.*
	15. Does not exhibit fear of unfamiliar people – fails to display "stranger anxiety"	**10 months** Mark only if child is **at least** this age.	✔	*Displays no appropriate fear of strangers.*	
	16. Does not seek others' attention in order to share an experience (e.g., bring an object to show or point out an item or person)	**13 months** Mark only if child is **at least** this age.			
	17. Has difficulty joining an activity with peers	**24 months** Mark only if child is **at least** this age.	✔	*Wanders away from circle time.*	*With prompting, Leigh Ann goes to her carpet square for circle time and is beginning to stay there for longer periods of time.*
	18. Makes no attempt to comfort others who are in obvious distress	**28 months** Mark only if child is **at least** this age.	✔	• *Does not seem to notice when sisters are in distress.* • *Does not notice when peers are upset.*	
	19. Does not show interest or shows little interest in interacting with peers	**30 months** Mark only if child is **at least** this age.	✔	*Shows little interest in her classmates. Walks away from circle time and often plays alone.*	*Will initiate brief interaction on her topics of interest.*
	20. Displays unusual eye contact (e.g., looks out of corner of eye or away from speaker)	**36 months** Mark only if child is **at least** this age.	✔	*Eye contact is fleeting.*	
	21. Has little or no interest in assuming "roles" in play interactions with others (e.g., "cooking" play pizza for peer at table) or between play objects (e.g., conversations between mom and dad dolls)	**48 months** Mark only if child is **at least** this age.	✔	*Play with others is limited to reciting names of the Disney princesses or movie lines.*	
	22. Other:				

INDIVIDUAL STRENGTHS AND SKILLS INVENTORY: SOCIAL

Please summarize or list the child's strengths in this area. Refer to the data written in the *Description of Mastered or Developing Skills* as a starting point:

Leigh Ann initiates some social interaction – she tells others about her princess dolls, points out "sparkly" objects, and prompts others to recite the names of Disney princesses and movie lines. She is able to identify some basic emotions of characters in movies. Leigh Ann will initiate short hugs with familiar people. With prompting and assistance, she will participate in group activities and play with others. She plays with her sisters and responds to parent praise.

Figure 3.12. Leigh Ann's UCC and ISSI (continued).

Area	Item	Age of Concern (refer to developmental norms)	✔	Notes (Describe behavior/characteristic in more detail)	Description of Mastered or Developing Skills
RESTRICTED PATTERNS OF BEHAVIOR, INTERESTS, AND ACTIVITIES	23. Seems to be unmotivated by customary rewards or social approval (e.g., stickers, praise, hug, smile)	**8 months** Mark only if child is **at least** this age.	✔		
	24. Stares intensely and for long periods of time at objects that move (e.g., stares at fan or rolling credits of television show/movie)	**12 months** Mark only if child is **at least** this age.			
	25. Attached to objects in an unusual manner (e.g., refuses to leave the house without a block, goes to bed while holding a plastic letter of the alphabet)	**21 months** Mark only if child is **at least** this age.	✔	*Always takes her princess backpack filled with toys when she leaves the home. Becomes distressed if she does not have her backpack with her.*	
	26. Uses objects in repetitive, atypical manner (e.g., meticulously lines up objects, spins objects repeatedly)	**21 months** Mark only if child is **at least** this age.	✔	*Lines up princess dolls.*	
	27. Has intense preoccupations (e.g., trains, letters, shapes, electronics, doors) – to the exclusion of play or family activities – and is difficult to distract	**21 months** Mark only if child is **at least** this age.	✔	*Interested in Disney princess movies and related toys.*	*Remembers names of princesses. Recites lines from favorite movies.*
	28. Displays atypical repetitive motor movements (e.g., flaps hands, rocks body side-to-side, flicks fingers)	**24 months** Mark only if child is **at least** this age.	✔	*Wiggles fingers close to her face, shakes objects close to her eyes, spins, jumps.*	
	29. Displays difficulty engaging in activities other than intense special interests	**30 months** Mark only if child is **at least** this age.	✔	*Yes!*	*Is spending more time with peers with assistance and prompting.*
	30. Has excessive difficulty transitioning from a preferred activity	**30 months** Mark only if child is **at least** this age.			
	31. Has strong need for closure or difficulty stopping a task before it is completed	**30 months** Mark only if child is **at least** this age.			
	32. Repeats specific sounds, words, phrases, or music frequently (e.g., repeats parts of movies or phrases from books)	**36 months** Mark only if child is **at least** this age.			
	33. Becomes upset easily with interruption to routines or unanticipated changes in events (e.g., taking a different route to a destination, moving a familiar object from "its place," using a different color plate for meals)	**42 months** Mark only if child is **at least** this age.	✔	*A few months ago, Leigh Ann would cry for hours when there was a change. She calms more quickly now.*	*Leigh Ann is usually able to adjust to a change in activity when we "count down" the time.* *Is beginning to participate in transition songs such as "Clean Up, Clean Up"*
	34. Other:				

INDIVIDUAL STRENGTHS AND SKILLS INVENTORY: BEHAVIOR, INTERESTS, AND ACTIVITIES

Please summarize or list the child's strengths in this area. Refer to the data written in the *Description of Mastered or Developing Skills* as a starting point:
Leigh Ann has a good memory. She spends more time with others with assistance and prompting. She is improving in her ability to cope with change in routine at home and school and is beginning to participate in classroom routines such as clean-up time. Leigh Ann responds well to structure such as use of a count down before transitioning. She displays a special interest in princesses and prefers activities that are routine/predictable.

Figure 3.12. Leigh Ann's UCC and ISSI (continued).

Area	Item	Age of Concern (refer to developmental norms)	✔	Notes (Describe behavior/characteristic in more detail)	Description of Mastered or Developing Skills
	35. Has current speech delay (e.g., no sounds of content, vowel-like sounds between 2-3 months; no babbling at 8 months; no single words by 12 months; no phrase speech by 24 months)	**3 months** Mark only if child is **at least** this age.	✔	*First delays noticed at what age?* *At 22 months first noticed language delay. Currently is able to speak in 4- to 5-word sentences; however, her communication tends to be repetitive.*	*Communicates best on topics of interest.*
	36. Atypically quiet; does not produce a variety of sounds other than crying (e.g., cooing)	**4 months** Mark only if child is **at least** this age.			
	37. Displays absence of a social smile or displays a "vacant" smile	**4 months** Mark only if child is **at least** this age.	✔	*Does not smile often.*	
	38. Does not imitate sound produced by a caregiver	**4 months** Mark only if child is **at least** this age.			
	39. Does not use varied voice intonation to express joy and pleasure	**5 months** Mark only if child is **at least** this age.			
	40. Does not respond or shows delayed response when name is called	**9 months** Mark only if child is **at least** this age.	✔	*When immersed in play, she is difficult to distract.*	
	41. Does not use turn-taking when vocalizing/ verbalizing with a partner that includes a comfortable to-and-fro	**10 months** Mark only if child is **at least** this age.	✔	*Communication is more one-sided.*	• *Able to take turns when answering "who is that?" questions.* • *Will take turns when reciting movie lines.*
	42. Has difficulty using basic gestures, facial expressions, and other expressions of "body language" to communicate feelings	**12 months** Mark only if child is **at least** this age.	✔		• *With prompting, Leigh Ann will respond to gestures like waving bye-bye.* • *Able to follow a point.*
	43. Fails to respond to verbal greetings or nonverbal gestures (e.g., wave bye-bye, raise arms to be picked up)	**12 months** Mark only if child is **at least** this age.	✔	*Not always attentive to others, so she misses gestures and greetings.*	
	44. Has difficulty or makes no attempt to make clear requests (e.g., does not lift arms to be picked up, only labels objects – does not request by name)	**12 months** Mark only if child is **at least** this age.			
	45. Has difficulty understanding labels or names for common objects/people (e.g., does not point to picture in book upon request)	**13 months** Mark only if child is **at least** this age.			
	46. Has difficulty following a variety of routine one-step directions	**13 months** Mark only if child is **at least** this age.			
	47. Demonstrates unusual voice or speech qualities (e.g., hums, grunts; uses "singsong" or mechanical speech)	**18 months** Mark only if child is **at least** this age.			

Figure 3.12. Leigh Ann's UCC and ISSI (continued).

Area	Item	Age of Concern (refer to developmental norms)	✔	Notes (Describe behavior/characteristic in more detail)	Description of Mastered or Developing Skills
COMMUNICATION	48. Fails to respond to verbal or nonverbal greetings by giving a verbal response (e.g., by saying "hi" and "bye")	**24 months** Mark only if child is **at least** this age.	✔	*Not always attentive to others, so she misses gestures and greetings.*	*With prompting, will say, "hi" and "bye."*
	49. Communicates wants and needs through tantrums that appear more extreme in frequency and/ or intensity than those of other children of the same age	**24 months** Mark only if child is **at least** this age.	✔	*Tantrums are decreasing.*	*Asks for food and preferred objects.*
	50. Makes sounds or states the same words or phrases repeatedly	**24 months** Mark only if child is **at least** this age.	✔	*Recites lines from movies.*	
	51. Talks to self excessively in place of communicating with others	**27 months** Mark only if child is **at least** this age.			
	52. Frequently uses "gibberish" with few recognizable words	**27 months** Mark only if child is **at least** this age.			
	53. Does not spontaneously comment or share experiences – may speak only when asked a direct question	**36 months** Mark only if child is **at least** this age.	✔	*Shares information limited to her own interests.*	*Points out sparkly objects.*
	54. Has difficulty with basic rules of conversation (e.g., asks inappropriate questions, makes poor eye contact, has difficulty maintaining conversation, wants to talk about own interests exclusively)	**36 months** Mark only if child is **at least** this age.	✔	• *Conversations are one-sided.* • *Often ignores peers' attempt to initiate.*	
	55. Displays immediate or delayed echolalia (e.g., repeats another person's questions or statements, recites lines from a favorite book or movie repetitively)	**36 months** Mark only if child is **at least** this age.	✔	*Recites movie lines.*	
	56. Uses words in odd or idiosyncratic manner (e.g., calling yellow objects "cheesy")	**36 months** Mark only if child is **at least** this age.			
	57. Asks repetitive questions	**36 months** Mark only if child is **at least** this age.			
	58. Makes frequent mistakes in use of pronouns (e.g., reverses *you* and *me* or refers to self by name)	**36 months** Mark only if child is **at least** this age.			
	59. Other:				

INDIVIDUAL STRENGTHS AND SKILLS INVENTORY: COMMUNICATION

Please summarize or list the child's strengths in this area. Refer to the data written in the *Description of Mastered or Developing Skills* as a starting point:

Leigh Ann communicates best on her topics of interest. She is able to take turns in conversation when answering simple, "who is that?" questions and when reciting movie lines. With prompting, Leigh Ann will respond to gestures such as waving bye-bye. She can follow gestures such as a point. With prompting, she will say "hi" and "bye." Leigh Ann requests food and preferred objects. She spontaneously points out when she sees sparkly objects.

Figure 3.12. Leigh Ann's UCC and ISSI (continued).

Area	Item	Age of Concern (refer to developmental norms)	✔	Notes (Describe behavior/characteristic in more detail)	Description of Mastered or Developing Skills
SENSORY DIFFERENCES	60. Often responds in a developmentally unusual manner to sounds (e.g., reacts as if has no hearing, ignores some sounds, turns up volume on TV, bangs toys and objects, or overreacts to noises such as crowds or sirens)	**3 months** Mark only if child is **at least** this age.	✔	*She is startled by unexpected sounds and has difficulty being in noisy rooms.*	
	61. Often responds in a developmentally unusual manner to pain (e.g., overreacts or seems unaware of an illness or injury)	**3 months** Mark only if child is **at least** this age.			
	62. Often responds in a developmentally unusual manner to temperature (e.g., prefers or avoids certain temperatures or fails to respond to temperature)	**3 months** Mark only if child is **at least** this age.			
	63. Often responds in a developmentally unusual manner to smells (e.g., may comment on smells that others do not notice or fails to notice strong smells)	**3 months** Mark only if child is **at least** this age.			
	64. Often shows an unusually strong desire to do activities that provide touch or pressure (e.g., tight swaddling; crashing body into bed, sofa, or people; banging toys together)	**3 months** Mark only if child is **at least** this age.	✔	*She jumps frequently.*	
	65. Often shows an unusually strong desire to do activities that provide movement (e.g., swinging, rocking, spinning body, running; or being rocked or bounced by others)	**3 months** Mark only if child is **at least** this age.	✔	*She frequently spins her body.*	
	66. Often shows an extreme overreaction to activities that provide touch or pressure (e.g., resists diaper changes, strongly dislikes hair washing or cutting, nail cutting, and/or tooth brushing; avoids touching foods or walking on grass)	**3 months** Mark only if child is **at least** this age.	✔	*• Able to initiate hugs, but has difficulty receiving them.* *• It is very difficult to brush her teeth, and she often takes off her shoes and socks.*	
	67. Often shows an extreme overreaction to activities that provide movement (e.g., avoids swinging, climbing, rocking, or pacing)	**3 months** Mark only if child is **at least** this age.			
	68. Often responds in a developmentally unusual manner to visual input (e.g., focuses on shiny items and reflections; ignores faces; shows preference for or strong dislike of certain colors; overreliance on salient visual features such as glasses and hair)	**4 months** Mark only if child is **at least** this age.	✔	*Distracted by straight lines such as DVD cases, corners of books, and piano keys. She wiggles her fingers near her eyes.*	

Figure 3.12. Leigh Ann's UCC and ISSI (continued).

Area	Item	Age of Concern (refer to developmental norms)	✔	Notes (Describe behavior/characteristic in more detail)	Description of Mastered or Developing Skills
SENSORY DIFFERENCES	69. Has had difficulty learning feeding skills and/or transitioning to more advanced feeding skills (e.g., from breast/bottle feeding to spoon feeding with smooth, thin purees and then to mixed textures)	**6 months** Mark only if child is **at least** this age.			
	70. Often responds in a developmentally unusual/rigid manner to taste (e.g., avoids many textures, foods, and flavors)	**7 months** Mark only if child is **at least** this age.			
	71. Frequently preoccupied with sensory exploration of objects (e.g., mouths, licks, chews, sniffs, holds close to eyes, rubs, squeezes, or uses object to make sounds)	**8 months** Mark only if child is **at least** this age.			
	72. Frequently makes noises such as humming, singing, or throat-clearing vocalizations	**36 months** Mark only if child is **at least** this age.			
	73. Other:				

INDIVIDUAL STRENGTHS AND SKILLS INVENTORY: SENSORY

Please summarize or list the child's strengths in this area. Refer to the data written in the *Description of Mastered or Developing Skills* as a starting point:

Eats a variety of foods. Does not chew objects or place objects in her mouth. Communicates when she is injured. Repetitive movement seems to be calming to her. Leigh Ann enjoys sand play.

Area	Item	Age of Concern	✔	Notes	Description
COGNITIVE DIFFERENCES	74. Takes longer to learn new skills or learns some skills much earlier than same-age peers (e.g., may be able to identify letters or numbers or read words at unusually young age)	**3 months** Mark only if child is **at least** this age.			
	75. Does not generalize learned skills to new settings or demonstrate them consistently upon request	**3 months** Mark only if child is **at least** this age.			
	76. Demonstrates inconsistent recall of information or routines (e.g., seems to forget what was previously learned)	**7 months** Mark only if child is **at least** this age.			
	77. Has difficulty engaging in adult-initiated activities	**8 months** Mark only if child is **at least** this age.			
	78. Has difficulty maintaining engagement in meaningful self-directed activities (e.g., persists with activities but only within preferred interests or remains engaged only in areas of restricted interests)	**10 months** Mark only if child is **at least** this age.			

Figure 3.12. Leigh Ann's UCC and ISSI (continued).

Area	Item	Age of Concern (refer to developmental norms)	✔	Notes (Describe behavior/characteristic in more detail)	Description of Mastered or Developing Skills
COGNITIVE DIFFERENCES	79. Recites, sings, lists, or labels with limited purpose or understanding (e.g., displays excellent memory for songs or stories)	**24 months** Mark only if child is **at least** this age.	✔	*Recites movie lines and names of all the Disney princesses.*	
	80. Has difficulty following new or unfamiliar directions	**24 months** Mark only if child is **at least** this age.			
	81. Displays little or no pretend and imaginative play – only uses objects for intended purpose (e.g., banana as food not telephone)	**36 months** Mark only if child is **at least** this age.	✔	*Lines up toys. Does not act out imaginative scenes.*	
	82. Other:				

INDIVIDUAL STRENGTHS AND SKILLS INVENTORY: COGNITIVE

Please summarize or list the child's strengths in this area. Refer to the data written in the *Description of Mastered or Developing Skills* as a starting point:

Leigh Ann has strong memory skills and is able to engage in self-directed play for hours. She is able to follow directions with prompting. She maintains learned skills.

Area	Item	Age of Concern	✔	Notes	Description of Mastered or Developing Skills
MOTOR DIFFERENCES	83. Demonstrates awkward motor movements (e.g., head flops backwards when placed into sitting position, crawls, walks or runs atypically for age, walks on toes)	**3 months** Mark only if child is **at least** this age.			
	84. Displays atypical activity level (e.g., overactive/hyperactive, underactive/very passive, or unusual stamina)	**3 months** Mark only if child is **at least** this age.	✔	• *Leigh Ann has a high activity level – she frequently jumps and spins – especially when she is in crowded places.* • *She has difficulty remaining in her place during circle time.*	
	85. Displays variability in gross-motor skills (e.g., able to engage in some age-appropriate physical activities but not others, may climb furniture but seeks support climbing stairs)	**3 months** Mark only if child is **at least** this age.			
	86. Has difficulty maintaining hold or actively resists grasping objects or a tool (e.g., chalk, crayon, marker, pencil, paintbrush) for purposeful activities	**5 months** Mark only if child is **at least** this age.			
	87. Displays unusual facial expressions or grimacing	**6 months** Mark only if child is **at least** this age.			
	88. Has extreme difficulty starting or stopping actions (e.g., difficulty feeding self, moving through environment, or playing with objects)	**7 months** Mark only if child is **at least** this age.			

Figure 3.12. Leigh Ann's UCC and ISSI (continued).

Area	Item	Age of Concern (refer to developmental norms)	✔	Notes (Describe behavior/characteristic in more detail)	Description of Mastered or Developing Skills
MOTOR DIFFERENCES	89. Has difficulty independently moving through environment and appropriately maneuvering around objects and people (e.g., difficulty crawling, moving room to room, walking on uneven surfaces, moving on/off a chair)	**12 months** Mark only if child is **at least** this age.			
	90. Has difficulty using hands for fine-motor tasks (e.g., holding a crayon, using eating utensils, turning a single page, fastening, buttoning, and zipping)	**18 months** Mark only if child is **at least** this age.			
	91. Displays variability in fine-motor skills (e.g., can accomplish some tasks but not others, may use one hand in a very precise manner to manipulate small objects, but does not use hands together for combined stabilizing and skill)	**18 months** Mark only if child is **at least** this age.			
	92. Displays unusual or repetitive body postures and movements (e.g., hand flapping, rocking, finger flicking, moving fingers in front of face, and spinning)	**24 months** Mark only if child is **at least** this age.	✔	She spins, wiggles fingers near face and jumps.	
	93. Other:				

INDIVIDUAL STRENGTHS AND SKILLS INVENTORY: MOTOR

Please summarize or list the child's strengths in this area. Refer to the data written in the *Description of Mastered or Developing Skills* as a starting point:

Leigh Ann is an energetic and strong child. She walks and runs with ease and is able to use her hands to color and cut. She enjoys jumping, running, spinning, and climbing.

Area	Item	Age of Concern (refer to developmental norms)	✔	Notes (Describe behavior/characteristic in more detail)	Description of Mastered or Developing Skills
EMOTIONAL VULNERABILITY	94. Exhibits more extreme emotional responses, in duration and/or intensity, than other children of the same age	**4 months** Mark only if child is **at least** this age.	✔	Cries when there is a change in routine. Is calming more easily now.	
	95. Demonstrates unusual fear response – lacks appropriate fears or is overly fearful	**4 months** Mark only if child is **at least** this age.	✔	Lacks appropriate fear of strangers. Will walk up to strangers and talk about her dolls.	
	96. Emotional responses are not related to the situation (e.g., laughs for no apparent reason)	**7 months** Mark only if child is **at least** this age.			
	97. Displays great difficulty being comforted by parents/caregivers when upset – is not easily calmed	**8 months** Mark only if child is **at least** this age.			

Figure 3.12. Leigh Ann's UCC and ISSI (continued).

Area	Item	Age of Concern (refer to developmental norms)	✔	Notes (Describe behavior/characteristic in more detail)	Description of Mastered or Developing Skills
EMOTIONAL VULNERABILITY	98. Has more difficulty expressing and/or controlling emotions than other same-age children	**9 months** Mark only if child is **at least** this age.	✔	*Leigh Ann does not smile much. She does not show emotions unless she is upset.*	
	99. Does not find pleasure in activities and interactions similar to children the same age; seems withdrawn	**9 months** Mark only if child is **at least** this age.	✔	*She prefers to play alone and requires prompting to participate in activities with others.*	*Will participate with peers with prompting and assistance.*
	100. Appears to purposefully injure self (e.g., bangs head, picks skin, bites nails until finger bleeds, bites self)	**11 months** Mark only if child is **at least** this age.			
	101. Becomes stressed when presented with a new task or situation (e.g., does not initially attempt new things)	**42 months** Mark only if child is **at least** this age.			
	102. Shows persistent aggressive behaviors with people and/or objects that do not readily respond to typical developmental interventions (e.g., persistently harms others or breaks objects)	**48 months** Mark only if child is **at least** this age.			
	103. Has low frustration tolerance	**48 months** Mark only if child is **at least** this age.			
	104. Other:				

INDIVIDUAL STRENGTHS AND SKILLS INVENTORY: EMOTIONAL

Please summarize or list the child's strengths in this area. Refer to the data written in the *Description of Mastered or Developing Skills* as a starting point:

Leigh Ann calms more easily now. It is easy to tell what she is upset about. She responds to being comforted by parents and her teacher.

Area	Description	Notes (Describe in more detail)	Description of Mastered or Developing Skills
KNOWN MEDICAL OR OTHER BIOLOGICAL FACTORS	**Sleep:** Has history of poor sleep patterns that are unusual for his/her age, culture, or family norms	*She did not sleep through the night until she was 36 months. Now, she sleeps through the night 5 out of 7 days.*	*Leigh Ann goes to sleep without protest as long as she is given a Cinderella doll.*
	Eating: Has a history of eating behaviors that are highly restrictive or unusual for his/her age, culture, or family norms		*She eats a variety of foods.*
	Development: Has a history of regression: loss of acquired skills (e.g., social, language, motor) at any age		
	Other medical issues (please specify):	*Leigh Ann is allergic to mangos and other tropical fruits.*	

INDIVIDUAL STRENGTHS AND SKILLS INVENTORY: BIOLOGICAL

Please summarize or list the child's strengths in this area. Refer to the data written in the *Description of Mastered or Developing Skills* as a starting point:

Leigh Ann is an energetic, strong, and healthy child. She sleeps well most nights, eats a variety of foods, and is meeting most developmental milestones with the exception of speech and socialization.

Figure 3.12. Leigh Ann's UCC and ISSI (continued).

Global Intervention Plan: Guide to Establishing Priorities

Ruth Aspy, Ph.D., and Barry G. Grossman, Ph.D.

Directions: Following completion of the UCC and ISSI, the next step is to identify UCC **areas** and **items** that will result in a *meaningful* Global Intervention Plan. Consideration of priorities and strengths for an individual facilitates selection of UCC areas and items. The following questions are provided as a guide.

Selecting UCC Areas

Vision   "Begin with the end in mind" – Stephen R. Covey

- What is the long- and short-term vision of/for the individual?
  Note that "long-term" and "short-term" may be defined differently in order to be meaningful.

  Long term (1 year):
  · Tell parents about an event that occurred at school
  · Make a friend
  · Attend classes in the general education setting

  Short term:
  · Play with peers
  · Pretend play on topics other than princesses
  · Increase communication skills - communicate with same-age peers

- ⊙ Which UCC **areas** would have the greatest impact on achieving this vision?

  Social, Communication, Sensory Differences, Restricted Patterns of Behavior Interests and Activities

Settings

- In what settings does the individual participate?

  School, home, family, church, OT

- ⊙ Which UCC **areas** have the greatest impact on the individual's ability to function in multiple settings?

  Social, Communication, Sensory Differences

Quality of Life

- What is most important to the individual? What provides a sense of well-being?
  Consider independence, relationships, play/leisure activities, safety, health, etc.

  Jumping, princesses, watching television/movies, structure, and predictability

- ⊙ Which UCC **areas** have the greatest impact on the individual's quality of life?

  Restricted Patterns of Behavior Interests and Activities

Key UCC Areas

Based on your answers to the questions above, place an X next to the key UCC **areas**.

*Transfer to the **Areas of Concern** section of the Ziggurat Worksheet.*

☒ Social
☒ Restricted Patterns of Behavior Interests, and Activities
☒ Communication
☒ Sensory Differences

☒ Cognitive Differences
☒ Motor Differences
☒ Emotional Vulnerability
☐ Known Medical or Other Biological Factors

Figure 3.13. Global Intervention Plan Guide completed by Leigh Ann's team.

Key UCC Items

Select key UCC **items** for *each* of the UCC **areas** listed above. Choose items that are essential (necessary for progress) and developmentally appropriate. Emphasize items that are pivotal (building blocks for additional skills). Avoid selecting redundant items.

Write key item numbers and descriptions below. These items will be used to develop interventions, keeping strengths and skills (identified on the ISSI) in mind.

*Transfer items to the **Selected UCC Item** section of the Ziggurat Worksheet and develop interventions.*

#1 *Appears to be unresponsive to others (e.g., unaware of the presence of others)*

#11 *Has difficulty using and perceiving nonverbal communication (e.g., tone of voice, gestures, facial expressions)*

#14 *Isolates self from others or chooses solitary play consistently and across settings*

#29 *Displays difficulty engaging in activities other than intense special interests*

#33 *Becomes upset easily with interruption to routines or unanticipated changes in events (e.g., taking a different route to a destination, moving a familiar object from "its place," using a different color plate for meals)*

#53 *Does not spontaneously comment or share experiences – may speak only when asked a direct question*

#54 *Has difficulty with basic rules of conversation (e.g., asks inappropriate questions, makes poor eye contact, has difficulty maintaining conversation, wants to talk about own interests exclusively)*

#60 *Often responds in a developmentally unusual manner to sounds (e.g., reacts as if has no hearing, ignores some sounds, turns up volume on TV, bangs toys and objects, or overreacts to noises such as crowds or sirens)*

#64, 65 *Often shows an unusually strong desire to do activities that provide touch, pressure, and movement*

#68 *Often responds in a developmentally unusual manner to visual input (e.g., focuses on shiny items and reflections; ignores faces; shows preference or strong dislike of certain colors; overreliance on salient features such as glasses and hair)*

Selecting UCC Items

Figure 3.13. Global Intervention Plan Guide (continued).

Ziggurat Worksheet

BEHAVIOR/AREAS OF CONCERN	FOR SPECIFIC INTERVENTION PLAN (Operationalized Behaviors)	SELECTED UCC ITEMS	CHECK ALL THAT APPLY		
			A	B	C
Social Restricted Patterns Communication Sensory Differences	ⓐ ⓐ ⓐ	#1 Appears to be unresponsive to others #11 Has difficulty using and perceiving nonverbal communication #14 Isolates self from others or chooses solitary play consistently and across settings #29 Displays difficulty engaging in activities other than intense special interests #33 Becomes upset easily with interruption to routines or unanticipated changes in events #53 Does not spontaneously comment or share experiences – may #54 Has difficulty with basic rules of conversation #60 Often responds in a developmentally unusual manner to sounds #64, 65 Often shows an unusual strong desire to do activities that provide touch, pressure, and movement #68 Often responds in a developmentally unusual manner to visual input	✓		
	Sensory and Biological Intervention:	• Provide sensory diet in the home and school settings. The diet should emphasize vestibular, proprioceptive, and oral motor activities and may include (a) using a thick straw with drinks; (b) sitting on a therapy ball or disco seat during activities; (c) activities that involve movement, such as jumping or hopping; (d) weighted vest for 10 minutes during seated activity; (e) helping to "set up" or put away activities; (f) work space clearly defined with boundary markers; (g) mini-trampoline use. Activities and supports should be part of the daily routine and NOT contingent upon Leigh Ann's behavior. Include sensory activities on Leigh Ann's visual schedule. • Provide a comfort item that can be held during stressful times such as circle time, conversation item, and speech therapy (use rounded rather than angular items to prevent her from becoming visually distracted): (a) princess doll clothing item; (b) a round princess tag with Leigh Ann's name on it; (c) princess-themed cloth; (d) princess bookmark with rounded edges. • Leigh Ann is easily distracted by sounds. As work becomes more challenging, allow her to use noise-reducing headphones and/or earplugs during work periods. Consider the use of headphones and/or earplugs during times where loud noises are expected. Understand that movement and heavy work activities may also help Leigh Ann to tolerate certain auditory input.			
Sensory and Biological	Underlying Characteristics Addressed:	#14 Isolates self from others or chooses solitary play consistently and across settings #29 Displays difficulty engaging in activities other than intense special interests #60 Often responds in a developmentally unusual manner to sounds #64, 65 Often shows an unusually strong desire to do activities that provide touch, pressure, and movement #68 Often responds in a developmentally unusual manner to visual input			

Figure 3.14. Ziggurat worksheet for Leigh Ann's global intervention plan.

Ziggurat Worksheet

			✓
		✓	
	✓		

Respectful Reinforcement	Reinforcement Intervention:	• Carefully identify a list of reinforcers for Leigh Ann. Be sure to incorporate her special interests. Maintain and update the list to keep her engaged in learning, communication, and social tasks. Use of a reinforcer menu/self-selection increases the effectiveness of reinforcers. Because some of the visual and movement distracters that are highly reinforcing for Leigh Ann are naturally available in the environment, she will need high levels of engineered reinforcement in order to compete with those that are freely accessible. When Leigh Ann enters class, place all princess items in "their castle so that they can be safe." They will remain in the "castle" all day. Conduct a reinforcer assessment daily using: (a) princess books, (b) princess silverware, (c) prisms, (d) kaleidoscope, etc. • Identify specific crunchy foods that are not included in her sensory diet to be used as reinforcers. These may vary and may be selected from a menu. Leigh Ann's food preferences include (a) carrots, (b) baked potato chips, (c) unsalted popcorn, (d) celery, (e) apples. • Use First-Then (first work, then reinforcer) to help increase task engagement. • Reinforce Leigh Ann for skills such as responding to peer initiations, remaining in group activities at school, and completing her morning schedule, including brushing her teeth. • Develop a box of reinforcement activities that include objects containing lines and/or angles (e.g., xylophone, mini-blinds, pickup sticks – items that differ from the reinforcer list above). Make a visual menu of the items in the box and have Leigh Ann earn access to an item from the box after participating in challenging activities such as communicating with peers. • Use video, such as clips from Disney princess movies, to teach about emotions and their causes. Emphasize cause and effect – pointing out how the characters feel and what caused them to feel that way. Narrate clips from Disney movies. For example, say, "She is smiling. She is happy because ___." "He is yelling. He is mad because ___." Help Leigh Ann to generalize to real people in real situations. • Structure play activities to include at least one selected/trained peer. Use activities involving Leigh Ann's interests, such as princess activity books. • Use princess sticker or stamp to reinforce interactions.
	Underlying Characteristics Addressed:	#1 Appears to be unresponsive to others #11 Has difficulty using and perceiving nonverbal communication #14 Isolates self from others or chooses solitary play consistently and across settings #29 Displays difficulty engaging in activities other than intense special interests #33 Becomes upset easily with interruption to routines or unanticipated changes in events #53 Does not spontaneously comment or share experiences – may speak only when asked a direct question #54 Has difficulty with basic rules of conversation

Figure 3.14. Ziggurat worksheet for Leigh Ann's global intervention plan (continued).

Ziggurat Worksheet

		✓	✓	✓

Structure & Visual/Tactile Supports

Structure & Visual/Tactile Support Intervention:	• Use a visual mini-schedule to depict tasks to complete for the morning and evening routines. The last item on the schedule should be a reinforcer. • Create a video schedule of school routines showing successful completion of activities such as circle time and centers. • Provide video modeling of social activities, such as turn taking and dramatic play, using a person in a princess costume as the model. The goal is for Leigh Ann to first imitate play from the video and then generalize the skills in order to create novel play scenarios. • Use video, such as clips from Disney princess movies, to teach about emotions and their causes. Emphasize cause and effect – pointing out how the characters feel and what caused them to feel that way. Narrate clips from Disney movies. For example, say, "She is smiling. She is happy because ____." "He is yelling. He is mad because ____." Help Leigh Ann to generalize to real people in real situations. • Structure play activities to include at least one selected/trained peer. Use activities involving Leigh Ann's interests, such as princess activity books. • During instruction, use a high level of visual strategies: show visual schedule to prepare for transitions; have Leigh Ann carry a visual to match to the designated activity area; etc. • In addition to Disney movies, a professionally developed video series – The Transporters (Baron-Cohen) – may be helpful in teaching Leigh Ann to identify others' feelings based on facial expressions. She may find the use of tracks (parallel lines) of high interest. • Use a visual support with symbols (such as Board Maker) to assist Leigh Ann in reporting daily activities. This can be used in both school and home environments. Leigh Ann can share school activities with her parents and home activities with her teacher. • Use an emotion check-in chart at the beginning of the day to begin to discuss emotions
Underlying Characteristics Addressed:	#1 Appears to be unresponsive to others #14 Isolates self from others or chooses solitary play consistently and across settings #29 Displays difficulty engaging in activities other than intense special interests #33 Becomes upset easily with interruption to routines or unanticipated changes in events #53 Does not spontaneously comment or share experiences – may speak only when asked a direct question #54 Has difficulty with basic rules of conversation

Figure 3.14. Ziggurat worksheet for Leigh Ann's global intervention plan (continued).

Ziggurat Worksheet

			✓
		✓	
	✓		

Task Demand Intervention:	• Decrease task demands through the use of structure and visual supports described above – video schedule, mini-schedule, movie clips, structured play activities, video modeling, visual communication supports. • Train peers to play with Leigh Ann. Peers should be taught how to model appropriate play and to keep her engaged. • Exaggerate your own facial expressions for Leigh Ann. Narrate and describe them. For example, say, "I'm smiling because I'm so glad to see you this morning." • Use First-Then (first work, then reinforcer) to help increase task engagement. • Monitor the sensory environment to ensure that it is not too demanding for Leigh Ann. Provide breaks and calming sensory activities as needed. • Leigh Ann is easily distracted by sounds. As work becomes more challenging, allow her to use noise-reducing headphones and/or earplugs during work periods. Consider the use of headphones and/or earplugs during times where loud noises are expected. Understand that movement and heavy work activities may also help Leigh Ann to tolerate certain auditory input. • Prompt interactions with peers and staff, as needed
Underlying Characteristics Addressed:	#1 Appears to be unresponsive to others #11 Has difficulty using and perceiving nonverbal communication #14 Isolates self from others or chooses solitary play consistently and across settings #29 Displays difficulty engaging in activities other than intense special interests #33 Becomes upset easily with interruption to routines or unanticipated changes in events #53 Does not spontaneously comment or share experiences – may speak only when asked a direct question #54 Has difficulty with basic rules of conversation #60 Often responds in a developmentally unusual manner to sounds #64, 65 Often shows an unusually strong desire to do activities that provide touch, pressure, and movement #68 Often responds in a developmentally unusual manner to visual input

Task Demands

Figure 3.14. Ziggurat worksheet for Leigh Ann's global intervention plan (continued).

Ziggurat Worksheet

Skills to Teach	Skill Intervention:		✓	✓
	• Use video, such as clips from Disney princess movies, to teach about emotions and their causes. Emphasize cause and effect – pointing out how the characters feel and what caused them to feel that way. Narrate clips from Disney movies. For example, say, "She is smiling. She is happy because _____." "Help Leigh Ann to generalize to real people in real situations.			
	• Structure play activities to include at least one selected/trained peer. Use activities involving Leigh Ann's interests, such as princess activity books.			
	• Provide speech therapy to teach expressive language skills, including responding to greetings and other peer initiations, language used in play activities, sharing about an experience, and other basic pragmatic language skills.			
	• Parents should set up play dates for Leigh Ann. Select an activity that both children will find enjoyable. Keep the play date brief to help ensure success. Build in reinforcers and make sure that Leigh Ann knows what she is working for. Supervise and narrate during the play to assist. Video the play and review with Leigh Ann.			
	• Teach Leigh Ann to play using video and trained peers (see Structure and Visual/Tactile Supports and Task Demands levels for detailed description).			
	• Provide video modeling of social activities, such as turn taking and dramatic play, using a person in a princess costume as the model. The goal is for Leigh Ann to first imitate play from the video and then generalize the skills in order to create novel play scenarios.			
	• Teach Leigh Ann skills for sensory activities, including jumping jacks, jumping rope, tricycle riding, and trampoline.			
	Underlying Characteristics Addressed:	#1 Appears to be unresponsive to others #11 Has difficulty using and perceiving nonverbal communication #14 Isolates self from others or chooses solitary play consistently and across settings #29 Displays difficulty engaging in activities other than intense special interests #53 Does not spontaneously comment or share experiences – may speak only when asked a direct question #54 Has difficulty with basic rules of conversation #64, 65 Often shows an unusually strong desire to do activities that provide touch, pressure, and movement		

Figure 3.14. Ziggurat worksheet for Leigh Ann's global intervention plan (continued).

Designing a Program to Address Specific Behavioral Needs

Individuals on the spectrum often display specific behavioral concerns that become the focus of intervention (e.g., class disruption, difficulty making friends, poor conversation skills, poor organizational skills, physical aggression, and rage). In order to develop an intervention plan, an assessment must be completed that consists of both the UCC/ISSI and the ABC-I. The UCC/ISSI identifies the features of autism and strengths and skills while the ABC-I is used to look at patterns and specific core features related to this behavior (taken from the UCC). The specific intervention plan form (Appendix D) is used to guide completion of the ABC-I. We will use the case of Ashley to illustrate this process.

Shortly after the school year began, Ashley's teachers were concerned because she frequently interrupted the lesson. She asked off-topic questions or shared comments that were unrelated to what was going on. Despite frequent private conversations about this behavior, Ashley continued to disrupt lessons. Her teachers found this behavior confusing. After reviewing and revising the UCC/ISSI (Figure 3.9), they completed the Specific Intervention Plan form and the ABC-I (see Figure 3.15).

The first step was to operationally define the behavior of concern by describing it in a manner that was observable and measurable and recognizable to others. Ashley's behavior, "disrupting class," was operationally defined as "asking off-topic questions during lecture" and "making off-topic comments during the lesson." Her questions and comments typically centered on her intense interest in animals. These were documented in the middle of the page under the behavior section of the ABC-I.

Next, her team identified antecedents for this behavior. They decided that more information was needed. They started out by interviewing Ashley, who seemed confused about her behavior. In order to gather more information, Ashley was observed in class. The team also spoke with other teachers to gather additional information about this behavior. Several antecedents were uncovered: (a) The behavior only occurred at school during class lecture. (b) It happened in most subjects that were difficult for her. (c) Her parents said that she seemed more restless lately and was not sleeping well.

Ashley's team continued the functional assessment by identifying consequences for her behavior. Recall that the term "consequence" simply refers to events that follow a behavior. Consequences can be positive, negative, or even neutral. Also, what may be rewarding or aversive to most may not be to an autistic individual. Most of Ashley's teachers simply talked to her about their concerns. One tried detention. Some peers laughed at her comments while others ignored them. Her daily participation grades were low, resulting in an overall decline in her academic progress.

Specific Intervention Plan: Guide to Establishing Priorities

Ruth Aspy, Ph.D., and Barry G. Grossman, Ph.D.

INSTRUCTIONS: Use the ABC-I when designing an intervention to address specific behavioral concerns. Complete the questionnaire below. Transfer information to the ABC-I form (using the numbers as a guide) and to the Ziggurat Worksheet as indicated. Once the information has been transferred to the Ziggurat Worksheet, develop interventions for each level of the Ziggurat and ensure that the intervention is complete (5 levels, 3 points, addresses underlying needs).

Behavior

What specific behavior is of greatest concern?   *Disrupting class*

Transfer behavior to the top of the ABC-I ❶ and to the upper left corner of the Ziggurat Worksheet

Next to the 👁 icon, describe the behavior in observable, measurable terms.

👁 *Asking off-topic questions in class*

👁 *Making off-topic comments during lessons*

Place observable, measurable behavior descriptions next to the 👁 icon on the ABC-I ❷ and on the Ziggurat Worksheet

Antecedent

When and where does the behavior occur? List what is happening at the time or just before.

- *Class lecture*
- *Often wakes up at night*
- *Difficult courses*

Transfer to the antecedent column of the ABC-I ❸

Consequences

List what usually happens after the behavior occurs.

- *Verbal redirection*
- *Peers laughing/ignoring*
- *Decline in academic performance*
- *Detention*
- *Low daily participation grades*

Transfer to the consequences column of the ABC-I ❹

Underlying Characteristics

Review **ALL** the checked UCC items. Identify underlying characteristics that may be associated with the behaviors described on the ABC-I. *List the UCC item numbers and a brief description of each item on the bottom of the ABC-I ❺ and next to the # icons in the "Selected UCC Items" section on the Ziggurat Worksheet.*

Function

Behavior serves a purpose. Common functions include:

- Escape/avoidance
- Sensory stimulation
- Adult/peer attention
- Access to preferred activity
- Tangible items
- Other

What is the hypothesized function of the behavior?   *Escape/avoidance*

Figure 3.15. Ashley's Specific Intervention Plan Guide and ABC-I.

Antecedent(s) ⟶ Behavior ⟶ Consequence(s)

❶ Disrupting Class

❸
- Class lecture
- Difficult courses
- Often wakes up at night

❷
- ◉ Asking off-topic questions in class
- ◉ Making off-topic comments during lesson

❹
- Verbal redirection
- Detention
- Peers laughing/ignoring
- Low daily participation grades
- Decline in academic performance

Specific Behaviors

Underlying Characteristics*

❺
#1 Difficulty recognizing feelings and thoughts of others (mindblindness)
#14 Eccentric or intense preoccupations
#15 Asks repetitive questions
#16 Seems to be unmotivated by customary rewards
#25 Has difficulty with rules of conversation (e.g., interrupts others, asking questions)
#28 Has difficulty starting, joining, and/or ending a conversation
#30 Makes irrelevant comments
#60 Attention problems
#89 Has difficulty managing stress and anxiety

*As determined through the UCC.

Figure 3.15. Ashley's Specific Intervention Plan Guide and ABC-I (continued).

The next step to complete the ABC-I was to identify specific items from the UCC that were related to this behavior. This can be a challenge; however, Ashley's teachers were able to determine several underlying characteristics, including mindblindness, difficulty managing stress and expressing feelings, and her strong interest in specific subjects. This was documented on the bottom of the ABC-I. The information was used to develop an intervention plan using the ZW (see Figure 3.16). The information from the ABC-I was transferred to the Ziggurat Worksheet according to the Specific Intervention Plan Guide provided in Appendix D. This plan will be implemented in conjunction with her general program.

Once the underlying characteristics related to the behaviors were identified, the team concluded that the attention difficulties, social challenges, and absence of meaningful reinforcers combined to overwhelm Ashley's ability to cope during challenging academic activities, especially when she was fatigued. They decided that the off-topic questions and comments served the purpose of avoiding these activities. In addition, they recognized that skills deficits related to mindblindness and conversation were factors.

The final stage of this process is the Comprehensive Autism Planning System (CAPS; Henry & Myles, 2007). The CAPS is the comprehensive daily schedule for the student that embeds the supports the student needs to be successful. As such, it is the ultimate goal of the interdisciplinary team.

Designing the Student's Daily Program
By Brenda Smith Myles and Shawn Henry (adapted for Ziggurat Model)

Up to this point, the interdisciplinary team has identified supports that address the student's "autism." Even though interventions have been identified, they will be not functional until they are transferred into the student's daily program. For example, the Ziggurat Worksheet may indicate that a student needs a fidget, a choice board, and visual schedule, but many educators, in particular general educators, do not know when such supports should be used during the student's day.

The CAPS ensures that when the supports are created, they are compatible not only with student's "autism," but also with the environment in which the student is expected to perform. This important consideration is all too often ignored. For example, if a student sits at a desk most of the time during a class, a visual support that is Velcroed® to her desk or to a notebook may be useful. If, on the other hand, the student moves frequently during class, she may need a visual support that moves with her or is accessible from all areas of the room. It is often helpful to photograph effective supports detailed in the CAPS (Figure 3.21).

Specifically, CAPS is designed to provide an overview of a student's daily schedule by time and activity as well as the supports that he needs during each period. Following the development of the student's Ziggurat Worksheet, all educational professionals who work with the student

Ziggurat Worksheet

BEHAVIOR/AREAS OF CONCERN	FOR SPECIFIC INTERVENTION PLAN (Operationalized Behaviors)	SELECTED UCC ITEMS	CHECK ALL THAT APPLY		
			A	B	C
Disrupting Class	◎ Asking off-topic questions in class ◎ Making off-topic comments during lesson	#1 Difficulty recognizing the feelings and thoughts of others (mindblindness) #14 Eccentric or intense preoccupations #15 Asks repetitive questions #16 Seems to be unmotivated by customary rewards #25 Has difficulty with rules of conversation (e.g., interrupts others, asking questions) #28 Has difficulty starting, joining, and/or ending a conversation #30 Makes irrelevant comments #60 Attention problems #89 Has difficulty managing stress and anxiety	✓		
Sensory and Biological	Sensory and Biological Intervention:	• Allow Ashley to use stress ball or fidgets in class to help her remain calm and attentive.			
	Underlying Characteristics Addressed:	#60 Attention problems #89 Has difficulty managing stress and anxiety			
Respectful Reinforcement	Reinforcement Intervention:	• Reinforce Ashley for making on-topic statements and asking relevant questions in class. • Reinforce Ashley for using coping skills.			✓
	Underlying Characteristics Addressed:	#1 Difficulty recognizing the feelings and thoughts of others (mindblindness) #14 Eccentric or intense preoccupations #15 Asks repetitive questions #16 Seems to be unmotivated by customary rewards #30 Makes irrelevant comments			
Structure & Visual/Tactile Supports	Structure & Visual/Tactile Support Intervention:	• Use a Comic Strip Conversation to illustrate what others think and feel when she interrupts the class activity (e.g., "It is frustrating when she asks those questions," "She's rude"). • Give Ashley a card that indicates the topic for the current activity. Reinforce her for remaining on topic in practice and in class. • Provide Ashley with a list of strategies to use when feeling stressed or anxious (e.g., take deep breaths, ask for help, squeeze stress ball). Reinforce for using skills.	✓	✓	✓
	Underlying Characteristics Addressed:	#1 Difficulty recognizing the feelings and thoughts of others (mindblindness) #15 Asks repetitive questions #30 Makes irrelevant comments			

Figure 3.16. Ashley's intervention program to address specific behavior.

Ziggurat Worksheet

Task Demands	Task Demand Intervention:	• Use topic card during class lecture. • Tell Ashley about topic in advance and ask her to think about questions/comments in advance. Review questions/comments and help her write relevant ones down prior to lecture. Reinforce Ashley for developing on-topic question/comments. • Provide Ashley with a list of strategies to use when feeling stressed or anxious (e.g., take deep breaths, ask for help, squeeze stress ball). Reinforce for using skills.	✓	✓	✓
	Underlying Characteristics Addressed:	#14 Eccentric or intense preoccupations #15 Asks repetitive questions #30 Makes irrelevant comments #60 Attention problems			
Skills to Teach	Skill Intervention:	• Teach Ashley the concept of interruption and how it makes others feel through the use of written words and visuals. • Teach coping skills. • Teach Ashley to recognize the feelings of others based on facial expressions and other clues (tone of voice and gestures). Reinforce for accurate identification in pictures and real life.		✓	✓
	Underlying Characteristics Addressed:	#15 Asks repetitive questions #30 Makes irrelevant comments #89 Has difficulty managing stress and anxiety			

Figure 3.16. Ashley's intervention program to address specific behavior (continued).

develop the CAPS. Thus, the CAPS allows professionals and parents to answer the all-important question for autistic students: *What supports does the student need for each activity?*

Components of the CAPS (modified to integrate with Ziggurat Model)

As shown in Figure 3.17, the CAPS (see also Appendix F) is simply a list of a student's tasks and activities, the times they occur, and a delineation of the supports needed to support student success. In addition, the CAPS includes space for making notations about data collection and how skills are to be generalized to others settings.

The CAPS consists of the following components developed from evidence-based practices for students on the spectrum:

1. *Time.* This section indicates the clock time when each activity takes place that the student engages in throughout the day.

2. *Activity.* Activities include *all* tasks and activities throughout the day in which the student requires support. Academic periods (e.g., reading, math), nonacademic times (e.g., recess, lunch), and transitions between classes would all be considered activities.

3. *Skills to Teach.* This may include IEP goals, state standards, and/or general skills that lead to school success. These skills can serve as the basis for measuring response to instruction or annual yearly progress. Some skills may be dropped into the CAPS Worksheet from the Skills to Teach section of the Ziggurat Worksheet.

4. *Task Demands & Positive Environment and Structure & Visuals/Tactile Supports.* This can encompass a wide variety of supports, including placement in the classroom, visual supports (e.g., choice boards, visual schedules), peer supports (e.g., Circle of Friends, peer buddies) and instructional strategies (e.g., priming, self-monitoring). These are dropped into the CAPS Worksheet from the Structure and Visual/Tactile Supports and Task Demands and Positive Environment sections of the Ziggurat Worksheet.

5. *Reinforcement.* Student access to specific types of reinforcement as well as reinforcement schedule is listed under the reinforcement section of the CAPS. The team places information from the Reinforcement section of the Ziggurat Worksheet.

6. *Sensory and Biological.* Sensory supports and strategies, identified by an occupational therapist from the Sensory and Biological section of the Ziggurat Worksheet, are listed in this CAPS area.

7. *Communication/Social Skills.* The Sensory and Biological, Structure and Visual/Tactile Supports, Task Demands and Positive Environment, and Skills to Teach areas of the Ziggurat Worksheet that contain relevant items are used in this section of the CAPS. Supports, which are also diverse, may encompass (a) language boards; (b) PECS (Picture Exchange Communication Systems; Frost & Bondy, 2002); or (c) other augmentative communication systems.

Comprehensive Autism Planning System (CAPS)

Child/Student: _____

Time	Activity	Skills to Teach	Task Demands & Positive Environment and Structure & Visual/ Tactile Supports	Respectful Reinforcement	Sensory & Biological	Communication/ Social Skills	Data Collection	Generalization Plan

From Henry, S. A., & Myles, B. S. (2007). *The Comprehensive Autism Planning System (CAPS) for Individuals with Asperger Syndrome, Autism, and Related Disabilities.* Shawnee Mission, KS: AAPC Publishing. Adapted and used with permission.

Figure 3.17. CAPS form.

Although a separate section is not included for this purpose on the Ziggurat Worksheet, this section of the CAPS serves as a reminder that each activity requires some type of communication and social supports.

8. *Data Collection*. Data collection includes gathering information on behavior(s) to be documented during a specific activity. Typically, this section relates directly to IEP goals and objectives, behavioral issues, and state standards.

9. *Generalization Plan*. Because individuals with ASD often have problems generalizing information across settings, this section of the CAPS was developed to ensure that generalization of skills is built into the child's program.

CAPS for Middle and High School

When students enter middle and high school, most change rooms and teachers for each general education class and may have as many as nine teachers in nine different classrooms. Despite their movement from classroom to classroom, the activities in which the students participate in each academic class are similar. That is, in each class students are likely to be required to participate in (a) independent work, (b) group work, (c) tests, (d) lectures, and (e) homework. From this standpoint, the activities in English class and Geometry are the same.

The Modified Comprehensive Autism Planning System (M-CAPS) was developed to serve as a means of communicating to educators who teach academic subjects the types of supports that students need during each activity (Sue Klingshirn, personal communication, April 2006). The interdisciplinary team who plans the program for a high school student on the spectrum who spends extensive time in general education classrooms develops the student's program using the M-CAPS. The result is that each of the student's academic teachers shares the same document. The M-CAPS used in Biology is the same as the M-CAPS used in Sociology. The supports are, likewise, the same. The M-CAPS is illustrated in Figure 3.18 (see blank form in Appendix G).

The benefits of using the M-CAPS in middle and high school are many and include the following:

1. The student uses the same types of supports across classes, which allows him to see the flexibility of supports. This, in turn, facilitates the student's understanding of the concept of generalization (i.e., "Whenever I am stressed, I can use my coping cards. It doesn't have to be only in Mr. Miu's room. I can use them in Ms. Allen's math class as well.").

2. Communication is fostered across academic teachers because teachers share the same documents and have access to the same types of supports.

3. The student's case manager and team can easily track successes and problems across academic subjects. For example, if Susan is experiencing problems during independent work

Modified Comprehensive Autism Planning System (M-CAPS)

Child/Student: _____

Activity	Skills to Teach	Task Demands & Positive Environment & Visual/Tactile Supports	Respectful Reinforcement	Sensory & Biological	Communication /Social Skills	Data Collection	Generalization
Independent Work							
Group Work							
Tests							
Lectures							
Homework							

From Henry, S. A., & Myles, B. S. (2007). *The Comprehensive Autism Planning System (CAPS) for Individuals with Asperger Syndrome, Autism, and Related Disabilities.* Shawnee Mission, KS: AAPC Publishing. Adapted and used with permission.

Figure 3.18. M-CAPS form.

in Psychology, the team can consult her other academic teachers to identify whether Susan also has problems with independent work in their classes.

Not all classes in middle and high school include (a) independent work, (b) group work, (c) tests, (d) lectures, and (e) homework. For these classes, the traditional CAPS can be used. Physical Education is a good example of a class that does not follow the aforementioned structure and for which the CAPS by time and activity would be most appropriate. For students who are involved in work experiences, community-based opportunities, and extracurricular activities, a traditional CAPS is completed for these activities.

CAPS for College

The M-CAPS is not just limited to middle and high school but can be a valuable tool for post-secondary education as well. Autistic students who enter a two- or four-year college or university may find that the M-CAPS provides the type of structure they need to be successful in their classes. This tool, which can be shared with Office of Disabilities staff and college professors, easily communicates what the student needs to be successful across activities. In addition, it supports and enhances self-advocacy. That is, autistic students can approach faculty members with the M-CAPS and use it as a starting point for discussing strengths and needs.

CAPS for the Workplace

When adults on the spectrum transition to the workplace, they will most likely need supports – whether it is in an independent or a supported environment. The Vocational Comprehensive Autism Planning System (V-CAPS), shown in Figure 3.19 (see also Appendix H), is an efficient and effective means to ensure that all areas of the individual's autism are addressed throughout the day. The Activity category, rather than the Time category, is used to identify the tasks in which the individual engages. While tasks vary depending on the type of job the individual has, certain basic work activities that need support may include (a) arrival, (b) break, (c) lunch, (d) the work task itself, (e) meetings, and (f) departure.

Creating an Archive of Supports

It is important to create a visual archive of supports for the student. After each support is created, purchased, or identified, a photograph of it should be taken and placed in the student's file. This becomes a mini-portfolio of the student's supports. Such a pictorial representation serves multiple purposes:

1. It links a given task to needed supports.

2. It provides a visual model for substitute teachers, paraeducators, and others who may work with the student throughout the day.

Vocational Comprehensive Autism Planning System (V-CAPS)

Name: _____

Activity	Skills to Teach	Task Demands & Positive Environment and Structure/ Tactile Supports	Respectful Reinforcement	Sensory & Biological	Communication /Social Skills	Data Collection	Generalization
Arrival at Work							
Work Activity							
Break							
Meetings							
Lunch							
Departure from Work							

Myles, B. S., & Henry, S. A. (2008). Adapted and used with permission.

Figure 3.19. V-CAPS form.

3. It can help the student's future teachers understand the supports that the student needed in each environment.

In this way, the CAPS with supporting visual representations, ensures current and future success for the student at school. Figure 3.18 provides an example of this concept.

Transferring Items from the Ziggurat Worksheet to the CAPS

The following steps are involved in completing the CAPS.

1. *Time and Activities.* The first step in completing a CAPS is filling in the Time and Activities columns. Activities include all academic and nonacademic subjects, including recess, lunch, and transitions – any activity in which the student is likely to need support (see #1 and #2 on Figure 3.22).

2. *Skills to Teach.* Next, the skills to be taught in each class are identified, including IEP goals, state standards, or general class rules and routines. These are stated globally so that they can be measured over time (see #3 on Figure 3.22).

3. *Data Collection.* This section delineates how student progress on the *Skills to Teach* column will be measured. Identify what data will be taken as well as how often data will be taken.

4. *Task Demands & Positive Environment and Structure & Visual/Tactile Supports, Reinforcement, Sensory Strategies, and Communication/Social Skills.* The interventions listed on the Ziggurat Worksheet are placed on the CAPS. All interventions are to be used somewhere in the CAPS. Many will be used in more than one activity (see Figure 3.20).

Ziggurat Worksheet		CAPS
Skills to Teach	→	Skills to Teach
Structure and Visual/Tactile Supports Task Demands & Positive Environment	→	Task Demands & Positive Environment and Structure & Visual/Tactile Supports
Reinforcement	→	Reinforcement
Sensory and Biological	→	Sensory and Biological
Sensory and Biological Reinforcement Structure and Visual/Tactile Supports Task Demands & Positive Environment Skills to Teach	→	Communication/Social Skills

Figure 3.20. Location of items from the Ziggurat Worksheet on the CAPS.

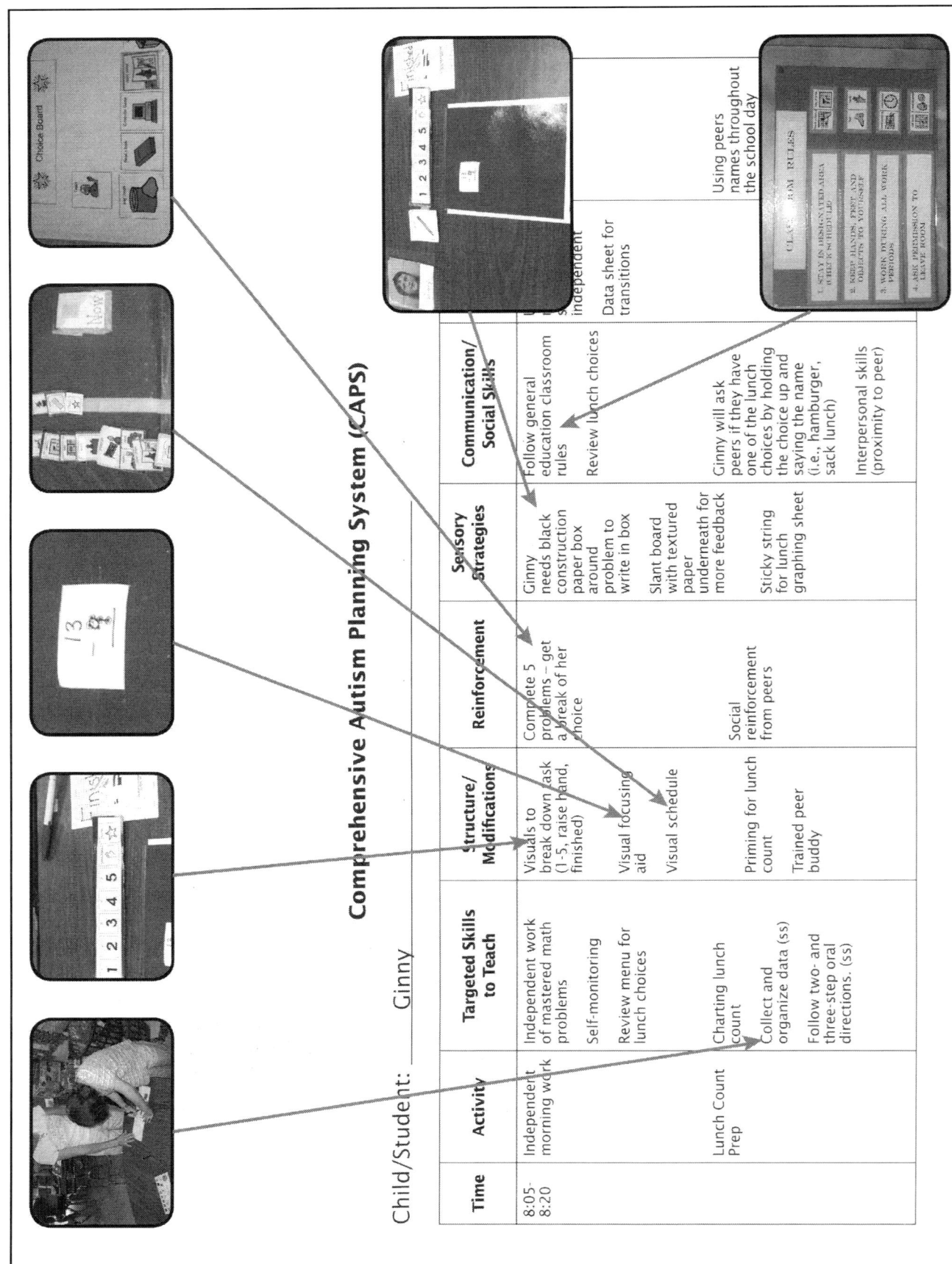

Comprehensive Autism Planning System (CAPS)

Child/Student: _____ Ginny _____

Time	Activity	Targeted Skills to Teach	Structure/Modifications	Reinforcement	Sensory Strategies	Communication/ Social Skills
8:05–8:20	Independent morning work	Independent work of mastered math problems Self-monitoring Review menu for lunch choices	Visuals to break down task (1–5, raise hand, finished) Visual focusing aid Visual schedule	Complete 5 problems – get a break of her choice	Ginny needs black construction paper box around problem to write in box Slant board with textured paper underneath for more feedback	Follow general education classroom rules Review lunch choices
	Lunch Count Prep	Charting lunch count Collect and organize data (ss) Follow two- and three-step oral directions. (ss)	Priming for lunch count Trained peer buddy	Social reinforcement from peers	Sticky string for lunch graphing sheet	Ginny will ask peers if they have one of the lunch choices by holding the choice up and saying the name (i.e., hamburger, sack lunch) Interpersonal skills (proximity to peer)

Data sheet for transitions

Using peers names throughout the school day

Figure 3.21. CAPS showing support materials needed.

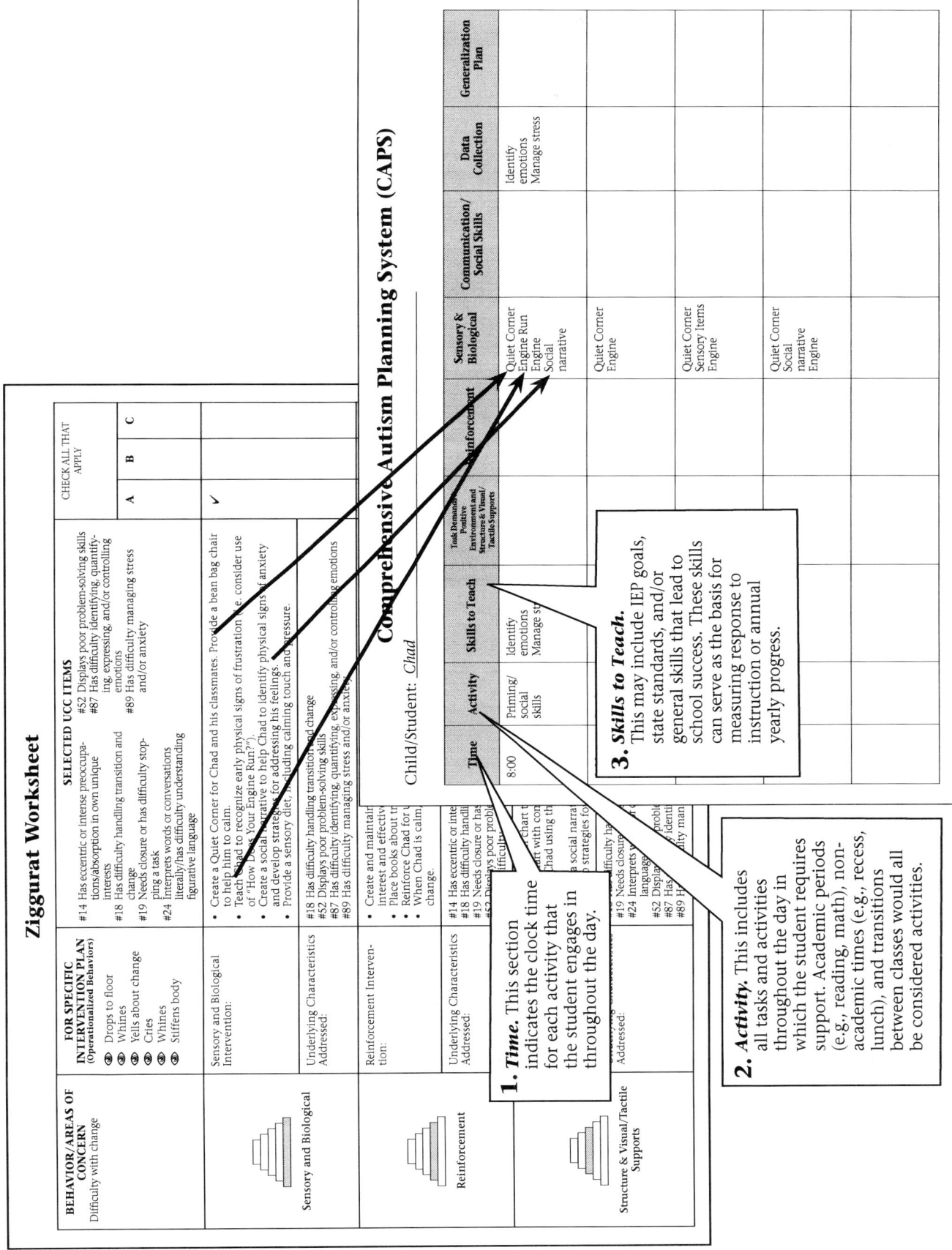

Figure 3.22. Transferring items from the Ziggurat Worksheet to the CAPS.

Figure 3.22 depicts how items are transferred from the Ziggurat Worksheet to the CAPS.

Ashley's CAPS
Ashley's M-CAPS is presented in Figure 3.23. Items generated from her interdisciplinary team using the Ziggurat Worksheet have been placed on the M-CAPS form. These interventions are then implemented in Ashley's general education classes.

Leigh Ann's CAPS
Leigh Ann's team helped to make her comprehensive plan a reality by creating a CAPS. Placing the strategies into her daily schedule helped her team to conceptualize when and how the interventions would take place. This step also increased the accountability for following through with the plan. Leigh Ann's CAPS is presented in Figure 3.24.

Summary
The CAPS for preschool and elementary students, the M-CAPS for middle school, high school students, and college students, and the V-CAPS for the workplace are developed from items on the Ziggurat Worksheet. The various forms of CAPS represent the student's daily schedule and indicates when specific interventions are needed to ensure success throughout the day.

Modified Comprehensive Autism Planning System (M-CAPS)

Child/Student: _Ashley_

Activity	Skills to Teach	Task Demands & Positive Environment and Structure & Visual/ Tactile Supports	Respectful Reinforcement	Sensory & Biological	Communication/ Social Skills	Data Collection	Generalization
Independent Work	• Work completion • Modified academic standards	• Provide starter sentences and graphics organizers • Allow to highlight or underline main ideas in passages • 50% of problems • Reduce writing required or allow for oral response, keyboarding • Use books on tape	• Drawing with peer after assignment completed • Provide starter sentences and graphic organizers • Verbal reinforcement for using coping cards	• Hand out materials and books • Coping cards • Incredible 5-Point Scale	• Help card • Peer buddy to assist and focus	• Work completion (Y/N) (M-F) • Modified academic standards (Grades, M-F)	• Peer buddy at lunch
Group Work	• Participation • E•motional regulation	• Time for drawing after group work • Provide a smaller group • Do not have Ashley write	• Time for drawing after group work • Verbal reinforcement for using coping cards	• Hand out materials and books • Coping cards • Incredible 5-Point Scale	• Conversation starter and manners cards • Help card • Assign a role • Peer buddy to assist and focus	• Participation (Y/N) (M,T) • Emotional regulation (# Rumble, Rage) (W,R)	• Conversation starter and manner cards at lunch
Tests	• Test completion • Emotional regulation	• Run errands before test • Take test in resource room • Reduce writing or allow for oral response, keyboarding	• Time to talk about animals or fantasy with a peer after test • Reinforcement menu for using coping cards	• Run errands before test • Coping cards • Incredible 5-Point Scale	• Conversation starter and manners cards	• Completed Test (Grades) • Emotional regulation (# Rumble, Rage) (F)	• NA

Figure 3.23. Ashley's M-CAPS.

Modified Comprehensive Autism Planning System (M-CAPS)

Activity	Skills to Teach	Task Demands & Positive Environment and Structure & Visual/Tactile Supports	Respectful Reinforcement	Sensory & Biological	Communication/ Social Skills	Data Collection	Generalization
Lectures	• Understanding main ideas • On-task	• Provide graphic organizers • Provide copies of lecture notes • Highlight or underline main ideas in lecture notes	• Verbal reinforcement for using coping cards	• Coping cards • Incredible 5-Point Scale	• Conversation starter and manners cards • Peer buddy to assist and focus	• Understanding main ideas (Highlighted Y/N) (W) • On-task (Y/N) (R)	• NA
Homework	• Homework completion • Turning in homework	• Use books on tape, as needed • 50% of problems • Highlight or underline main ideas in passages • Reduce amount of writing required or allow for oral response, keyboarding	• Reinforce homework completion (time to talk or draw about animals and her fantasy world)	• Down time before homework • Coping card	• NA	• Homework completion (Y/N) (Daily) • Turning in homework (Y/N) (Daily)	• NA

Figure 3.23. Ashley's M-CAPS (continued).

Comprehensive Autism Planning System (CAPS)

Time	Activity	Skills to Teach	Task Demands & Positive Environment and Structure & Visual/Tactile Supports	Respectful Reinforcement	Sensory & Biological	Communication/ Social Skills	Data Collection	Generalization
9:00	Circle/ Calendar Time	• Follow task strip/visual schedule • State standards • Orientation to speaker • Initiate, respond, comment with peers/adults	• Task strip of activities • Visual schedule • Turn-taking card	• Reinforcement menu (after task completion, transition) • Verbal • Princess stamp or sticker for communication with peers	• Carpet square or disco seat • Princess nametag, cloth (comfort item) • Help put away materials	• Match icon to schedule • Prompt initiate, respond, comment	• W: I/P steps of schedule • W: # (5 min) Initiate respond, comment	• Princess stickers for bedtime routine
9:30 10:30 1:20	Literacy/ Language/ Social Group	• Initiate, respond, comment • State standards • Recognize emotion • Independent transition to activity	• Task strip of activities • Visual schedule • Turn-taking card • Emotion cards	• Interacting with peers • Verbal • Turn-taking card • Reinforcer box	• Fidget • Carpet square or therapy ball • Princess nametag	• Transporters • *My Feelings* and related books • Match icons to match activity	• T: # (5 min) initiation, response, comment; • Grade book • T: # steps, T: I/P	• Read books at home
10:00 12:00	Centers	• Follow task strip/visual schedule • State standards	• Task strip of activity/ visual schedule	• Reinforcement menu (after task completion, transition)	• Fidget • Disco seat	• Video model center; pretend play center with peer; reading center; emotion center	• R: # steps (5 min) • Grade book, R: I/P	
10:50 12:50	Bathroom Break	• Complete bathroom steps independently	• Visual schedule	• Reinforcement menu (after bathroom steps)	• Fidget	• Language board	• D: # steps, greetings I/P	• Visual schedule at home

Note. I/P=Independent/Prompt; D = Daily; M, T, W, R, F = Days of the week.

Figure 3.24. Leigh Ann's CAPS.

Time	Activity	Skills to Teach	Task Demands & Positive Environment and Structure & Visual/Tactile Supports	Respectful Reinforcement	Sensory & Biological	Communication/ Social Skills	Data Collection	Generalization
11:00	Lunch	• Follow task strip • Orientation to speaker • Ask for help	• Visual schedule/task strip • Seat in quiet area of cafeteria	• Reinforcement menu (completing steps, asking for help)	• Headphones • Seat in quiet area of cafeteria, allow to leave if agitated	• Labeled area with icons to match schedule		• Task strip at home for meals
11:30	Recess	• Join an activity with prompting • Initiate, respond, comment	• Task strip of activities • Visual schedule	• Interacting with peers • Verbal • Reinforcement menu	• Running, jumping	• Video model at the beginning of the activity (if differs from center) • Prompt to interact with others	• T: # (5 min) initiations, responses, comments • Grade book • T: # steps, I/P	• Set up structured play dates for short periods of time
1:00	Snack	• Initiate/request respond, comment	• Visual schedule • Turn-taking card	• Verbal reinforcement • Activity is reinforcing	• Crunchy foods • Disco seat	• Help, listen card		
1:50	Pack up	• Complete departure steps independently • Say good-bye • Emotion check	• Task strip of arrival steps • Emotion check-in poster	• Reinforcement menu assessment (after arrival steps)	• Movement	• Prompt to greet (fade)	• D: # steps, greetings I/P • Emotion (y/n)	• Task strip at home for bedtime routine

Note. I/P=Independent/Prompt; D = Daily; M, T, W, R, F = Days of the week.

Figure 3.24. Leigh Ann's CAPS (continued).

STRENGTHS OF THE ZIGGURAT AND CAPS MODELS

The Ziggurat Model is consistent with research-based trends in the treatment of ASD. In a review of the literature on behavior interventions for autistic children, a recent study identified four developments in behavior intervention (see Figure 3.25): prevention, functional assessment, comprehensive intervention, and systems change (Horner, Carr, Strain, Todd, & Reed, 2002). The advantages of the Ziggurat Model can be outlined in light of these four developments.

Four developments in behavior intervention (Horner et al., 2002)

- Prevention
- Functional assessment
- Comprehensive intervention
- Systems change

Figure 3.25. **Four developments in behavior intervention.**

Prevention

Recent trends in the literature highlight the importance of changing the environment to meet the needs of the individual in order to prevent problem behaviors from occurring (Reeve & Carr, 2000). Use of the Ziggurat Model facilitates the development of comprehensive and proactive interventions.

To begin, the strengths and challenges identified through assessment become the foundation of prevention-based interventions. The ABC-I examines patterns of behavior and underlying characteristics of ASD. Knowing the pattern helps us to recognize the cause and purpose of behavior. This recognition serves as the foundation for prevention. Lastly, a basic premise of the model is that multiple aspects of the environment must be addressed concurrently. Chapters 4 through 8 present the five levels of the Intervention Ziggurat that provide a framework to guide environmental changes consistent with the emphasis on prevention.

Functional Assessment

Functional assessment used in planning interventions is important and results in reduction of problem behaviors (Carr et al., 1999; Ellingson, Miltenberger, Stricker, Galensky, & Garlinghouse,

2000). As discussed in Chapter 2, the ABC-I helps to identify patterns of behavior through the use of an FBA. The process is enriched by incorporating the underlying characteristics of ASD into the FBA, allowing examination of behavior patterns with more precision than does either in isolation. Thus, behaviors are viewed within the context of the disorder. Once the hypotheses are tested and confirmed, interventions are developed across the five levels of the Ziggurat. *This augmentation of the FBA process results in a more authentic understanding of individual needs and behaviors and more effective treatment plans.*

Comprehensive Intervention

Recently, there has been a shift from interventions based on research on isolated behaviors in unrealistic settings to using broader and more comprehensive approaches (Horner et al., 2002). According to Horner et al., this shift is driven by increasing expectations and needs of parents, teachers, and autistic children. These increased expectations likely result from the complexity of ASD and the frequent co-occurrence of other clinical conditions (e.g., ADHD, depression).

To address all needs across settings, thorough assessment is required. To that end, the ZM includes the UCC/ISSI assessment and the enhanced FBA process (ABC-I). The model is also comprehensive, leading to implementation of multiple research-supported interventions on five levels. Use of the levels results in interventions without limitations – ones that can be implemented by multiple caregivers across settings in order to address a broad range of needs. Such a comprehensive approach is an appropriate match for the complexity of the disorder. No single solution is adequate to resolve complex needs.

Systems Change

In describing the latest developments in behavior intervention, Horner et al. (2002) recommend an emphasis on changing systems. The first systems-level change is the expectation that the reduction of problem behavior is accompanied by skill development and increased opportunities to participate in the social milieu. The ZM meets this expectation. Because it goes beyond a problem focus, the resulting treatment plans encourage growth, skill development, and participation.

The second systems-level change is the requirement that the environment adjust to the needs of the child – not the reverse. As stated by Horner et al. (2002), "The net result has been a shift from viewing behavior support as a process by which individuals were changed to fit environments, to one in which environments are changed to match the behavioral needs of people in the environments" (p. 425). Use of the ZM results in this type of system change. It requires knowledge, training, and resources consistent with Gill's suggestion that, "Almost everything we think, do, say, and plan needs to be adapted" (2003, p. 200).

The third systemic change required for the multidimensional interventions outlined by the ZM to be fully realized is at the organizational level – funding, staff training, and structure. The ZM requires consideration of effective practices across areas. This meshing of knowledge decreases the isolation of subspecialties and encourages cooperative work across fields. Furthermore, the ZM facilitates organizational changes in a school system, emphasizing the unique characteristics of ASD.

Applying the ZM requires that skills to be taught, task demands, reinforcement systems, and the level of structure be designed to address the unique needs of this population. School systems must educate staff and provide environments and curriculum conducive to meeting these needs. No longer is it sufficient to simply instruct students in the "three Rs." Schools must also address skills that will impact a student's ability to transition into adulthood. Critical for this group are social skills, communication skills, recreational skills, coping skills, and vocational skills. This most often will mean expanding the continuum of services available in a school system. Once these systemic changes are made, autistic students will no longer be the "orphans" of the school system.

SUMMARY

The Ziggurat Model facilitates the development of comprehensive intervention plans to address specific behavioral needs and global interventions. The IZ incorporates five critical levels, structured in a hierarchy: Sensory and Biological, Reinforcement, Structure and Visual/Tactile Supports, Task Demands & Positive Environment, and Skills to Teach. According to the ZM, an intervention plan is considered to be comprehensive or complete when intervention (a) occurs on all five levels of the Ziggurat, (b) addresses underlying characteristics, and (c) includes antecedent, behavior, and consequence strategies. The Comprehensive Autism Planning System (CAPS) is the companion to the Ziggurat Model. CAPS ensures that when the supports are created, they are compatible not only with a student's "autism," but also with the environment in which the individual is expected to perform. The Ziggurat Model may be used alone or in combination with the CAPS. Either of these models is strong, but together they are even stronger.

CHAPTER HIGHLIGHTS

- *The IZ incorporates five critical levels, structured in a hierarchy: Sensory and Biological, Reinforcement, Structure and Visual/Tactile Supports, Task Demands, and Skills to Be Taught.*

- *The development of effective behavior intervention programs requires consideration of biological factors and inclusion of interventions to address needs at this level.*

- *Reinforcement is essential to the process of acquiring new skills.*

- *Structure and visual/tactile supports increase the ability of individuals on the spectrum to predict and understand the world around them.*

- *The ZPD refers to skills that can currently only be accomplished with assistance. Presenting tasks within the ZPD is appropriate when trying to teach new concepts that build on known skills and when seeking to generalize previously mastered skills to new settings.*

- *Participation of an interdisciplinary team increases the effectiveness of interventions.*

- *A complete intervention is one that occurs on all five levels of the Ziggurat, addresses underlying characteristics, and includes antecedent, behavior, and consequence strategies.*

- *The Ziggurat Model may be used to both address specific behavioral needs (targeted intervention planning) and design global or general programs.*

- *The interventions from the five Ziggurat levels are incorporated into the daily schedule using the CAPS. Use of the CAPS ensures that the comprehensive intervention plan becomes a reality.*

- *The strengths of the Ziggurat and CAPS models are evidenced in the multiple functions that they may serve. These models may be useful for prevention, functional assessment, comprehensive intervention, and systems change.*

4 Sensory and Biological

"The last thing one knows in constructing a work is what to put first."

– Blaise Pascal

The five levels of the Ziggurat outline critical areas required for a comprehensive intervention. This chapter describes the foundation level and reviews interventions to address fundamental internal factors that impact all functioning – sensory and biological. First, sensory and motor differences and sensory integration techniques are discussed. Next, research on medications and other biological interventions are reviewed. The chapter closes by applying interventions on the first level of the Ziggurat to two case scenarios.

SENSORY AND MOTOR INTERVENTIONS

Although sensory differences are not currently included as core symptoms of ASD, they can result in some of the greatest challenges for individuals on the spectrum. Thus, anxiety (Edelson, Edelson, Kerr, & Grandin, 1999; Pfeiffer & Kinnealey, 2003), distractibility, overactivity, impulsivity, perseveration, delayed receptive and expressive language skills, poor social skill development, and poor eye contact have all been related to impaired sensory functioning (Lane, Young, Baker, & Angley, 2010; Stackhouse, Graham, & Laschober, 2002). Motor differences such as low muscle tone, oral-motor differences, repetitive movements, and motor planning deficits create additional challenges.

Intervention design requires careful attention to the sensory state of the individual and to the sensory and motoric demands of environments and activities (Cook, 1990; Myles et al., 2000). Because these needs tend to be less visible, they are often overlooked as critical elements of intervention plans. A person who is hungry or in pain, or whose senses are overwhelmed, cannot respond to an otherwise excellent intervention plan. It is for this reason that Sensory and Biological appear on the first level of the Ziggurat.

The field of occupational therapy has led in the development of approaches to ameliorate the impact of sensory and motor differences. The field's greatest impact on the ASD population has perhaps been the theory of sensory integration (SI) – the ability to organize information received through the senses. The eight sensory systems are listed in Figure 4.1. SI dysfunction results when neural and physiological differences disrupt the capacity to receive and process sensory input (Dunn, 1999). SI theory was developed by Jean Ayres in the 1970s. Ayres (1979) held that differences in the processing of sensory information resulted in behavioral difficulties. She believed that many of the symptoms seen in individuals on the autism spectrum could be explained by sensory integration theory (Stackhouse et al., 2002).

Sensory System	Function
Proprioceptive	Indicates location of body parts in relation to each other based on information from muscles and joints
Vestibular	Detects movement and guides eye-hand movements; provides information about balance, gravity, and posture
Tactile/Touch	Discriminates texture, temperature, touch, pain, or pressure for protection and comfort/bonding
Visual/Sight	Detects color, depth, spatial orientation, and brightness
Olfactory/Smell	Gathers information about odors in the environment and contributes to sense of taste
Auditory/Sound	Gathers information about sounds in the environment
Gustatory/Taste	Detects bitter, sweet, salty, and sour; distinguishes safe from noxious foods
Interoception	Internal body signals (e.g., hunger, pain, thirst, anxiety)

Figure 4.1. **The eight sensory systems and their functions.**

SI dysfunction may take the form of overresponsiveness (hypersensitivity) or under-responsiveness (hyposensitivity). *Hypersensitivity* to sensory input, sometimes called sensory defensiveness, results in a negative reaction or alarm reaction to stimuli that are generally not aversive or threatening. Behaviors caused by sensory defensiveness vary, depending on the sense or senses involved. For example, children who are hypersensitive to movement (a characteristic sometimes called gravitational insecurity) may resist exploring the environment (e.g., engaging in childhood activities such as climbing or swinging). Distractibility, covering the ears, noise-making, and hiding are possible indicators of oversensitivity to sound. Similarly, oversensitivity to visual stimuli may result in decreased scanning and tracking of the environment, gaze aversion, or poor eye contact (Stackhouse et al., 2002).

In contrast to hypersensitivity, *underresponsiveness,* or *underarousal,* leads to delayed or passive responses. For example, autistic individuals may fail to register or orient to certain stimuli – most often visual or auditory. Deficits in communication and social skill development are likely related to differences in sensory processing (Ayres, 1987; Baranek, 2002). According to Baranek, this relationship is not yet well understood.

Sensory Integration Approaches

The application of SI theory to ASD has been explored more in practice than in research. One study of sensory modulation (i.e., over- or underresponse to sensory input) provides support for application of SI theory to high-functioning ASD. The researchers found that children and adolescents diagnosed with high-functioning ASD with higher levels of hyper- or hyposensitivity to sensory input had decreased adaptive functioning in the areas of community (integrating into community environments) and social skills (interacting with others) (Pfeiffer, Kinnealey, Reed, & Herzberg, 2005).

Sensory responses tend to fluctuate. What is overwhelming to the senses on one day may be easily tolerated the next. Additionally, an individual may be alternately overresponsive and underresponsive to input from one sensory system. For example, a child may comment on the distracting sound of the fluorescent lights in a room and then fail to respond when being called by her name. This variation in responses is often seen in individuals on the spectrum.

These fluctuations, along with the cumulative impact of sensory stressors, make it difficult to predict when situations are overwhelming and may result in rages or behavior changes that, therefore, *seem* random. For example, a child who is overresponsive to touch may make it through the bustle of recess and P.E. in the morning without incident but later cry when he is accidentally bumped in line. Without awareness of the cumulative impact of sensory experiences, one might conclude that hypersensitivity to touch cannot be the underlying factor because the student was successful in recess and P.E.

The SI approach to occupational therapy may be used with individuals of all ages. Case-Smith and Bryan (1999) describe three main components of therapy for school-aged children with ASD.

1. Therapists assist parents in understanding the sensory differences exhibited by their child and the impact of those differences on the child's behavior.
2. Therapists assist both teachers and parents in modifying the environment to address the child's sensory differences.
3. Therapists help the child to organize his or her response to sensory stimuli. This is accomplished through providing sensory input through tactile, proprioceptive, or vestibular modes to decrease or increase arousal.

These areas are the three largest sensory systems and the central focus of sensory integration therapy. According to Cook (1990), "The primary goal when using a sensory integrative approach with autistic children is to facilitate interaction with a variety of environments and people in a functional, more satisfying way" (p. 5).

Two SI-based approaches often used with school-aged children are the sensory diet and the Alert Program. These programs are designed to be used under the leadership and guidance of occupational therapists.

- A *sensory diet* provides sensory-based activities selected to address the specific needs of an individual (e.g., movement, touch, auditory). These activities are provided in a systematic, prescriptive manner (Baranek, 2002; Robbins & Miller, 2007).
- The *Alert Program* uses cognitive-behavioral strategies to teach students to recognize their levels of arousal and to use SI strategies in order to maintain an optimal level of arousal (Williams & Shellenberger, 1996). Williams and Shellenberger also developed the Sensory-Motor Preference Checklist, which may be used by adolescents and adults to determine individualized strategies that are likely to be effective in modulating their levels of alertness.

Research Support

As mentioned, there is a scarcity of empirical evidence to support the use of SI therapy.

- *Deep-pressure techniques* have been addressed in a number of studies but with very few subjects. Studies with individual subjects conducted in the early 1990s examined the impact of applying deep pressure (McClure & Holtz-Yotz, 1991; Zisserman, 1992). Results for one child included increased calm and increased ability to interact (McClure & Holtz-Yotz). In another study, deep pressure was associated with an 11.8% decrease in self-injurious behavior (Zisserman). Yet another study found that deep pressure had a calming effect on learners with autism, especially those with anxiety-related behaviors (Edelson, Edelson, Kerr, & Grandin, 1999).

  More recent studies have examined the use of weighted vests as a method of applying deep pressure. Ferter-Daly, Bedell, and Hinojosa (2003) conducted a study of the impact of weighted vests on self-stimulatory behavior in preschool children. They found a decreased duration of self-stimulatory behaviors in four out of the five subjects as well as improved attention. Contradictory results were found in a study using weighted vests with four children between the ages of 8 and 11 who were diagnosed with autism or PDD-NOS. No decrease in repetitive behaviors was found, and the ability to attend to task was not improved. In fact, the vests had a negative impact on the behaviors of three of the four subjects. Pfeiffer and colleagues (2005) concluded that the use of a weighted vest to decrease repetitive behaviors or to increase attention was not supported. Others have studied the use of weighted vests, including Hodgetts, Magill-Evans, and Misiaszek (2011), Myles et al. (2004), and Vandenberg (2001).

Temple Grandin, one of the best known individuals on the spectrum, invented a "hug machine" designed to apply pressure to the sides of the body. It was used in a study investigating the behavioral and physiological effects of deep pressure on children with autism. Researchers found a significant decrease on the Tension Scale of the Conners Parent Rating Scale, indicating that anxiety was decreased (Edelson et al., 1999).

- *Application of SI theory in the school setting* was reviewed in a recent study (Schilling & Schwartz, 2004). The researchers replaced traditional, inflexible seating in the classroom with large therapy balls and found that participation and in-seat behavior increased significantly for students with ASD.

- *More global approaches* to SI therapy have been used in other studies. For example, Pfeiffer and Kinnealey (2003) examined the effectiveness of a protocol for treating sensory defensiveness in adults (not identified on the autism spectrum). The protocol included training in sensory defensiveness, followed by an individually designed sensory diet, including daily activities that provided tactile, vestibular, and proprioceptive input. Decreases in sensory defensiveness and anxiety were found following treatment. Treatment benefits were also noted in a study of the effects of occupational therapy with an SI emphasis on preschool-age children with autism. Positive effects included decreased frequency of staring, wandering, or stereotypic movements as well as increased goal-directed play (Case-Smith & Bryan, 1999).

Considerations for Incorporating Sensory Strategies

Simply understanding that the capacity to receive or organize sensory input is often disrupted for autistic individuals is valuable both for those on the spectrum and for those who seek to help them. Such understanding provides a possible explanation for many of the behavioral and emotional differences presented. It has also led to the SI approach to intervening.

In spite of the scarcity of empirical support, Dunn (1999) rated SI therapy as a promising practice. SI techniques have been widely applied in practice for a number of years with few adverse results. Positive outcomes are widely reported, although much more research is needed in order to establish SI therapy as a scientifically validated approach to helping individuals on the spectrum.

SI interventions have a number of advantages.

- They are individualized in design, based on the particular behaviors exhibited and responses to stimuli (Myles et al., 2000).

- SI-based interventions and modifications can occur in various environments and do not require a clinical setting.
- When used with children, these interventions may resemble play and may readily incorporate reinforcing items or interests.
- Some sensory techniques may be used independently once learned; however, it is important to note that extensive training in neurological systems and physiological systems is required in order to design and monitor SI interventions (Dunn, 1999).

PHARMACOTHERAPY

Unlike other interventions discussed here, pharmacological treatments cannot simply be studied and implemented by users of this book. Thus, this section is designed to inform readers of medical interventions. All medication decisions must be discussed with a physician, and risks, costs, and benefits must be carefully considered. If pharmacotherapy is used, frequent monitoring by a medical professional will be required. Additionally, physicians should make decisions regarding dosage adjustment.

The information in this section should not be considered a replacement for medical advice. Further, due to ongoing research and new developments, the information presented here will rapidly become outdated. We recommend consulting physicians who have expertise in working with psychiatric conditions for a specific age group. Family physicians, pediatricians, and general practitioners may not have the same amount of experience as a psychiatrist who focuses on children and adolescents or adults on the spectrum.

It is important to note that because many studies do not differentiate between specific groups on the autism spectrum (e.g., AS, HFA, PDD-NOS), this section provides a summary of selected research on the use of pharmacotherapy as a treatment for all ASDs. This is not a comprehensive review of all medications. For a more in-depth review, see Handen and Lubetsky (2005).

The use of psychotropic medications (drugs that affect the mind, behaviors, and emotions) is one of the most common forms of treatment for autistic individuals. One research study surveyed members of the Autism Society of Ohio and found that approximately 46% of individuals with ASD were prescribed one medication while roughly 21% were taking two or more (Aman, Lam, & Collier-Crespin, 2003). This study also found medication use to increase with age. The most common type of drugs taken were antidepressants, followed by antipsychotics, antiepileptics, antihypertensives, and stimulants, sedatives, and mood stabilizers.

It is generally believed that pharmacotherapy cannot address the core features of ASD (social and communication impairments, and restricted, repetitive behaviors); however, research supports its efficacy in treating specific behavioral and comorbid psychiatric concerns. Hollander, Phillips, and Yeh (2003) refer to this as a "targeted" treatment approach and suggest that practitioners focus on treating specific symptoms by drawing on effective treatments from other disorders that share symptoms. For example, Hollander et al. note that obsessive and compulsive traits seen in individuals with ASD may be ameliorated with medications that help individuals with Obsessive-Compulsive Disorder (OCD). Experts agree that while pharmacotherapy may be beneficial, it should be used as part of a broader treatment approach (Buitelaar & Willemsen-Swinkels, 2000; Handen & Lubetsky, 2005; Towbin, 2003). Figure 4.2 contains a selective list of several medications reviewed in this section.

DRUG TYPE	DRUG NAME
ANTIDEPRESSANTS	TRICYCLICS • Clomipramine (Anafranil®) • Amitriptyline (Elavil®)
	SELECTIVE SEROTONIN REUPTAKE INHIBITORS • Fluvoxamine (Luvox®) • Fluoxetine (Prozac®) • Sertraline (Zoloft®)
ANTIPSYCHOTICS	TYPICAL • Haloperidol (Haldol®)
	ATYPICAL • Risperidone (Risperdal®) • Olanzapine (Zyprexa®) • Aripiprazole (Abilify®) • Quetiapine (Seroquel®)
STIMULANTS	• Methylphenidate (Ritalin®, Concerta®) • Dextroamphatamine (Adderall®)

Figure 4.2. **Selective list of medications often used for autistic individuals.**

Antidepressants

Antidepressants are used to treat a variety of conditions, including depression, anxiety, OCD, enuresis, and inattention. As a group, antidepressants either directly or indirectly affect the concentration of serotonin, a neurotransmitter in the brain. Serotonin is believed to impact mood, anxiety, sleep, aggression, social interaction, and obsessive-compulsive traits. Some antidepressants also impact other neurotransmitters – norepinephrine or dopamine.

There are different types of antidepressants. The most current are called selective serotonin reuptake inhibitors or SSRIs. Other forms of antidepressants include the tricyclics (TCAs) and monoamine oxidase inhibitors (MAOIs). In general, the SSRIs have fewer negative side effects than other types of antidepressants.

Research Support

Role of Serotonin in Autism

A growing body of research suggests that serotonin may play a role in the development of autism.

- Studies indicate that approximately 30% of individuals with autism exhibit higher levels of serotonin in the blood (known as hyperserotonemia) than those without autism (Anderson et al., 2002; Anderson, Horne, Chatterjee, & Cohen, 1990; Schain & Freedman, 1961).
- One author explored the hypothesis that hyperserotonemia causes developmental differences in the brain that results in some characteristics of autism (Whitaker-Azmitia, 2005). Specifically, she asserts that during the fetal stages of development, before the blood-brain barrier is operational, the elevated level of serotonin in the blood results in a high concentration of serotonin in the brain. At this point, the heightened level of serotonin negatively impacts the development of specialized serotonin neurons in the brain. These neurons develop fewer terminals (structures responsible for transmitting/releasing serotonin in order to communicate with other neurons in different areas of the brain). As a result of the reduced number of terminals, less serotonin is available in the brain.
- One study found developmental differences in the brain's ability to synthesize serotonin. Specifically, prior to the age of 5, children with autism have a decreased capacity to create serotonin compared with age mates without autism (Chugani et al., 1999). Thus, where typically developing children experience a period of heightened brain serotonin synthesis, children with autism do not. While this study estab-

lished decreased synthesis in the whole brain, another study examined the level of serotonin synthesis within different areas of the brain (left cortex and right cortex). Among the findings, the research revealed that decreased serotonin synthesis in the left hemisphere of the brain was associated with severe language impairments while decreased serotonin synthesis in the right hemisphere was related to left and mixed handedness (Chandana et al., 2005). Based on these results, the authors proposed that decreased serotonin results in structural differences in the brain.

- The hypothesis that serotonin plays a role in autism is further strengthened by studies on human beings and animals. One investigation intentionally reduced the amount of serotonin in the brains of adults with autism and found an increase in repetitive behaviors (e.g., flapping, pacing), agitation, and anxiety (McDougle, Naylor, Cohen, Aghajanian et al., 1996). In animal studies prenatal exposure to a higher concentration of serotonin in the blood resulted in heightened auditory and tactile sensitivity as well as seizures and repetitive motor behaviors (Kahne et al., 2002).

Effects of Antidepressant Medications for Individuals on the Spectrum

Antidepressant medications, especially those that impact serotonin, have been shown to be helpful for individuals on the autism spectrum. Some studies have found that clomipramine (Anafranil®), a tricyclic antidepressant, was associated with improved social relations, decreased obsessive and ritualized behaviors, aggression, and impulsivity (McDougle, Price et al., 1992). Other studies have found similar improvements (Gordon, Rapoport, Hamburger, State, & Mannheim, 1992; Gordon, State, Nelson, Hamburger, & Rapoport, 1993). The McDougle et al. study also found a significant decrease in trichotillomania (pulling out one's hair).

SSRIs have shown similar benefits and reportedly have fewer side effects. Because some of these medications are relatively new, less research has been conducted, especially on children and adolescents. McDougle, Naylor, Cohen, Volkmar, et al. (1996) studied the use of fluvoxamine (Luvox®) on adults with autism and found a reduction in repetitive thoughts and behaviors and aggression, with improvements in social relations and use of language. Different results were found when it was administered to children and adolescents. Fewer patients responded – none demonstrated improvements in target behaviors and more experienced negative side effects (McDougle, Kresch, & Posey, 2000).

A similar study was conducted with children and adolescents using a different SSRI, fluoxetine (Prozac®). Using a lower dosage, a significant reduction in repetitive behaviors was found (Hollander et al., 2005). Other studies of children (4 to 7 years old) revealed fewer repetitive motor movements (stereotypies) and ritualistic behaviors with improved social functioning (DeLong, Teague, & McSwain, 1998; Perel, Margarita, & Inmaculada, 1999). In addition, Delong et al. found improvements with language acquisition and mood. In small or single-case studies, another SSRI, sertraline (Zoloft®), has demonstrated benefits such as reduced aggression (Buck, 1995) and compulsive and repetitive behaviors as well as a reduction in symptoms of co-occurring depression and anxiety (Ozbayrak, 1997).

A study of adults with autism, PDD-NOS, and AS found that sertraline resulted in improvements in repetitive behaviors and aggression; however, only those patients with autism and PDD-NOS responded to the medication (McDougle, Brodkin, Naylor, Carlson, Cohen, & Price, 1998). The researchers believed that those with AS did not respond because they were relatively less impaired prior to the start of the study.

Case studies of paroxetine (Paxil®) have been promising. For example, one 7-year-old boy with autism showed a significant decrease in tantrums and time spent discussing his preoccupations. Sleep and mood also improved (Posey, Litwiller, Koburn, & McDougle, 1999). The authors noted that this boy did not respond well to other medications. Another case, involving an adolescent with autism, showed a reduction in self-injurious behaviors (Snead, Boon, & Presberg, 1994). While these case studies are encouraging, additional well-controlled group studies need to be conducted on paroxetine before more definitive conclusions may be drawn.

One study examined the benefits of citalopram (Celexa®) on children with autism and AS. Couturier and Nicolson (2002) found improvements in anxiety, preoccupations, aggression, and repetitive behaviors; however, no benefits were found in the core areas of social interaction and communication. Another study examined children and adolescents with ASD and found improvements in symptoms of autism, mood, and anxiety (Namerow, Thomas, Bostic, Prince, & Monuteaux, 2003). Hollander, Kaplan, Cartwright, and Reichman (2000) examined the use of venlafaxine (Effexor®) in individuals with ASD and found low dosages to be effective in addressing repetitive behaviors and interests, language, inattention, and hyperactivity.

Antipsychotics

As discussed above, antipsychotics are commonly prescribed for individuals with ASD (Aman et al., 2003). This family of drugs is used to treat a variety of conditions, including psychosis, mania (bipolar disorder), and Tourette's. It has also commonly been used to treat behavioral concerns such as aggression, impulsivity, hyperactivity, repetitive behaviors, and communication deficits in individuals on the autism spectrum.

There are two types of antipsychotics – typical and atypical. The latter are relatively newer medications and are considered to have fewer side effects (Erickson, Stigler, Posey, & McDougle, 2005; Posey & McDougle, 2000). Antipsychotics work by reducing the neurotransmitters serotonin and/or dopamine (Tarascon, 2005). (The function of serotonin was reviewed above.) Dopamine is involved with movement, learning, and reward behaviors. It also impacts attention and has been implicated in ADHD (Madras, Miller, & Fischman, 2005; Maher, Marazita, Ferrell, & Vanyukov, 2002).

Research Support

Haldol®
According to Posey and McDougle (2000), the earliest studies on medications for treatment of children with autism were conducted on antipsychotics. One typical antipsychotic, haloperidol (Haldol®), has been extensively researched. Reviews of these studies indicate multiple benefits, including a reduction in repetitive movements, hyperactivity, and irritability and an increase in attention span and socialization (Handen & Lubetsky, 2005; Posey & McDougle, 2000). Haloperidol has also been found to enhance learning (Posey & McDougle). Several potential serious side effects have been associated with haloperidol. As a result, atypical antipsychotics, which are considered to be safer, have become more widely used.

Risperdal®
By far, the most well-researched atypical antipsychotic is risperidone (Risperdal®), which works by reducing both serotonin and dopamine. Erickson and colleagues (2005) reviewed all current studies on the use of these medications with individuals with PDD, including ASD, and found a number of improvements, such as reduction in anger, aggression, irritability, and impulsivity. Furthermore, a recent study demonstrated long-term benefits of the use of risperidone on children with ASD (Troost et al., 2005). A reduction in repetitive behaviors has also been reported for children (McDougle, Scahill et al., 2005; Research Units on Pediatric Psychopharmacology Autism Network, 2002) while a decrease in symptoms of anxiety and depression was found in one study on adults with ASD (McDougle, Holmes et al., 1998).

Other Antipsychotics
Other atypical antipsychotics have shown promising results. One study on olanzapine (Zyprexa®) examined children with ASD and found improvements in hyperactivity, ir-

ritability, as well as speech and communication (Kemner, Willemsen-Swinkels, DeJonge, Tuynman-Qua, & Van Engerland, 2002). A case report was conducted on five children and adolescents with ASD using aripiprazole (Abilify®). The authors reported improvements, including decreased aggression, agitation, anger, hyperactivity, and irritability (Stigler, Posey, & McDougle, 2004). Improved socialization and a reduction in irritability, rigidity, repetitive behaviors, and anxiety were reported on one adult with autism using this drug (Staller, 2003). One study looked at children and adolescents with pervasive developmental disorders taking quetiapine (Seroquel®) and found significant improvements in conduct, hyperactivity, inattention, and anxiety (Hardan, Jou, & Handen, 2005).

Stimulants

Psychostimulants are used in the treatment of ADHD and narcolepsy. They are commonly prescribed for individuals with ASD to address inattention and hyperactivity. Stimulants work by increasing norepinephrine and dopamine in the brain.

Research Support

Handen and Lubetsky (2005) note that while the results of early studies on the use of stimulants were not positive, more recent studies have found stimulants to be beneficial. One study examining the use of methylphenidate in children and adolescents with PDD showed a significant reduction in hyperactivity and impulsivity with associated improvements in oppositional behaviors and tantrums (Di Martino, Melis, Cianchetti, & Zuddas, 2004). Another study examined the use of methylphenidate (such as Ritalin®) in children with autism who also exhibited characteristics of ADHD (Handen, Johnson, & Lubetsky, 2000). In this well-controlled study, significant reduction in hyperactivity as well as decreased repetitive movements and inappropriate speech was observed; however, global ratings of symptoms of autism did not decrease.

One recent large group study on psychostimulants found that most participants did not respond to the medication. In looking at patterns, the researchers discovered that individuals with AS appeared to be more likely to benefit from stimulants than those with autism or other PDDs (Stigler, Desmond, Posey, Wiegand, & McDougle, 2004).

Considerations for Incorporating Pharmacotherapy in Treatment

Regardless of the type of drug used, all medications have potential side effects and should be monitored closely by medical professionals.

The use of antidepressants requires an additional consideration. While used widely, there are several concerns associated with the use of antidepressants, especially in children and adolescents. After analyzing the combined results of studies, the Food and Drug Administration (FDA) found a heightened risk of suicidal thoughts and behaviors during the first few months of treatment for children and adolescents (FDA, 2004a). As a result, the FDA published a health advisory statement that "The average risk of such events on drug was 4%, twice the placebo risk of 2%. No suicides occurred in these trials," and issued a "black-box" warning for specific antidepressants.

The decision to use medications often presents a dilemma – especially for parents of children or adolescents. It is difficult to recognize when the benefits of treatment outweigh the costs. Parents often fear significant side effects – both medical and social. Those who seek medical assistance may be perceived as "lazy" or even "sinful" by some cultural standards. Contributing to the community's attitude is the media, which tends to report sensational or negative accounts of pharmacological treatments for children and adolescents. Due to these pressures, some may not receive medical interventions that could result in a better quality of life for them and their families.

We encourage those dealing with these decisions to recognize that pharmacotherapy may be one of the most powerful tools available to aid those who struggle with this pervasive disorder. Pharmacological treatment is not appropriate for every individual on the autism spectrum, but when medication is recommended by a physician, the possibility that the benefits outweigh the risks should not be easily dismissed.

OTHER BIOLOGICAL INTERVENTIONS

Many noteworthy biological factors not specific to autism impact behaviors. For example, hunger, pain, fatigue, illness, nutrition, and general health influence everyone's behavior. There is little information about interventions in these areas specific to this population;

however, it is no less important to address these biological and sensory factors. Often, the impact of these factors will be discovered by finding the patterns through a functional behavioral assessment – part of the ABC-I. The antecedents, in particular, are of key importance here. Once identified, these factors can be addressed through careful problem solving, as illustrated in the following example.

Joanie

Joanie often lost her temper at school in the morning. Her teacher and parents first thought that she was having difficulty transitioning to school. As a result, they tried starting her day off with some fun activities and frequent rewards, and her teacher created a visual chart to map out her day.

After a few weeks, Joanie's behavior had not improved. Her teacher met with Joanie's parents and they discussed that the morning routine was difficult for her. By the time they got her ready for school, Joanie's breakfast consisted of a granola bar that she ate in the car on the way to school. Her parents said that they have seen Joanie lose her temper when she was hungry. Her teacher and parents decided to let Joanie eat breakfast at school with her peers. Improvement was seen the first day of this new intervention.

APPLICATION OF THE ZIGGURAT MODEL

This chapter and several that follow emphasize research-based interventions for each of the five levels of the Ziggurat. In order to become proficient in using the ZM, it is necessary to see it applied to case examples. Two case examples are presented here – Steve and Penny. These case examples will be revisited in subsequent chapters to demonstrate the application of each level of the ZM in order to illustrate the development of comprehensive intervention plans.

Case Study
Steve Goes to College

Steve is in his first semester of college. He was first diagnosed with autism when he was in fifth grade and received services through special education. He made progress with the support of his parents and professionals at school. Steve did not have friends at first. He rarely spoke to his peers. Over time, he learned to greet others. In the past, Steve became anxious and upset in large crowds and had difficulty with changes in his routine. He cried and rocked back and forth when required to be in the gymnasium or assemblies for a long period of time.

By the time he reached high school, Steve had made many improvements and was considered by most to be "eccentric." He found a niche in the school computer club and made a few friends with whom he shared an interest in *Star Trek*. Steve excelled academically with intensive organizational and study support through special education and his mother. His parents were hesitant to send him to college; however, he received several scholarships, and they decided that he should take advantage of this opportunity.

Transitioning to college was difficult for Steve. He did not realize how different the study requirements would be. Steve was assigned a roommate in the dorms. He rarely left his room except to go to class. Steve did not socialize with others and did not know the names of anyone on his hall. He had a difficult time getting along with his roommate, Mark. Steve demanded complete silence when he studied – even the sound of music coming from Mark's headphones upset him. He was also disturbed by the sound of the beds and asked Mark to not turn over during the night. One day, he told Mark that his alarm was too loud. He asked Mark to turn it down or muffle it under his pillow. When Mark explained that there was no volume setting and that he could not sleep with a clock under his pillow, Steve exclaimed, "I don't see why you won't compromise with me!"

Small changes such as Mark having company over or occasionally putting his backpack in a place where he did not normally put it caused Steve to become very upset. He would comment, "It upsets my homeostasis!" He demanded that Mark move his backpack. Steve was disorganized and frequently lost books, keys, and even freshly washed clothing. On one occasion, he "lost" his sweater. He systematically knocked on every door on his floor until he found Mark. Steve yelled, "Where did you put my sweater?" Mark was surprised but told Steve that it was hanging to dry by the window. Instead of thanking Mark for his help, Steve blamed Mark for "stealing" the sweater.

Steve became increasingly anxious over the course of the semester and had difficulty concentrating when studying. Instead of focusing on academics, he often spent extended periods of time playing chess on-line or reading *Star Trek* novels. He felt uncomfortable attending large classes and would not ask for help from the teaching assistants. Despite the fact that Steve was very intelligent, his grades were poor. He frequently phoned his parents and told them he worried about failing school and not making friends. They saw that he was having great difficulty with the recent changes.

Intervention

After receiving several frantic phone calls from their son, Steve's parents contacted the school to obtain the name of a student sponsor at the student support center – the department responsible for assisting students with special needs. They gave Steve the phone number and encouraged him to make an appointment with the sponsor, Nicole, who was knowledgeable about autism. He consented to allow Nicole to speak with his parents to get their input in completing the UCC/ISSI and provide the documentation needed for Steve to receive special accommodations in the classroom (see Figure 4.3).

Note: This example was completed prior to publishing the two UCC-Self-Reports (Adolescent and Adult). At the time, Steve's input was gathered in collaboration with his parents in completing the UCC-HF.

Later Nicole met with Steve. Using the Global Intervention Plan Guide, Steve outlined his long- and short-term vision and considered factors that would improve his quality of life (see Figure 4.4). Together, Steve and Nicole prioritized areas of the UCC to focus on, in order to make his college life more rewarding and enjoyable. For example, they developed several strategies to address his sensory needs, including using earplugs or noise-canceling headphones, selecting smaller classes, engaging in regular physical activities, and using relaxation strategies (see Figure 4.5). The sponsor also recommended that Steve make an appointment with a doctor at the student health center to explore possible medical interventions to address the significant anxiety and attention problems he experienced.

UNDERLYING CHARACTERISTICS CHECKLIST-HF

Ruth Aspy, Ph.D., and Barry G. Grossman, Ph.D.

NAME: *Steve* COMPLETED BY: *Steve and parents*

DATE: *8-18* FOLLOW-UP DATE:

DIRECTIONS: Place check beside all items that apply and describe behaviors observed.

Area	Item	✔	Notes	Follow-Up
SOCIAL	1. Has difficulty recognizing the feelings and thoughts of others (mindblindness)	✔		
	2. Uses poor eye contact	✔		
	3. Has difficulty maintaining personal space, physically intrudes on others			
	4. Lacks tact or appears rude	✔	• *Accuses roommate of stealing* • *Makes unusual requests*	
	5. Has difficulty making or keeping friends	✔	*Has not made any friends since starting school. Does not know anyone in the dorm except for roommate.*	
	6. Has difficulty joining an activity	✔		
	7. Is naïve, easily taken advantage of, or bullied			
	8. Tends to be less involved in group activities than most same-age individuals	✔	*Feels socially isolated.*	
	9. Has difficulty understanding others' nonverbal communication (e.g., facial expressions, body language, tone of voice)	✔	*Not able to read the facial expressions of others. Does not respond appropriately to others when they are upset.*	
	10. Has difficulty understanding jokes			
	11. Other			
RESTRICTED PATTERNS OF BEHAVIOR, INTERESTS, AND ACTIVITIES	12. Expresses strong need for routine or "sameness"	✔	*Do not tolerate even small changes. I like to know what to expect every day.*	
	13. Expresses desire for repetition			
	14. Has eccentric or intense preoccupations/absorption in own unique interests	✔	*Star Trek. Chess.*	
	15. Asks repetitive questions			
	16. Seems to be unmotivated by customary rewards			
	17. Displays repetitive motor movements (e.g., flaps hands, paces, flicks fingers in front of eyes)			
	18. Has problems handling transition and change	✔	*Difficulty transitioning to college.*	
	19. Has strong need for closure or difficulty stopping a task before it is completed			
	20. Other			

Figure 4.3. UCC and ISSI for Steve.

Area	Item	✔	Notes	Follow-Up
COMMUNICATION	21. Makes sounds or states words or phrases repeatedly [non-echolalic] (e.g., humming, "well actually")			
	22. Makes up new words or creates alternate meanings for words or phrases			
	23. Displays immediate or delayed echolalia (e.g., recites lines from movies, repeats another person's questions or statements, repeats sounds)			
	24. Interprets words or conversations literally/has difficulty understanding figurative language			
	25. Has difficulty with rules of conversation (e.g., interrupts others, asks inappropriate questions, makes poor eye contact, has difficulty maintaining conversation)			
	26. Fails to initiate or respond to social greetings			
	27. Has difficulty using gestures and facial expressions			
	28. Has difficulty starting, joining, and/or ending a conversation	✔	*Do not engage in casual conversation with others. I have trouble talking to others.*	
	29. Has difficulty asking for help			
	30. Makes irrelevant comments			
	31. Has difficulty expressing thoughts and feelings			
	32. Speaks in an overly formal way			
	33. Gives false impression of understanding more than he/she actually does	✔	*He is highly intelligent. People do not understand that his social skills are not equivalent.*	
	34. Talks incessantly, little back-and-forth			
	35. Uses an advanced vocabulary			
	36. Uses mechanical, "singsong" voice or speech sounds unusual in other ways (e.g., prosody, cadence, tone)			
	37. Has difficulty following instructions			
	38. Has difficulty understanding language with multiple meanings, humor, sarcasm, or synonyms	✔		
	39. Has difficulty talking about others' interests	✔	*Carries on one-sided conversations on his interests.*	
	40. Other			

Figure 4.3. UCC and ISSI for Steve (continued).

Area	Item	✔	Notes	Follow-Up
SENSORY DIFFERENCES	41. Responds in an unusual manner to sounds (e.g., ignores sounds or over-reacts to sudden, unexpected noises, high-pitched continuous sounds, or complex/multiple noises)	✔	*Many sounds are aversive to him, including large crowds, alarm clocks, his roommate rolling over in bed, and the music from head-phones worn by roommate. Loud places bother me. I don't like alarm clocks or loud music.*	
	42. Responds in an unusual manner to pain (e.g., overreacts or seems unaware of an illness or injury)			
	43. Responds in an unusual manner to taste (e.g., resists certain textures, flavors, brands)			
	44. Responds in an unusual manner to light or color (e.g., focuses on shiny items, shadows, reflections, shows preference or strong dislike for certain colors)			
	45. Responds in an unusual manner to temperature			
	46. Responds in an unusual manner to smells (e.g., may comment on smells that others do not detect)			
	47. Seeks activities that provide touch, pressure, or movement (e.g., swinging, hugging, pacing)			
	48. Avoids activities that provide touch, pressure, or movement (e.g., resists wearing certain types of clothing, strongly dislikes to be dirty, resists hugs)			
	49. Makes noises such as humming or singing frequently			
	50. Other			
COGNITIVE DIFFERENCES	51. Displays extensive knowledge in narrow areas of interest	✔	*Chess tournament history, Star Trek.*	
	52. Displays poor problem-solving skills	✔	*Steve's "solution" to many problems was insuf-ficient (alarm clock, not finding clothes, etc.).*	
	53. Has poor organizational skills	✔	*Not budgeting enough time to study for tests and complete assignments.*	
	54. Withdraws into complex inner worlds/fantasizes often			
	55. Is easily distracted by unrelated details – has difficulty knowing what is relevant or makes off-topic comments			
	56. Displays weakness in reading comprehension with strong word recognition			
	57. Knows many facts and details but has difficulty with abstract reason-ing (i.e., weak central coherence)	✔	*Grades are falling perhaps because of the expectation of a deeper understanding of the material.*	

Figure 4.3. UCC and ISSI for Steve (continued).

Area	Item	✔	Notes	Follow-Up
COGNITIVE DIFFERENCES	58. Has difficulty applying learned skills in new settings	✔		
	59. Has academic skills deficits			
	60. Has attention problems	✔	*Distracted by sounds.*	
	61. Displays very literal understanding of concepts			
	62. Recalls information inconsistently (i.e., seems to forget previously learned information)			
	63. Has difficulty understanding the connection between behavior and resulting consequences	✔		
	64. Other			
MOTOR DIFFERENCES	65. Has balance difficulties			
	66. Resists or refuses handwriting tasks			
	67. Has poor handwriting			
	68. Has poor motor coordination (e.g., accident prone, difficulty using fasteners)	✔		
	69. Writes slowly	✔	*I type faster than I can write.*	
	70. Displays atypical activity level (e.g., over-active/hyperactive, under-active/hypoactive)			
	71. Has athletic skills deficits			
	72. Displays an awkward gait			
	73. Displays unusual body postures and movements or facial expressions (e.g., odd postures, stiffness, "freezing," facial grimacing)			
	74. Has difficulty starting or completing actions (e.g., may rely on physical or verbal prompting by others)			
	75. Other			

Figure 4.3. UCC and ISSI for Steve (continued).

Area	Item	✔	Notes	Follow-Up
EMOTIONAL VULNERABILITY	76. Is easily stressed – worries obsessively	✔	*Stressed by changes in his environment and routine.*	
	77. Appears to be depressed or sad	✔		
	78. Has unusual fear response (e.g., lacks appropriate fears or awareness of danger or is overly fearful)			
	79. Appears anxious	✔	*I feel anxious about school.*	
	80. Exhibits rage reactions or "meltdowns"	✔		
	81. Injures self (e.g., bangs head, picks skin, bites nails until they bleed, bites self)			
	82. Makes suicidal comments or gestures			
	83. Displays inconsistent behaviors			
	84. Has difficulty tolerating mistakes			
	85. Has low frustration tolerance	✔	*Easily upset by small things.*	
	86. Has low self-esteem, makes negative comments about self			
	87. Has difficulty identifying, quantifying, expressing, and/or controlling emotions (e.g., can only recognize and express emotions in extremes or fails to express emotions – "emotionally flat")			
	88. Has a limited understanding of own and others' emotional responses	✔		
	89. Has difficulty managing stress and/or anxiety	✔	*Easily overwhelmed.*	
	90. Other	✔		

Area	Description	Notes	Follow-Up
KNOWN MEDICAL OR OTHER BIOLOGICAL FACTORS			

Figure 4.3. UCC and ISSI for Steve (continued).

Individual Strengths and Skills Inventory

Ruth Aspy, Ph.D., and Barry G. Grossman, Ph.D.

When designing an effective intervention plan, it is important to consider individual strengths. Please describe strengths in the following areas:

Social

- Has friends who share similar interests
- Initiates interactions with familiar individuals

Behavior, Interests, and Activities

- Has strong interests (e.g., computer, science fiction, chess)
- Able to follow complex instructions

Communication

- Able to greet others well
- Asks for help
- Verbally expresses feelings of frustration

Sensory

- Eats a wide range of foods
- Has no issues with clothing textures

Cognitive

- Makes good grades
- Studies hard
- Demonstrates good reading comprehension

Motor

- Has good keyboarding skills
- Demonstrates typical activity level

Emotional

- Has learned to set goals and work towards them
- Expresses enthusiasm about his interests

Biological

- Has responded well to anti-anxiety medication in the past
- Has no history of major illnesses or hospitalization

Figure 4.3. UCC and ISSI for Steve (continued).

Global Intervention Plan: Guide to Establishing Priorities

Ruth Aspy, Ph.D., and Barry G. Grossman, Ph.D.

Directions: Following completion of the UCC and ISSI, the next step is to identify UCC **areas** and **items** that will result in a *meaningful* Global Intervention Plan. Consideration of priorities and strengths for an individual facilitates selection of UCC areas and items. The following questions are provided as a guide.

<table>
<tr><td rowspan="3">Selecting UCC Areas</td><td>

Vision   "Begin with the end in mind" – Stephen R. Covey

- What is the long- and short-term vision of/for the individual?
  Note that "long-term" and "short-term" may be defined differently in order to be meaningful.

<u>Long-term</u>: *Graduate college, get a good job, participate in chess tournament.*
<u>Short-term</u>: *Make good grades, make one friend, feel less anxious about college, get along better with roommate.*

⊙ Which UCC **areas** would have the greatest impact on achieving this vision?

Social, Restricted Patterns of Behavior, Sensory Differences, Cognitive Differences, Emotional Vulnerability

Settings

- In what settings does the individual participate?

Class, dormitory, campus, home, scholastic clubs

⊙ Which UCC **areas** have the greatest impact on the individual's ability to function in multiple settings?

Social, Sensory Differences, Cognitive Differences, Emotional Vulnerability

Quality of Life

- What is most important to the individual? What provides a sense of well-being?
  Consider independence, relationships, play/leisure activities, safety, health, etc.

My interests (sci-fi, chess), learning, having friends

⊙ Which UCC **areas** have the greatest impact on the individual's quality of life?

Social, Restricted Patterns of Behavior, Cognitive Differences, Emotional Vulnerability

Key UCC Areas

Based on your answers to the questions above, place an X next to the key UCC **areas**.
*Transfer to the **Areas of Concern** section of the Ziggurat Worksheet.*

☒ Social
☒ Restricted Patterns of Behavior Interests, and Activities
☐ Communication
☒ Sensory Differences

☒ Cognitive Differences
☐ Motor Differences
☒ Emotional Vulnerability
☐ Known Medical or Other Biological Factors

</td></tr>
</table>

<table>
<tr><td>Selecting UCC Items</td><td>

Key UCC Items

Select key UCC **items** for *each* of the UCC **areas** listed above. Choose items that are essential (necessary for progress) and developmentally appropriate. Emphasize items that are pivotal (building blocks for additional skills). Avoid selecting redundant items.

Write key item numbers and descriptions below. These items will be used to develop interventions, keeping strengths and skills (identified on the ISSI) in mind.

*Transfer items to the **Selected UCC Item** section of the Ziggurat Worksheet and develop interventions.*

#1 Mindblindness
#4 Lacks tact
#5 Difficulty making or keeping friends
#8 Tends to be less involved in group activities
#12 Expresses strong need for routine or sameness
#18 Problems with transition and change

#41 Responds in unusual manner to sounds
#52 Displays poor problem solving skills
#53 Has poor organizational skills
#60 Has attention problems
#76 Is easily stressed
#89 Has difficulty managing stress and/or anxiety

</td></tr>
</table>

Figure 4.4. Global Intervention Plan Guide completed by Steve and Nicole.

ZIGGURAT WORKSHEET

BEHAVIOR/AREAS OF CONCERN — Social, Restricted Patterns of Behavior, Sensory Differences, Cognitive Differences, Emotional Vulnerability	FOR SPECIFIC INTERVENTION PLAN (Operationalized Behaviors)	SELECTED UCC ITEMS	A	B	C
	👁 👁 👁 👁	#1 Has difficulty recognizing the feelings and thoughts of others (mindblindness) #4 Lacks tact or appears rude #5 Has difficulty making or keeping friends #8 Tends to be less involved in group activities #12 Expresses strong need for routine or sameness #18 Has problems handling transition and change #41 Responds in an unusual manner to sounds #52 Displays poor problem-solving skills #53 Has poor organizational skills #60 Has attention problems #76 Is easily stressed #89 Has difficulty managing stress and/or anxiety			
Sensory and Biological	Sensory and Biological Intervention: • Use noise-canceling headphones while studying and soft earplugs on days when roommate has to wake early. • Make an appointment with a doctor at the student health center to discuss medications for your symptoms of anxiety and attention problems. • Try to sign up for early morning or late evening classes where class size is typically smaller. • Get involved in regular physical activities to help keep mind/body alert prior to studying and attending lectures. • Prior to attending large lecture classes, take time to relax and prepare yourself by taking deep breaths and reminding yourself that you can handle the crowd for the duration of class. Arrive to class early and select a seat away from "traffic." If you need to, take a quick break.		✓	✓	
	Underlying Characteristics Addressed:	#41 Responds in an unusual manner to sounds #60 Has attention problems #89 Has difficulty managing stress and/or anxiety			

Figure 4.5. Ziggurat worksheet for Steve's global intervention.

Case Study
Penny and Her Insects

Penny is in the fourth grade. She was diagnosed with high-functioning ASD last year and receives special education services through her school. Her parents and teachers describe her as a "tomboy." Penny will only wear shorts and short-sleeved shirts – regardless of the temperature or weather. She will not wear dresses, pants, or skirts. She frequently argues with her parents over clothing choices. Because Penny prefers certain colors and fabrics (cotton), when her parents are able to find an acceptable type of shirt, they buy in "bulk." Unfortunately, girls at school tease her because they think that she wears the same "boy clothes" every day.

Penny does not have many friends at school. She is very active and her interests are atypical when compared to girls in her grade. Penny plays better with boys than girls her age. She has an intensive interest in animals and insects and incessantly reads about them. Penny likes to spend her recess time searching for insects. She knows many great details about this interest and recites facts to anyone who will listen (or appear to do so). She also disrupts class discussions by making unrelated comments about this interest. At the beginning of fourth grade, Sarah, a classmate, would occasionally accompany Penny on her searches for bugs. After Sarah commented that she thought that praying mantises were ugly, Penny hit her and told the teacher. When her teacher encouraged the two to play together, Penny said she could not play with an "insect hater" and has refused to play with Sarah since that time. In an attempt to increase peer interactions, her teacher encouraged Penny to join the children playing soccer. This was not successful. Penny cried and complained that her peers were not playing "fair." Throughout the recess, she constantly "reported" small rule infractions to the teacher.

Penny frequently asks her parents why she does not have any friends. Her parents are concerned because she cries and complains about a lack of friends almost daily. Penny is enrolled in soccer and Girl Scouts. Her mother decided to be the Scout leader so she could "coach" Penny and help her interact successfully with her peers.

Penny is a gifted student. She easily learns the concepts but struggles to complete her work. Writing tasks are always a source of frustration. She is very creative but has great difficulty putting her thoughts down on paper. Her principal has discovered that Penny needs a "special" teacher with the right perspective. If the teacher is too strict, Penny will appear more oppositional. If the teacher is too spontaneous in her scheduling, Penny anxiously immerses herself in her animal books. This year, her teacher, Ms. Simpson, seems to offer the right balance. She is structured and very nurturing and understanding.

Penny's parents have noticed that their daughter has difficulty with major transitions. For example, she has great difficulty at the start of each school year. Mondays and returning to school after holiday breaks can also be problematic. During these times, she appears more frustrated and angry. At home, her parents have difficulty getting her up and ready for school in the morning. In the classroom, she may vocally refuse to do work by making statements such as "I don't have to do worksheets; my mother says that only bad teachers use them." She also disrupts class more after a weekend or holiday. Penny makes negative comments about her peers when they answer questions. She recently commented, "I can't believe you missed that – it was a second-grade question!" She also has more difficulty working with peers, making comments such as, "I don't want him on my team, he's not good at math."

Intervention

Penny's parents completed the UCC and the ISSI and gave them to her teacher to add information from her perspective (see Figures 4.6).

A meeting was held at school with Penny's team (parents, teacher, speech therapist, psychologist, and occupational therapist). The team reviewed the UCC and ISSI responses from all team members. Together, they completed the Global Intervention Plan Guide and selected UCC items that will help Penny to achieve the long- and short-term vision (see Figure 4.7). Building on Penny's strengths, identified with the ISSI, they began to develop a comprehensive intervention plan (see Figure 4.8).

The occupational therapist recommended that she observe and work with Penny in order to determine whether sensory or motor factors could be impacting her difficulty with writing. Subsequently, she helped to develop a sensory diet and instructed Penny's teachers and parents in how to implement it in both school and home environments. Due to their concerns with Penny's frustration and sadness, Penny's parents decided to seek consultation from a pediatric psychiatrist to determine whether medical interventions would be appropriate.

Penny displayed one specific behavior at school – class disruption – that her teacher wanted to understand better so she could address it. She completed the Specific Intervention Plan Guide to assist her in this process (see Figure 4.9). Ms. Simpson observed Penny and also asked her about this behavior. She found that Penny could not tell that her comments were hurtful to peers and disrespectful to her teacher. It was clear that Penny enjoyed the attention gained through class participation; however, she needed assistance in order to make appropriate contributions. Further, Ms. Simpson learned that Penny's refusal to write may have served the purpose of delaying the activity; however, she also recognized, with the assistance of the UCC, that Penny's writing difficulties were genuine and part of her ASD. In summary, the function of Penny's behavior (escape/avoidance) is best understood in light of her skill deficits. Specifically, the presence of skill deficits, including mind reading skills, coping skills, and handwriting skills, is the appropriate focus of intervention. That is, rather than limiting the focus of intervention to Penny's class disruption, her plan must address the underlying skill deficits.

Ms. Simpson completed an ABC-I (see Figure 4.10). As noted on the ABC-I, She recognized that Penny's peers were becoming less accepting of Penny as they grew older. Penny remained mystified about the connection between her behaviors and the rejection by her peers. Ms. Simpson developed a specific intervention plan for this important behavior with the assistance from others on Penny's team (see Figure 4.11). While some of the interventions were similar to those in Penny's global plan, additional strategies were developed to assist her in learning to recognize her own body cues in order to manage her feelings more successfully in the school environment. The ABC-I was used to ensure that underlying characteristics, associated with class disruption, were addressed through the interventions.

UNDERLYING CHARACTERISTICS CHECKLIST-HF
Ruth Aspy, Ph.D., and Barry G. Grossman, Ph.D.

NAME: *Penny*   COMPLETED BY: *Mr. and Mrs. Smith and Ms. Simpson*

DATE: *8-10*   FOLLOW-UP DATE:

DIRECTIONS: Place check beside all items that apply and describe behaviors observed.

Area	Item	✔	Notes	Follow-Up
SOCIAL	1. Has difficulty recognizing the feelings and thoughts of others (mindblindness)	✔	*Not aware of the teacher's reaction to her comments to peers in class.*	
	2. Uses poor eye contact			
	3. Has difficulty maintaining personal space, physically intrudes on others			
	4. Lacks tact or appears rude	✔	*Makes negative comments about peers.*	
	5. Has difficulty making or keeping friends	✔		
	6. Has difficulty joining an activity	✔	*Often plays alone. Needs parent assistance to participate with peers.*	
	7. Is naïve, easily taken advantage of, or bullied			
	8. Tends to be less involved in group activities than most same-age individuals	✔	*Searches for bugs during recess by herself.*	
	9. Has difficulty understanding others' nonverbal communication (e.g., facial expressions, body language, tone of voice)			
	10. Has difficulty understanding jokes			
	11. Other			
RESTRICTED PATTERNS OF BEHAVIOR, INTERESTS, AND ACTIVITIES	12. Expresses strong need for routine or "sameness"	✔	*Insists on wearing the same color shirts every day.*	
	13. Expresses desire for repetition			
	14. Has eccentric or intense preoccupations/absorption in own unique interests	✔	*Animals and insects.*	
	15. Asks repetitive questions			
	16. Seems to be unmotivated by customary rewards	✔	*Inconsistently responds to praise.*	
	17. Displays repetitive motor movements (e.g., flaps hands, paces, flicks fingers in front of eyes)			
	18. Has problems handling transition and change	✔	*Has difficulty with major changes such as starting school after summer break.*	
	19. Has strong need for closure or difficulty stopping a task before it is completed			
	20. Other			

Figure 4.6. **UCC and ISSI for Penny completed by her parents and teacher.**

Area	Item	✔	Notes	Follow-Up
COMMUNICATION	21. Makes sounds or states words or phrases repeatedly [non-echolalic] (e.g., humming, "well actually")			
	22. Makes up new words or creates alternate meanings for words or phrases			
	23. Displays immediate or delayed echolalia (e.g., recites lines from movies, repeats another person's questions or statements, repeats sounds)			
	24. Interprets words or conversations literally/has difficulty understanding figurative language			
	25. Has difficulty with rules of conversation (e.g., interrupts others, asks inappropriate questions, makes poor eye contact, has difficulty maintaining conversation)	✔	*Disrupts class with comments.*	
	26. Fails to initiate or respond to social greetings			
	27. Has difficulty using gestures and facial expressions			
	28. Has difficulty starting, joining, and/or ending a conversation	✔	*Walks up to peers and adults and starts reciting facts about insects.*	
	29. Has difficulty asking for help	✔	*May act out or shut down instead of asking for help.*	
	30. Makes irrelevant comments			
	31. Has difficulty expressing thoughts and feelings			
	32. Speaks in an overly formal way	✔	*Sounds like she is "lecturing" on animals and insects.*	
	33. Gives false impression of understanding more than he/she actually does	✔	*Because she is so bright and articulate, people expect her to know more about her social world than she does.*	
	34. Talks incessantly, little back-and-forth	✔		
	35. Uses an advanced vocabulary	✔		
	36. Uses mechanical, "singsong" voice or speech sounds unusual in other ways (e.g., prosody, cadence, tone)	✔	*Sounds mechanical.*	
	37. Has difficulty following instructions			
	38. Has difficulty understanding language with multiple meanings, humor, sarcasm, or synonyms			
	39. Has difficulty talking about others' interests	✔	*Conversations are one-sided.*	
	40. Other			

Figure 4.6. UCC and ISSI for Penny completed by her parents and teacher (continued).

Area	Item	✔	Notes	Follow-Up
SENSORY DIFFERENCES	41. Responds in an unusual manner to sounds (e.g., ignores sounds or over-reacts to sudden, unexpected noises, high-pitched continuous sounds, or complex/multiple noises)			
	42. Responds in an unusual manner to pain (e.g., overreacts or seems unaware of an illness or injury)			
	43. Responds in an unusual manner to taste (e.g., resists certain textures, flavors, brands)			
	44. Responds in an unusual manner to light or color (e.g., focuses on shiny items, shadows, reflections, shows preference or strong dislike for certain colors)	✔	*Notices colors. Comments on colors and has a strong preference for the color of her clothing.*	
	45. Responds in an unusual manner to temperature			
	46. Responds in an unusual manner to smells (e.g., may comment on smells that others do not detect)			
	47. Seeks activities that provide touch, pressure, or movement (e.g., swinging, hugging, pacing)	✔	*Penny is rather active and sometimes paces.*	
	48. Avoids activities that provide touch, pressure, or movement (e.g., resists wearing certain types of clothing, strongly dislikes to be dirty, resists hugs)	✔	*Insists on wearing shorts and short-sleeved shirts.*	
	49. Makes noises such as humming or singing frequently			
	50. Other			
COGNITIVE DIFFERENCES	51. Displays extensive knowledge in narrow areas of interest	✔	*Animals, interests, and reading.*	
	52. Displays poor problem-solving skills			
	53. Has poor organizational skills			
	54. Withdraws into complex inner worlds/fantasizes often			
	55. Is easily distracted by unrelated details – has difficulty knowing what is relevant or makes off-topic comments			
	56. Displays weakness in reading comprehension with strong word recognition			
	57. Knows many facts and details but has difficulty with abstract reasoning (i.e., weak central coherence)	✔	*Penny's all-or-nothing reasoning about peers reflects her inability to see the big picture. Sarah was labeled as an "insect hater" and dismissed as a friend despite other qualities.*	

Figure 4.6. UCC and ISSI for Penny completed by her parents and teacher (continued).

Area	Item	✔	Notes	Follow-Up
COGNITIVE DIFFERENCES	58. Has difficulty applying learned skills in new settings			
	59. Has academic skills deficits			
	60. Has attention problems			
	61. Displays very literal understanding of concepts			
	62. Recalls information inconsistently (i.e., seems to forget previously learned information)			
	63. Has difficulty understanding the connection between behavior and resulting consequences	✔	*Blames others for her own behavior.*	
	64. Other			
MOTOR DIFFERENCES	65. Has balance difficulties			
	66. Resists or refuses handwriting tasks	✔		
	67. Has poor handwriting			
	68. Has poor motor coordination (e.g., accident prone, difficulty using fasteners)			
	69. Writes slowly	✔		
	70. Displays atypical activity level (e.g., over-active/hyperactive, under-active/hypoactive)			
	71. Has athletic skills deficits			
	72. Displays an awkward gait			
	73. Displays unusual body postures and movements or facial expressions (e.g., odd postures, stiffness, "freezing," facial grimacing)			
	74. Has difficulty starting or completing actions (e.g., may rely on physical or verbal prompting by others)			
	75. Other			

Figure 4.6. UCC and ISSI for Penny completed by her parents and teacher (continued).

Area	Item	✔	Notes	Follow-Up
EMOTIONAL VULNERABILITY	76. Is easily stressed – worries obsessively			
	77. Appears to be depressed or sad	✔	*Complains about not having friends.*	
	78. Has unusual fear response (e.g., lacks appropriate fears or awareness of danger or is overly fearful)			
	79. Appears anxious			
	80. Exhibits rage reactions or "meltdowns"			
	81. Injures self (e.g., bangs head, picks skin, bites nails until they bleed, bites self)			
	82. Makes suicidal comments or gestures			
	83. Displays inconsistent behaviors			
	84. Has difficulty tolerating mistakes			
	85. Has low frustration tolerance	✔	• *Writing and "too much" school work upset her.* • *Becomes upset if she does not have the "right" clothes clean and ready to wear.*	
	86. Has low self-esteem, makes negative comments about self			
	87. Has difficulty identifying, quantifying, expressing, and/or controlling emotions (e.g., can only recognize and express emotions in extremes or fails to express emotions – "emotionally flat")			
	88. Has a limited understanding of own and others' emotional responses			
	89. Has difficulty managing stress and/or anxiety	✔	*Transitions are especially stressful.*	
	90. Other			

Area	Description	Notes	Follow-Up
KNOWN MEDICAL OR OTHER BIOLOGICAL FACTORS	*Fatigue*	*Penny doesn't sleep well on weekends – seems "grumpy" on Mondays.*	

Figure 4.6. UCC and ISSI for Penny completed by her parents and teacher (continued).

Individual Strengths and Skills Inventory

Ruth Aspy, Ph.D., and Barry G. Grossman, Ph.D.

In designing effective intervention plans, it is important to be aware of individual strengths. Please describe strengths in the following areas:

Social

- Plays well with boys
- Wants friends
- Eye contact has improved
- Respects others' personal space
- Enjoys sharing her interests with others

Behavior, Interests, and Activities

- Interested in animals and insects
- Participates well in Girl Scouts
- Respects rules

Communication

- Seeks assistance from adults
- Has strong vocabulary
- Initiates conversation with adults
- Speaks clearly

Sensory

- Tolerates heat, movement, noise, and touch well

Cognitive

- Loves to read
- Remembers facts well
- Curious
- Gifted student
- Creative

Motor

- Athletic – well coordinated

Emotional

- Affect is consistent with emotions
- Responds to nurturing approach and structure

Biological

- Energetic
- Generally healthy

Figure 4.6. UCC and ISSI for Penny completed by her parents and teacher (continued).

Global Intervention Plan: Guide to Establishing Priorities

Ruth Aspy, Ph.D., and Barry G. Grossman, Ph.D.

Directions: Following completion of the UCC and ISSI, the next step is to identify UCC **areas** and **items** that will result in a *meaningful* Global Intervention Plan. Consideration of priorities and strengths for an individual facilitates selection of UCC areas and items. The following questions are provided as a guide.

Selecting UCC Areas

Vision   "Begin with the end in mind" – Stephen R. Covey

- What is the long- and short-term vision of/for the individual?
  Note that "long-term" and "short-term" may be defined differently in order to be meaningful.

Long-term: College, have a group of friends, hold a job, have a family
Short-term: Complete assignments, read and understand others' feelings, cope with change

⊙ Which UCC **areas** would have the greatest impact on achieving this vision?

Social, Communication, Restricted Patterns of Behavior, Motor Differences, Emotional Vulnerability

Settings

- In what settings does the individual participate?

School (classroom, playground, etc.), home, Girl Scouts, soccer

⊙ Which UCC **areas** have the greatest impact on the individual's ability to function in multiple settings?

Social, Communication, Emotional Vulnerability

Quality of Life

- What is most important to the individual? What provides a sense of well-being?
  Consider independence, relationships, play/leisure activities, safety, health, etc.

Insects, animals, sports, making friends, "being smart"

⊙ Which UCC **areas** have the greatest impact on the individual's quality of life?

Social, Restricted Patterns of Behavior, Cognitive Differences, Emotional Vulnerability

Key UCC Areas

Based on your answers to the questions above, place an X next to the key UCC **areas**.

*Transfer to the **Areas of Concern** section of the Ziggurat Worksheet.*

☒ Social	☐ Cognitive Differences
☒ Restricted Patterns of Behavior Interests, and Activities	☒ Motor Differences
☒ Communication	☒ Emotional Vulnerability
☐ Sensory Differences	☐ Known Medical or Other Biological Factors

Selecting UCC Items

Key UCC Items

Select key UCC **items** for *each* of the UCC **areas** listed above. Choose items that are essential (necessary for progress) and developmentally appropriate. Emphasize items that are pivotal (building blocks for additional skills). Avoid selecting redundant items.

Write key item numbers and descriptions below. These items will be used to develop interventions, keeping strengths and skills (identified on the ISSI) in mind.

*Transfer items to the **Selected UCC Item** section of the Ziggurat Worksheet and develop interventions.*

#1 Mindblindness	# 25 Difficulty with rules of conversation
#4 Lacks tact	# 47 Seeks touch, pressure, or movement
#5 Difficulty making or keeping friends	# 57 Difficulty with abstract reasoning
#8 Tends to be less involved in group activities	# 77 Appears depressed or sad
#14 Has eccentric or intense preoccupations	# 85 Low frustration tolerance
#18 Problems with transition and change	

Figure 4.7. **Global Intervention Plan Guide for Penny.**

ZIGGURAT WORKSHEET

BEHAVIOR/AREAS OF CONCERN	FOR SPECIFIC INTERVENTION PLAN (Operationalized Behaviors)	SELECTED UCC ITEMS	CHECK ALL THAT APPLY		
			A	B	C
Social, Restricted Patterns of Behavior, Communication, Motor Differences, Emotional Vulnerability		#1 Difficulty recognizing the feelings and thoughts of others (mindblindness) #4 Lacks tact or appears rude #5 Difficulty making or keeping friends #8 Tends to be less involved in group activities #14 Has eccentric or intense preoccupations/absorption in own unique interests #18 Has difficulty handling transition and change #25 Has difficulty with rules of conversation #47 Seeks activities that provides touch, pressure, or movement #66 Resists or refuses handwriting tasks #77 Appears to be depressed or sad #85 Has low frustration tolerance			
	Sensory and Biological Intervention:	• Seek consultation from the occupational therapist (OT) to assess handwriting, including sensory factors and hand fatigue. • Provide Penny with a sensory diet with direction of an OT to help address anxious or agitated behaviors. • Seek medical consultation regarding possible need for pharmacotherapy.	✓		
Sensory and Biological	Underlying Characteristics Addressed:	#47 Seeks activities that provides touch, pressure, or movement #66 Resists or refuses handwriting tasks #77 Appears to be depressed or sad #85 Has low frustration tolerance			

Figure 4.8. Ziggurat worksheet for Penny's global intervention.

Specific Intervention Plan: Guide to Establishing Priorities

Ruth Aspy, Ph.D., and Barry G. Grossman, Ph.D.

INSTRUCTIONS: Use the ABC-I when designing an intervention to address specific behavioral concerns. Complete the questionnaire below. Transfer information to the ABC-I form (using the numbers as a guide) and to the Ziggurat Worksheet as indicated. Once the information has been transferred to the Ziggurat Worksheet, develop interventions for each level of the Ziggurat and ensure that the intervention is complete (5 levels, 3 points, addresses underlying needs).

Behavior

What specific behavior is of greatest concern?   *Class Disruption*

Transfer behavior to the top of the ABC-I ❶ *and to the upper-left corner of the Ziggurat Worksheet*

Next to the 👁 icon, describe the behavior in observable, measurable terms.

👁 *Says, "I don't have to do this work"*

👁 *Insults peers*

👁 *Does not complete writing tasks*

Place observable, measurable behavior descriptions next to the 👁 *icon on the ABC-I* ❷ *and on the Ziggurat Worksheet*

Antecedent

When and where does the behavior occur? List what is happening at the time or just before.

- *Transitions (e.g., mornings, Mondays, vacations)*
- *Written assignments*
- *Class discussions*

Transfer to the antecedent column of the ABC-I ❸

Consequences

List what usually happens after the behavior occurs.

- *Peer rejection/isolation from peers*
- *Loss of recess time*
- *Attention/opportunity to participate*
- *Private conversation with teacher*
- *Delay of task*

Transfer to the consequences column of the ABC-I ❹

Underlying Characteristics

Review **ALL** the checked UCC items. Identify underlying characteristics that may be associated with the behaviors described on the ABC-I. *List the UCC item numbers and a brief description of each item on the bottom of the ABC-I* ❺ *and next to the # icons in the "Selected UCC Items" section on the Ziggurat Worksheet.*

Function

Behavior serves a purpose. Common functions include:

- Escape/avoidance
- Sensory stimulation
- Adult/peer attention
- Access to preferred activity
- Tangible items
- Other

What is the hypothesized function of the behavior?   *Escape/avoidance (skill deficits are key to understanding this function)*

Figure 4.9. Penny's Specific Intervention Plan Guide.

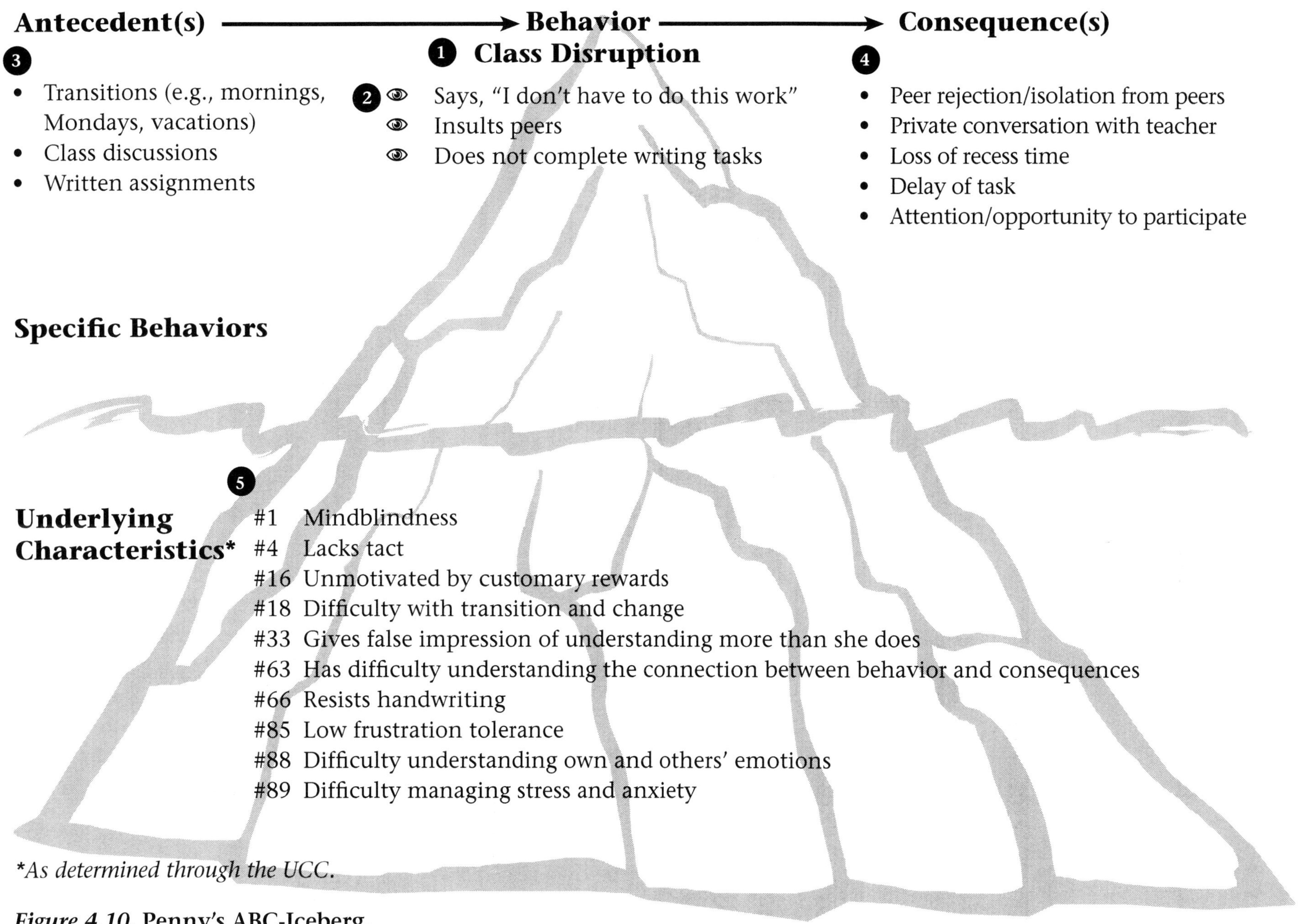

Antecedent(s) ⟶

3
- Transitions (e.g., mornings, Mondays, vacations)
- Class discussions
- Written assignments

Behavior ⟶
❶ Class Disruption

2
- Says, "I don't have to do this work"
- Insults peers
- Does not complete writing tasks

Consequence(s)

4
- Peer rejection/isolation from peers
- Private conversation with teacher
- Loss of recess time
- Delay of task
- Attention/opportunity to participate

Specific Behaviors

Underlying Characteristics*

5
#1   Mindblindness
#4   Lacks tact
#16 Unmotivated by customary rewards
#18 Difficulty with transition and change
#33 Gives false impression of understanding more than she does
#63 Has difficulty understanding the connection between behavior and consequences
#66 Resists handwriting
#85 Low frustration tolerance
#88 Difficulty understanding own and others' emotions
#89 Difficulty managing stress and anxiety

*As determined through the UCC.

Figure 4.10. Penny's ABC-Iceberg.

ZIGGURAT WORKSHEET

BEHAVIOR/AREAS OF CONCERN	FOR SPECIFIC INTERVENTION PLAN (Operationalized Behaviors)	SELECTED UCC ITEMS	CHECK ALL THAT APPLY		
			A	B	C
Class disruption	② Says, "I don't have to do this work." ② Insults peers ② Does not complete writing tasks	#1 Mindblindness #4 Lacks tact #16 Unmotivated by customary rewards #18 Difficulty with transition and change #33 Gives false impression of understanding more than she does			
		#63 Has difficulty understanding the connection between behavior and consequences #66 Resists handwriting #85 Low frustration tolerance #88 Difficulty understanding own and others' emotions #89 Difficulty managing stress and anxiety	✓	✓	
Sensory and Biological	Sensory and Biological Intervention: • Seek consultation from the occupational therapist (OT) to assess handwriting, including sensory factor and hand fatigue. • Provide Penny with a sensory diet with direction of an OT to help address anxious or agitated behaviors. • Provide a calming sensory activity prior to giving lengthy writing task. • Teach Penny to recognize body cues that indicate stress or frustration (e.g., muscle tension, heart rate, breathing pattern). • Teach Penny strategies to address her stress and frustration (e.g., engage in sensory calming strategy; ask for help, take slow, deep breaths). *Note.* This intervention applies to multiple levels.				
	Underlying Characteristics Addressed:	#66 Resists handwriting #85 Low frustration tolerance #88 Difficulty understanding own and others' emotions #89 Difficulty managing stress and anxiety			

Figure 4.11. Ziggurat worksheet for Penny's specific intervention.

SUMMARY

Chapter 4 began a discussion of the five hierarchal levels of the Ziggurat. The ZM begins with Sensory and Biological because this level is believed to be fundamental. The chapter also reviewed sensory integration, consequences of SI dysfunction, as well as research on SI approaches. Pharmacotherapy is one of the most common forms of treatment for individuals on the spectrum. Research-supported benefits and risks of three classes of medications were reviewed – antidepressants, antipsychotics, and stimulants. Other biological factors and interventions were discussed. The chapter closed by applying interventions on the first level of the Ziggurat to two case scenarios.

CHAPTER HIGHLIGHTS

- *Based on the Ziggurat, the first and most fundamental level is Sensory and Biological.*

- *Sensory differences are often associated with autism and can result in anxiety, distractibility, overactivity, impulsivity, perseveration, language delays, and poor social skills.*

- *Motor skill differences, such as low muscle tone, oral motor differences, repetitive movements, and motor planning deficits, create additional challenges.*

- *SI dysfunction may take the form of overresponsiveness (i.e., sensory seeking) or underresponsiveness (i.e., sensory defensiveness) to sensory input. SI dysfunction is believed to be related to several behaviors. Sensory responses tend to fluctuate, making it difficult to predict when situations will be overwhelming for an individual.*

- *At this time, only a few SI therapy approaches have empirical support; however, it is considered by some to be a "promising" practice for autistic individuals .*

- *The use of psychotropic medications is one of the most common forms of treatment for autistic individuals.*

- *Serotonin is believed to play a role in brain development and behavioral manifestations associated with autism. Antidepressants (most of which impact serotonin) have been shown to help a variety of symptoms of autism, including improving social relations and decreasing repetitive behaviors and movements, aggression, tantrums, depression, and anxiety.*

- *There are two types of antipsychotics – typical and atypical. The latter refer to newer medications that are considered to be safer. Antipsychotics have been used to address aggression, impulsivity, hyperactivity, repetitive behaviors, and communication in autistic individuals.*

- *Stimulants work by increasing norepinephrine and dopamine. They have been found to reduce hyperactivity, impulsivity, repetitive movements, oppositional behaviors, and tantrums.*

- *Other biological factors such as hunger, pain, fatigue, illness, nutrition, and health influence behavior and also should be addressed.*

5 Respectful Reinforcement

*"The way positive reinforcement
is carried out is more important
than the amount."*

– B. F. Skinner

In the mid 1900s, B. F. Skinner advanced the field of behaviorism – the study of observable behaviors – by carefully examining the nature of the relationship between behavior and consequences – reinforcement and punishment. Through his work, a detailed description of this relationship emerged. The principles identified by Skinner became the basis of applied behavioral analysis (ABA) interventions, including discrete trial training (DTT) and pivotal response training (PRT). Simpson et al. (2005) classify each of these behavioral approaches as scientifically based practices for autistic individuals. Thus, a broad range of behavioral interventions based on Skinner's principles is effective with individuals across the autism spectrum. The behavioral research on reinforcement is emphasized on the second level of the Intervention Ziggurat, Reinforcement.

Without reinforcement, there is no intervention. A reinforcer is, by definition, something/anything that follows a behavior and increases the likelihood that the behavior will occur. A reinforcer can increase any behavior – positive or negative. The ultimate goal of any intervention plan is a change in behavior. If a decrease of an inappropriate behavior is sought, an alternative or replacement *behavior must be increased* to take the place of the unwanted behavior. If, on the other hand, the goal is to acquire a new skill to improve functioning, then the skill or *behavior must be taught and increased*. Only one element in an intervention ensures the increase of a behavior–*reinforcement*.

After a brief introduction of reinforcement as an alternative to punishment, this chapter describes exemplary reinforcement-based interventions specifically designed to be effective with individuals on the autism spectrum. Research support for the use of token reinforcement systems and reinforcers related to obsessive interests with those on the spectrum is then discussed. Selection of meaningful reinforcers and careful timing of delivery is emphasized. Five guidelines for effective use of reinforcement are outlined. The chapter ends with application of the Reinforcement level of the IZ to specific cases.

REINFORCEMENT AS AN ALTERNATIVE TO PUNISHMENT

It is possible to use the principles of reinforcement to decrease undesirable behaviors by rewarding other or incompatible behaviors. This technique is called *differential reinforcement*. There are various types of differential reinforcement: differential reinforcement of other behaviors (DRO), differential reinforcement of incompatible behaviors (DRI), and differential reinforcement of lower rates of behavior (DRL).

- *DRO.* Using DRO, an individual would be observed for a period of time and then reinforced for the absence of a specific behavior. For example, a young child who injures himself by banging his head during the first 30 minutes of the school day could be rewarded for refraining from this behavior for a specific interval of time. One disadvantage of this approach is that while the specific behavior may not occur, other inappropriate behaviors that occur during the interval will be reinforced.

- *DRI.* Using DRI, a teacher can help a child decrease touching her peers in line by rewarding her for keeping her hands in her pockets. A teenager who is depressed and makes negative remarks about himself can be rewarded for making positive self-statements. In both examples, the desired replacement behavior is incompatible with the undesirable or "target" behavior.

- *DRL.* Using DRL, a teacher can reward a student for making fewer requests to go to the restroom or for reciting television programs for less time. Over time, rewards are given for fewer and fewer occurrences (or less time). In this strategy, the goal is a reduction of a behavior rather than its extinction.

In brief, the use of differential reinforcement results in a decrease of undesirable behavior as reinforcement is strategically delivered to increase desirable behavior. Thus, punishment and its side effects are avoided through the selective use of reinforcement.

Exemplary Reinforcement-Based Interventions

Social Stories™ and Social Articles™

Reinforcement plays a central role in some of the most successful interventions for autistic individuals. For example, Carol Gray (2000) has developed a technique for teaching social skills, Social Stories™ for children and Social Articles™ for adults. Her approach includes reinforcement by ensuring that at least every other story or article delivers a social reinforcer for positive behavior. Additionally, through the use of special "perspective" sentences (e.g., "When you respect others' personal space, they will want to play with you more"), Social Stories™ incorporate reinforcement by articulating the positive thoughts and feelings of others (rewards) that result from exhibiting a desired behavior. According to Gray, "at least 50% of all the stories developed for any person should congratulate or applaud current skills/abilities/personality traits/ or concepts that the person does well" (Hoekman, n.d.).

Red and Green Choices®

Another example of effectively incorporating the principles of reinforcement is the Red and Green Choices® positive behavioral strategy (Green, 2003). Designed for use with individuals across a wide age range, this system uses the colors green and red as visual cues to indicate appropriate and inappropriate behaviors. Goal behaviors are either drawn or written in green whereas inappropriate target behaviors are represented in red. Consequences for either type of behavior are also included.

The Red and Green Choices® system incorporates many basic behavioral principles. Green (2003) describes specific elements of the system: establishing behavioral trust, shaping, practicing, and establishing the criteria for earning a reinforcer.

- *Establishing behavioral trust.* First, Green recognizes the importance of establishing a positive relationship as an essential step in an intervention program. Once a relationship is established, social reinforcement is meaningful. Green refers to this as "behavioral trust."

- *Shaping.* Many goal behaviors must be learned in steps. To successfully teach new skills, reinforcement should not be delayed until the final "product" is produced; therefore, Green uses the principle of shaping, or successive approximations, in which the goal behavior is broken down into smaller, more easily attainable, parts. The learner receives reinforcement for displaying the parts of the desired skill until the goal behavior is eventually accomplished.

- *Practicing.* Practicing each skill may be necessary. Green recognizes the importance of reinforcing efforts during the learning or practicing of a new skill.

- *Establishing the criteria for earning a reinforcer.* Lastly, Green encourages careful consideration of the criteria for earning a reinforcer. Tasks that are challenging require more valuable or more frequent reinforcers than easier tasks to establish a fair "trade." That is, if the task is very difficult (i.e., the price is high), a small reinforcer may not be sufficient to motivate the desired behavior.

The Red and Green Choices® system can be applied to Penny, the fourth-grade student with disruptive behaviors in Ms. Simpson's class we met earlier. Penny's teacher decided to help her build the skills necessary to eventually participate successfully in group discussions using this system. Ms. Simpson had already established a good working relationship with Penny. Since Penny did not have the skills necessary to successfully participate in group, Ms. Simpson knew that she could not wait for the goal behavior to occur before reinforcing. She had to reinforce successive approximations of the behavior. Using the principle of shaping, she broke the goal of participating in a group into smaller steps (see Figure 5.1).

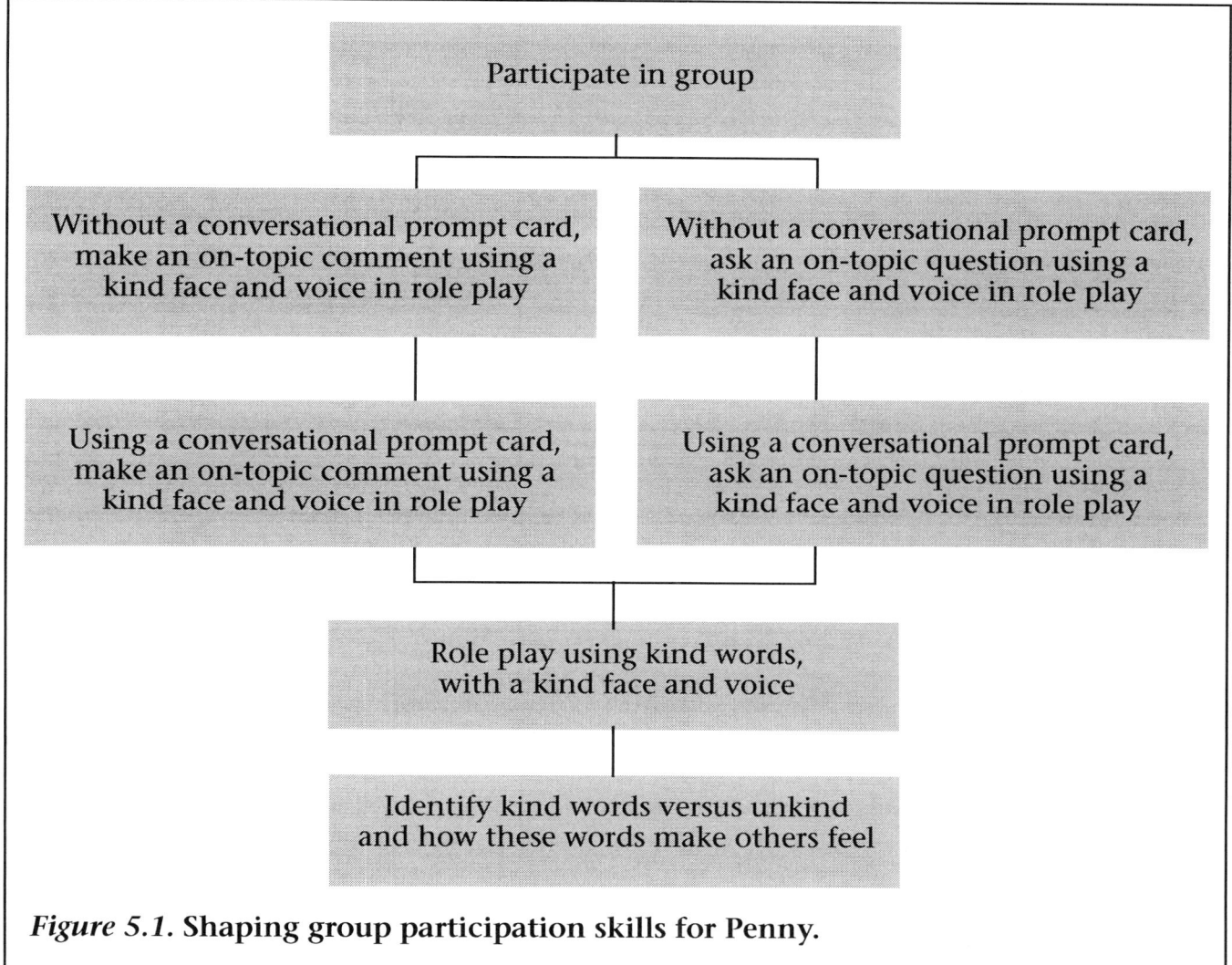

Figure 5.1. **Shaping group participation skills for Penny.**

Each step was taught and rehearsed through role play and reinforced using Penny's reinforcer menu (Figure 5.2). Ms. Simpson wrote out the green (expected) behaviors as well as red (inappropriate) behaviors. She established that green behaviors would be rewarded while no reinforcer would be earned for red behaviors.

Penny first learned to identify kind versus unkind words. Ms. Simpson taught her how her words made others feel. During role plays, she used a red and a green card as visual cues to indicate whether or not Penny was exhibiting the new skill, and Penny selected a reinforcer from her menu following successful role plays. Mrs. Simpson continued to teach, practice, and reinforce each new skill in order to shape Penny's behavior so that she would ultimately be able to be successful during group time with her peers. Ms. Simpson also followed Gray's recommendation that special stories be used to reinforce success. She wrote stories to celebrate Penny's progress as she accomplished each step.

The Way to A

Another reinforcement strategy, this one designed to specifically address aggression and tantrums, is described in a book, *The Way to A* (Manasco, 2006). This strategy is somewhat similar to Red and Green Choices®. The book provides positive alternatives to aggression and incorporates reinforcement to help children choose between "A" (appropriate) and "B" (inappropriate) behaviors. In this system, the adult and child first read through a special book describing positive and negative choices to problem situations. Pages and words are color-coded: green (positive) and red (negative). Together, they fill in blanks indicating consequences for appropriate and inappropriate behaviors. A flow chart is provided to visually reinforce the pathway between behavior and consequence. Color-coded "A" and "B" cue cards are also provided to be used as a prompt for an upset child to choose between "A" and "B" behaviors.

In the previous examples, an adult monitors performance and then provides a reinforcer. Another technique involves the child herself monitoring and reinforcing her own behavior. This approach, *self-management*, has long been established as effective (McDougall, 1998) and has been applied successfully to individuals with PDD (Kaplan, Hemmes, & Motz, 1996) and autism (Koegel & Koegel, 1990; Stahmer & Schreibman, 1992).

Self-management is beneficial because it encourages independence (Schreibman & Ingersoll, 2005). It also addresses a common concern in this population – generalization (Koegel, Frea, & Surratt, 1994). This technique is particularly effective with higher functioning individuals with ASD who have more adequate language skills (Schreibman & Ingersoll).

Research Support

Decades of behavioral research have resulted in well-established techniques for addressing behavior concerns for individuals on the autism spectrum. Careful attention to reinforcement is central to the success of these techniques. A review of the literature indicates that effective behavior intervention programs deliver reinforcers for positive behaviors and minimize reinforcement of problem behaviors (Horner et al., 2002). Researchers have given special consideration to the use of obsessive interests as reinforcers. A series of studies examining this process is reviewed here.

Obsessive Interests

For individuals on the autism spectrum, obsessions are often more effective reinforcers than are food reinforcers (Charlop-Christy, Kurtz, & Casey, 1990). Materials or activities related to obsessions have been used effectively to decrease inappropriate behavior through DRO. In DRO designs, access to the reinforcer is provided after a period without inappropriate behaviors. This approach has proven effective for decreasing negative behaviors without the side effects of punishment by focusing on increasing alternative behaviors through the use of reinforcement.

The use of obsessive interests as reinforcers has additional advantages. Individuals on the spectrum are much less likely to become satiated when rewarded with obsessive interests than when receiving food or other reinforcers. The use of an obsessive interest as a reinforcer has not been found to increase the time spent engaged in the obsessive interest. Care should be taken to use age-appropriate materials related to obsessions so that the reinforcement process does not set the child apart from peers (Charlop-Christy & Hamyes, 1996).

Token System

A token reinforcement system is used when an established reinforcer is not immediately available after a given behavior. Thus, the token signals that a reinforcer will be delivered at a later time. In some instances, a specified number of tokens may be required to obtain or "buy" the reward. Eventually, the token becomes a reinforcer in itself (i.e., *secondary reinforcer*). The reinforcement value of the token may be increased by the nature of the token. That is, using a token related to an obsessive interest increases the reinforcement value of the token. For example, an insect sticker might be an ideal token for Penny. A child who is fascinated by trains might benefit from a reinforcement system using cars or trains as tokens. When the train is complete, the child is allowed to play with it.

Studies have found that reinforcement systems that use tokens related to an obsession are more effective than a generic token system in increasing on-task behaviors in children on the autism spectrum (Charlop-Christy & Hamyes, 1998).

Considerations for Incorporating Reinforcement

It is important to keep in mind the definition of reinforcement – *a reinforcer is something that increases the likelihood of a behavior.* This definition is deceptively simple. Often attempts at reinforcement fail. Common difficulties are listed on the following page.

- Reinforcement increases both desired and undesired behaviors; therefore, if a negative behavior increases, it is important to identify the reinforcer(s) and remove them.

- Reinforcement may occur without being planned. For example, if Penny misses a written task by going to the school nurse, she may increase her frequency of asking to go to the nurse (because she escaped/avoided written work). Similarly, encouraging Penny to interact with her peers at recess may be especially difficult because of the challenge of finding a reinforcer strong enough to compete with the unplanned reward that she receives from her isolated search for bugs.

- Reinforcement is not effective without meaningful reinforcers delivered in an effective manner.

Effective reinforcement requires effort. As stated by B. F. Skinner, "The way positive reinforcement is carried out is more important than the amount" (http://creativequotations. com/one/219.htm). Selection of reinforcers, schedule of delivery, and general guidelines are discussed below.

Identification of Reinforcers

In order for any behavior plan to be successful, it is necessary to identify effective reinforcers. There are several types of reinforcers, including primary, activity, social, material, and token.

- *Primary reinforcers* are those that are innately desirable such as food and water.
- *Activity reinforcers* include computer time, video game time, television, and other privileges.
- *Social reinforcers* are praise, hugs, and other forms of positive interaction.
- *Material reinforcers* include toys, games, and other desired items.
- *Tokens.* There are times when it is not possible to provide one of these reinforcers immediately after a behavior. For example, it may be too disruptive to a group lesson if the teacher allows a student to leave and play a video game. Instead, a token is given. The token signals that a reinforcer will be delivered at a later time. Token reinforcers can include stickers, chips, stamps, and so on. A specified number of tokens may be required in order to obtain or "buy" the reward. The token becomes a reinforcer in itself.

There are many ways to identify meaningful reinforcers. One of easiest is to observe what students do during their free time as these activities or items are often the strongest reinforcers. Another way to identify reinforcers is to simply ask the child what he would like to earn. This may be done in a conversation or through completion of a written checklist, also called a reinforcement survey. This process can be a good opportunity to teach the concepts of compromise and negotiation.

Based on the information gathered about potential reinforcers, a reinforcer "menu" may be developed. Such a menu consists of a set of reinforcers from which the child may select the item he wishes to work for at any given time. Because preferred items do not always hold the same value (e.g., a soda is more valuable when you are thirsty, a computer game may have more value if it is new), a menu ensures that an effective reinforcer is available. An individual's selection of reinforcers from the menu can provide important information regarding the value of reinforcers. If a reinforcer on a menu is not selected for a long period of time, a new assessment should be completed to find current salient reinforcers. Lastly, a visual reinforcer menu serves as a reminder of the link between the expected behavior and consequence (reward).

Figure 5.2 depicts a reinforcer menu that Penny's teacher developed to address Penny's behaviors in school. As illustrated, Penny's narrow interest in insects became key to her reinforcement plan. Several items on the menu are related to her interest, and the menu itself was designed to incorporate her interest in insects.

🪲 **What I want to work for:**
Circle choice for this morning
🐞   **Insect book break**
🐞   **Computer game with peer**
🐞   **Wear baseball cap at recess**
🐞   **Take bug net to recess**
🐞   **Watch ant farm**
🐞   **Chew gum**
🐞   **Science lab assistant**
🐞   **Other**
Notes: *Penny wrote 4 sentences today!*
Great Job! <u>Ms. Simpson</u> **(teacher signature)**
Figure 5.2. Penny's reinforcement menu.

Schedules of Reinforcement

When developing a reinforcement system, one important consideration is determining when to provide a reinforcer. There are different schedules of reinforcement – continuous and intermittent.

As implied in the term, when using a *continuous schedule,* a reinforcer is provided every time a behavior occurs. For example, on a continuous schedule, Penny receives an item off of her menu every time she finishes a writing task.

Intermittent schedules are based on either a certain number of responses (*ratio*) or a duration of time (interval). They can be fixed or variable. For example, if Ms. Simpson were to use a *fixed-ratio schedule,* Penny would receive a reinforcer based on a determined ratio (e.g., after three assignments are complete). If she used a *variable-ratio schedule,* the number of assignments required for her reward would not be consistent. Providing reinforcement after one hour illustrates a fixed-interval schedule while varying the time is consistent with a variable-interval schedule. Figure 5.3 summarizes the different schedules of reinforcement.

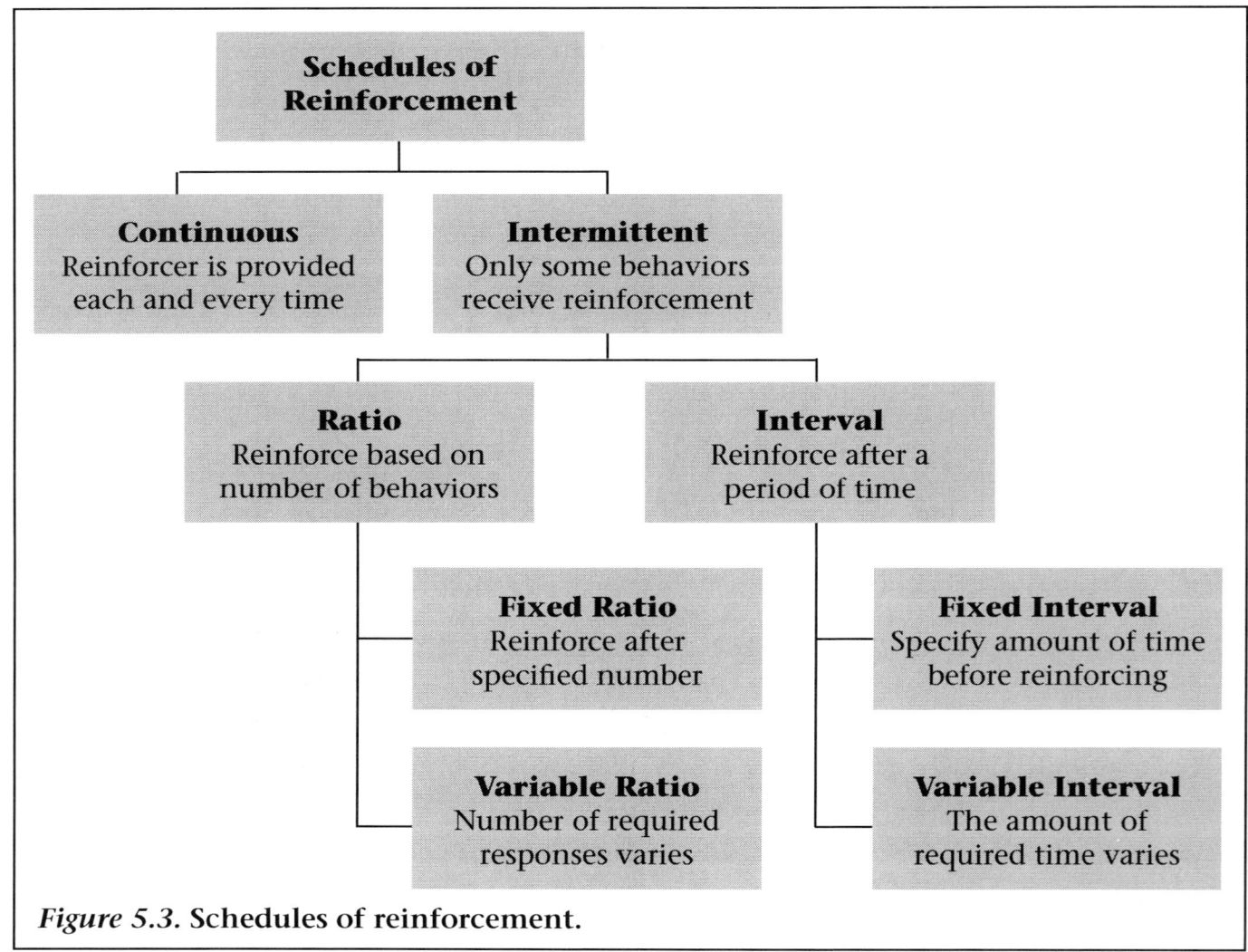

Figure 5.3. Schedules of reinforcement.

Continuous schedules are best when teaching new skills, because in order to learn new skills, reinforcers must be delivered at the highest possible rate – every time. A skill is considered fluent when the behavior is performed both accurately and quickly. Once the skill becomes fluent, maintenance becomes the goal. This is accomplished by moving to an intermittent schedule. Intermittent schedules help students to learn to wait longer for the payoff (Alberto & Troutman, 2003).

It is often a goal for students to be able to produce behaviors independent of a specialized reinforcement system. That is, ideally, naturally occurring reinforcers eventually replace those that are contrived. To that end, the reinforcement schedule can be thinned by requiring an increasing number of appropriate behaviors in order to earn the reinforcer or by lengthening the time between opportunities to earn reinforcers (Alberto & Troutman, 2003).

We have been discussing the importance of the ratio of reinforcers to correct responses. It is perhaps more important to consider the ratio of positive feedback to negative. No reinforcement system, regardless of how well designed, is effective if negative feedback outweighs the positive. The necessary ratio of positives to negatives is estimated to be somewhere between 4:1 and 10:1.

Guidelines for Reinforcement

Years of research have led to a set of guidelines for effective use of reinforcement.

1. *Make certain that reinforcement is contingent on appropriate behaviors.* When a critical skill is to be taught, it is often helpful to reserve a strong reinforcer to be delivered only when a desired behavior related to that skill is exhibited.

2. *Pair activity or material reinforcers with social reinforcement.* This is especially important with individuals on the autism spectrum who often need to be directly taught the value of social reinforcers such as smiles, hugs, praise, and so on.

3. *When possible, take advantage of natural reinforcers to increase desired behaviors.* These are consequences that are an ordinary result of a behavior. For example, earning free time after homework is complete, receiving good grades for studying, and increased social acceptance/inclusion as a result of treating others kindly. The advantage of these reinforcers is that because they are "built" into the environment, they do not have to be delivered by an adult. Because the same reinforcer is available in multiple settings, natural reinforcers help to promote generalization of skills.

4. *Use a preferred activity to reinforce one that is less preferred.* This basic principle of reinforcement is known as the Premack Principle, or "grandma's rule." For example, "You can only eat dessert if you finish your green beans." Or, "You can go outside and play after you have finished your homework." In other words, participation in the preferred activity becomes the reward. Knowing that Penny dislikes writing tasks, for example, her teacher can structure classroom lessons such that writing is followed by activities of high interest or something from her reinforcer menu.

   Despite its simplicity, the Premack Principle is underutilized. To apply it, one must notice what is reinforcing to an individual and then restrict access to the reinforcer until completion of a goal behavior.

5. *Keep in mind that the value of a reinforcer may change over time.* A reinforcer that is used repeatedly may lose its effectiveness through satiation. This is especially true with primary reinforcers such as edibles. In order to prevent satiation: (a) use small amounts of a reinforcer; (b) use a variety of reinforcers; (c) require several responses for each delivery of a reinforcer; and (d) use a token system (Sundberg, 2005).

In general, fresh or novel items have greater reinforcement value than familiar items. Updating reinforcer surveys on an ongoing basis is a helpful way to add novel items and assess their reinforcement value.

APPLICATION OF THE ZIGGURAT MODEL

Sensory and biological interventions for Steve and Penny were outlined in Chapter 4. Reinforcement is the second fundamental level of the Ziggurat. It helps set the stage for other interventions and make learning and maintaining skills possible. In the following we will illustrate this level of the ZM as applied to Steve and Penny.

Steve's Reinforcement Interventions

Steve, the college student we met earlier, is having great difficulty his first semester. Studying is difficult, and his grades are declining. He has not made any friends and frequently experiences conflict with his roommate. Upon his parents' suggestion, he met with Nicole, a sponsor at the student support center. After prioritizing goals for Steve, Nicole helped Steve develop several interventions using reinforcement (Figure 5.4).

ZIGGURAT WORKSHEET

BEHAVIOR/AREAS OF CONCERN	FOR SPECIFIC INTERVENTION PLAN (Operationalized Behaviors)	SELECTED UCC ITEMS	CHECK ALL THAT APPLY		
			A	B	C
Social, Restricted Patterns of Behavior, Sensory Differences, Cognitive Differences, Emotional Vulnerability	👁 👁 👁 👁 👁	#1 Has difficulty recognizing the feelings and thoughts of others (mindblindness) #4 Lacks tact or appears rude #5 Has difficulty making or keeping friends #8 Tends to be less involved in group activities #12 Expresses strong need for routine or sameness #18 Has problems handling transition and change #41 Responds in an unusual manner to sounds #52 Displays poor problem-solving skills #53 Has poor organizational skills #60 Has attention problems #76 Is easily stressed #89 Has difficulty managing stress and/or anxiety			
Sensory and Biological Intervention:		• Use noise-canceling headphones while studying and soft earplugs on days when roommate has to wake early. • Make an appointment with a doctor at the student health center to discuss medications for your symptoms of anxiety and attention problems. • Try to sign up for early morning or late evening classes where class size is typically smaller. • Get involved in regular physical activities to help keep the mind/body alert prior to studying and attending lectures. • Prior to attending large lecture classes, take time to relax and prepare yourself by taking deep breaths and reminding yourself that you can handle the crowd for the duration of class. Arrive to class early and select a seat away from "traffic." If you need to, take a quick break.	✓	✓	
Sensory and Biological	Underlying Characteristics Addressed:	#41 Responds in an unusual manner to sounds #60 Has attention problems #76 Is easily stressed			
	Reinforcement Intervention:	• Develop a self-reinforcement system. Monitor your own progress on specific goals (e.g., study goals, academic goals, and social goals). For example, reward yourself with a timed game of chess on the Internet after you finish reading a chapter. • Join clubs in your area of interests such as movie club or chess club to provide yourself with rewarding social opportunities. • Tell yourself that you have done a good job after you notice a minor change in your dorm room and handle it without complaining.		✓	✓
Respectful Reinforcement	Underlying Characteristics Addressed:	#5 Has difficulty making or keeping friends #8 Tends to be less involved in group activities #52 Displays poor problem-solving skills #53 Has poor organizational skills #60 Has attention problems #69 Writes slowly			

Figure 5.4. Ziggurat worksheet for Steve's global intervention.

Nicole taught Steve how to use a self-management system to address study habits and grades, as well as social goals. First, realistic, measurable goals were written. Nicole helped Steve to create a study schedule and a reinforcer menu, ensuring that the items were reasonable and would not interfere with his social functioning (Figure 5.5). Because Steve enjoyed playing chess, she encouraged him to reserve this strong reinforcer for what he considered to be his most difficult goal – studying.

To begin, Steve will use a *continuous reinforcement schedule*. After completing his scheduled study time, he will note the start and end times on his calendar and select a reinforcer from his *menu*. After Steve demonstrates fluency with his new study skills, Nicole will recommend that he change his schedule of reinforcement to a *fixed ratio*. Based on her experience with other college students, Nicole defines fluency as starting to study within 15 minutes of the planned schedule and remaining on task until the study session is complete. After three successful sessions, Steve will select a reinforcer from his menu.

My Rewards
• Timed game of Internet chess
• Watching one program on the Sci Fi network
• Thirty minutes of time to browse the web
• Soda
• Ice cream sandwich
• One chapter of leisure reading
• Pizza

Figure 5.5. **Reinforcer menu for Steve.**

This reinforcement system will also be used to address Steve's social goals, such as joining a club and successfully resolving roommate issues. For each of these goals, Steve will monitor his progress and document and reward himself as appropriate. In the event that he fails to demonstrate success, he will withhold his reinforcer. Nicole realizes that, especially for these goals, the activity itself can serve as a reinforcer; therefore, for these goals, it may eventually be desirable to thin (i.e., slowly remove) the reinforcement system.

Penny's Reinforcement Interventions

Reinforcements were incorporated into Penny's global intervention plan in order to address social skill development and work completion (see Figure 5.6).

Penny's parents and school team (speech therapist, psychologist, and occupational therapist) decided that she needed meaningful reinforcers to motivate her to learn and use social skills and to work on writing tasks that she considered difficult. The team decided that a *menu* would help ensure that Penny would always have a variety of effective reinforcers available to choose from. Ms. Simpson met with Penny and administered a *reinforcement survey*. From the information gathered, a school menu was developed (see Figure 5.2). Penny's parents also developed a reinforcement menu for home.

The team decided to start out targeting two behaviors: (a) identifying kind versus unkind words and (b) starting writing tasks without complaining. A *token system* was developed. Penny would earn insect stamps when she demonstrated goal behaviors. Once the pre-determined number of stamps were earned, she could select an item from her reinforcement menu. Because this was a positive system, it was decided that stamps would never be taken away. Furthermore, if the chart was not complete by the end of the day, it would be carried over to the next day.

It is important to note that Penny's token chart was designed to be flexible based on her skill level during the shaping process (refer to Figure 5.7). When learning a new skill that requires frequent practice and reinforcement, Penny will earn an insect stamp for imitating or role-playing the behavior. Later, she will earn stamps on her token chart for independently using the skill in actual situations. The completion of each chart will correspond with the delivery of a reinforcer from her menu. Figure 5.7 depicts a token chart assuming that Penny has acquired the ability to independently demonstrate these two skills.

Additional reinforcement was built into Penny's intervention plan. For example, it was decided to reinforce social success by pairing social interaction with a well-established reinforcer. Ms. Simpson planned to arrange an opportunity for Penny to create and present a project on praying mantises to the third grade during their unit on insects.

Penny's parents wanted to use a similar token system at home to address getting ready for school. They will break up the morning routine into a checklist. Penny will receive a stamp for each completed item with reminders. If she follows the schedule independently,

ZIGGURAT WORKSHEET

BEHAVIOR/AREAS OF CONCERN Social, Restricted Patterns of Behavior, Communication, Motor, Emotional Vulnerability	FOR SPECIFIC INTERVENTION PLAN (Operationalized Behaviors)	SELECTED UCC ITEMS	A	B	C
	② ② ② ②	#1 Difficulty recognizing the feelings and thoughts of others (mindblindness) #4 Lacks tact or appears rude #5 Difficulty making or keeping friends #8 Tends to be less involved in group activities #14 Has eccentric or intense preoccupations/absorption in own unique interests #18 Has difficulty handling transition and change #25 Has difficulty with rules of conversation #47 Seeks activities that provide touch, pressure, or movement #66 Resists or refuses handwriting tasks #77 Appears to be depressed or sad #85 Has low frustration tolerance			
 Sensory and Biological	Sensory and Biological Intervention: • Seek consultation from the occupational therapist (OT) to assess handwriting, including sensory factors and hand fatigue. • Provide Penny with a sensory diet with direction of an OT to help address anxious or agitated behaviors. • Seek medical consultation regarding possible need for pharmacotherapy.		✓		
	Underlying Characteristics Addressed:	#47 Seeks activities that provide touch, pressure, or movement #66 Resists or refuses handwriting tasks #77 Appears to be depressed or sad #85 Has low frustration tolerance			
 Respectful Reinforcement	Reinforcement Intervention: • Develop a positive behavior management plan to address social skills and work completion. Have Penny help to select items for a reinforcer menu. Reinforcers are earned both in home and school. Penny should have frequent opportunities to "cash in" by selecting reinforcers from her menu. • Reinforce Penny for being able to categorize statements as "rude" or "kind." • Provide reinforcement for initiating work on a writing assignment without negative comments. Also reinforce her for working for an increasing length of time. • Reinforce social success by pairing social interaction with a well-established reinforcer. For example, arrange an opportunity to create and present a project on praying mantises to the third grade during their unit on insects. • Develop a token reinforcement system to address transitioning to school. Use alligator or other favorite animal stamps in Penny's token reinforcer system. Parents will provide Penny with a visual checklist/schedule for the morning routine and transition to school. Make the last item on the checklist a school task (e.g., put backpack away). Reinforce Penny at school for following checklist/schedule. Provide additional reinforcement for following the schedule independently. *Note.* This intervention applies to multiple levels.	✓	✓	✓
	Underlying Characteristics Addressed:	#4 Lacks tact or appears rude #5 Difficulty making or keeping friends #8 Tends to be less involved in group activities #14 Has eccentric or intense preoccupations/absorption in own unique interests #25 Has difficulty with rules of conversation #77 Appears to be depressed or sad			

Figure 5.6. Ziggurat worksheet for Penny's global intervention.

she will receive two stamps. The final items on the checklist will be entering the classroom at school and putting her backpack away. Her teacher will provide Penny with additional stamps for completing the final items on her morning checklist.

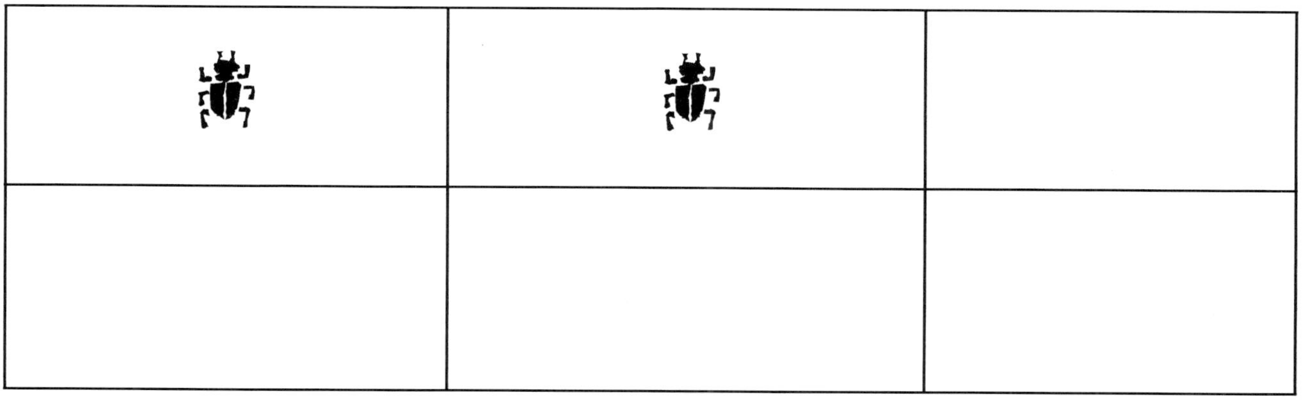

🪲	🪲	

- **Use kind words**
- **Start work without complaining**

Figure 5.7. Penny's token chart for her two goals: starting work without complaining and using kind words.

Ms. Simpson continued to augment the global intervention with a specific intervention to address disruptive behaviors (Figure 5.8). One plan included a strategy to help Penny transition to school after the weekend by providing a special Monday reinforcer. Additionally, a speech therapist will develop a list of guidelines for listening and contributing during class discussions. When Penny follows the guidelines, she will receive stamps on her token chart. (This strategy employs visual aspects – a red and a green color-coded card – and will be discussed further in the chapter on structure and visual supports.)

ZIGGURAT WORKSHEET

BEHAVIOR/AREAS OF CONCERN	FOR SPECIFIC INTERVENTION PLAN (Operationalized Behaviors)	SELECTED UCC ITEMS	CHECK ALL THAT APPLY		
			A	B	C
Class disruption	⌦ Says, "I don't have to do this work" ⌦ Insults peers ⌦ Does not complete writing tasks	#1 Mindblindness #4 Lacks tact #16 Unmotivated by customary rewards #18 Difficulty with transition and change #33 Gives false impression of understanding more than she does #63 Has difficulty understanding the connection between behavior and consequences			
  Sensory and Biological	Sensory and Biological Intervention:	• Seek consultation from the occupational therapist (OT) to assess handwriting, including sensory factors and hand fatigue. • Provide Penny with a sensory diet with direction of an OT to help address anxious or agitated behaviors. • Provide a calming sensory activity prior to giving lengthy writing task. • Teach Penny to recognize body cues that indicate stress or frustration (muscle tension, heart rate, breathing pattern, etc.). • Teach Penny strategies to address her stress and frustration (engage in sensory calming strategy, ask for help, take slow, deep breaths, etc.). *Note.* This intervention applies to multiple levels.	✓	✓	
	Underlying Characteristics Addressed:	#66 Resists handwriting #85 Low frustration tolerance #88 Difficulty understanding own and others' emotions #89 Difficulty managing stress and anxiety			
  Respectful Reinforcement	Reinforcement Intervention:	• Develop a positive behavior management plan to address social skills and work completion. Have Penny help to select items for a reinforcer menu. Reinforcers are earned both in home and school. Penny should have frequent opportunities to "cash in" by selecting reinforcers from her menu. • Reinforce Penny for being able to categorize statements as "rude" or "kind." • With the assistance of a speech therapist, develop a card that lists rules for class discussion. During a class discussion, give Penny a card. One side is green (with rules for appropriate class discussion; e.g., no insults, on-topic remarks). The other side is red (with a list of appropriate listening behaviors). Begin each class discussion with the green side up. Turn card to red if Penny makes an inappropriate contribution. Remove card at the end of class discussion. Reinforce Penny for following the rules on either side of the card. *Note.* This intervention applies to multiple levels. • Provide reinforcement for initiating work on a writing assignment without negative comments. Also reinforce her for working for an increasing amount of time. • Develop a token reinforcement system to address transitioning to school. Use alligator or other favorite animal stamps in Penny's token reinforcer system. Parents will provide Penny with a visual checklist/schedule for the morning routine and transition to school. Make the last item on the checklist a school task (e.g., put backpack away). Reinforce Penny at school for following checklist/schedule. Provide additional reinforcement for following the schedule independently. *Note.* This intervention applies to multiple levels. • Provide Penny with a strong reinforcer on Mondays when she arrives to school with her completed morning home checklist.	✓	✓	✓
	Underlying Characteristics Addressed:	#4 Lacks tact #16 Unmotivated by customary rewards #18 Difficulty with transition and change #66 Resists handwriting #85 Low frustration tolerance			

Figure 5.8. Ziggurat worksheet for Penny's specific intervention.

SUMMARY

As we stated at the beginning of this chapter, *without reinforcement, there is no intervention.* The ZM emphasizes the careful selection and use of reinforcement and is designed to avoid and discourage punitive approaches. The Reinforcement Level helps to set the stage for effective use of structure and visual supports and to make learning and maintaining skills at later levels possible.

CHAPTER HIGHLIGHTS

- *A reinforcer is, by definition, something/anything that follows a behavior and increases the likelihood that the behavior will occur.*

- *A reinforcer can increase any behavior – positive or negative.*

- *Differential reinforcement may be used to decrease undesirable behaviors by rewarding other or incompatible behaviors.*

- *Effective behavior intervention programs deliver reinforcers for positive behaviors and minimize reinforcement of problem behaviors.*

- *A token reinforcement system is used when an established reinforcer is not immediately available after a given behavior. The token signals that a reinforcer will be delivered at a later time.*

- *Reinforcement systems that use tokens related to an obsession are more effective than a generic token system in increasing on-task behaviors in children on the autism spectrum.*

- *In order to increase the desired behavior, reinforcement should be contingent on that behavior.*

- *Natural reinforcers are "built" into the environment and do not have to be delivered by an adult. Natural reinforcers help to promote generalization of skills.*

- *A preferred activity may be used to reinforce one that is less preferred. This is called the Premack Principle, or "grandma's rule."*

- *The value of a reinforcer may change over time. In general, fresh or novel items have greater reinforcement value than familiar items.*

---

6 Structure and Visual/Tactile Supports

"And it is best if you know a good thing is going to happen, like an eclipse or getting a microscope for Christmas. And it's bad if you know a bad thing is going to happen, like having a filling or going to France. But I think it is worst if you don't know whether it is a good thing or a bad thing which is going to happen."

– Christopher John Francis Boone,
from *The Curious Incident of the Dog in the Night-Time*, by Mark Haddon (2003)

"I like everything still. It gives you a full feeling. It gives you a full attention. With something quick you don't get the full idea of it. With something still you take a look at it and you get to know the whole look and feeling."

– Warden, from *Rage for Order* (BBC, 1996)

Structure and Visual/Tactile Supports is the third level of the Intervention Ziggurat. This level of the Ziggurat draws on the strength of visual processing and addresses the need for order and routine that is fundamental to autistic individuals. The term "structure" refers to a purposeful, systematic arrangement of the environment from physical layout of a room to routines used. Structure provides the predictability and organization individuals on the spectrum need and can prevent behavior difficulties from arising. Similarly, by using the "first language" and strength of autistic individuals – visual communication – visual supports provide structure and aid in teaching skills. Visual supports – from a daily schedule or checklist to a small cue card with a list of social skills – create opportunities for success, facilitate learning, and foster independence. It is important to note that not all autistic individuals have a strength in visual processing; however, structure is critical and must be addressed. If the visual mode is not a strength (e.g., individuals with a visual impairment), alternative approaches that rely on known strengths (e.g., auditory, kinesthetic, tactile) must be developed. Given this, we have also included tactile in the name of this level, as many students (particularly those with visual impairments) require this additional type of support.

This chapter opens with quotations by two young men – one factual, one fictional. Each has been diagnosed with a autism and is high functioning. When the fictional character, Christopher John Francis Boone, states that it is better to know that something bad is going to happen than not to know that something good is going to happen, he is describing his need for predictability, or assistance in understanding the context in which he is expected to function. Knowing what will happen before it actually occurs allows time to prepare, ask questions, and process the upcoming situation. For individuals with weak central coherence and a strong need for sameness, predictability improves the ability to function and decreases anxiety.

In the second quote, when Warden states, "With something still, you take a look at it and you get to know the whole look and feeling," he is referring to his habit of pausing videotapes to study facial expressions. Warden has found a way to learn about the thoughts and feelings of others. This information, which most others are able to access naturally, is lost to him. Due to mindblindness, he cannot access many social cues in "real time." By taking visual information and pausing it, he discovers the wealth of social information available through facial expressions and gestures. In this way, a paused videotape provides a visual support for Warden.

In this chapter, the crucial role of structure and visual/tactile supports in a complete intervention program is discussed. Specific interventions to be discussed include video and photography, Social Stories™, cartooning, Structured Teaching, priming, modeling, virtual environments, and other visual supports (e.g., visual schedules and the Power Card strategy).

VIDEO AND PHOTOGRAPHY

Video and photographs are key elements in the development of many structure and visual supports interventions for autistic individuals. Video may be incorporated in some of the specific techniques, including Social Stories™, priming, modeling, and virtual environments, to be discussed below. Video and photographic media may be used to facilitate the development of mind-reading skills and can provide a safe way of practicing these skills.

Deficits in theory of mind, also called mindblindness, refer to an inability to understand the thoughts and feelings (mental states) of others. As discussed earlier, this is a common deficit for individuals on the spectrum. Video and photographs can easily be incorporated into a teaching intervention to address this area of need. For example, an adult may present a photograph or video and ask the child, "What do you think he is feeling?," "Why is she crying?," or facilitate a discussion of these concepts.

Research on the use of photographs for this purpose is sparse; however, some promising findings are beginning to emerge. Parsons and Mitchell (2002) reviewed a number of studies that have demonstrated that photographs can be used to facilitate development of some basic principles of theory of mind. Research supporting the use of video is discussed in the sections that follow. Video and photographs are valuable and versatile tools for use in visual supports. Given the contribution that they can make to a comprehensive intervention plan, we consider them to be vastly underutilized in general practice.

SOCIAL STORIES™

On the surface, communication appears simple; however, closer inspection reveals that it is a complex process. In order to understand one another, we must take into consideration spoken and unspoken, as well as literal and implied, messages and then integrate them into a meaningful whole. For example, you may say one thing ("I'm happy to do that for you"), but your body language (arms crossed over your chest and a dour expression on your face) tells that you mean the opposite. It is often difficult for those on the spectrum to understand the complexities inherent in social exchanges. As a result, they miss important messages and easily become "lost" in social situations.

Teaching social skills is a common intervention; however, because teaching is most often a social or interpersonal activity, this method may hinder the ability of those on the spectrum to learn these skills.

In the early 1990s, Carol Gray developed the Social Story™, an individualized or student-specific tool for teaching relevant social information and appropriate responses (1998). More recently, Gray expanded and adapted this approach for adults, Social Articles™ (Gray, 2000). In contrast to teaching through a traditional interactive format (e.g., direct instruction, group), by putting the lesson in a story, the individual has greater access to the material because the requirement for social interaction is minimized (Sanosti, Powell-Smith, & Kincaid, 2004). The Social Story™ provides a type of task analysis – breaking down complex information into distinct parts – written at the learner's level of comprehension and from the learner's perspective (Barry & Burlew, 2004). Because Social Stories™ describe or establish routines, they are a good fit for individuals on the spectrum, who often seek out rules and thrive on routines (Scattone, Wilczynski, Edwards, & Rabian, 2002).

Creation of quality Social Stories™ requires thorough observation of the student in the environment with careful attention to the language used, details of the learner's behavior, and specifics of the situation to be addressed. Social Stories™ are comprised of the following types of sentences (Sanosti et al., 2004).

Type	Description
Descriptive	Provide factual information – what, why, when, where, who.
Directive	Describe desired behaviors or goals for a situation.
Perspective	Describe the feelings, thoughts, and reactions of characters in the story.
Affirmative	Provide reassurance or state a rule or law.
Control	State an analogy identified by the student/learner to help in remembering the story.
Cooperative	Identify those who will provide support in following through with the story.

Gray has established a Social Story™ Formula: The writer is to include at least two to five other types of sentences for every directive sentence in a Social Story™ (1998). As a matter of fact, an effective Social Story™ may not include any directive sentences. In addition, Gray recommends that at least half of the stories developed emphasize successes or strengths of the learner (Hoekman, n.d.).

Research Support

In 2004, a review of eight case studies using Social Stories™ found them to be effective in addressing targeted behaviors (Sanosti et al., 2004). Although the authors expressed several concerns regarding the design of the studies, they termed the results "preliminary support" for the Social Story™ method. In another study, Hagiwara and Myles (1999) found that computers may be effectively used to deliver Social Stories™. Further, research has shown that Social Stories™ are effective in teaching positive social skills such as greeting and sharing (Crozier & Tincani, 2005), reducing disruptive behavior (Barry & Burlew, 2004; Lorimer, Simpson, Myles, & Ganz, 2002), and reducing tantrums (Thieman & Goldstein, 2001).

Considerations for Incorporating Social Stories™
The use of Social Stories™ has many benefits, including the following.

- Because stories are a typical part of the school experience, Social Stories™ hold a low risk of stigmatizing the learner (Crozier & Tincani, 2005).

- Social Stories™ may be delivered in a variety of ways – videotape, song, audiotape, computer-based, or the written word (Sanosti et al., 2004). The optimal method of delivery may be determined based on developmental and intellectual factors as well as the interests of the specific learner.
- The accessibility of Social Stories™ facilitates their use for pre-teaching or priming (Crozier & Tincani, 2005).
- Social Stories™ are time and cost effective (Gray & Garand, 1993).
- Social Stories™ may be used by a range of individuals who are familiar with the autism spectrum and the needs of the specific individual for whom the story is prepared (Gray & Garand, 1993).

While Social Stories™ are readily used by a range of individuals, Sanosti et al. (2004) warn against directly using a prepared story from a general collection since these are not sufficiently individualized. In other words, collections of stories should serve as a resource for writing an individualized story, not presented as is.

Once the story is delivered, students should be asked a series of questions to ensure that they comprehend the story. To enhance learning and facilitate generalization of skills, it is also beneficial to role play elements of the story. Finally, the learner's progress in applying the lesson in the story should be monitored (Gray & Garand, 1993).

An additional caveat regarding the Social Story™ Formula is necessary. Unfortunately, the term "Social Story" has been used to describe many forms of intervention that do not adhere to Gray's guidelines. One of the most high-risk and common diversions from the accepted form has been the tendency to write a list of rules or expectations and label it a "Social Story."

For example, Ms. Guess wrote what she thought was a Social Story for one student who had difficulty during assemblies at school:

When I go to an assembly, I will stay with my class, pay attention, use my best inside voice, and keep quiet. If I need to go to the bathroom, I should ask before the assembly starts.

This approach fails to describe elements important to an understanding of the situation. Worse, such an approach may increase the anxiety level of the learner, who now feels pressure to adhere to a list of rules, yet has not received assistance in understanding her social environment.

CARTOONING

Another type of visual support combines words with simple drawings in order to explain a social concept. This approach is referred to as cartooning. Comic Strip Conversations™, an application of cartooning developed by Carol Gray, are a modification of the Social Story™ using simple figures and symbols in a comic strip format (1994). The Comic Strip Conversation™ is used to process a situation in which the student participated and to brainstorm alternative behaviors (Pierson & Glaeser, 2005). Missed social information is provided through a concrete visual representation of thought, often incorporating a "thought bubble" as seen in published comic strips. The conversation may be written by an individual on the spectrum or by an adult helper.

Research Support

While research supports the use of visually based interventions for individuals with ASD, few studies have been conducted on cartooning (e.g., Rogers & Myles, 2001). However, recent investigations have examined the effectiveness of a related element, thought bubbles. In two studies with children ages 5 through 18, Wellman et al. (2002) found that thought bubbles improved the performance on tasks requiring an understanding of beliefs and feelings. Another study found that three 3-year-olds with autism were able to represent the mental states (awareness of thoughts and feelings) of others on a false-belief task when given the visual support of a thought bubble (Kerr & Durkin, 2004). This is especially important because it is well established that children do not begin to develop this skill until the age of 4.

Considerations for Incorporating Cartooning

Cartooning interventions provide social information in a format that allows reflection time as opposed to real-time social interactions. Further, cartooning is inexpensive and may be used across a variety of settings (Rogers & Myles, 2001). Not only can cartooning increase the social understanding of the individual with ASD, but the process of cartooning assists the participating adult in understanding the perspective of that individual and, therefore, may provide invaluable insight for additional intervention. A collection of cartoons may be created and kept available for review and discussion in a variety of settings (Glaeser, Pierson, & Fritschman, 2003).

STRUCTURED TEACHING

In the 1960s, the founder of Treatment and Education of Autistic and Communication handi-capped Children (TEACCH), Schopler, conducted a series of studies to refute the theory that parents, especially cold and rejecting mothers, were causing autism in their children (Mesibov et al., 2004). Not surprisingly, Schopler found that parents were being scape-goated. In addi-tion to this important insight, his research confirmed the role of cognitive and perceptual fac-tors in autism. From this series of studies grew the principles of TEACCH, including respect for the culture of autism and family collaboration (Mesibov et al.).

TEACCH, now a statewide program in North Carolina, was designed to address the needs of individuals with autism (Mesibov et al., 2004). Eric Schopler founded the program, and Gary Mesibov later became its director. The TEACCH program has led in the development and use of structure and visual supports for individuals with autism.

Structured Teaching, a critical element of TEACCH, is grounded in an understanding of the cognitive and behavioral characteristics of autism. Thus, it capitalizes on strengths such as the desire to complete a task, attention to visual details, and intense interests. The predictability of the learning environment is increased through the use of visual supports, organization, and routines (Mesibov et al.).

According to Mesibov and Shea (2006), Structured Teaching includes the following four components:

1. *Provides structured and predictable environments and activities*. The physical environment is carefully arranged to increase structure. For early learners, the entire classroom is ar-ranged strategically to minimize distractions and to create physical boundaries. Care is taken to use specific areas for certain tasks. Visual cues such as color coding, label-ing, and highlighting also provide structure. For learners who are higher functioning or older, Structured Teaching may provide quiet or safe areas in the classroom and/or areas with minimal distraction. Predictability is increased with the use of visual sched-ules that aid in transitioning from one activity to another and are used to encourage independence by decreasing the need for prompts. Predictability in the schedule has been shown to decrease anxiety for the learner (Mesibov et al., 2004).

2. *Utilizes strength in visual skills to encourage task engagement*. Because autistic individuals often possess a strength in visual processing, the use of visual supports, such as

written directions, photographs, and pictures, is an effective strategy. Visual strategies are used to increase the structure of the learning environment. These strategies include providing instructions in a visual format, maintaining a visually organized workspace, and designing materials that incorporate visual cues.

For example, structured activity systems include visual cues that help students to recognize the beginning, middle, and end of a task and to know what will happen after the task is completed. Figure 6.1 illustrates a sample of visually structured activities.

3. *Emphasizes social communication that is functional and meaningful.* TEACCH encourages the use of communication systems such as signs, pictures, and speech to facilitate expressive language.

4. *Incorporates special interests to increase motivation and encourage learning.* As discussed in Chapter 5, obsessive interests can be powerful reinforcers for individuals with ASD and maintain their effectiveness longer than are other types of reinforcers (Charlop-Christy, Kurz, & Casey, 1990). Based on this and other research support, TEACCH utilizes these powerful reinforcers to promote learning.

Visual Strategy	Description	Purpose	Examples
Visual Instructions	Written directions and/or materials that show completed product	• Provides mechanism for change in approach to task by changing written instructions • Emphasizes visual-perceptual skills and minimizes demand on language skills	• Sample of completed product • Written step-by-step instructions • Symbol or picture sequences (for young, pre-literate learners)
Visual Organization	Orderly and minimally stimulating design of materials	• Decreases anxiety • Decreases distraction • Decreases complexity of task	• Colored folders • Binder • Trays/bins • Dividers
Visual Clarity	Visually distinctive materials presented in limited numbers	• Prevents confusion • Prevents overwhelming the learner	• Color coding materials • Folding a page to remove distractions • Highlighting • Cutting and pasting items to increase the visual space between them

Figure 6.1. **Visually structured activities based on TEACCH.**

Research Support

Although research on a complex system of interventions such as TEACCH is a daunting task, a substantial body of studies exists to support the approach. Indeed, Mesibov and Shea state, "The TEACCH approach, which is based on theory, supported by empirical research, enriched by extensive clinical expertise, and notable for its flexible and person-centered support of individuals of all ages and skill levels can rightfully be considered an Evidence-Based Practice for autism" (2006, p. 19). A sample of studies supporting TEACCH is summarized in Figure 6.2.

In one study, included in Figure 6.2, researchers compared the progress of children served in a preschool program accompanied by Structured Teaching in the home setting to the progress of children receiving preschool services only. Results showed that the children who received Structured Teaching at home made more progress than those who received school programming only. The researchers also found that receiving two different forms of intervention (Structured Teaching at home and standard preschool services) did not prevent students from making progress in either setting (Ozonoff & Cathcart, 1998).

Another study summarized in Figure 6.2 compared the progress of children served in a TEACCH program to the progress of children in the general education setting. The former made greater progress on measures of cognitive skills, imitation, gross-motor skills, and perceptual functioning (Panerai, Ferrante, & Zingale, 2002). While this study provides encouraging results, it is important to note that the subjects were diagnosed with intellectual disability in addition to autism; therefore, the applicability of the results to a higher functioning group on the autism spectrum is unknown.

Considerations for Incorporating Structured Teaching
The TEACCH model has been used across the United States and worldwide. No risks are associated with the use of this model in serving individuals on the autism spectrum. TEACCH is founded on research-based principles and is appropriately considered to be an evidence-based practice.

TEACCH Component	Studies That Address the Component
Structuring the environment and activities to reduce distress, confusion, disorganization, and overstimulation	Ferguson, Myles, & Hagiwara, 2005; Marcus, Lansing, Schopler, Andrews, & Schopler, 1978; Ozonoff & Cathcart, 1998; Panerai, Ferrante, & Zingale 2002; Rutter & Bartak, 1973; Schopler, Brehm, Kinsbourne, & Reichler, 1971; Short, 1984; Van Bourgondien, Reichle, & Schopler, 2003
Utilizing strength in visual skills to encourage task engagement	Boucher & Lewis, 1989; Bryan & Gast, 2000; Dettmer, Simpson, Myles, & Ganz, 2000; Dooley, Wilczenski, & Torem, 2001; Hagiwara & Myles, 1999; Hume & Odom, in press; Krantz, MacDuff, & McClannahan, 1993; Krantz & McClannahan, 1998; MacDuff, Krantz, & McClannahan, 1993; Marcus, Lansing, Schopler, Andrews, & Schopler, 1978; Massey & Wheeler, 2000; Mesibov, Browder, & Kirkland, 2002; Morrison, Sainato, Benchaaban, & Echo, 2002; Ozonoff & Cathcart, 1998; Panerai, Ferrante, & Zingale, 2002; Pierce & Schreibman, 1994; Rogers & Myles, 2001; Sarokoff, Taylor, & Poulson, 2001; Schmit, Alper, Raschke, & Ryndak, 2000; Short, 1984; Stromer, Kimball, Kinney, & Taylor, 2006; Thiemann & Goldstein, 2001
Emphasizing social communication that is functional and meaningful	Aldred, Green, & Adams, 2004; Carr, Binkhoff, Kologinsky, & Eddy, 1978; Carr & Durand, 1985; Charlop-Christy, Carpenter, Le, LeBlanc, & Kellet, 2002; Durand & Merges, 2001; Foley & Staples, 2003; Ganz & Simpson, 2004; Kiernan, 1983; Magiati & Howlin, 2003; Marcus, Lansing, Schopler, Andrews, & Schopler, 1978; Ozonoff & Cathcart, 1998; Panerai, Ferrante, & Zingale, 2002; Schwartz, Garfinkle, & Brauer, 1998; Short, 1984; Van Bourgondien, Reichle, & Schopler, 2003
Incorporating special interests to increase motivation and encourage learning	Baker, 2000; Baker, Koegel & Koegel, 1998; Boyd, 2005; Charlop-Christy & Haymes, 1996, 1998; Charlop-Christy, Kurtz, & Casey, 1990; Delprato, 2001; Hung, 1978; Keeling, Myles, Gagnon, & Simpson, 2003; Marcus, Lansing, Schopler, Andrews, & Schopler, 1978; Ozonoff & Cathcart, 1998; Short, 1984; Sugai & White, 1986; Van Bourgondien, Reichle, & Schopler, 2003; Wolery, Kirk, & Gast, 1985

Figure 6.2. Sample of studies that support the TEACCH approach.

PRIMING

Priming is a technique used to help autistic individuals by making the environment more structured and predictable. Essentially, priming involves preparing a person through exposure to a situation or skill in a safe setting in advance. Sakai (2005) outlines the following steps to priming as used with children on the autism spectrum.

1. *Explanation.* Describe the schedule of events.
2. *Visual aids.* Use picture schedules, cartooning, or written lists.

3. *Schedule.* Use a timeline and stick to it.
4. *Reward.* Tell about the reward or negotiate what will be received at the end for reasonable compliance, or "going with the program."

Adapted with permission from *Finding Our Way* (p. 44), by K. Sakai, 2005. Shawnee Mission, KS: AAPC Publishing.

For example, in order to prepare their daughter Lauren for a school trip to the museum, her parents can describe the sequence of events (e.g., ride bus from school, see exhibits, eat lunch at museum, see more exhibits, ride bus home). Lauren's parents may then show her photographs of a bus and a museum the night before a school field trip to the museum and review behavioral expectations. For example, Lauren's parents can explain, "It is okay to talk and sing on the bus but not in the museum." In this situation, her parents could also talk about the museum exhibit so that their daughter will have meaningful comments to share the following day. Exposing Lauren to the photographs helps to prepare her for this activity and the change in the typical school schedule. Once the schedule has been discussed, it is important to adhere to it closely to make the event as predictable as possible. Last, her parents may negotiate with Lauren for rewards to be earned for a successful trip to the museum.

Research Support

Priming has been shown to be an effective method of reducing disruptive behaviors and improving class participation in children with autism (Koegel & Koegel, 1992, cited in Schreibman, Whalen, & Stahmer, 2000; Koegel, Koegel, Frea, & Green-Hopkins, 2003). One study also found increased spontaneous social interactions with peers as a result of priming (Zanolli, Daggett, & Adams, 1996). Finally, a study successfully used priming to introduce toilet training to a child with autism (Bainbridge & Myles, 1999).

In a unique study, videos were created to depict specific transitions, such as leaving the home or going shopping, from the child's visual perspective (Schreibman et al., 2000). The researchers then primed children by having them watch videos of the transitions. The children exhibited fewer behavior problems during the actual transitions and even generalized the skills to other situations. In explaining the effectiveness of this approach with children with ASD, the authors note that video draws on a known strength for visual presentation of information. Also, through the reproduction of sights and sounds, video provides a more thorough and realistic representation of events than is possible through verbal description. Finally, training is not required to benefit from videos and watching them may be reinforcing.

Considerations for Incorporating Priming

Difficulty dealing with transitions and changes is one of the most common characteristics observed in individuals on the autism spectrum. In our two sample cases, both Penny and Steve encountered problems as a result of transition and change – even a subtle difference, such as his roommate putting his backpack in a different place in the room, resulted in great distress for Steve. Zanolli et al. (1996) highlight three requirements for successful priming.

1. Priming must occur before the event using the same materials. For example, parents can read their daughter a story the night before she is expected to read and discuss it at school.
2. Demands should be reduced when priming. That is, success should be easily attained.
3. A variety of reinforcers should be available.

Priming is an effective method of preparing for upcoming events. It is much easier to intervene on the front end (antecedent/prevention) than on the back end (after problems occur). Sadly, while priming is easy to implement, it is greatly underutilized in general practice.

MODELING

Modeling is another type of visual strategy, which involves learning skills through either real-life (in vivo) or video observations. This technique is based on social learning theory, which asserts that individuals can learn by observing and then imitating the actions of others (Bandura, 1977). Different types of modeling have been described, including *direct modeling* (simply copying the model), *synthesized modeling* (combining several observations to create a new behavior), and *symbolic modeling* (copying fictional characters from television, books, etc.) (Goetz, Alexander, & Ash, 1992).

Bandura (1977) demonstrated that watching others receive consequences for their behaviors can vicariously serve to reinforce or punish the viewer. For example, if Joshua sees that others in his class receive praise for sitting at their desks, he will likely sit nicely in order to receive the reinforcer. In another example, Kim is notorious for arriving home late. One day, her parents decided to enforce harsher consequences. Kim watched as her sister, Rosie, was grounded for two weeks for arriving home late. Kim immediately began to be more punctual. In this case, Rosie's consequence served as a vicarious punisher because it reduced Kim's late-arrival behavior. These principles of social learning theory contribute to the effectiveness of modeling interventions.

Unlike these instances, individuals with ASD do not spontaneously pick up information from their environment. Modeling has been used to address this need. Video modeling (Charlop-Christy, Le, & Freeman, 2000; Stahmer, Ingersoll, & Carter, 2003) and live modeling (Stahmer et al.) have been found to be effective methods for teaching individuals with ASD new behaviors and increasing demonstration of these new skills across settings.

- *Video modeling* typically involves taping adults or children engaging in specific target behaviors. The learner subsequently watches the video several times and is then observed to see if he can demonstrate the target behaviors.
- *Video self-modeling* is an alternative to video modeling. Here the learner is first videoed performing the goal behaviors. The video is then edited to ensure that only images of the learner performing the task without prompting are depicted. The learner repeatedly views the video to learn the goal behavior.
- *Live modeling* involves the use of live performances depicting specific skills such as cooperative play or conversations. Role play can also be incorporated. After viewing the models, the learner uses a written script and substitutes for one of the models.

Research Support

Video modeling has been found to be effective for teaching skills to individuals with ASD, including:

• Play	Charlop-Christy et al., 2000; Nikopoulos & Keenan, 2004; D'Ateno, Mangiapanello, & Taylor, 2003
• Communication and conversation skills	Apple, Billingsley, & Schwartz, 2005; Charlop & Milstein, 1989; Nikopoulos & Keenan, 2003, 2004; Sherer et al., 2001; Taylor, Levin, & Jasper, 1999; Wert & Neisworth, 2003
• On-task behaviors	Lasater & Brady, 1995
• Perspective taking	Charlop & Daneshvar, 2003
• Academics	Kinney, Vedora, & Stromer, 2003
• Adaptive skills	Alcantara, 1994; Haring, Kennedy, Adams, & Pitts-Conway, 1987

Models used in these videos include other children and adults, or even the learner (i.e., video self-modeling). The use of video clips integrated within a computer program has been found to result in rapid improvements in targeted social skills (Simpson, Langone & Ayres, 2004).

The effects of live modeling have also been investigated. One study found that, used in conjunction with verbal description of others' behavior and actual practice, live modeling resulted in increased cooperative play and generalization of skills (Jahr, Eldevik, & Eikeseth, 2000). Another study compared live versus video modeling and found video to be superior (Charlop-Christy et al., 2000). Specifically, children who watched videos learned the skills more quickly. Additionally, those who watched videos generalized skills while children who were exposed to live modeling did not. The authors hypothesized that video was superior to live modeling because it reduced the amount of distracting cues – the camera automatically focused on the essential aspects. Alternatively, they proposed that television might be intrinsically reinforcing.

Considerations for Incorporating Modeling

Video modeling can be used to address a broad range of needs for children, adolescents, and adults. Given the strength of the research supporting the use of video modeling – in particular, findings of rapid skill acquisition and generalization – this technique should more often be incorporated into intervention plans. Unfortunately, the use of video tends to be an overlooked and underutilized intervention technique.

Because modeling can be highly effective, caution must be exercised in choosing what to show. For example, researchers have found that observing violent television (Coyne, Archer, & Eslea, 2003; Hughes & Hasbrouck, 1996) and playing video games with violent themes (Sherry, 2001) resulted in increased violence in children. Alternatively, prosocial television has been found to increase positive social behaviors and reduce aggression (Mares & Woodard, 2005). Given the tendency for autistic individuals to exhibit obsessive thoughts and to experience difficulty in understanding the big picture (i.e., real consequences for violence), this caution is especially relevant for this population. Additionally, Schreibman and Ingersoll (2005) note that video modeling should not be used in isolation. It should always be coupled with real-life instruction and opportunities.

VIRTUAL ENVIRONMENTS

The use of virtual environment computer technology has been described as a promising approach to helping individuals understand the mental states of others (Moore, Cheng, McGrath, & Powell, 2005; Parsons & Mitchell, 2002). Virtual environment "(VE) technology allows construction of realistic 3D representations of real world environments which can be interacted with and explored in real time" (Cobb et al., 2002, p. 12). This technology provides a method of role playing in the safety of a computer environment. Some programs, known as collaborative virtual environments (CVE), provide opportunities for a group of people to interact in the virtual world (Moore et al.).

Research Support and Considerations for Incorporating Virtual Environments

Research to date has largely focused on the ability of those on the spectrum to use and understand the technology. The efficacy of this approach was the focus of one study. The researchers found that individuals with ASD could quickly learn how to use the computer equipment required for training (Parsons et al., 2004). Moreover, virtual environments were, in fact, seen by participants as representing reality. One study found that individuals with ASD were able to accurately identify facial expressions of computer avatars and perform tasks such as predicting emotions based on scenarios (Moore et al., 2005). The authors state that these initial results suggest that this technology may one day be useful for helping individuals with ASD.

OTHER VISUAL AND STRUCTURAL SUPPORTS

Many other visual strategies are used to provide structure and predictability for autistic individuals. Visual schedules are widely used and easy-to-implement tools that depict an individual's day or a series of activities in words and/or pictures. Mesibov, Browder, and Kirkland (2002) describe several uses for schedules, including reducing behavior problems when transitioning to new activities, facilitating independent completion of tasks, describing the sequence of activities in a day, and structuring leisure time.

Daily Schedule

Recall the example of Penny, who experienced difficulty transitioning from home to school on Mondays and after holidays. Changes in her schedule at school resulted in heightened anxiety and increased immersion in one of her obsessive interests – reading animal books. Ms. Simpson developed a daily schedule to help her with transitions (see Figure 6.3).

Because Penny's speech teacher was out sick, Ms. Simpson spoke to Penny using the schedule to create a visual representation of the change. She crossed through "speech" and wrote "library" to indicate where Penny would be in the afternoon. The schedule helped Penny to adjust to the change and made her day predictable so she could transition more smoothly to new activities.

Ms. Simpson wanted Penny to gain independence in coping with changes. To that end, she and Penny agreed on the symbol of a compass to symbolize a change in the schedule. Ms. Simpson will prepare Penny's schedule using this symbol to indicate a change. Over time, she will reduce and eventually eliminate the time spent in the morning reviewing the schedule together.

Penny's Schedule	
Date: *Monday, December 8*	
✦ Means there is a change and that's okay.	
8:00-8:15	**Morning routine:** ☐ Put away backpack ☐ Make lunch selection ☐ Check helper chart ☐ Turn in homework ☐ Take out journal
8:15-8:30	Write in journal
8:30-9:15	Math
9:15-10:00	Specials (circle one): Music Art P.E.
10:00-10:15	Restroom break
10:15-10:30	Snack and read book
10:30-11:00	Reading/Language Arts
11:00-11:30	Spelling
11:30-12:00	Lunch
12:00-12:30	Recess
12:30-1:00	Speech ✦ *Library today because Ms. Jones is out sick*
1:00-1:45	Science
1:45-2:15	Social Studies
2:15-2:30	Story time
2:30-2:45	Pack to go home
Thought for the day: *Ms. Jones is out today, but that is okay. I will go to the library instead and see Ms. Jones on my speech day when she feels well.*	

Figure 6.3. **Penny's daily schedule. Note the revision made by her teacher to reflect a change for today.**

Mini-Schedule

The mini-schedule is another type of visual schedule that can be helpful in providing structure and fostering independence. Mini-schedules depict a portion of a day and are used in conjunction with a daily schedule (Hodgdon, 1995). Returning to the example of Penny, to assist her in lunch time routines, Ms. Simpson gave her a mini-schedule that listed events that would occur: wash hands, wait in line, eat with the class, and clean tray. Penny was able to follow the schedule independently. Similarly, Penny's parents developed a morning mini-schedule that depicted her daily routine at home. It included tasks such as getting dressed, brushing teeth, and ended with putting away her backpack at school (see Figure 6.4). Because the morning was structured and visually represented in a schedule, Penny was able to successfully follow the list without adult supervision.

Check	Activity
☐	Wash face
☐	Eat breakfast
☐	Brush teeth
☐	Get dressed
☐	Get backpack
☐	Watch TV until 7:40
☐	Put backpack away at school

😊 I followed my list.

😐 I followed my list all by myself (no reminders).

Figure 6.4. **Penny's weekday mini-schedule.**

Schedules can also be used to structure leisure time (Mesibov et al., 2002). This may take many forms. For example, Penny's parents could set aside a block of reward time as a potential re-inforcer. Penny would be instructed to select an activity and write it into her home schedule. She will earn reward time when she successfully completes the task. Alternatively, her parents could create a mini-schedule for unstructured time and Penny could list the sequence of activities that she would accomplish during that block (e.g., complete homework, eat snack, watch television).

Power Card Strategy

A unique visual strategy, Power Cards, employs a child's special interests to teach skills (Gagnon, 2001). This technique was developed based on the principles of priming and modeling discussed earlier in this chapter. Essentially, a brief story or "script" is written that incorporates characters based on an area of high interest or an identifiable hero. The character in the story resolves a problem or demonstrates a specific skill (modeling) related to the behavior to be addressed. The rationale for the skill as well as key points to remember are provided in the script, and a Power Card is created based on this information.

The Power Card is approximately the size of a standard note card or a trading card. One side contains pictures or other visuals. The other side of the card contains a brief summary and list of key elements for solving a similar problem or demonstrating a similar skill. Encouraging notes are also included (see Figure 6.5). An adult reviews the script (priming) prior to an activity and then the Power Card is presented as a visual reminder of the steps to follow.

Sam

Sam is a highly intelligent sixth-grade student with a diagnosis of Asperger Syndrome. Sam hopes one day to attend Harvard and often speaks of this plan to anyone willing to listen. But even though Sam is intelligent, he has developed few organizational strategies. Specifically, he doesn't ask questions about course requirements and therefore often fails to turn in assignments on time. The following scenario and POWER CARD were introduced to Sam by his mother to provide him with organizational strategies.

A Harvard Student
by Becky Heinrichs

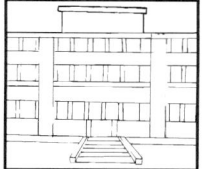

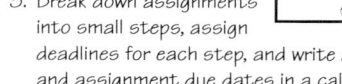

1. Take class notes and write all assignments in a calendar.
2. Ask questions when you don't understand.
3. Break down assignments into small steps, assign deadlines for each step, and write all deadlines and assignment due dates in a calendar.

Dave is proud to be a student at Harvard. He spent many hours studying throughout middle school and high school so he could achieve his dream. He always had difficulty with organization and relied on his mother to keep track of course requirements, paperwork, and due dates. When Dave got to Harvard, he realized that he was having difficulty with organization. He scheduled a meeting with his English professor and explained his problems to him and received the following advice:

1. *Take class notes and write all assignments in a calendar.*
2. *Ask questions when you don't understand.*
3. *Break down assignments into small steps, assign deadlines for each step, and write all deadlines and assignment due dates in a calendar.*

You do not have to wait to get to Harvard to practice these three steps. Dave now knows that he would have enjoyed middle school and high school much more if he would have tried these things earlier.

***Figure 6.5.* Example Power Card.**

From *Power Cards: Using Special Interests to Motivate Children and Youth with Asperger Syndrome and Autism* (pp. 47-48), by E. Gagnon, 2001, Shawnee Mission, KS: AAPC Publishing. Copyright 2001 by AAPC. Adapted and used with permission.

Personal Digital Assistant

A personal digital assistant (PDA) is a small computer that incorporates a calendar, task list, and date book. These visual devices can help depict daily schedules and tasks and remind the user of important events through the use of audible and visual alarms. As such, they can help individuals to function more independently. Due to their general widespread use, PDAs may be used by individuals on the spectrum without attracting undue notice.

Timers, T-Charts, and Checklists

Other tools that provide structure and visual support are widely used in practice. While there is currently no research on these strategies, many build on a known strength for individuals on the spectrum – visual processing. The following is a brief description of these techniques.

- *Timers* are effective for some individuals who have difficulty remaining on task or transitioning. Some companies make special timers that are visual in nature; however, traditional auditory timers that make a sound when the set time has elapsed are also effective.

  Timers can be used to indicate when an activity change will occur. For example, the timer may sound when there are five minutes remaining before the next task is due to begin. This warning serves to make the upcoming change more predictable and less challenging for those who need high levels of structure. Additionally, timers can be a helpful way of promoting on-task behavior. Use of a timer may become a part of the daily structure and provide a cue of the behavior expected during a given interval of time.

- T-charts are a helpful way of depicting contrasting information such as "kind/unkind words," "things you say to teachers/peers," and "home/school topics." The chart can be amended as new skills are learned or incidents occur.

  Simple lists can serve a similar purpose. For example, a running list can be kept of "sensitive topics," "things that we run out of," or "words that mean the same thing." Figures 6.6 and 6.7 depict examples of common formats for charts.

Kind words	Rude words
☺	☹
Good job! Great idea Nice job Awesome Yeah	So what You're stupid That was dumb That stinks Duh!

Figure 6.6. Kind versus rude words.

P.E. & Gym

Break & Snack time

Complete & Finished

Ms. Wells & Substitute Teacher

Recess & Outside

Figure 6.7. **List of words that mean the same thing.**

- *Checklists* are essentially mini-schedules that can be useful memory tools for a variety of purposes. For example, a bathroom routine or criteria for determining when the kitchen is clean may be put in checklist form. Reinforcers can even be included as an item on a checklist (see Figure 6.8) and can be delivered by an adult or the user herself (self-reinforcement). The latter strengthens the ability of schedules to build independence, always an important consideration.

Check	Activity
☐	Put away backpack
☐	Make lunch selection
☐	Complete helper chart
☐	Turn in homework
☐	Take out journal
☐	Pick reward from your menu 

Figure 6.8. **Penny's morning routine checklist.**

It is often helpful to put other important information in writing and make it accessible. For example, teachers can write down specific rules for an activity, such as walking instead of running in the hallway, and quickly review them prior to students leaving the classroom. When coupled with reinforcement, this type of intervention can be very effective. Information can even be written on small, portable "cue" cards.

For example, Penny's speech therapist may write down prompts for starting a conversation on a card. Penny can take the card with her to recess or the cafeteria and refer to it as needed. Before starting a class discussion, Penny's teacher can place a card on her desk with a brief list of participation rules (raise hand and wait to be called on, make on-topic remark, do not say mean things about others' comments). When the class starts an independent assignment, her teacher can place a card indicating the rules for this activity (raise your hand for help, do not speak with your neighbor, and work hard).

In summary, visual cues are very helpful for creating structure and predictability and facilitating independence.

Research Support

Visual schedules have been shown to (a) increase the speed of transitions (Dettmer, Simpson, Myles, & Ganz, 2000); (b) decrease behavior problems during transitions (Dettmer et al.; Dooley, Wilczenski, & Torem, 2001); (c) increase on-task behaviors (Bryan & Gast, 2000); (d) increase independence (Bryan & Gast; Kranz, MacDuff, & McClannahan, 1993; Pierce & Schreibman, 1994); and (e) facilitate following a routine (Clarke, Dunlap, & Vaughn, 1999). One study found schedules to help individuals to self-select and independently engage in leisure activities (Krantz, MacDuff, & McClannahan, 1993).

To date, one study has been conducted on Power Cards (Keeling, Myles, Gagnon, & Simpson, 2003). By using the Power Card technique, the researchers were successful in teaching sportsmanship skills to a young girl with autism. Generalization of the skill was also observed.

Finally, one case study explored the use of a PDA with an adolescent with AS. The researchers found that the device increased independent task completion at home and school (Ferguson, Myles, & Hagiwara, 2005).

Considerations for Incorporating Visual and Structural Supports

Visual schedules can be very helpful when used properly. Unfortunately, they are not always well designed and/or implemented. Necessary considerations include location/accessibility of the schedule, literacy skills of the user, and training needed for optimal use of the schedule. At times, a student's schedule is nothing more than a class schedule mounted on a bulletin board across the room. This does not meet the criteria for a visual schedule referred to in this discussion. Ideally, the schedule is individualized and easily available to a student. Mesibov, Browder, and Kirkland (2002) recommend that the literacy skills of the user be considered when developing a schedule. Schedules may be presented using objects, pictures or symbols, or written words depending on the user's reading level. Finally, individuals need to be taught how to use visual schedules.

Reviewing the schedule daily, especially when there are significant changes, can be an effective method of reducing behavior problems. One of the most common mistakes we have observed is for the schedule to be underutilized or even discontinued because the student does not appear to need it. Most adults use a calendar to record important appointments. Regardless of how well this strategy works, they never stop using it. In short, *visual schedules should be individualized, amended, and not discontinued.*

While the Power Card strategy builds on established techniques such as priming and modeling, research is sparse but positive. Similarly, the use of other visual strategies appears beneficial; however, such strategies have not yet undergone scientific scrutiny.

APPLICATION OF THE ZIGGURAT MODEL

Steve's Structure and Visual/Tactile Support Interventions

Increased structure and the use of visual supports were recommended largely to address academic concerns. Steve's sponsor, Nicole, realized that Steve's grades were not likely to improve without more structure (see Figure 6.9).

In order to effectively communicate with Steve, she provided a detailed written description of her recommendations. Additionally, when possible, she showed Steve examples. She suggested that Steve buy a PDA or use a detailed paper calendar to record daily reading and homework assignments in addition to dates of tests and projects. To illustrate, Nicole shared her calendar with Steve and gave him a pamphlet instructing him on how to effectively use a calendar. She said that he should schedule or block off time each day to study while ensuring that across the week, adequate time was allotted for each subject. Nicole recommended that, while studying, Steve create a running list of questions to ask his professor or teaching assistant. Additionally, she suggested that Steve allocate plenty of time before tests to meet with his professors and teaching assistants. Finally, she also taught him to include time to reward himself after studying.

ZIGGURAT WORKSHEET

BEHAVIOR/AREAS OF CONCERN Social, Restricted Patterns of Behavior, Sensory, Cognitive, Emotional Vulnerability	FOR SPECIFIC INTERVENTION PLAN (Operationalized Behaviors)	SELECTED UCC ITEMS	CHECK ALL THAT APPLY		
			A	B	C
	② ② ②	#1 Has difficulty recognizing the feelings and thoughts of others (mindblindness) #4 Lacks tact or appears rude #5 Has difficulty making or keeping friends #8 Tends to be less involved in group activities #12 Expresses strong need for routine or sameness #18 Has problems handling transition and change	#41 Responds in an unusual manner to sounds #52 Displays poor problem-solving skills #53 Has poor organizational skills #60 Has attention problems #76 Is easily stressed #89 Has difficulty managing stress and/or anxiety			
Sensory and Biological	Sensory and Biological Intervention:	• Use noise-canceling headphones while studying and soft earplugs on days when roommate has to wake early. • Make an appointment with a doctor at the student health center to discuss medications for your symptoms of anxiety and attention problems. • Try to sign up for early morning or late evening classes where class size is typically smaller. • Get involved in regular physical activities to help keep the mind/body alert prior to studying and attending lectures. • Prior to attending large lecture classes, take time to relax and prepare yourself by taking deep breaths and reminding yourself that you can handle the crowd for the duration of class. Arrive to class early and select a seat away from "traffic." If you need to, you can take a quick break.	✓		
	Underlying Characteristics Addressed:	#41 Responds in an unusual manner to sounds #60 Has attention problems #76 Is easily stressed			
Respectful Reinforcement	Reinforcement Intervention:	• Develop a self-reinforcement system. You will need to monitor your own progress on specific goals (e.g., study goals, academic goals, and social goals). For example, reward yourself with a timed game of chess on the Internet after you finish reading a chapter. • Join clubs in your area of interests such as movie club, or chess club, in order to provide yourself with rewarding social opportunities. • Tell yourself that you have done a good job after you notice a minor change in your dorm room and handle it without complaining.		✓	✓
	Underlying Characteristics Addressed:	#5 Has difficulty making or keeping friends #8 Tends to be less involved in group activities #12 Expresses strong need for routine or sameness #52 Displays poor problem-solving skills #53 Has poor organizational skills #60 Has attention problems #76 Is easily stressed			

Figure 6.9. Ziggurat worksheet for Steve's global intervention.

ZIGGURAT WORKSHEET

Structure & Visual/Tactile Supports		✓	✓	✓
	Structure & Visual/Tactile Support Intervention:			
	• Purchase small handheld computer (PDA) or paper calendar. Record all assignments and tests. Schedule time to study each day. Schedule time to meet with professor or assistant before tests. Review schedule daily. *Note.* This intervention applies to multiple levels. • Schedule reinforcement time after tasks are completed. • Make written notes of questions to ask teaching assistant or professor when attending office hours. • Review list of relaxation/coping skills (provided) when feeling upset. • Place items (clothing, book bag, etc.) in the same location to avoid losing them.			
	Underlying Characteristics Addressed:			
	#52 Displays poor problem-solving skills #53 Has poor organizational skills #76 Is easily stressed			

Figure 6.9. Ziggurat worksheet for Steve's global intervention (continued).

To address anxiety, Nicole and Steve reviewed several relaxation skills and created a list of ideas to help when Steve is stressed or anxious. This list, written on Steve's Ziggurat Worksheet, states:

> Prior to attending large lecture classes, take time to relax and prepare yourself by taking deep breaths and reminding yourself that you can handle the crowd for the duration of class. Arrive to class early and select a seat away from "traffic." If you need to, you can take a quick break.

Last, Nicole gave Steve a list of strategies to help him keep organized. Because he tends to lose things, she suggested that he create labels to indicate a specific place for his belongings. These and other suggestions are included on the Ziggurat Worksheet as illustrated below:

- Make written notes of questions to ask teaching assistant or professor when attending office hours.
- Review list of relaxation/coping skills (provided) when feeling upset.
- Place items (clothing, book bag, and so on) in the same location to avoid losing them.

Penny's Structure and Visual/Tactile Support Interventions

As discussed, Penny's teacher and parents designed visual strategies to address her difficulty with transitions (see Figures 6.3 and 6.4). After reviewing the UCC, her team determined that her rude statements are likely related to mindblindness. They decided to use several visual strategies to help her to gain a better understanding of her comments and how they make others feel (see Figures 6.10 and 6.11).

First, Ms. Simpson selected a recent incident in which Penny made an insensitive comment – she told a peer that he missed an easy question. Ms. Simpson will use a Comic Strip Conversation™ to help Penny understand the thoughts and feelings of her peers. Because Penny is not able to read social cues, the intervention team realized that she may not know which words are considered kind or unkind. Therefore, her parents and school staff plan to help Penny to create a T-chart to depict these categories (see Figure 6.6 for an example). A list will be kept and updated as kind and unkind words occur in Penny's environment (peers, movies, etc.).

ZIGGURAT WORKSHEET

BEHAVIOR/AREAS OF CONCERN	FOR SPECIFIC INTERVENTION PLAN (Operationalized Behaviors)	SELECTED UCC ITEMS	CHECK ALL THAT APPLY — A	B	C
Social, Restricted Patterns of Behavior, Sensory Differences, Emotional Vulnerability	① ② ③	#1 Difficulty recognizing the feelings and thoughts of others (mindblindness) #4 Lacks tact or appears rude #5 Difficulty making or keeping friends #8 Tends to be less involved in group activities #14 Has eccentric or intense preoccupations/absorption in own unique interests #18 Has difficulty handling transition and change #25 Has difficulty with rules of conversation #47 Seeks activities that provide touch, pressure, or movement #66 Resists or refuses handwriting tasks #77 Appears to be depressed or sad #85 Has low frustration tolerance	✓		
Sensory and Biological — Sensory and Biological Intervention:	• Seek consultation from the occupational therapist (OT) to assess handwriting, including sensory factors and hand fatigue. • Provide Penny with a sensory diet with direction of an OT to help address anxious or agitated behaviors. • Seek medical consultation regarding possible need for pharmacotherapy.				
Underlying Characteristics Addressed:		#47 Seeks activities that provide touch, pressure, or movement #66 Resists or refuses handwriting tasks #77 Appears to be depressed or sad #85 Has low frustration tolerance			
Respectful Reinforcement — Reinforcement Intervention:	• Develop a positive behavior management plan to address social skills and work completion. Have Penny help to select items for a reinforcer menu. Reinforcers are earned both in home and school. Penny should have frequent opportunities to "cash in" by selecting reinforcers from her menu. • Reinforce Penny for being able to categorize statements as "rude" or "kind." • Provide reinforcement for initiating work on a writing assignment without negative comments. Also reinforce her for working for an increasing length of time. • Reinforce social success by pairing social interaction with a well-established reinforcer. For example, arrange an opportunity to create and present a project on praying mantises to the third grade during their unit on insects. • Develop a token reinforcement system to address transitioning to school. Use alligator or other favorite animal stamps in Penny's token reinforcer system. Parents will provide Penny with a visual checklist/schedule for the morning routine and transition to school. Make the last item on the checklist a school task (e.g., put backpack away). Reinforce Penny at school for following checklist/schedule. Provide additional reinforcement for following the schedule independently. *Note.* This intervention applies to multiple levels.		✓	✓
Underlying Characteristics Addressed:		#4 Lacks tact or appears rude #5 Difficulty making or keeping friends #8 Tends to be less involved in group activities #14 Has eccentric or intense preoccupations/absorption in own unique interests #25 Has difficulty with rules of conversation #77 Appears to be depressed or sad			

Figure 6.10. Ziggurat worksheet for Penny's global intervention.

ZIGGURAT WORKSHEET

Structure & Visual/Tactile Supports	Structure & Visual/Tactile Support Intervention:	✓	✓	✓
	• Create visual chart "Rude versus kind words." Update as kind/unkind words occur and keep a copy at home and in school. • Use a Comic Strip Conversation to help illustrate the thoughts and feelings of others in the context of a problem situation. For example, teach Penny to recognize the response of others to her comments. *Note.* This intervention applies to multiple levels. • Parents will provide Penny with a visual checklist/schedule for the morning routine and transition to school (see Reinforcement level for description). • Provide Penny with a weekly schedule to increase predictability.		✓	
	Underlying Characteristics Addressed:	✓		
	#1 Difficulty recognizing the feelings and thoughts of others (mindblindness) #4 Lacks tact or appears rude #5 Difficulty making or keeping friends #18 Has difficulty handling transition and change #85 Has low frustration tolerance			

Figure 6.10. Ziggurat worksheet for Penny's global intervention (continued).

ZIGGURAT WORKSHEET

BEHAVIOR/AREAS OF CONCERN	FOR SPECIFIC INTERVENTION PLAN (Operationalized Behaviors)	SELECTED UCC ITEMS	CHECK ALL THAT APPLY		
			A	B	C
Class disruption	⊛ Says, "I don't have to do this work" ⊛ Insults peers ⊛ Does not complete writing tasks	#1 Mindblindness #4 Lacks tact #16 Unmotivated by customary rewards #18 Difficulty with transition and change #33 Gives false impression of understanding more than she does #63 Has difficulty understanding the connection between behavior and consequences #66 Resists handwriting #85 Low frustration tolerance #88 Difficulty understanding own and others' emotions #89 Difficulty managing stress and anxiety	✓		
[Sensory and Biological]	Sensory and Biological Intervention: • Seek consultation from the occupational therapist (OT) to assess handwriting, including sensory factors and hand fatigue • Provide Penny with a sensory diet with direction of an OT to help address anxious or agitated behaviors. • Provide a calming sensory activity prior to giving lengthy writing task. • Teach Penny to recognize body cues that indicate stress or frustration (muscle tension, heart rate, breathing pattern, etc.). • Teach Penny strategies to address her stress and frustration (e.g., engage in sensory calming strategy; ask for help, take slow, deep breaths, etc.). *Note.* This intervention applies to multiple levels.		✓	✓	
	Underlying Characteristics Addressed:	#66 Resists handwriting #85 Low frustration tolerance #88 Difficulty understanding own and others' emotions #89 Difficulty managing stress and anxiety			
	Reinforcement Intervention: • Develop a positive behavior management plan to address social skills and work completion. Have Penny help to select items for a reinforcer menu. Reinforcers are earned both in home and school. Penny should have frequent opportunities to "cash in" by selecting reinforcers from her menu. • Reinforce Penny for being able to categorize statements as "rude" or "kind." • With the assistance of a speech therapist, develop a card that has rules for class discussion. During a class discussion, give Penny a card – one side is green (with rules for appropriate class discussion; no insults, on-topic remarks, etc.) and the other side is red (with a list of appropriate listening behaviors). Begin each class discussion with the green side up. Turn the card to red if Penny makes an inappropriate contribution. Remove card at the end of class discussion. Reinforce Penny for following the rules on either side of the card. *Note.* This intervention applies to multiple levels. • Provide reinforcement for initiating work on a writing assignment without negative comments. Also reinforce her for working for an increasing amount of time. • Develop a token reinforcement system to address transitioning to school. Use alligator or other favorite animal stamps in Penny's token reinforcer system. Parents will provide Penny with a visual checklist/schedule for the morning routine and transition to school. Make the last item on the checklist a school task (e.g., put backpack away). Reinforce Penny at school for following checklist/schedule. Provide additional reinforcement for following the schedule independently. *Note.* This intervention applies to multiple levels. • Provide Penny with a strong reinforcer on Mondays when she arrives to school with her completed morning home checklist.		✓	✓	✓
[Respectful Reinforcement]	Underlying Characteristics Addressed:	#4 Lacks tact #16 Unmotivated by customary rewards #18 Difficulty with transition and change #66 Resists handwriting #85 Low frustration tolerance			

Figure 6.11. Ziggurat worksheet for Penny's specific intervention.

ZIGGURAT WORKSHEET

				✓
			✓	✓
		✓	✓	
Structure & Visual/ Tactile Supports	Structure & Visual/ Tactile Support Intervention:	• Create visual chart "Rude versus kind words." Update as kind/unkind words occur and keep a copy at home and in school. • Videotape a same-age class during discussion time. Prior to taping, remind all students of behavioral expectations. Show Penny the tape, stopping to view specific skills (raising hand, refraining from negative comments when peers answer incorrectly, etc.) and to explore facial expressions and gestures of the peer models. Practice skills with Penny and reinforce. Provide Penny with a visual reminder of class discussion rules and reinforce her for successfully following them. • Use red/green class discussion card (see Reinforcement level for description). • Create a visual chart for tracking her progress on earning rewards. For example, use a drawing of a bug. Let Penny color in a segment each time she earns a reinforcer for being on-task or making appropriate comments in class. Penny may select a reinforcer from the menu when the drawing is completely colored. • Use a Comic Strip Conversation to help illustrate the thoughts and feelings of others in the context of a problem situation. For example, teach Penny to recognize the response of others to her comments. *Note.* This intervention applies to multiple levels. • Parents will provide Penny with a visual checklist/schedule for the morning routine and transition to school (see Reinforcement level for description). • Provide Penny with a weekly schedule to increase predictability.			
	Underlying Characteristics Addressed:	#1 Mindblindness #4 Lacks tact #16 Unmotivated by customary rewards #18 Difficulty with transition and change #33 Gives false impression of understanding more than he/she actually does #63 Has difficulty understanding the connection between behavior and consequences #88 Difficulty understanding own and others' emotions			

Figure 6.11. Ziggurat worksheet for Penny's specific intervention (continued).

Understanding the power of video modeling, the team also decided to create a short video for Penny depicting appropriate behavior during class discussions. After first reviewing behavioral expectations with her students, Ms. Simpson will ask a colleague to help record a class discussion. She will then review the video with Penny and practice explicit skills. While watching the tape, Ms. Simpson will point out subtle aspects of interaction, including facial expressions, gestures, absence of negative comments, and use of non-literal language.

Before class discussions, Ms. Simpson will give Penny a small card with one side colored green and the other red. The card, developed with the assistance of Penny's speech therapist, will contain a brief list of class discussion rules to help Penny to be more successful. The green side will contain a list of rules for sharing ideas and being polite to others while the red side of the card will contain a list of appropriate listening behaviors. Ms. Simpson will permit Penny to participate in class discussions provided that she follows the rules listed on the green side. If Penny breaks a rule, the card will be turned over to the red side, and Penny will not be allowed to share comments for the remainder of the activity but will be able to participate in the discussion by listening to others. Using a visual reward chart and menu, Ms. Simpson will provide Penny with praise and reinforcement for following the rules on *either* side of the card. In this way, Penny will be successful as a talker and/or listener.

SUMMARY

In the next chapter we will see that careful consideration must be given to the match between task requirements and the characteristics and needs of the individual expected to perform the task. Because all interventions at the Structure and Visual/Tactile Supports level are a direct response to the needs of those on the spectrum, these interventions may also be considered to be Task Demand interventions. They are set apart on a distinct level in the ZM because of their importance. The predictability and information that structure and visual supports make available to those on the spectrum are critical aspects of every comprehensive intervention plan.

CHAPTER HIGHLIGHTS

- *Structure and Visual/Tactile Supports is the third level of the Intervention Ziggurat. This level draws on the strength of visual processing and addresses the need for order and routine that is fundamental to individuals on the spectrum.*

- *Social Stories™ are an individualized visual tool for teaching relevant social information and appropriate responses.*

- *Comic Strip Conversations™ are a modification of Social Stories™ using simple figures and symbols. The Comic Strip Conversation™ is used to process a situation in which the student participated and to brainstorm alternative behaviors.*

- *In Structured Teaching, an element of TEACCH, the predictability of the learning environment is increased through the use of visual supports, organization, and routines.*

- *Priming involves preparing a person by pre-exposure to a situation or skill in a safe setting.*

- *Modeling is a type of visual strategy that involves learning skills through either real-life or video observations.*

- *Video is a highly effective and underutilized visual support for individuals on the spectrum.*

- *Visual schedules are widely used and easy-to-implement tools that depict an individual's day or a series of activities in words and/or pictures.*

- *The Power Card technique, which employs a child's special interests to teach skills, was developed based on the principles of priming and modeling.*

7 Task Demands and Positive Environment

"In the middle of every difficulty lies opportunity."

– Albert Einstein

Barney is an 8-year-old boy with on the spectrum. His family is flying to Florida to go to Disney World. Barney's parents are concerned that the trip will be difficult for him. He has never flown before and has difficulty coping in large crowds. Barney sometimes flaps his arms when he is nervous or excited. He frequently uses a loud voice, and his parents are concerned that other people will not respond with patience and kindness to their son. Barney does not like to be touched or bumped. His parents anticipate that a crowded airplane and lines at Disney World may overwhelm him. Last, Barney has a difficult time managing his feelings. Any changes in routine are particularly distressing to him.

The fourth tier of the Intervention Ziggurat, Task Demands and Positive Environment, is the last to be completed to set the stage for skill development. It is critical to consider the level of difficulty of a task. Every activity may be considered to be a task with varying levels of demands or a range of potential obstacles. Depending on the individual's characteristics, any given demand may constitute an obstacle.

It is clear that the planned trip to Disney World presents many obstacles for Barney that would not be challenging for most of his typically developing peers. The demands associated with flying on an airplane and going to an amusement park may be beyond Barney's current ability. His parents recognize that in order for Barney (and his family) to have a positive experience, they must find a way to lower the task demands – to remove the obstacles to his success.

Three essential questions are introduced in this chapter to help the reader to determine how task demands must be adjusted. Intervention on this level involves identifying skill deficits, reducing task demands, and providing necessary supports to facilitate success. To that end, the chapter discusses the importance of conducting a task analysis to identify prerequisite and component skill deficits that need to be taught. Skills to be taught should be prioritized, and the environment should be adapted to foster success. Methods for reducing the demands in seven key areas are discussed. The chapter ends by revisiting Steve and Penny and designing interventions for them on this level of the Ziggurat.

THREE ESSENTIAL QUESTIONS

The continuum of task demands was introduced in Chapter 3 and is depicted again in Figure 7.1. As illustrated, it is important to take into consideration the level of task difficulty. For example, even if students can accomplish easy tasks independently, such activities do not facilitate the learning of new information or generalization of known skills. On the other hand, when demands are excessive, they can result in failure and behavior problems. *For learning to occur, demands must fall between being too easy and too excessive, within the range known as the zone of proximal development (ZPD).*

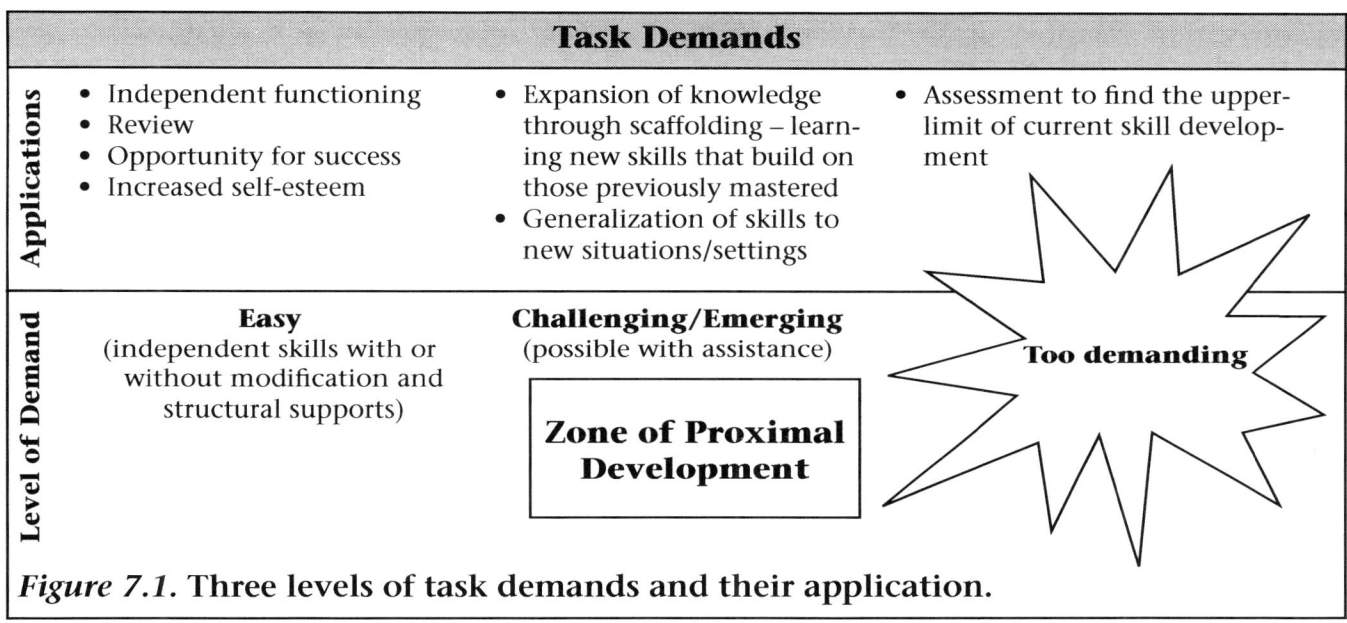

Figure 7.1. **Three levels of task demands and their application.**

Three questions must be answered in order to ensure the appropriate level of task demand.

1. Are you asking for performance of a skill that is too hard?
2. Are you asking for performance of a skill that has not been taught?
3. Are you asking for a task to be accomplished without the necessary supports?

Interventions on this level of the Intervention Ziggurat involve *identifying* prerequisite and component skill deficits (Question 1 and 2) and *reducing the demands* of a task (Question 3). Asking these questions is especially important when working with autistic students, whose areas of competence may mask underlying skill deficits. Thus, because they appear competent, teachers tend to hold the same expectations for these students as for their age-mates. For example, while working in a small group may not be hard for most 15-year-olds, it may be for a student on the spectrum. Regardless of how competent the student appears, she may not be ready because she has not yet learned basic cooperative skills (Question 1).

In contrast, while having the ability to refrain from picking her nose in public, an autistic 15-year-old might persist with this behavior because he has not been told *why* you do not pick your nose in public (because it upsets others and impacts your reputation with peers) (Question 2).

Finally, most 15-year-olds do not need to write in their weekly schedule three days in advance that their teacher will be absent and a substitute will be filling in. However, for students on the spectrum for whom change and transitions pose challenges, such preparation helps support them when the change does occur (Question 3). Placing students in situations for which they are ill prepared or poorly supported is a recipe for behavior problems.

In order to answer these three fundamental questions, it is necessary to determine the difficulty level of a task as well as the steps needed to complete it – this is known as task analysis. Determining the prerequisite skills is one form of task analysis (Question 1). If the student has not mastered all the *prerequisite skills,* the task is too difficult for him. A second form of task analysis involves identifying the *components of a skill* (Question 2). This means breaking down a task into sequential steps. If someone has the skills for a given task but has not been taught the steps to accomplish it, the demands are too high.

While the first two approaches to reducing task demands involve addressing the learner's skill level, the third involves changing some aspect of the task to meet the learner wherever he or she is. It is essential for the first two questions to be answered fully in order to identify the supports necessary to compensate for the missing prerequisite and component skills. If the necessary supports are absent (Question 3), the task demands are too high.

Answering the Questions

The following interventions from the Task Demands section of Penny's global Ziggurat Worksheet (Figure 7.2) demonstrate how the three questions were addressed.

- Ask Penny to be responsible for taking the soccer ball out on the playground and give her a visual script for how to start playing the game at recess. Teach the playground soccer rules to Penny and remind her that the "playground" rules differ from "league" rules.

- Train a peer to be Penny's "buddy" at recess. The peer will help to integrate her into ongoing play activities such as soccer.

ZIGGURAT WORKSHEET

BEHAVIOR/AREAS OF CONCERN	FOR SPECIFIC INTERVENTION PLAN (Operationalized Behaviors)	SELECTED UCC ITEMS	A	B	C
Social, Restricted Patterns of Behavior, Communication, Motor, Emotional Vulnerability	① ② ③	#1 Difficulty recognizing the feelings and thoughts of others (mindblindness) #4 Lacks tact or appears rude #5 Difficulty making or keeping friends #8 Tends to be less involved in group activities #14 Has eccentric or intense preoccupations/absorption in own unique interests #18 Has difficulty handling transition and change #25 Has difficulty with rules of conversation #47 Seeks activities that provide touch, pressure, or movement #66 Resists or refuses handwriting tasks #77 Appears to be depressed or sad #85 Has low frustration tolerance			

(CHECK ALL THAT APPLY — A, B, C columns)

Sensory and Biological	Sensory and Biological Intervention:	• Seek consultation from the occupational therapist (OT) to assess handwriting, including sensory factor and hand fatigue. • Provide Penny with a sensory diet with direction of an OT to help address anxious or agitated behaviors. • Seek medical consultation regarding possible need for pharmacotherapy.	✓		
	Underlying Characteristics Addressed:	#47 Seeks activities that provide touch, pressure, or movement #66 Resists or refuses handwriting tasks #77 Appears to be depressed or sad #85 Has low frustration tolerance			
Respectful Reinforcement	Reinforcement Intervention:	• Develop a positive behavior management plan to address social skills and work completion. Have Penny help to select items for a reinforcer menu. Reinforcers are earned both in home and school. Penny should have frequent opportunities to "cash in" by selecting reinforcers from her menu. • Reinforce Penny for being able to categorize statements as "rude" or "kind." • Provide reinforcement for initiating work on a writing assignment without negative comments. Also reinforce her for working for an increasing length of time. • Reinforce social success by pairing social interaction with a well-established reinforcer. For example, arrange an opportunity to create and present a project on praying mantises to the third grade during their unit on insects. • Develop a token reinforcement system to address transitioning to school. Use alligator or other favorite animal stamps in Penny's token reinforcer system. Parents will provide Penny with a visual checklist/schedule for the morning routine and transition to school. Make the last item on the checklist a school task (e.g., put backpack away). Reinforce Penny at school for following checklist/schedule. Provide additional reinforcement for following the schedule independently. _Note._ This intervention applies to multiple levels.		✓	✓
	Underlying Characteristics Addressed:	#4 Lacks tact or appears rude #5 Difficulty making or keeping friends #8 Tends to be less involved in group activities #14 Has eccentric or intense preoccupations/absorption in own unique interests #25 Has difficulty with rules of conversation #77 Appears to be depressed or sad			

Figure 7.2. Ziggurat worksheet for Penny's global intervention.

ZIGGURAT WORKSHEET

Structure & Visual/Tactile Supports	Structure & Visual/ Tactile Support Intervention:	• Create visual chart "Rude versus kind words." Update as kind/unkind words occur and keep a copy at home and in school. • Use a Comic Strip Conversation to help illustrate the thoughts and feelings of others in the context of a problem situation. For example, teach Penny to recognize the response of others to her comments. *Note.* This intervention applies to multiple levels. • Parents will provide Penny with a visual checklist/schedule for the morning routine and transition to school (see Reinforcement level for description). • Provide Penny with a weekly schedule to increase predictability.	✓	✓	✓
	Underlying Characteristics Addressed:	#1 Difficulty recognizing the feelings and thoughts of others (mindblindness) #4 Lacks tact or appears rude #5 Difficulty making or keeping friends #18 Has difficulty handling transition and change #85 Has low frustration tolerance			
Task Demands	Task Demand Intervention:	• The speech therapist will provide Penny with a small note card with prompts for starting a conversation with peers. Keep note cards on preferred peers and their interests. *Note.* This intervention applies to multiple levels. • Have Penny be responsible for taking the soccer ball out on the playground and give her a visual script for how to start playing the game at recess. Teach the playground soccer rules to Penny and remind her that the "playground" rules differ from "league" rules. *Note.* This intervention applies to multiple levels. • Train a peer to be Penny's "buddy" at recess. The peer will help to integrate her into ongoing play activities such as soccer.	✓	✓	
	Underlying Characteristics Addressed:	#5 Difficulty making or keeping friends #25 Has difficulty with rules of conversation #85 Has low frustration tolerance			

Figure 7.2. Ziggurat worksheet for Penny's global intervention (continued).

Because soccer is a prominent activity for fourth-graders and Penny plays in a league, the intervention team felt that encouraging this activity might help Penny interact successfully with her peers at recess and reduce the time she spends independently immersed in her current interest – bugs. A previous attempt by Ms. Simpson to involve her in soccer appeared to fail. Not recognizing that playground rules were different than league rules, Penny cried and complained that her peers were not playing fair. These interventions were designed to improve and increase Penny's successful interactions with her peers at recess.

Question #1: Are you asking for performance of a skill that is too hard (lack of prerequisite skills)?

Identifying prerequisite skills deficits is an important element in addressing task demands. Moreover, before a skill can be taught (Skills to Teach intervention), deficits must be identified. For Penny, the question is whether playing with peers at recess is too hard for her. Are prerequisite skills lacking before Penny can successfully engage in play?

Task analysis resulted in the following list of prerequisite skills for playing with peers during recess:

- Tolerate sensory input of a playground (noise, temperature)
- Know how to seek assistance
- Know how to follow unwritten and written rules
- Know how to join or start activities

The team agreed that Penny does not currently have all the prerequisite skills. While she is able to tolerate the sensory demands, seek assistance, and follow rules, she does not yet know how to join or start activities.

Now that a skill deficit has been identified, it will become a target for skills instruction discussed in Chapter 8 – Skills to Teach. As such, this intervention falls on two levels – Task Demands (identifying needed skills) and Skills to Teach (instruction in skills).

Question #2: Are you asking for performance of a skill that has not been taught (lack of component skills)?

Some skills are not necessarily too difficult, but they simply must be taught as illustrated in the following example.

Beth

Beth is an autistic kindergarten student. She loves to be around other children but has difficulty maintaining appropriate personal space. Specifically, Beth hugs her classmates, which is not uncommon at her age; however, her classmates cry because she does not let them go. Indeed, the other children have become fearful of her approaching them because they do not know how to get her to let them go.

Her teacher recognized that Beth needed to be taught a key element of hugging – letting go. At a later developmental stage it will be important to teach her whom to hug and when it is appropriate to hug. At this point, Beth is ready to learn how to hug, but she has not been taught.

In a second type of task analysis, a task or skill is broken down into its components, and the components are listed in the order in which they must occur. Because learners differ in their level of mastery of the subcomponents of a given task, awareness of the specific sub-skills allows targeted instruction.

For example, Beth's teacher broke down hugging into simple, concrete behaviors. Then she taught Beth that there were four steps to hugging: (a) Put your arms around someone; (b) gently squeeze them; (c) count to three; and (d) let go. Beth knew the first two steps; however, the final two were the key to Beth's success with this skill.

Returning to Penny, while she has the ability to follow rules (prerequisite), she has not been taught the specific "playground" rules for soccer. Furthermore, she has not been taught the concept that rules can differ based on the setting. The staff will need to perform a task analysis to identify sequential components of the skill. Identifying the missing components sets the stage for teaching the skill.

Recall Steve, the college student who confronted his roommate about the alarm clock. When Mark refused to muffle the sound of his alarm by sleeping with it under his pillow, Steve was angered at his unwillingness to "compromise." Clearly, Steve had the ability to engage in some give-and-take; however, it appears that he did not fully understand the concept. A compromise entails each side yielding in order to attain some of what they both need. Offering the option for Mark to sleep with his alarm clock under his pillow was not a realistic offer on his part (no doubt Mark would not need an alarm to wake him because he would not be able to sleep with a large clock under his head). Steve appeared to expect Mark to submit to his demands rather than having to work out an equitable solution. His mentor plans to teach him the definition of "compromise" and steps required. Once he has an understanding of the seemingly obvious meaning of compromise, he can master negotiating conflict with more success.

Question #3: Are you asking for a task to be accomplished without the necessary supports?

In contrast to addressing task demands by teaching prerequisite and component skills as described in the previous two questions, it is possible to simply reduce the demands of a task by providing adult or peer support, or by changing the task in other ways (such as shortening an assignment, providing copies of notes, etc.). This is the third way of adjusting task demands.

In many situations, some aspect of the environment must be changed in order for a student to demonstrate emerging and existing skills. Without these changes, the task demands are still too high, but with the necessary supports, it becomes possible for the individual to perform the task. In other words, supports can complement efforts to develop prerequisite and component skills by reducing the demands so learned skills can be displayed. For example, after teaching a student how to start a conversation in a therapy session, a speech therapist can write down the steps to facilitate generalization in the classroom. Having a list of steps reduces the demand of displaying this developing skill outside of the therapy setting without a therapist.

The following examples illustrate how the demands of a task may quite easily be reduced.

Joshua

Problem:
- Joshua had many friends in school but "shut down" in the cafeteria because of the noise level.

Solution:
- He could wear soft earplugs in the cafeteria, or be permitted to eat in a quieter location (classroom, picnic table outside) with a few friends.

Penny

Problem:

- Penny does not know how to initiate play.

Solution:

- Until Penny is ready to learn how to initiate play with others, her teacher could ask a few peers to play with Penny. This way, the goal of having her play with peers at recess will be accomplished by removing the one skill she currently lacked (initiating play with others).

Steve

Problem:

- Steve is quite bright, but he has difficulty writing for long periods of time. This is impacting his performance because his notes are often incomplete.

Solution:

- Steve could be allowed to type or tape record class lectures. Alternatively, his professor could provide him with copies of the lecture notes. In doing so, the demands of learning are reduced so Steve's grades will reflect his intellect rather than his ability to take good notes.

Other Task Demand Considerations

One essential aspect of the Task Demands level is providing strategies and supports to foster a positive environment. It is kind to incorporate non-contingent positives such as warm, caring relationships or including preferred interests and enjoyable activities that are not earned. All of these are included on this level.

Tasks do not occur in a vacuum. Sometimes unforeseeable aspects of the environment itself become so overwhelming that a student cannot exhibit certain skills even if the demand level has been carefully selected. That is to say, aspects of the environment can serve as antecedents that make a task too demanding. For example, the presence of a substitute teacher can temporarily impair a student's ability to perform tasks that she is otherwise capable of performing independently. Excessive noise caused by construction at work may overwhelm an individual's capacity to focus, preventing him from completing a project. In both examples, an antecedent (presence of substitute/excessive noise) resulted in increasing the demand of a task that was not otherwise too demanding.

TASK DEMAND INTERVENTIONS

As discussed above, interventions on this level take two forms: (a) identifying prerequisite and component skill deficits, and (b) reducing the demands of a task.

In the following we will look at approaches to reducing the demands of tasks. Some task demand interventions address behaviors and consequences, but most are antecedent-based. Pure task demand interventions, by nature, are considered antecedent interventions because they change events that occur before the behaviors. Changing the precipitating events sometimes results in behavior change.

To develop targeted antecedent interventions, a functional behavioral assessment should be completed as part of the ABC-I (discussed in Chapter 2). Figure 7.3 depicts Penny's ABC-I for disruptive class behaviors. The following antecedents were identified: transitions, class discussions, and written assignments. Her teacher could develop several antecedent strategies, such as providing a visual schedule or verbal reminders of transitions, giving her a list of rules to follow for class discussions, and reducing written assignments or allowing Penny to respond orally.

The key diagnostic characteristics of autism identified on the UCC – social functioning, repetitive behavior and preoccupations, communication, sensory, and associated features such as cognitive, motor, and emotional vulnerability – may be thought of as areas of demands to be addressed on this level of the Ziggurat.

Social

Participation in social activities is particularly challenging for individuals on the spectrum as it places demands in every area of functioning – communication, cognitive, emotional, sensory, and so on.

One way to decrease demands or stressors is to carefully select the participant group. Students on the autism spectrum are most often delayed in their social skills. Their interests may be dissimilar to their same-age peers' as well; therefore, they are often left out or bored when grouped only with children their age. Unfortunately, children tend to be grouped by age for social activities. According to Siegel (2003), this arrangement may present an "insurmountable challenge" for children on the spectrum.

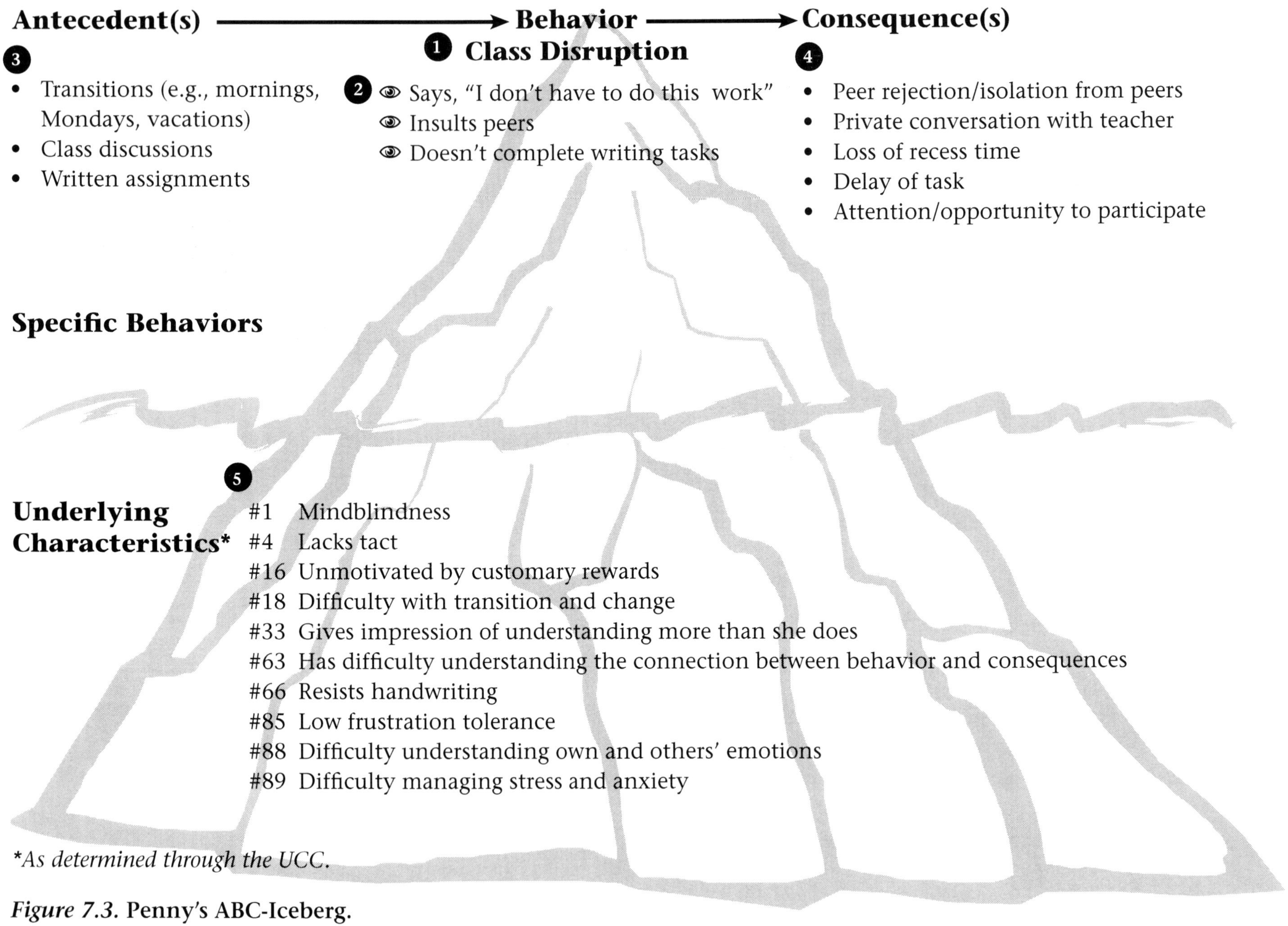

Antecedent(s) ⟶ **Behavior** ⟶ **Consequence(s)**

❶ Class Disruption

❸
- Transitions (e.g., mornings, Mondays, vacations)
- Class discussions
- Written assignments

❷
- ⓐ Says, "I don't have to do this work"
- ⓐ Insults peers
- ⓐ Doesn't complete writing tasks

❹
- Peer rejection/isolation from peers
- Private conversation with teacher
- Loss of recess time
- Delay of task
- Attention/opportunity to participate

Specific Behaviors

Underlying Characteristics*

❺
- #1   Mindblindness
- #4   Lacks tact
- #16 Unmotivated by customary rewards
- #18 Difficulty with transition and change
- #33 Gives impression of understanding more than she does
- #63 Has difficulty understanding the connection between behavior and consequences
- #66 Resists handwriting
- #85 Low frustration tolerance
- #88 Difficulty understanding own and others' emotions
- #89 Difficulty managing stress and anxiety

*As determined through the UCC.

Figure 7.3. Penny's ABC-Iceberg.

Instead, allowing children to interact with mixed-age or developmentally similar (younger) children may decrease task demands for some activities. Typically developing children, 6 years of age or older, often have developed skills for "repairing" a social interaction – the skills needed to assist others when they struggle in a social situation. For example, an older child might notice a child playing alone and take her hand to guide her through an activity, whereas younger children without the skill for repairing might move on to play with others. Consequently, having older children present may be beneficial to children on the spectrum under the age of 6.

In the following we will look at a variety of grouping formats, including peer network, circle of friends, peer buddies, play dates, and Integrated Play Groups.

Peer Network

Some studies have examined the benefits of structured peer contact. Two studies investigated the impact of peer networks on social skills in children with autism. In the first, a "network" was created by having children with ASD and their peers tutor younger children. The researchers found that students with ASD not only learned to be tutors but also benefited socially because their peers modeled good social skills (Kamps, Dugan, Potucek, & Collins, 1999).

In the second study, a small group of peers was selected to participate in structured activities such as tutoring, lunch, and recess. Training, reinforcement, and social scripts were used. The study resulted in similar positive findings with regard to social interaction (Kamps, Potucek, Lopez, Kravits, & Kemmerer, 1997).

Circle of Friends

A similar technique, known as "circle of friends," essentially creates a peer network to support a student with special needs. Peers are most often selected by asking for volunteers during a special class discussion about the target child when he or she is not present (Frederickson, Warren, & Turner, 2005). Peers often receive training to help them understand autism and can even be taught how to deal with specific behaviors.

Findings related to circle of friends are somewhat mixed. While studies have found improvements in peers' acceptance of target children as a result of this type of intervention (Frederickson & Turner, 2003; Frederickson et al., 2005), no additional benefits were observed from weekly circle-of-friends meetings (Frederickson et al.). Further, improvements in peers' level of acceptance were not sustained over time. Most disconcerting, with one exception, significant behavior changes were not observed in the target children (Frederickson & Turner; Frederickson et al.). Neither of these studies specifically examined individuals on the spectrum.

Other studies have documented improvements in behavior as a result of circle of friends, however. For example, using a circle-of-friends technique with five children with autism, Kalyva and Avramidis (2005) found significant improvements in initiation of communication as well as appropriate responses to others' initiation. Fewer unsuccessful initiations or responses to others' attempts were also noted. Gold (1994) used the same technique to aid an adult with special needs. Having a "circle" was very meaningful to the recipient, and participants enjoyed being friends with her and supporting her. Miller, Cooke, Test, and White (2003) used a similar technique called "friendship circles" with three children with mild disabilities. A significant increase in appropriate social interactions was observed during lunch for all students and during recess for two of the three.

Peer Buddies

The use of peer buddies has also been investigated. Researchers paired students on the spectrum with a buddy and taught them that buddies stay and play together and talk to one another. Appropriate social interaction increased, such as asking for objects, waiting one's turn, and looking at the speaker (Laushey & Heflin, 2000).

Play Dates

The use of structured and unstructured play dates has also been examined as an intervention technique (Koegel, Werner, Vismara, & Koegel, 2005). In the structured version, a graduate student facilitated interaction through the use of mutually reinforcing activities that involved cooperation from each child (such as cooking). No assistance was provided during unstructured play dates. The children chose their own activities. The researchers found improvements in reciprocal interactions and mood for supported play dates. It appeared that selecting intrinsically motivating activities and providing adult support reduced the demands of the task (reciprocal play) such that success could be attained.

Integrated Play Groups

Wolfberg (2003) and Wolfberg and Schuler (1993, 1999) emphasize the importance of play skills in the development of positive peer relationships and social understanding, and they designed a special model used to help facilitate these relationships – Integrated Play Groups (IPG). This model involves placing children with autism into small groups with peers who are more adept at play.

Adults assist play through monitoring and guidance. Specifically, adults first observe in order to identify the child's current ability level. Then support is provided, as necessary, consistent with the child's zone of proximal development (ZPD). For example, Wolfberg and Schuler (1999) note that a guide may first act as an interpreter by helping participants understand one another. Later the guide may model specific behaviors, provide scripts to enhance socialization, or assign roles. Adult guides work to push children a little beyond their current abilities, consistent with the ZPD, so that they learn new skills. Over time, adult support is diminished.

Results of research on IPGs are promising. In one study, Wolfberg and Schuler (1993) found that participation resulted in a reduction of stereotyped play and isolated play with an increase in social play (e.g., playing near or beside others, and sharing materials) as well as symbolic or pretend play. Moreover, skills were observed to generalize beyond the play group setting.

Wolfberg and Schuler (1999) reviewed other studies, documenting benefits, including improvements in language as well as social and pretend play in one girl with autism. Additionally, several benefits for play group participants without autism were found, such as a positive attitude and increased sensitivity to the needs of their playmates with autism. Given the support of Integrated Play Groups, Wolfberg and Schuler assert that children on the spectrum can develop pretend play skills and reduce their isolation from peers.

Peer networks, circle of friends, peer buddies, and Integrated Play Groups all help to reduce social demands. Each involves careful selection of peers who are supportive. The addition of peer support makes socialization less challenging and facilitates joining and initiating play and conversations. Additionally, all of these techniques involve structure, which adds predictability and routine, resulting in a decrease in demands. Lastly, while not specifically researched, it seems plausible that these techniques would help to increase acceptance and reduce bullying of students on the spectrum.

Considerations for Addressing Social Task Demands
Creating successful peer supports requires organization and effort, including the following:

- Responsible peers need to be selected. For school-aged individuals, teachers and counselors may provide valuable assistance in identifying appropriate peers. For adults on the spectrum, peers may be drawn from volunteer organizations, religious groups, and family friends.
- It is not enough to simply provide opportunities for peers to gather. They need sufficient training in order to *support* the target individual. This means, when age-appropriate, they should learn about autism as well as how to respond to behavioral concerns.
- Adult guides who assist with IPG require training in order to carefully monitor children and properly facilitate play.

Restricted Patterns of Behavior, Interests, and Activities

The tendency for autistic individuals to prefer predictability and routine and to be preoccupied with limited areas of interest often poses challenges in everyday life. The world is not always predictable, and routines necessarily must be adjusted. Further, others in the social environment do not always share interests in specialized areas. As a result, the tasks of daily life and social interactions often present greater demands for those on the spectrum than for their neurotypical peers, leading to stress, anxiety, and sometimes behavioral challenges.

Following are approaches to decreasing the task demands by using restricted interests and increasing predictability in order to address these specific areas of difference.

Motivation

Understanding that students on the spectrum may be highly motivated to engage in tasks or activities related to their restricted areas of interest is beneficial. When possible, classroom teachers can reduce the demands of a task by integrating these interests. Attwood (1998) refers to this as a "constructive application" of special interests (p. 96). For example, Ms. Simpson will be more successful in getting Penny to write if she permits Penny to select a topic about insects. Even math could be enhanced for Penny by incorporating her interest (e.g., word problems involving insects). Ms. Simpson can also help to facilitate Penny's peer relationships by giving her the opportunity to make class presentations on her area of interest.

Demands of Difficult Activities

Restricted interests can also be used to reduce the demands of difficult activities such as school, work, or attending a large social gathering. It is often helpful to set aside time prior to a stressful activity to engage in restricted interests. The activities may be quite calming and foster success.

Reinforcement

Additionally, as discussed in Chapter 5, restricted interests can serve as highly salient re-inforcers. Students should be permitted to select their reward prior to participating in the activity in order to use the reward as an antecedent intervention.

Transitioning

Parents and teachers often report that autistic students have difficulty transitioning from one activity to another, especially when the new activity is less preferred. For many, tran-sitioning from vacation back to school, or even from the weekend to Monday can be difficult. Another common observation is that it can be exceptionally challenging for them to stop an activity before it is complete. While it is not possible to prevent Monday from following a weekend and other transitions from occurring, the demands of transition can be reduced.

Building predictability is one effective method of decreasing the difficulty of transition. Predictability may be increased through a range of interventions.

- *Written or pictorial schedules* can effectively depict daily events and eliminate the unknown. Often a simple prompt to look at the schedule can help prevent behavior problems. The schedule can even include statements, such as "It's okay if your work is not finished" or "Incomplete work can be finished during study hall," to further reassure students.
- *Timers* can be used to visually and auditorally depict when an activity change will occur.
- *During or following transitions, tasks can be altered* to prevent problems. For example, Penny had more behavioral difficulties on Mondays and following holidays. Ms. Simpson could reduce her workload or provide more adult or peer assistance on Monday mornings (or the whole day) in order to help prevent behavior problems.

Sameness

Many individuals on the spectrum have a strong need for sameness, fostering "rigidity." As a result, they have great difficulty when required to be flexible and adjust to changes.

David and Shari

David is a 12-year-old boy on the spectrum. In his last visit with the speech therapist, he noticed that she wore her hair differently. While it was not readily apparent, he was upset by the change. He had difficulty working during the session and asked her how she would wear her hair the next time they met.

The need for routine appeared differently in Shari. Every Tuesday, she asked her teacher if it was pizza day. Even though her teacher confirmed that it was, Shari returned later and asked the same question. The questioning was rather frustrating for her teacher as it continued until Shari entered the cafeteria in the afternoon. Often, her teacher raised her voice and told Shari to sit down.

The demands of dealing with changes can be reduced by either avoiding change, when possible, or creating routine/predictability. For example, David's speech teacher can build a routine of ending the session by asking if he has any questions about their next meeting and providing factual answers. Discussions of upcoming changes will help prepare David by making the future more predictable.

Similarly, Shari's teacher can work to create a routine. Shari needs reassurance. She has learned to predict that her questions will result in an answer. In other words, questioning has made her world more predictable. Her teacher can create an alternate routine that will serve the same purpose – making her world predictable. The teacher can acknowledge how important it is for Shari to know that it is pizza day but teach her that others cannot ask the teacher questions if Shari continues to come to her desk. Her teacher can then give her one ticket (to purchase an answer) and write down "pizza day" on Shari's daily schedule. She can check the schedule as many times as she likes. In order to fully address this concern, her teacher must identify and target the underlying social information that Shari appears to lack – understanding that repeated questioning can make others feel untrusted and annoyed. Also, it may upset her peers because her questioning takes much of her teacher's time. (This topic will be discussed in depth in Chapter 8.)

Considerations for Using Restricted Interests and Predictability to Reduce Task Demands

As discussed above, it is possible to use special interests to motivate individuals on the spectrum to engage in activities that are not intrinsically rewarding to them. Additionally, setting time aside to engage in restricted interests was recommended. Some caution should be used when employing these strategies, however.

Because restricted interests are often solitary, it is important to monitor and control the amount of time a person is permitted to spend in these activities. If a student is too immersed in her pursuits, more harm than good may result. Furthermore, providing opportunities to socialize through the use of interests may be detrimental if there is no accompanying communication skills instruction. That is, peers and adults alike will likely grow tired of one-sided conversations.

Communication

Participating in conversation requires multiple expressive language skills such as initiation, turn-taking, and sharing a topic. Ways to provide support in these areas include scripts, careful selection of communication partners, and other considerations.

Scripts

Prepared scripts are an effective way to decrease the demands of conversing. Scripts in a variety of forms have been found to be effective. These include verbal rehearsal of scripts prior to conversation (Goldstein & Cisar, 1992); video modeling (Charlop & Milstein, 1989); written scripts; words written into activity schedules (Krantz & McClannahan, 1993); and audiotaped scripts (Stevenson, Krantz, & McClannahan, 2000).

Charlop-Christy and Kelso (2003) used scripts written on cue cards to facilitate conversation in 8- and 11-year-olds with reading skills. The cue cards provided scripts for conversations on abstract topics (pertaining to objects or activities not present at the time). The researchers found a rapid increase in conversational speech that was maintained after the removal of the cue cards. They also found that the conversation skills generalized to unrehearsed questions and to new conversation partners.

Communication Partners

Careful selection of communication partners and activities is another way to decrease the demands in this area. For example, selecting peers who share similar interests can help develop conversational exchanges and make conversing more rewarding for both parties. Selection of activities may also reduce communication demands. For example, working or playing on a computer, sharing a listening station, and watching a movie or sporting event all allow social success without extensive conversational demands.

As discussed earlier, many interventions that facilitate social interaction by providing peer support or increasing structure also reduce communication demands. Thus, responsibility for initiating and joining is shifted more towards the selected peer or adult facilitator.

Other Strategies

Additional strategies to reduce demands in communication include avoiding or limiting the use of sarcasm and abstract language and providing additional time to process verbal information and formulate responses. Limiting directions to one or two steps and writing them down can also be beneficial.

Considerations for Addressing Communication Task Demands

Deficits in communication are present across the autism spectrum. While those with high-functioning ASD may be more skilled than others on the spectrum, they still have significant communication needs. For example, pragmatic (social) language and nonverbal communication (understanding and use of tone of voice, cadence, facial expressions, and gestures) are often areas of weakness. Given the complexity of communication, it is highly recommended that speech-language pathologists be included in developing and planning interventions. Their unique expertise includes knowledge of prerequisite and component skills as well as language interventions.

Sensory Differences

The sensory demands of activities are also important. As discussed in Chapter 4, many on the spectrum exhibit hypersensitivity (sensory defensiveness) and/or hyposensitivity (underresponsiveness). For example, the humming of fluorescent light, which is imperceptible to most, can be overwhelming to someone on the spectrum. In contrast, other sensations (e.g., the sound of one's name being called or a whistle blowing, touch, pain) may not register, resulting in delayed or passive responses.

Antecedent strategies, such as individually designed sensory diets, are reported to be beneficial for many. Diets include activities to address targeted sensory systems. For example, one student who experienced difficulty focusing on school work was given gum to chew and permitted to take short breaks to walk.

Other strategies that help to reduce sensory demands include the use of earplugs, seat cushions, oral sensory "tools" (e.g., gum, sports bottles that require sucking, chewy candy or snacks), and other fidgets (e.g., squeeze balls, "squishy" toys). Avoiding or limiting time in settings that are overdemanding can be effective as well.

Considerations for Addressing Sensory Aspects of Task Demands

While many sensory interventions appear easy to develop and implement, some activities may have an effect that is opposite of what was intended. For example, activities that are calming for one individual may be stimulating for another. Because strategies need to be individualized, it is recommended that an occupational therapist be involved when possible.

Cognitive Differences

It is important to capitalize on the cognitive strengths that many autistic individuals present, such as intense interests and strong rote memory and visual spatial processing. At the same time, deficits in executive functioning, weak central coherence, unevenness of skills, and difficulty with abstract concepts create difficulties in academic settings. Academic demands must be adjusted in order to minimize the impact of these and other deficits.

Uneven Skill Development

Due to uneven skill development, many students on the spectrum already have mastered grade-level material. If pretests indicate that a student has an understanding of the concepts to be taught to the class, alternative assignments should be provided. While such alternative assignments may be more demanding academically, because they prevent boredom and allow opportunities for growth, they may be less demanding behaviorally.

Attention Deficits

Deficits in attention are prominent among individuals on the spectrum and may have significant impact on academics. The following tips have been found to be helpful in this regard.

- Provide frequent reinforcement. This decreases the demand for sustained attention. That is, having to work for 1 hour to earn a reinforcer is much more difficult than working for 10 minutes.
- Break larger projects into smaller, more manageable parts to facilitate work completion.
- Increase the pace of instruction in some subjects, vary instructional methods, and provide a variety of activities.

- Select activities of high interest or allow flexibility in topic choice to help reduce demands on attention.
- Reduce distraction by designating a quiet place to work.
- Allow movement in the classroom and provide fidgets, snacks, or drinks of water.

Transitioning

In order to facilitate transition to new tasks, it is often helpful to expose the student to the materials to be used ahead of time or to provide an overview of the topic of an upcoming lesson. This type of priming (see Chapter 5) increases the predictability of an academic task and, thus, is ideal for students on the spectrum.

For some students, it may be necessary to decrease demands by removing a task required of other students or by shortening assignments. This consideration becomes especially important in decisions regarding homework assignments. It is not uncommon for parents of a student who appears to be coping well during the school day to report that at home, the child expresses frustration, even rage, related to school experiences. These students may require significant reduction or even removal of homework demands. One approach to reduction of work is to prioritize assignments and require that only the most essential be completed.

Central Coherence Deficits

Central coherence deficits result in difficulty recognizing a theme or major point. For those with weak central coherence, all details may seem equally important and relationships among details may not be understood. Thus, an understanding of the "big picture" is impeded by a focus on the details.

The following interventions make tasks less demanding for students with weak central coherence.

- *Graphic organizers* or spatial learning strategies such as webbing and mapping clarify relationships among important concepts and help to make abstract material more concrete.
- *Word banks* offer sets of words from which to select answers. This intervention "limits the forest" so that the student does have to think of and rule out all possibilities.
- *Color coding* uses the strength in visual processing to organize subjects or concepts by color.
- *Highlighted materials* aid the learner in recognizing key concepts among the other details.

Considerations for Addressing Cognitive Task Demands

The school day presents social, sensory, and cognitive experiences that are more demanding for students on the spectrum than they are for their typically developing peers. Recognizing and responding to this fact is critical to effective intervention. At times a decrease in academic demands or workload may be necessary to keep the school experience from becoming overwhelming.

Motor Differences

As discussed in Chapter 1, motor skill deficits are a common associated feature of ASD (Ghaziuddin & Butler, 1998; Page & Boucher, 1998; Rapin, 1996). Some researchers place a major emphasis on the role of motor differences for daily functioning. Considering how prevalent these differences are, most comprehensive intervention plans will likely include strategies to address them.

Handwriting

Handwriting is often challenging for individuals on the spectrum. Providing alternatives to handwriting decreases the level of demand for these tasks. For example, note-taking may be decreased by selecting a peer to copy notes, providing lecturer or teacher copies of notes, or by permitting audio taping for later review. Demands of tasks that require a composition may be reduced by accepting an audiotape of the product or by permitting the student to dictate the material. Additionally, keyboarding is often much less demanding than handwriting for those on the spectrum and, therefore, offers a beneficial support.

Without the demand for handwriting, it becomes possible for the student to exhibit mastery of concepts and content and to express creativity. These alternatives and modifications may be necessary during the educational process and throughout work life. When it is not possible to provide such interventions, demands may be decreased by evaluating material on content rather than on presentation.

Catatonia

Chapter 1 reviewed the research on catatonia, a movement disorder characterized by slowness in movements and verbal responses, difficulty in initiating and completing actions, and increased need for prompting. Shah and Wing (2006) suggest the following interventions as ways to reduce demands and help those experiencing catatonia:

- Reduce stress
- Provide verbal and physical prompts
- Maintain routine and structure
- Educate caregivers
- Consider medication

Catatonia is a potentially life-threatening condition. Professional medical assistance may be necessary if symptoms appear to be severe or unresponsive to nonmedical interventions.

Other Motor Differences

Other motor differences such as poor coordination, clumsiness, and an awkward gait are often observed. Activities that require these skills can be adapted to reduce demands. When these differences are significant, specialists such as occupational therapists, physical therapists, or adaptive P.E. teachers may need to participate in intervention planning.

Considerations for Addressing Motor Task Demands

Luckily, in the technological era in which we live, it is possible to be highly functional without having highly developed handwriting skills. Therefore, the continuing emphasis on and requirement for handwriting in the school setting may be misplaced. Indeed, Freedman (2005) reports that public schools are spending less time teaching handwriting skills and more time teaching language and math in response to the increased use of standardized tests to measure academic progress. For those who struggle with handwriting, the mental effort required to produce the handwriting diminishes the quality of the content (Graham & Harris, 2005). To reduce task demands, early introduction of functional alternatives (e.g., keyboarding skills, audio/videotape, and dictation) should be considered more often for those on the spectrum who experience motor differences that impact the development of handwriting skills.

Emotional Vulnerability

Individuals on the spectrum are often emotionally fragile. Daily demands may overwhelm their capacity to cope, resulting in feelings of anxiety, frustration, anger, and depression, as well as emotional "meltdowns" and rage. In general, as stressors increase, the ability to modulate emotions decreases. The tendency for individuals on the spectrum to be less flexible, coupled with an often immature understanding and expression of feelings, can make it impossible for them to resolve the issue at hand and move ahead. This may manifest as repetitive questioning, complaining, and even rage. Reducing demands across areas of functioning (e.g., social, restricted patterns, communication, sensory, cognitive, and motor) is often necessary to prevent emotional overload. However, it may not be sufficient. Additional interventions that target emotional vulnerability directly will be discussed here.

Individuals on the spectrum sometimes cannot identify for themselves or communicate to others how they are feeling and, therefore, may need assistance in this process. Strategies include the following:

- Tools such as a feeling word bank and faces depicting emotions can help reduce the demands of recognizing and appropriately expressing their feelings.
- When perseverative feelings are present, one teacher suggests that writing or drawing in a journal may be a helpful way of working through the feelings well enough to resolve them (A. L. De Ville, personal communication, February 4, 2006). This strategy is a lifelong skill useful for individuals of all ages. For younger children and adolescents, De Ville suggests creating a "happiness" box or book. The box or book is simply a collection of pictures and objects representing favorite interests. When the child feels a negative emotion, she can be prompted to use items from the collection to calm and change focus and redirect emotions. Over time, the child will learn to use this coping skill independently. Other visual supports that depict feelings in a range of intensity such as a thermometer may also decrease the demands for communication (see Figure 7.4).

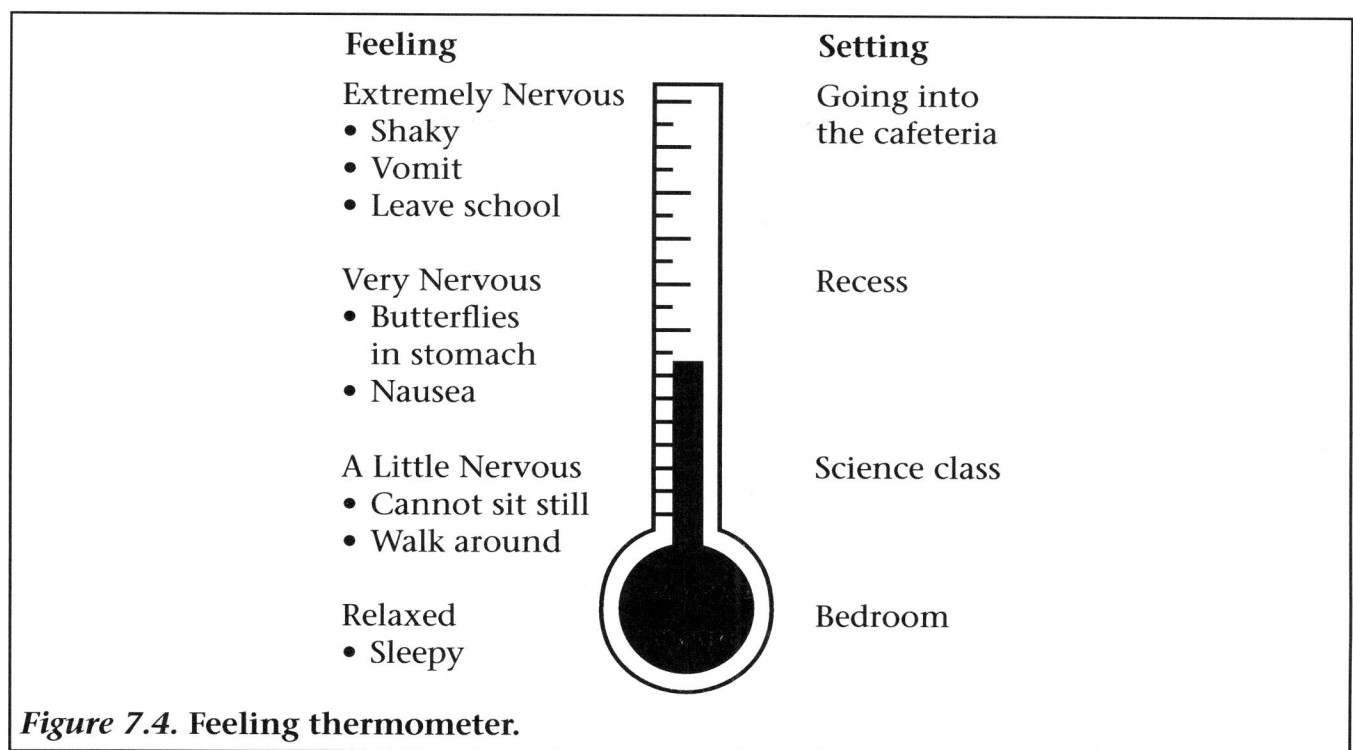

Feeling		Setting
Extremely Nervous		Going into
• Shaky		the cafeteria
• Vomit		
• Leave school		
Very Nervous		Recess
• Butterflies in stomach		
• Nausea		
A Little Nervous		Science class
• Cannot sit still		
• Walk around		
Relaxed		Bedroom
• Sleepy		

Figure 7.4. Feeling thermometer.

Anxiety

Anxiety is often a precursor to feelings of anger and rage. In many instances, simply providing adequate structure and predictability can help to reduce or eliminate anxiety and prevent behavioral concerns from arising. This may be accomplished by preparation for change, pre-exposure, practicing, and creation of routines.

- *Visual schedules* are one method for preparing for change, such as Penny's, depicted in Chapter 6. Schedules often include a special symbol that signal a change in routine (see Figure 6.3).
- *Providing advanced warnings* of transitions or alterations of routines can also help. Some people need days to prepare for a change in routine while others may only require a five-minute warning.
- *Pre-exposure* involves preparing an individual by walking him or her through an activity before it occurs. For example, a seventh-grade boy who was a first-year band student expressed anxiety about the upcoming concert. The teacher took him into the auditorium and allowed him to stand on the stage where he would be on the evening of the performance. The teacher described and demonstrated the lighting and sound and reviewed the program brochure.
- *Practicing*, also known as pre-teaching, is another technique used to help prepare for change. Using this approach, the individual is allowed to practice an activity in advance. For example, the band teacher could bring his students into the auditorium for rehearsal

a few days before the actual concert. In another example, to help her daughter adjust to starting high school, a parent took her to school during the summer. Together, they practiced opening her locker and navigating through the building to each of her classes.

- Finally, *routines* can be created to help build predictability, especially during activities that inherently have less structure. Parents can create routines for getting ready for school, bedtime, homework, and meals. Teachers can use routines for getting started in the morning and participating in groups.

The presence of routines and structure is not always sufficient to prevent anxiety. At times, factors that cannot be predicted occur or situations are too demanding in spite of adequate structure. Learning to recognize and address anxiety early can often prevent increasing anxiety and more serious behaviors.

Myles and Southwick (2005) describe the stages of a rage cycle. The first stage, "rumbling," is signaled by increased anxiety. It is sometimes followed by rage and then recovery. Interventions that prevent the progression to rage include antiseptic bouncing (i.e., removing an individual from the anxiety-provoking situation to allow him to calm), proximity control, use of humor, and provision of a safe place or "home base" (Myles & Southwick). Similarly, identifying a person to offer support and providing ongoing permission to seek help can be beneficial. For example, a school counselor can be designated as a helper, and the student can be given a pass to use when needing to seek out the helper.

Sadness, Depression, and Frustration
The presence of feelings of sadness, depression, and frustration also makes tasks challenging and can result in behavioral difficulties. Addressing or alleviating these feelings reduces the demands on coping resources. Sadness is only one of a number of symptoms that make up depression. Depression can also include lethargy, withdrawal, loss of interest in activities, severe irritability, low self-esteem, poor concentration, and sleep and appetite disturbance.

Strategies that are effective for treating depression in typically developing individuals are also helpful for those on the spectrum. However, they may require more supports in order to benefit from the intervention. For example, while talk therapy is often effective in treating depression, the "talk" in talk therapy may be a barrier to someone who struggles with communication. For autistic individuals, the therapy may be modified by using visual or activity-based techniques.

Encouraging and requiring increased activity and time with others is helpful for addressing depression in general. For autistic individuals, however, these strategies can present additional obstacles. For example, placing a child on the spectrum in a soccer league or Boy

Scouts, or guiding an adult to join a club without adequate support, may lead to more failure experiences and result in increased depression.

Some triggers for frustration among children on the spectrum are predictable, such as losing a game, changes in routine, and being wrong. In some situations, these triggers can be removed. For example, activities may be selected or designed to be cooperative instead of competitive, activities may be selected to increase opportunities for success, and changes in routine can sometimes be minimized or even avoided. However, at other times, triggers are unavoidable. Making mistakes is inevitable and some changes in routine are inescapable. In these circumstances, as described above, preparation is appropriate.

Considerations for Addressing the Emotional Aspects of Task Demands

In addressing emotional vulnerability, it is often helpful to enlist the participation of trained mental health professionals in the intervention planning process. Given that high-functioning autistic individuals are at a high risk for developing clinical anxiety and depression, additional help of professionals knowledgeable about autism may be necessary. Formal counseling by psychologists or counselors or medical consultation with a physician is often beneficial.

Additional Considerations

Social, communication, sensory, cognitive, motor, and emotional demands vary greatly from activity to activity. Individuals on the spectrum have increased success when demands are monitored and well matched to their needs and skills. Unfortunately, these considerations are often overlooked when making programming decisions for schoolchildren on the spectrum. As students who are served outside of the general education setting increase in skills, school staff begin to consider adding opportunities in the mainstream. Very often, the activities selected for inclusion are those least well matched to the needs of children on the autism spectrum and, therefore, are the most demanding. Indeed, Volkmar identifies what he describes as "almost a Holy Trinity of main-streaming opportunities" – gym, recess, and cafeteria (National Public Radio, 2004). According to Volkmar, these are the "three worst places to mainstream a child with AS." Volkmar suggests that children on the spectrum often need adult support in order to be successful in meeting the demands of these environments. Likewise, adults with ASD experience more success in activities in which the demands are not overwhelming to their ability to function and cope.

The number of people participating in an activity impacts the level of demand. With increased numbers of participants come increased demands for mind reading, conversation, turn-taking, and so on. The demands of a group activity may be reduced simply by decreasing the size of the group. If the majority of children in a class are able to work successfully in groups of five, children on the spectrum may benefit from working in groups of three or in pairs.

Research Support

As mentioned, the interventions discussed in this chapter are primarily antecedent-based. While there is no specific research support for some of them, all these interventions alter the setting events and, as such, are grounded in research. Antecedent strategies are well supported in the literature (Reeve & Carr, 2000). Horner and colleagues (2002) describe antecedent interventions as one critical element for addressing behavior problems. Moreover, they note a growing trend for using these interventions.

APPLICATION OF THE ZIGGURAT MODEL

Steve's Task Demand Interventions

During her conversation with Steve, Nicole, the student sponsor at the student support center, prioritized the following key areas from his UCC to adjust demands: cognitive, social, and emotional vulnerability. She believed that helping Steve to be more successful with school and his roommate would result in reduced anxiety and lessen the demands on his ability to cope. She asked the three questions discussed at the beginning of this chapter:

1. Are you asking for performance of a skill that is too hard?
2. Are you asking for performance of a skill that has not been taught?
3. Are you asking for a task to be accomplished without the necessary supports?

With regard to academics, Nicole and Steve agree that his high SAT scores and grade point average in high school indicate that he has most of the prerequisite skills to be successful in college. In high school, Steve's parents and teachers helped him to be organized, provided class notes, and structured his study time for him. Now that he is in college, he is struggling to accomplish this for himself. Component skills were reviewed. Nicole determined that the increased independence required for college-level academics was the key missing component. Furthermore, while Steve was able to write and take notes, doing so for an extended period of time was excessively fatiguing for him. Nicole decided that until Steve could gain these prerequisite and component skills, he would need increased supports.

Together, Nicole and Steve developed a plan to help reduce academic demands (see Figure 7.5). First, she recommended that he enroll in classes that have study sessions and teaching assistants. Such courses usually provide extra help, tutorials, test review sessions, and office hours, all of which will be helpful for Steve. Due to his difficulty in writing, Nicole arranged for Steve's professors to provide him with copies of lecture notes. She also recom-

ZIGGURAT WORKSHEET

BEHAVIOR/AREAS OF CONCERN Social, Restricted Patterns of Behavior, Sensory Differences, Cognitive Differences, Emotional Vulnerability	FOR SPECIFIC INTERVENTION PLAN (Operationalized Behaviors)	SELECTED UCC ITEMS	CHECK ALL THAT APPLY A	B	C
		#1 Difficulty recognizing the feelings and thoughts of others (mindblindness) #4 Lacks tact or appears rude #5 Has difficulty making or keeping friends #8 Tends to be less involved in group activities #12 Expresses strong need for routine or sameness #18 Has problems handling transition and change #41 Responds in an unusual manner to sounds #52 Displays poor problem-solving skills #53 Has poor organizational skills #60 Has attention problems #76 Is easily stressed #89 Has difficulty managing stress and/or anxiety			
Sensory and Biological	Sensory and Biological Intervention:	• Use noise-canceling headphones while studying and soft earplugs on days when roommate has to wake early. • Make an appointment with a doctor at the student health center to discuss medications for your symptoms of anxiety and attention problems. • Try to sign up for early morning or late evening classes where class size is typically smaller. • Get involved in regular physical activities to help keep the mind/body alert prior to studying and attending lectures. • Prior to attending large lecture classes, take time to relax and prepare yourself by taking deep breaths and reminding yourself that you can handle the crowd for the duration of class. Arrive to class early and select a seat away from "traffic." If you need to, you can take a quick break.	✓	✓	
	Underlying Characteristics Addressed:	#41 Responds in an unusual manner to sounds #60 Has attention problems #76 Is easily stressed			
Respectful Reinforcement	Reinforcement Intervention:	• Develop a self-reinforcement system. You will need to monitor your own progress on specific goals (e.g., study goals, academic goals, and social goals). For example, reward yourself with a timed game of chess on the Internet after you finish reading a chapter. • Join clubs in your area of interests such as movie club, or chess club, in order to provide yourself with rewarding social opportunities. • Tell yourself that you have done a good job after you notice a minor change in your dorm room and handle it without complaining.		✓	✓
	Underlying Characteristics Addressed:	#5 Has difficulty making or keeping friends #8 Tends to be less involved in group activities #12 Expresses strong need for routine or sameness #52 Displays poor problem-solving skills #53 Has poor organizational skills #60 Has attention problems #76 Is easily stressed			

Figure 7.5. Ziggurat worksheet for Steve's global intervention.

ZIGGURAT WORKSHEET

Structure & Visual/Tactile Supports	Structure & Visual/Tactile Support Intervention:	• Purchase small handheld computer (PDA) or paper calendar. Record all assignments and tests. Schedule time to study each day. Schedule time to meet with professor or assistant before tests. Review schedule daily. *Note.* This intervention applies to multiple levels. • Schedule reinforcement time after tasks are completed. • Make written notes of questions to ask teaching assistant or professor when attending office hours. • Review list of relaxation/coping skills (provided) when feeling upset. • Place items (clothing, book bag, etc.) in the same location to avoid losing them.	✓	✓	✓
	Underlying Characteristics Addressed:	#52 Displays poor problem-solving skills #53 Has poor organizational skills #76 Is easily stressed			
Task Demands	Task Demand Intervention:	• Enroll in classes that have study sessions and teaching assistants. • Arrange through student support center to have professors provide you copies of their class notes to reduce the amount of writing you will do or get a copy of peer's notes or record lecture. • Use PDA or paper calendar to record assignments and tests and schedule time to study (see Structure and Visual/Tactile Supports level for description). • Attend office hours and study sessions. • Read script (provided) how to address concern with roommate (e.g., "Could you please help me find my sweater?"). *Note.* This intervention applies to multiple levels. • Educate the Resident Assistant (RA) on your floor about autism. Notify him when there is conflict between you and your roommate. When possible, have the RA mediate by helping you understand how your roommate feels or how your behavior may have impacted Mark.	✓	✓	
	Underlying Characteristics Addressed:	#1 Difficulty recognizing the feelings and thoughts of others (mindblindness) #53 Has poor organizational skills #60 Has attention problems #76 Is easily stressed			

Figure 7.5. Ziggurat worksheet for Steve's global intervention (continued).

mended that Steve obtain copies of a peer's notes or use a laptop computer to take his own notes during lectures. Finally, to assist in organization and planning, Nicole recommended that Steve use a PDA (personal digital assistant) or a paper calendar. (This strategy was listed earlier on the worksheet in the Structure and Visual/Tactile Supports section.)

With regard to Steve's social skills, they determined that he did not have the prerequisite skills to resolve conflict with his roommate. Steve has not developed the ability to predict others' response to his behaviors (mindblindness) and does not recognize when his statements or questions sound rude or accusatory. Because social demands are unavoidable, supports must be provided until Steve has learned new skills (see Figure 7.5). Steve's resident assistant will be enlisted to moderate in conflicts between Steve and Mark. Nicole will also provide some written scripts for predictable situations that may arise while living in the dormitory.

Penny's Task Demand Interventions

Penny's team reviewed her UCC and discussed her prerequisite and component skills. After reviewing her UCC, they decided to focus on reducing social and communication demands.

As the team discussed Penny's social and communication skills, it became apparent that she was not independently successful in any setting, home or school. Had Penny attained success with siblings or some peers, it would be clear that she had mastered prerequisite skills, and the team would have focused on helping her to expand and generalize those skills. However, because her social skills were so immature, it was determined that she was missing prerequisite and component skills. To be able to successfully participate in academic and social activities, Penny would need added supports. They simultaneously identified skills to teach and supports to put in place until those skills were learned.

The peer buddy and soccer ball responsibility supports (discussed earlier) will be provided until Penny learns how to join play and accept group rules. Penny may always need some level of peer support in demanding social situations. As such, the emergence of social success should not be an indicator to remove her support systems. Until Penny learns how to initiate and maintain conversations with others, she will need supports such as scripted cue cards to start conversation, as well as notes about peers' interests.

Ms. Simpson reviewed the ABC-I (Figure 7.3) to better understand Penny's disruptive behavior in the classroom. As discussed, several antecedents were identified, including transitions, class discussions, and written assignments. Skill deficits, including mindblindness, low frustration tolerance, and difficulty with transition and change, had been determined earlier using the UCC (Figure 4.5). Recognizing that Penny was emotionally vulnerable and lacked the prerequisite coping, social, and communication skills, Ms. Simpson realized that additional supports would be required, at least until she mastered those skills. The addition of Task Demand interventions for Penny is depicted in Figure 7.6.

Ms. Simpson and Penny's speech therapist developed a visual system to reduce the communication and coping demands inherent in class discussions. The red/green class discussion card was discussed in detail in Chapter 6. The card helps to decrease communication demands by providing a visual reminder of the expected behaviors for participating in class discussion (raise hand and wait to be called on, make on-topic remark, do not say mean things about others' comments) and listening to others (raise your hand for help, do not speak with your neighbor, work hard). Ms. Simpson also provided Penny with a list of sentence starters to help reduce writing difficulties and demands on her frustration tolerance. Finally, recognizing the importance of keeping Penny "emotionally intact" in class, Ms. Simpson reduced the length of writing assignments and even allowed her to respond orally at times.

ZIGGURAT WORKSHEET

BEHAVIOR/ AREAS OF CONCERN	FOR SPECIFIC INTERVENTION PLAN (Operationalized Behaviors)	SELECTED UCC ITEMS	CHECK ALL THAT APPLY		
			A	B	C
Class disruption	• Says, "I don't have to do this work." • Insults peers • Does not complete writing tasks	#1 Mindblindness #4 Lacks tact #16 Unmotivated by customary rewards #18 Difficulty with transition and change #33 Gives false impression of understanding more than she does #63 Has difficulty understanding the connection between behavior and consequences #66 Resists handwriting #85 Low frustration tolerance #88 Difficulty understanding own and others' emotions #89 Difficulty managing stress and anxiety	✓	✓	
Sensory and Biological	Sensory and Biological Intervention: • Seek consultation from the occupational therapist (OT) to assess handwriting, including sensory factors and hand fatigue. • Provide Penny with a sensory diet with direction of an OT to help address anxious or agitated behaviors. • Provide a calming sensory activity prior to giving lengthy writing task. • Teach Penny to recognize body cues that indicate stress or frustration (muscle tension, heart rate, breathing pattern, etc.). • Teach Penny strategies to address her stress and frustration (e.g., engage in sensory calming strategy, ask for help, take slow, deep breaths). *Note.* This intervention applies to multiple levels.			
	Underlying Characteristics Addressed:	#66 Resists handwriting #85 Low frustration tolerance #88 Difficulty understanding own and others' emotions #89 Difficulty managing stress and anxiety	✓		
Respectful Reinforcement	Reinforcement Intervention: • Develop a positive behavior management plan to address social skills and work completion. Have Penny help to select items for a reinforcer menu. Reinforcers are earned both in home and school. Penny should have frequent opportunities to "cash in" by selecting reinforcers from her menu. • Reinforce Penny for being able to categorize statements as "rude" or "kind." • With the assistance of a speech therapist, develop a card that has rules for class discussion. During a class discussion, give Penny a card – one side green (with rules for appropriate class discussion; e.g., no insults, on-topic remarks) and the other side is red (with a list of appropriate listening behaviors). Begin each class discussion with green side up. Turn card to red if Penny makes an inappropriate contribution. Remove card at the end of class discussion. Reinforce Penny for following the rules on either side of the card. *Note.* This intervention applies to multiple levels. • Provide reinforcement for initiating work on a writing assignment without negative comments. Also reinforce her for working for an increasing length of time. • Develop a token reinforcement system to address transitioning to school. Use alligator or other favorite animal stamps in Penny's token reinforcer system. Parents will provide Penny with a visual checklist/ schedule for the morning routine and transition to school. Make the last item on the checklist a school task (e.g., put backpack away). Reinforce Penny at school for following checklist/schedule. Provide additional reinforcement for following the schedule independently. *Note.* This intervention applies to multiple levels. • Provide Penny with a strong reinforcer on Mondays when she arrives to school with her completed morning home checklist.		✓	✓
	Underlying Characteristics Addressed:	#4 Lacks tact #16 Unmotivated by customary rewards #18 Difficulty with transition and change #66 Resists handwriting #85 Low frustration tolerance	✓	✓	

Figure 7.6. Ziggurat worksheet for Penny's specific intervention.

ZIGGURAT WORKSHEET

			✓	✓	✓

	Structure & Visual/ Tactile Support Intervention:	• Create visual chart "Rude versus kind words." Update as kind/unkind words occur and keep a copy at home and in school. • Videotape a same-age class during discussion time. Prior to taping, remind all students of behavioral expectations. Show Penny the tape, stopping to view specific skills (raising hand, refraining from negative comments when peers answer incorrectly, etc.) and to explore facial expressions and gestures of the peer models. Practice skills with Penny and reinforce. Provide Penny with a visual reminder of class discussion rules and reinforce her for successfully following them. • Use red/green class discussion card (see Reinforcement level for description). • Create a visual chart for tracking her progress on earning rewards. For example, use a drawing of a bug. Let Penny color in a segment each time she earns a reinforcer for being on-task or making appropriate comments in class. She selects a reinforcer from the menu when the drawing is completely colored. • Use a Comic Strip Conversation to help illustrate the thoughts and feelings of others in the context of a problem situation. For example, teach Penny to recognize the response of others to her comments. *Note.* This intervention applies to multiple levels. • Parents will provide Penny with a visual checklist/schedule for the morning routine and transition to school (see Reinforcement level for description). • Provide Penny with a weekly schedule to increase predictability.	✓	✓	✓
Structure & Visual/Tactile Supports	Underlying Characteristics Addressed:	#1 Mindblindness #4 Lacks tact #16 Unmotivated by customary rewards #18 Difficulty with transition and change #33 Gives false impression of understanding more than he/she actually does #63 Has difficulty understanding the connection between behavior and consequences #66 Resists handwriting #88 Difficulty understanding own and others' emotions			
	Task Demand Intervention:	• Use red/green class discussion card (see Reinforcement level for description). The card explicitly lists the steps for discussion for Penny to use as a guide/reminder. • Provide Penny with list of sentence starters she can use when writing. • Teacher may shorten some lengthy writing assignments or allow Penny to type or respond orally.	✓	✓	✓
Task Demands	Underlying Characteristics Addressed:	#1 Mindblindness #63 Has difficulty understanding the connection between behavior and consequences #66 Resists handwriting			

Figure 7.6. Ziggurat worksheet for Penny's specific intervention (continued).

SUMMARY

It is not acceptable to place individuals in situations where the demands exceed their ability. This chapter discussed the importance of addressing task demands in all interventions in order to ensure success. The continuum of task demands was discussed in depth, and three questions were introduced to facilitate consideration of prerequisite and component skill deficits in addition to supports necessary for success. A number of methods for reducing task demands in key areas were also discussed. Identification of skill deficits is the fist step to remediation. Chapter 8 will focus on evidence-based strategies to teach skills in each of the seven areas.

CHAPTER HIGHLIGHTS

- *The level of demand must be appropriate for the individual and the goal of the task. If independence is desired, the demand must be easy. If the goal is to expand knowledge, the demand must be adjusted to fall within the learner's zone of proximal development (ZPD).*

- *Intervention on this level of the Ziggurat involves identifying prerequisite and component skill deficits (Questions 1 and 2) and reducing the demands of a task (Question 3).*

- *Task analysis can be used to identify and target prerequisite and component skill deficits to remediate. This involves first breaking down the requirements to accomplish a task or skill. Next, the activity should be broken down into its components.*

- *An essential aspect of the Task Demands level is fostering a positive environment. This includes non-contingent strategies such as providing a warm, caring relationship or incorporating preferred interests and enjoyable activities into the day.*

- *Necessary supports must be in place. If supports are absent, the demands of a task will be too high.*

- *Use of special interests can provide motivation that will reduce the demands of some tasks. Additionally, building in predictability can address demands for those who are sensitive to transition and change.*

- *Use of sensory diets and sensory tools can help address sensory needs.*

- *Examining and addressing academic demands is important for success. Also, reducing the demand for sustained attention and providing frequent reinforcement can help address focus issues.*

- *Use of visual strategies such as graphic organizers, word banks, and color-coded and highlighted materials can help address central coherence deficits.*

- *Many individuals on the spectrum are emotionally fragile. It is important to provide assistance with processing and coping with feelings.*

- *The use of antecedent strategies – those that alter the setting events – is well supported in the literature.*

8 Skills to Teach

"All the stuff that everybody seems to know, but nobody has ever told you."

– Judy Endow

Angela

Angela is an exceptionally bright fifth-grade student on the spectrum. She reads at the college level and excels in science. Today, her teacher called on students to read portions of the chapter aloud. She then asked the class if there were "any questions." Angela raised her hand and asked, "Why did you call on Bekah to read? She is the worst reader in the class." Bekah immediately burst into tears. The teacher asked Angela to apologize. Angela turned to Bekah and said, "I'm sorry she called on you."

The teacher later met with Angela in private and asked her to explain why Bekah cried. Angela replied, "Because you shouldn't have asked her to read." Angela's "refusal" to acknowledge her guilt confirmed to the teacher that she was obstinate. Because Angela was seen as a bright student, it never occurred to the teacher that Angela might have such a poor understanding of what had happened.

In the quote above, Endow refers to "all the stuff that everybody seems to know" to describe the mysterious information to which others had access. Myles et al. describe this as the "hidden curriculum" (2004). These concepts refer to the lessons that typically developing persons learn simply through living but that are often missed by autistic people.

When adults working with individuals on the spectrum find themselves feeling irritable and impatient, it is necessary to stop and ask the following questions:

- What is it about the situation that comes naturally to everyone else but is missing for this person? Why is it that others do not show the same behavior?

- What is it that has not occurred to me to teach?

That is the seemingly obvious. *That* is the thing to teach.

Ideally, Angela's teacher would have recognized the seemingly obvious prior to feeling irritable and impatient. Unfortunately, she was unable to see the autism in Angela's behavior. As a result, she assumed that Angela was being obstinate. Angela's poor understanding of the non-literal meaning of "any question" in this context and her lack of ability to accurately decode Bekah's response were hidden in plain sight. The fact that she was academically gifted essentially masked her uneven social skill development. It is no surprise that such skills have been called the "hidden" curriculum (Myles & Simpson, 2001; Myles et al., 2004).

Skills to Teach is the final level of the Intervention Ziggurat. The first four tiers set the stage for this most important level – skill development. It is essential to identify and teach the obvious as well as the "seemingly obvious" skills. Learning skills allows for growth. When the sensory system is calm, reinforcement is available, the environment is made predictable through structure and visual supports, and task demands are carefully designed, skills can be effectively taught and learned.

The key diagnostic characteristics of autism identified on the UCC – social functioning, repetitive behavior and preoccupations, communication, sensory, and associated features such as cognitive, motor, and emotional vulnerability – may be thought of as areas of skills deficits to be addressed on this level of the Ziggurat. This chapter will review skill interventions in each of these areas.

SOCIAL

"Social and communicative dysfunctions are arguably the most handicapping conditions associated with Asperger syndrome" (Paul, 2003, p. 87). In many respects, success in all stages of life hinges on how well we relate to and communicate with others. During the early school years, children on the spectrum are often social isolates and may be victims of bullying. Failure in the broader social world, coupled with a keen self-perception of being "different," is likely associated with the increase in anxiety and depression frequently observed to develop by adolescence (Klin & Volkmar, 1997). For adults, success in college and the working world is highly dependent on "people skills."

It is difficult to separate social skills from communication. Paul (2003) points out that all communication is considered social because it implies an "exchange of information between a speaker and listener" (p. 87). Success in the workplace means more than having content knowledge of a field. One must also be able to interface with colleagues, customers, and executives.

Several strategies have been used to teach social skills. These include direct instruction, modeling, role play, video-taped role play with feedback, communication scripts, playing games, structured activities, homework, and coaching. When conducting training, it is important to know which skills to teach.

As discussed in Chapter 7, conducting a task analysis is a helpful way to identify deficits in requisite skills as well as specific component skills to teach. Coucouvanis (2005) provides a sequential curriculum for social skill development from basic to advanced. Skills are broken down into discrete steps (task analysis) for instruction. This section will review ways to address several key social skills supported by research.

Theory of Mind Skills and Analysis of Social Situations

Theory of Mind (ToM) refers to the ability to understand the thoughts and feelings of others and to apply this understanding to predict their actions. It underlies the ability to understand figurative language and deceit, show empathy, recognize the intent of others (accidental versus intentional), and to enter and maintain a conversation. It is difficult to imagine that a person with severe mindblindness could experience social success without intervention.

In *Teaching Children with Autism to Mind-Read*, Howlin, Baron-Cohen, and Hadwin (1999) present a curriculum for teaching ToM skills using visual supports and direct instruction. They outline hierarchies of emotional understanding and informational state understanding that contribute to having ToM. As depicted in Figures 8.1 and 8.2, each level is increasingly more complex and represents skills to teach.

Emotional Understanding

1. Recognize feelings from photographs of faces.

2. Recognize feelings from drawings of faces.

3. Recognize feelings that result from situations (i.e., predict how someone will feel as the result of an event).

4. Recognize feelings resulting from desires being fulfilled or unfulfilled.

5. Recognize feelings based on perception of whether an individual's desires are fulfilled or unfulfilled.

Figure 8.1. Hierarchy of emotional understanding (Howlin et al., 1999).

Informational State Understanding

1. Demonstrate the basic ability to judge another person's visual perspective (i.e., understand that people can see different things based on their own perspective).

2. Demonstrate the basic ability to judge what another person can see and how it appears to him/her (e.g., if a picture of an object is right side up or upside down).

3. Demonstrate the understanding that experiences such as seeing are the basis for knowing.

4. Predict the actions of others based on his/her knowledge.

5. Predict the actions of others based on a false belief.

Figure 8.2. **Hierarchy of informational state understanding (Howlin et al., 1999).**

Myles and Southwick (2005) note the importance of teaching individuals with high-functioning ASD how to interpret social situations. Several cartooning techniques have been developed to help understand the emotions and perspectives of others (see Chapter 6 for a review). Myles and Southwick outline another method for teaching social interpretation – the social autopsy. Immediately following a social "incident," the adult assists the individual in performing a social autopsy by identifying and understanding errors in order to create a plan to avoid mistakes in the future. Visual techniques, such as written words or drawings, are often incorporated in conducting social autopsies.

Research Support

Research is beginning to provide evidence that ToM is a teachable skill. Not all approaches currently being used have been investigated; however, a few studies have found positive effects. Cartooning is a visual method of assisting others in perspective taking. Research supporting the use of cartooning techniques was reported in Chapter 6.

Ozonoff and Miller (1995) conducted a social skills intervention that specifically targeted perspective-taking skills (ToM). Children participated in a social skills group focusing on conversational and theory of mind skills. Training included modeling, videotape, and practice with feedback and reinforcement. Children demonstrated improvements on ToM tasks; however, skills did not generalize outside the training setting, suggesting that participants may not have made gains in their perspective-taking abilities.

Fisher and Happé (2005) were also able to teach ToM skills to children. They used a visual technique whereby they taught children that thoughts are like having a picture in the head. The examiners inserted photographs into slots on dolls' heads to represent their thoughts or beliefs. This study did not examine whether skills generalized outside the training setting.

Specific Social Skills

Play serves as an early training ground for human development. For typically developing children, it forms the foundation for learning the cognitive, emotional, language, and social skills necessary for understanding and interacting in the social world. However, autistic children display characteristics, such as repetitive behaviors, rigidity, motor skill deficits, communication deficits, and social withdrawal, that limit the development of appropriate play. Pretend play is an advanced play skill and is believed to be linked to ToM (Howlin et al., 1999). The levels of pretend play development are outlined in Figure 8.3 in a hierarchy, which is helpful in both assessing and targeting skills to teach.

Levels of Pretend Play

1. Simple repetitive use of toy (e.g., banging, shaking, sucking, lining up)
2. Conventional use of toy (e.g., use car as intended, sweeping with broom)
3. Expanded repertoire of conventional toy use (at least three or more during 10-minute play session)
4. Appearance of basic pretend play
   i. One object can represent another (e.g., stick becomes magic wand)
   ii. Incorporate imaginary characteristics of objects (e.g., change doll's diaper, pretend that play stove is hot, pretend that car engine is broken)
   iii. Incorporating imaginary objects (e.g., put gas in tank, spill tea)
5. Expanded repertoire of spontaneous pretend play

Figure 8.3. Five levels of pretend play (Howlin et al., 1999).

One of the challenges in identifying which social skills to teach is recognizing that most people on the spectrum require lessons on skills that others are never discretely taught or skills that are usually taught and mastered at a much younger age. This is illustrated in the case of Penny, who makes negative comments about her peers in class. Unlike her peers, Penny needs to explicitly be taught the rules for participation in group discussions, how to identify how others feel, and why her statements hurt their feelings.

The previous section addressed skills fundamental to social understanding (ToM). The next section will discuss several basic and advanced social skills, including greetings, group participation (e.g., taking turns, sharing, complimenting others), and play.

Research Support

The effectiveness of techniques for teaching a range of social skills have been examined in the research literature. Research on approaches to teaching social engagement skills, basic social skills, advanced social skills, and play skills are reviewed here.

Social Engagement Skills

The social isolation often experienced by autistic people is an initial obstacle for social skills training. The following are research-supported approaches to addressing social isolation.

- Priming has been used to increase spontaneous social initiation (Zanolli et al., 1996).
- Increasing interaction with others provides an opportunity for social skills instruction and practice.
- Using trained peers as facilitators has been found to be a successful approach to increasing social interactions of children with ASD (Goldstein, Kaczmarek, Pennington, & Shafer, 1992).

Basic Social Skills

Success in the social world depends on more than simply spending time engaged with others. Quality social interactions require specific skills. Research has demonstrated that it is possible to teach basic skills through formal social skill groups. Through this method, children and adolescents have learned skills for greeting and conversation (Barry et al., 2003; Kamps et al., 1992; Mesibov, 1984), and taking turns and sharing (Kamps et al.). Group social skills training used with adults with ASD has resulted in significant improvements in conversation and social skills (Howlin & Yates, 1999; Mesibov). Family members and participants also reported a perception of increased self-confidence and independence following the training (Howlin & Yates).

Social skills, such as sharing, following directions, and social greetings, have been shown to improve following the use of video modeling with a computer program (Simpson et al., 2004). Apple and colleagues (2005) used video modeling in conjunction with self-management (self-monitoring and reinforcement) to teach children with high-functioning ASD how to give compliments.

Advanced Social Skills

More advanced skills have also been taught using a variety of methods. One formal social skills program that has undergone scientific scrutiny is SCORE. The SCORE Skills Strategy was first developed for adolescents with learning disabilities and was later adapted for individuals with ASD (Webb, Miller, Pierce, Strawser, & Jones, 2004). The program emphasizes five social skills:

- Share ideas
- Compliment others
- Offer help or encouragement
- Recommend changes nicely
- Exercise self-control and associated body language expectations (e.g., use pleasant tone of voice and facial expression, make eye contact)

Research found that participants made significant gains on the five skills taught, and generalization was observed (Webb et al.).

Specific Play Skills

As discussed above, play contributes to the development of numerous social skills in typically developing children. Due to the importance of play, some researchers have sought to develop techniques for teaching these skills to children with ASD. One such technique, video modeling, is well supported by the research literature. Studies have found improvements in solitary and cooperative play (Charlop-Christy et al., 2000) through video modeling. Improved social play (Charlop-Christy et al.; Nikopoulos & Keenan, 2004), as well as conversational manners such as eye contact and topic maintenance, has also been observed (Charlop & Milstein, 1989; Ogletree & Fischer, 1995).

Terpstra, Higgins, and Pierce (2002) highlight several research-supported methods for teaching children with autism to play that can be used in classrooms, including teaching skills in isolation, using scripts and peers, integrated play, and pivotal response training.

It is often appropriate to teach play skills in an isolated setting in order to increase success in real-play situations such as the playground. Terpstra et al. (2002) note several benefits of this format, including adult instruction, prompting, and reinforcement. They highlight research that has demonstrated that children perform beyond their measured competence when instructed in isolation (Lifter, Sulzer-Azaroff, Anderson, & Cowdery, 1993) and generate more ideas during play when prompted by adults (Lewis & Boucher, 1995). Several specific recommendations were suggested, including selecting toys that are intrinsically motivating, modeling appropriate play, and adjusting the amount of prompting based on needs. The use of scripts was discussed in Chapter 7. This technique has successfully been used to teach play skills (Goldstein & Cisar, 1992; Thomas & Smith, 2004; Wolfberg & Schuler, 1999) and communication. Scripts contain both dialogue and related actions for play. For example, Goldstein and Cisar taught children to enact a carnival scene. One child played a game booth attendant while the other played the customer. Both dialogue and actions were taught. In this study, children with autism were trained along with their typical peers. All of the children displayed the targeted behaviors and generalized the skills.

One study combined the use of isolated training and scripts. Thomas and Smith (2004) investigated the effectiveness of a technique called Tabletop Identiplay for teaching play skills to preschool children with an ASD. This technique involves dividing a tabletop into two visually discrete areas using tape and providing identical toys to the facilitator and the child. The facilitator repeats a structured narrative while modeling a simple play sequence. If the child produces a new play sequence, the adult joins and imitates the child's activity. This approach to teaching play skills resulted in increased functional use of toys and increased time participating in joint attention play.

Several studies discussed in this section have demonstrated that peers can effectively be used to help children with ASD learn social skills and increase their social interaction (Goldstein et al., 1992; Zhang & Wheeler, 2011). Integrated Play Groups, discussed in Chapter 7, capitalize on the powerful influence of skilled peers (Wolfberg, 2003; Wolfberg & Schuler, 1999). This model also incorporates other techniques previously mentioned, such as adult prompting and use of scripts to help facilitate the development of skills. Research supporting Integrated Play Groups was discussed in the previous chapter.

One unique approach to teaching social and play skills is pivotal response training (PRT). This technique targets essential or "pivotal" areas that are believed to be central to other behaviors. Thus, by directly teaching a few key skills, it is believed that a multitude of others will be impacted (Koegel, Koegel, Harrower, & Carter, 1999). PRT combines behavioral and developmental approaches and emphasizes providing natural (rather than contrived) learning opportunities (Koegel & Kogel, 2006).

A few studies have investigated the use of PRT and play. Thorp, Stahmer, and Schreibman (1995) found a significant increase in sociodramatic play associated with improvements in language and social responses (e.g., comply with request, social initiation). Pierce and Schreibman (1995) noted an increase in play initiation and time spent engaged in play.

Considerations for Teaching Social Skills

Those who are most familiar with individuals on the spectrum often find their sometimes idiosyncratic style of interaction charming or endearing, making statements such as, "That's just William." While acceptance is critical to well-being and self-esteem, in the long run ignoring social behaviors that are considered by others to be awkward or rude will result in failure or even harm for those on the spectrum.

The responsibility for teaching social skills belongs to family, school, speech therapists, psychologists, job coaches, employers, and others. In fact, as stated in the Individuals with Disabilities Education Act (IDEA) of 2004, the purpose of special education services is "to ensure that all children with disabilities have available to them a free appropriate public education that emphasizes special education and related services designed to meet their unique needs and *prepare them for further education, employment and independent living*" (Individuals with Disabilities Education Act, 2004, Section 300.1; emphasis added).

It is impossible to prepare individuals for employment and independence in adulthood without addressing social skills. In fact, when employers were asked to list the top 10 characteristics sought in potential applicants, 5 of the top 10 skills listed were social in nature (i.e., communication skills, interpersonal abilities, leadership skills, multicultural sensitivity/awareness, and teamwork) (Hansen & Hansen, n.d.).

Once the importance of teaching social skills has been recognized, a correct balance between training in contrived or instructional settings and natural settings must be found. Skills that do not exist cannot be generalized; therefore, it is necessary to explain, model, practice, and reinforce social skills in an instructional setting.

After this initial phase, opportunities to practice in natural settings are required. Participation of same-age peers in the social skills training process creates a more natural environment for practice of social skills. It is important to train typically developing peers to interact, initiate, reinforce, and prompt their peers on the spectrum to engage in positive social interactions (Terpstra et al., 2002). Without instruction, typically developing individuals may become frustrated and eventually reject or ignore their peers on the spectrum. Alternatively, they may develop the role of caretakers, compensating for the social deficits exhibited by their peer, rather than the role of facilitators aiding in the development of skills for independent functioning in the social world.

As in other skill areas, preferred topics or interests may be an ideal starting point for social skills instruction. Building social activities around these topics may increase the reinforcement available in otherwise challenging experiences. This approach also may allow the individual on the spectrum to demonstrate his or her strengths and thus build self-esteem and positive peer regard.

RESTRICTED PATTERNS OF BEHAVIOR, INTERESTS, AND ACTIVITIES

Repetitive behaviors are considered to be symptomatic when they interfere with adaptive functioning. Sometimes they serve a self-stimulatory role and may help a person to regain physiological balance or homeostasis (Conroy, Asmus, Sellers, & Ladwig, 2005). Some repetitive behaviors may occur as a method for calming the nervous system. For example, when meeting new people (something that makes her nervous), Penny is likely to increase her comments about bugs and alligators because these interests offer comfort to her. They are familiar, distracting, and calming. At other times, repetitive behaviors may be exhibited as an effort to increase alertness or stimulate the nervous system. The repetitive behaviors that occur most frequently among individuals with ASD include repetitively talking about one subject; obsessive thinking about a narrow area of interest; repeatedly watching a video; and adherence to routines and rituals (South, Ozonoff, & McMahon, 2005).

While symptoms in the other core areas of autism such as social and communication generally become less severe over time, symptoms related to circumscribed interests become more severe (South et al., 2005). Among the most frequent obsessive interests are Japanese animation; gadgets/devices; dinosaurs; space/physics; natural disasters; and historical events (South et al.). Persons on the spectrum often talk about their interests at length without awareness of the listener's level of interest.

While others learn to recognize the response of the conversation partner and to adjust their own behavior through experience, individuals on the spectrum must be explicitly taught these skills. Role play, coaching, modeling, and videotaped practice may be incorporated in these lessons. Attwood (2003a) suggests that specific scripts designed to monitor the listener's level of interest be taught (e.g., "I hope this isn't boring you." "What are your thoughts and opinions on this?").

Some obsessive interests focus on unacceptable topics, including warfare, explosives, sex, and death, which may result in harmful, dangerous, or even illegal behaviors. Attwood recommends that Social Stories™ and Comic Strip Conversations™ be utilized to help change this type of obsessive interests. These techniques should include a description of the individual's perspective on the topic of interest and teach the perspectives of family members, friends, school staff, and legal authorities on the same topic. Through appealing to the individual's maturity or intelligence, Attwood suggests that it may be possible to prompt a related but more appropriate interest. For example, an interest in warfare may be redirected into the pursuit of knowledge of history (Attwood, 2003a).

Daniel

A third-grade student on the spectrum, Daniel, asked his teacher and parents repetitive questions about how animals and people die. On the way to school one morning, he asked his mother to pull the car over so that he could look at a squirrel that had been run over. Daniel's mother and teacher sought the help of the speech therapist and psychologist at school. Together, they developed a Social Story™ that described how other people feel when Daniel focuses on death. They encouraged Daniel to use his impressive intelligence to pursue an interest in biology. The teacher located software on how the body works. Daniel was able to shift his interest in this more productive direction. Over time, books on biology became a strong reinforcer for him.

Research Support

Researchers have examined methods for limiting repetitive behaviors and obsessive interests. For example, researchers have found that visual cue cards are effective for teaching elementary-school students to distinguish between appropriate and inappropriate times to engage in repetitive behaviors (Conroy et al., 2005). A visual symbol indicating "no" was presented during times when repetitive behaviors would be most disruptive to learning and was replaced at other times with a symbol indicating "yes." Students learned to limit repetitive behaviors to the periods when the "yes" symbol was present (Conroy et al.). Schreibman, Whalen, and Stahmer (2000) examined the use of videos as a method of priming or preparing children with autism for future events. Videos of difficult transitions were shown to three children who exhibited severe behavior problems when required to transition (e.g., leave the home or shop in a public place). The tapes were filmed from the perspective of a child walking through these situations. After watching the videos, the children displayed fewer behavior problems.

Considerations for Teaching Skills to Address Restricted Patterns of Behavior, Interests, and Activities

Skills for controlling and harnessing restricted interests and repetitive behaviors make a key difference for individuals on the spectrum. It is unlikely that these obsessions and behaviors can be eliminated. In fact, this may be undesirable, because such fascinations often represent a strength and an avenue for successful participation in the educational, social, and work worlds. The exception here is when interests involve unacceptable or illegal behavior.

COMMUNICATION

Weaknesses in two key areas – joint attention and symbol use – underlie social communication difficulties in individuals on the spectrum.

Joint attention is defined as the ability to coordinate attention and share focus on an event or object. Through joint attention, for example, we gain an understanding of the meanings of eye gaze, facial expressions, voice, and gestures. As such, joint attention is the basis for early social behavior and the precursor to language skills, play, and imitation. The development of later conversational skills such as selection of topics, initiation, turn-taking, and repairing breakdowns in communication also requires joint attention skills.

Symbol use is defined as the set of abilities that are necessary for developing an understanding and use of language and nonverbal communication, and adhering to social conventions. For example, symbol use underlies social problem solving and conversation skills such as shifting topics appropriately and terminating a conversation. More advanced skills that require the foundation of symbol use include collaboration and the ability to regulate arousal and emotions (Rubin & Lennon, 2004).

Research is beginning to point to effective methods for teaching these foundational and advanced skills of social communication.

Research Support

The effectiveness of techniques for teaching a range of communication skills has been examined in the research literature. Research on approaches to teaching joint attention, social initiation, and maintenance of conversations is reviewed here.

Joint Attention

In typically developing infants, joint attention skills begin to emerge around the age of 9 months. Deficits in these important skills are observed in children with autism prior to their first birthday (Jones & Carr, 2004) and are believed to represent one of the earliest symptoms of this disorder (Shic, Bradshaw, Klin, Scassellati, & Chawarska, 2011). As mentioned, it is thought that joint attention skills are important precursors to language development. Indeed, early vocabulary development (Morales et al., 2000) and response to language intervention (Bono, Daley, & Sigman, 2004) are positively associated with these skills.

A few studies have demonstrated that it is possible to teach joint attention skills to children with ASD. Whalen and Schreibman (2003) explicitly taught children the components required to respond to joint attention (responds to examiner placing child's hand on object, responds to examiner tapping object, follows a point, etc.) followed by training to initiate joint attention with the examiner. In this small-group study, children demonstrated improvement in initiating joint attention, and the skills generalized outside the research setting. Kasari, Gulsrud, Wong, Kwan, and Locke (2010) taught caregivers to follow and maintain their toddler's interests. They found improvement in joint attention of the two children in the study in addition to improved social and communication skills.

Social Initiation

Recognizing the importance of early social interaction, Hwang and Hughes (2000) reviewed 16 studies that examined interventions for social initiation in order to analyze patterns. The use of time delay and environmental factors were found to be effective in increasing skills. Time delay is an intervention in which the adult (parent or examiner) presents a desired object and waits briefly before prompting the child to make an appropriate request for it. Reinforcement is provided for requesting. As success is attained, the time delay for prompting is gradually increased. This technique was found to promote requesting, greetings, as well as responses during play activities (see Hwang & Hughes, for review). Environmental factors, such as providing preferred items and choices, have also resulted in an increase in requesting.

Similar to time delay, pivotal response training (PRT) has been used to increase initiation of communication in children with autism (Harper, Symon, & Frea, 2008; Koegel, Carter, & Koegel, 1998; Masiello, 2007). In one study (Koegel et al.), a desirable object was placed within sight of a child and delivered when the child asked, "What is that?" After training, children continued to use the question to identify new objects and generalized the skill to the home setting. The study found that children's expressive vocabulary was also increased (Koegel et al.).

Other methods have been found to be effective for teaching communication skills. For example, peer buddies have been used to promote initiation of interactions such as asking for objects, waiting one's turn, and looking at the speaker (Laushey & Heflin, 2000). Using written scripts, Kranz and McClannahan (1993) successfully taught children to initiate interactions with their peers. Thiemann and Goldstein (2004) designed a unique study that allowed for comparison between peer training and written text instruction (i.e., direct instruction using visual supports such as written scripts or pictures with written information). Most children demonstrated improvements in social initiation as a result of playing with trained peers; however, additional gains were observed when written text instruction was added.

Maintaining Conversations

Being able to maintain conversations is perhaps equally as important as being able to initiate them. Research has shown that children can learn scripted conversations by watching videotapes and then use them with a variety of people in a range of settings (Charlop & Milstein, 1989). D'Ateno et al. (2003) taught one girl with autism appropriate comments and actions for play by watching videotape.

Research on communication skills and autism is abundant; however, the bulk of this research focuses on early language development. Unfortunately, "the full complement of language skills that come into play as the demands of development and new situations expand has yet to be defined adequately, let alone addressed in treatment studies" (Goldstein, 2002, p. 392). More advanced communication skills are complex and involve subtleties that evade definition. It is these more subtle demands of communication, including pragmatic skills, that challenge high-functioning individuals on the spectrum. Increased research applicable to the needs of the higher functioning population will likely emerge as the understanding of more complex aspects of communication develops.

Considerations for Teaching Communication Skills

Because communication is transactional, it is not enough to provide instruction. Programs should include training and support of communication partners (Rubin & Lennon, 2004). Trained same-age peers are especially effective in improving communication skills (Paul, 2003). Communication partners may facilitate learning through making explicit that which is often only implied. For example, exaggerated cues or direct statements may be used. Rather than relying on subtle or nonverbal messages, conversation partners may be helpful by clearly stating their level of interest, explaining the meaning of their body language, or giving direct feedback. Comments, such as "I'm holding my hand up to ask you to pause so that I can ask a question" or "I am ready to talk about something else. I am not very interested in the skeletal structure of the manatee," may send messages that autistic individuals rarely perceive through less direct means. Without such information, they are unable to adjust and improve their communication skills. Communication partners may also be trained to use visual supports such as written lists of their own interests, or visual cues to speak more slowly or to allow their partner time to respond (Rubin & Laurent, 2004).

The learner's age and developmental level is an additional consideration. To children between the ages of 3 and 5, communication skills are often taught within the context of play activities. During the school-age years, activities such as games with rules, crafts, and shared interests become the context for teaching new skills. Communication training for adolescents may center on discussion groups and teaching skills for talking on the phone (Paul, 2003). Finally, in adulthood, communication skills for employment and leisure settings become appropriate targets.

Paul (2003) discusses several additional considerations for teaching communication skills to individuals with high-functioning ASD. First, she emphasizes the need to include opportunities for practice in naturalistic environments to encourage generalization. Further, it is important not to overlook the importance of visual supports in teaching communication skills. Finally, Paul points out that because prosody, the rhythm and rise and fall of speech, impacts social and vocational success, it must be directly addressed as a critical aspect of communication skills.

SENSORY DIFFERENCES

Some level of sensory input is inherent in all activities. It is not always possible to manage or decrease sensory input through the antecedent or task demand interventions discussed in Chapter 7. It is important to teach those on the autism spectrum to recognize and manage their response to the sensory environment.

Williams and Shellenberger (1996) developed the How Does Your Engine Run? program using the analogy of an engine to teach self-regulation skills. One book uses cartoon characters named "the Sensory Gang" to represent each sense and explain the complex sensory system (Culp, 2011). It may also be helpful for individuals on the spectrum to learn that differences in sensory function are often associated with autism and that, therefore, their sensory needs may differ from those of most others in their environment. Without such awareness, unnecessary tension or conflict often results. For example, an autistic student and a related hypersensitivity to sounds may complain that his classmates are too loud. If his teacher considers the volume level to be appropriate, she may not respond to the complaint as he had expected. The student then may become irate because his teacher "refused to tell them to be quiet."

In this scenario, it would be helpful to teach the student on the spectrum that it is *his* auditory sensitivity that is different from others' and that his classmates are not purposefully being loud to annoy him. The others in the room consider the volume level to be comfortable and appropriate for the classroom activity. With this understanding, the student may then be taught options such as moving to a quieter area to work or wearing headphones.

Research Support and Considerations for Teaching Skills to Address Sensory Needs

While research supporting specific sensory interventions is emerging, data on the effectiveness of teaching self-regulation skills are not yet available. The models for teaching skills for sensory regulation are, by necessity, oversimplified. It is important to maintain a consultative relationship with the experts on sensory functioning, primarily occupational therapists.

COGNITIVE DIFFERENCES

There is a wide range of cognitive differences in autism. In response to these differences, instruction often must be individualized or differentiated. In the following we will look at learning disabilities in math and reading, differences in executive functioning, as well as other common cognitive differences among individuals on the spectrum.

Learning Disability in Math

Approximately half of students with high-functioning ASD have a specific learning disability in math (Reitzel & Szatmari, 2003). Other difficulties in math are often observed as well. While computation tends to be a strength for those with high-functioning ASD, applying these skills to real tasks or problem solving (generalization) is often challenging. Therefore, direct instruction in applying math to life activities such as shopping, construction, or cooking is required.

Some students on the spectrum may dislike practicing computational skills that they feel they have "mastered" or writing out steps to problems that they are able to solve in their minds. It is necessary to teach the logic for the assignment or to adjust the requirements when they are actually unnecessary for specific individuals. It is sometimes helpful to allow the student to serve as a peer tutor. Through this process, the student will review the material and have an opportunity to practice social and communication skills (Jordan, 2003).

Learning Disability in Reading

Approximately one fifth of students with high-functioning ASD have a disability in reading (Reitzel & Szatmari, 2003). Techniques that are effective in teaching reading skills to students with dyslexia are also effective in teaching students with ASD (Jordan, 2003). Other reading challenges are frequently observed. For example, difficulties with understanding the motivation of characters and following the narrative structure are often present. Jordan suggests that teachers narrate stories with puppets to teach early reading comprehension. Through the use of such visual supports, children learn to associate the plot of the story with specific characters. As reading skills develop, students may be taught to highlight the information in the story related to a specific character as an aid to understanding the plot (Jordan). The skill of drawing meaning from literature or experience can be taught through systematically pointing out the theme or the overall meaning of a reading selection or activity. The use of drama and role playing from written scripts also advances comprehension skills (Jordan).

Differences in Executive Functioning

Many of the skills mentioned above are part of the group of mental processes called executive functions (EF). As discussed in Chapter 1, deficits in these processes, including working memory, behavior inhibition, planning, mental flexibility (shifting sets), task initiation and performance monitoring, and self-regulation, are often seen in individuals on the spectrum.

Dawson and Guare (2003) outline steps for teaching executive functions.

1. Accurately describe problems and set goals.
2. Develop a checklist of steps to reach the goal.
3. Supervise the learner as he follows the checklist, with prompting and feedback provided as needed.
4. Evaluate the process and, if necessary, make changes (such as adding cues or further breaking down the task).
5. Fade supervision. Cues and prompts are decreased until the learner is able to do the task independently.

Over time, through teaching and external supports, executive skills will become increasingly internalized.

Other Cognitive Differences

Other difficulties that impact learning are also common among students on the spectrum. Tasks that require abstract thinking, creativity, sustained attention, cognitive flexibility, or problem solving are often particularly difficult (Reitzel & Szatmari, 2003). Further, time management and organizational deficits compound these cognitive challenges.

The strong rote memory skills exhibited by many of the same individuals tend to mask these difficulties. For example, individuals on the spectrum may be able to repeat facts or rules that they are unable to apply in actual situations. Myles and Adreon (2001) state that this "lack of symmetry between verbalizations and actions" is often misinterpreted as willful defiance (p. 13).

Research Support

Theory of mind has dominated the research on cognitive skills of autistic individuals. This research is part of the social skills discussion earlier in this chapter. Current literature includes descriptions of methods for teaching cognitive skills in other areas such as central coherence and EF; however, to date, research support for these methods is sparse.

Two studies of literacy skills in students with autism used computer-generated multimedia study materials to augment the general classroom instruction. Results included significant gains in reading and phonological awareness along with more rapid reading. These findings indicate that the provision of opportunities to explore literature through multiple modes, coupled with targeted teacher interactions, is an effective approach for improving reading skills in children with autism spectrum disorder (Tjus, Heimann, & Nelson, 1998, 2004).

Considerations for Teaching Academic and Executive Functioning Skills to Individuals with Cognitive Differences

The approach to teaching cognitive or academic skills must be individualized. Strengths and interests should be harnessed and challenges related to the autism should be recognized and addressed. It is especially important to distinguish understanding from repetition, comprehension from word recognition, and noncompliance from being overwhelmed.

MOTOR DIFFERENCES

As discussed in Chapter 7, it is often necessary to decrease motor and handwriting demands in order for those on the spectrum to experience success. Alternatively, motor clumsiness and poor handwriting may be addressed through teaching new motor skills.

In the gross-motor area, skills for participation in aerobic and fitness activities should be emphasized while deemphasizing competitive sports (Griffin, Griffin, Fitch, Albera, & Gingras, 2006; Williams, 2001). These suggestions are based on the presence of poor motor skills and coordination and an accompanying increased risk of failure and teasing. During the school years, teachers who are knowledgeable at addressing special needs (i.e., adaptive physical education teachers) may be helpful in this process.

In the fine-motor area, teaching handwriting skills may be facilitated through hand-over-hand copying of letters accompanied by a verbal script. Use of guidelines or highlighting of lined paper can also be helpful in encouraging uniform writing (Williams, 2001). Attwood (1998) recommends that keyboard skills be taught early as an alternative to handwriting. During the school years, occupational therapists may be helpful in the transition to keyboarding.

Research Support

Baranek conducted an extensive review of the literature on sensory and motor interventions (2002). She notes the paucity of literature on these topics compared to other areas of study, and states that many existing studies suffer from methodological flaws. It seems clear that more research in motor interventions specific to autism is needed. Fortunately, the early 2000s has marked a period of increased interest in the motor area. It is hoped that the information gap will soon be bridged.

Considerations for Teaching Motor Skills

It is important to be mindful that motor differences are a biological reality for many individuals on the spectrum; therefore, a balance between adjusting demands and teaching skills must be found.

EMOTIONAL VULNERABILITY

In many respects, some of the challenges associated with autism set the stage for poor social and emotional adjustment. Not surprisingly, autistic individuals often experience difficulty understanding and expressing emotions. Scientists have learned much about the neurological basis for these challenges.

The Social Brain

In a review, Baron-Cohen and Belmonte (2005) note that one researcher used the term "social brain" to describe three special regions, including the amygdala, orbitofrontal and medial frontal cortices, and the superior temporal sulcas and gyrus (Brothers, 1990). Together, these areas are responsible for several fundamental components of social behavior, including processing and interpreting facial expressions (for review, see Schultz, 2005). Bachevalier and Loveland (2006) assert that the orbitofrontal amygdala, in particular, is responsible for self-regulation of social behaviors. They define self-regulation as "The ability to select and initiate complex behaviors in response to the specific conditions of the social environment" (p. 98). Essentially, in order to make social decisions and respond appropriately, one must first accurately interpret the behaviors of others; however, the neurological underpinnings of ASD are believed to impair this process (Bachevalier & Loveland).

Emotional Consequences

The emotional consequences of living with a severe social disorder can be profound.

- Many display *explosive anger and aggressive behaviors* that serve to isolate them further from family and peers.
- The presence of *clinically significant depression and anxiety* is also relatively common. Studies have found that children with high-functioning ASD experience both depression (Kim et al., 2000) and anxiety (Kim et al.; Russell & Sofronoff, 2005) at a higher rate than would be expected in the general population.
- Sadly, there also appears to be a *heightened risk of suicidal behaviors* among this group (Ghaziuddin, 2002; Lainhart, 1999; Tantum, 2003).

Teaching Skills for Preventing Rages

Myles and Southwick (2005) discuss the following three approaches to preventing rages:

- instruction
- interpretation
- restructuring

The first refers to *instructing in areas of skills deficits* and requires identifying deficient skills by conducting a task analysis as discussed in the previous chapter. Myles and Southwick recommend using pre-developed scope and sequences, available for a variety of skills that impact rages (emotional awareness, calming skills, etc.). They also outline essential methods for teaching skills, including providing the rationale for using a skill, breaking down information into small parts, incorporating both visual and auditory presentation, modeling, monitoring skill acquisition, and planning for generalization (see Myles & Southwick, 2005, for review).

Interpretation refers to providing assistance in understanding oneself within the social world. The authors discuss teaching individuals with ASD to recognize those body cues that inform them of their emotional states (Myles & Southwick, 2005). Understanding one's feelings is the first step to appropriately dealing with them. Comic Strip Conversations™ and social autopsies are suggested as methods for assisting in the understanding of others' thoughts and feelings, unwritten social rules, and the world in general.

Last, *restructuring* describes accommodations to restructure the environment in order to reduce demands. These techniques are consistent with the concept of Task Demands discussed in Chapter 7.

Increasing Social and Emotional Understanding

Several curricula have been developed to facilitate social and emotional understanding. For example, *Navigating the Social World* (McAfee, 2002), *Playing It Right!* (Bareket, 2006), and *Super Skills* (Coucouvanis, 2005) contain lessons that encourage the development of specific social and communication skills as well as emotional awareness and self-management. *My Book Full of Feelings* (Jaffe & Gardner, 2006) is a workbook that teaches children how to identify and deal with emotions. Also, *The 5-Point Scale* (Buron & Curtis, 2022) is helpful for teaching students awareness and self-regulation in a variety of situations.

In the field of psychology several effective interventions have been developed to address emotional concerns. One technique, in particular, cognitive behavior therapy (CBT), has received much attention. CBT is based on the premise that perception of an event impacts feelings and, ultimately, behavior (Beck, 1995). For example, after incorrectly answering a question in class, Cindy thinks to herself, "I'm stupid!" As a result, she feels depressed and throws her book on the ground.

The link between thinking, feeling, and behavior is a core assumption underlying this technique. Thus, the purpose of CBT is to help alter *thinking* so it becomes healthier. That is, the individual learns skills to reinterpret situations in order to reduce negative feelings and maladaptive behaviors.

While the benefits of CBT are established, studies have only recently begun to examine its use with individuals on the spectrum. Attwood (2003b) suggests that CBT is well suited for this population because it addresses thinking, which is often distorted. Indeed, Attwood has developed two CBT programs (2004a, 2004b) for children and adolescents with high-functioning ASD that may also be adapted for use with adults. One program addresses anger; the other focuses on anxiety. Components include affective education and cognitive restructuring.

Affective education teaches about feelings, including giving proper names for feelings, identifying different feelings, recognizing that feelings exist on a continuum (as opposed to all or nothing), identifying feelings based on facial expression, tone of voice, and body language, and identifying body cues that signal feelings.

Cognitive restructuring teaches participants to challenge distorted thinking by collecting and using "evidence" to correct irrational thoughts (Attwood, 2004a, 2004b). Comic Strip Conversations™ are used to help understand the perspective of others (Gray, 1998). Additionally, children are taught skills to add to their "emotional toolbox," which helps them learn techniques to address and change feelings independently.

Research Support

Cognitive behavior therapy is a well-researched method for teaching skills to address emotional vulnerability. CBT has been shown to be effective with a variety of disorders, including depression, anxiety, panic disorder, Obsessive-Compulsive Disorder, and social phobia (Butler, Chapman, Forman, & Beck, 2006). Attwood's programs (2004a, 2004b) represent an adaptation of CBT for use with individuals with ASD. These programs may be implemented by parents, teachers, and other professionals without psychological training.

Research supports Attwood's program. For example, Sofronoff, Attwood, and Hinton (2005) examined the effectiveness of the CBT program for anxiety in children with AS. After receiving six 2-hour group sessions, the children were significantly less anxious as reported by their parents. Furthermore, the children were able to generate coping strategies for a character in a scenario, suggesting that skills for emotional regulation could be generalized to novel situations.

Considerations for Teaching Strategies to Address Emotional Vulnerability

In order to teach individuals on the spectrum to identify and regulate emotions, it is necessary to understand the nature and impact of mindblindness and be knowledgeable of the scope and sequence of the skills to be taught. The inability to recognize and understand feelings in others is often associated with an inability to recognize and understand those feelings in oneself.

Theory of mind skills are the foundation upon which emotion regulation is built. If we cannot recognize our emotional states, we are unable to deal with them. Often maladaptive behaviors (e.g., rage, flat affect) emerge as a means of coping. Many individuals on the spectrum display an "all-or-nothing" emotional expression, which can manifest as intense mood swings. Because they are often only able to recognize the feelings of others when they are in an extreme form, it is not surprising that their ability to emote mirrors what they are capable of seeing.

This highlights the importance of teaching ToM skills. It is essential first to identify where the skill deficits lie. This process can be facilitated through the use of scope-and-sequence materials (e.g., *Teaching Children with Autism to Mind-Read* – Howlin, Baron-Cohen, & Hadwin, 1999; and *Super Skills* – Coucouvanis, 2005).

The ability to understand others' feelings and to regulate or control one's own emotional states are life skills that effect adaptation in multiple settings, including home, work, school, and community. Mastery of these skills is necessary to experience success. Learning to recognize and regulate emotion is an ongoing process. Skills needed at 8 years old differ from those required at the age of 28. Because typically developing individuals often do not have to work to learn these skills, they can seem deceptively simple. Yet, identifying, regulating, and responding to emotions are complex, multi-layered skills. For example, in order to show empathy, one must accurately identify another's emotional state (reading facial expression, voice tone, and body cues), associate that with one's personal experiences, and devise an appropriate expression of understanding.

When conducting any kind of training or teaching, it is important to consider the learner's emotional state. Being calm is a prerequisite for learning new skills. A person who is in a rage is not able to learn coping skills at that time. Motivation is an additional consideration. As discussed in Chapter 5, if there is no reinforcement, there is no lesson. In order for skills to be learned and displayed, one must provide meaningful rewards.

APPLICATION OF THE ZIGGURAT MODEL

Skills to Teach Interventions – Steve

After Nicole helped Steve to determine skill deficits currently impacting him, they developed a plan to increase his skills in these key areas (Figure 8.4).

With regard to academics, while Steve is bright, he does not possess the skills for independent study. He lacks organizational and study skills and communicates his needs poorly to his professors (i.e., requesting help with coursework, copies of notes, etc.). Knowing that Steve is very concrete or rule-governed, Nicole suggested that he attend a special seminar on organization and study skills entitled "The Five Rules for College Success." As discussed previously, she also recommended that he use an electronic or paper calendar. She believed the seminar would teach skills to help him to more fully utilize a paper or computer organization system.

Nicole recognized that Steve's lack of communication with his professors and teaching assistants contributed to his failing grades and increasing level of anxiety. In high school, his special education monitoring teacher and his mother helped to keep Steve organized and current in all his classes. If he made a poor grade on a test, they assigned him activities to remediate the skill (e.g., speak with the teacher, review the answers to the test, reread the

ZIGGURAT WORKSHEET

BEHAVIOR/AREAS OF CONCERN Social, Restricted Patterns of Behavior, Sensory Differences, Cognitive Differences, Emotional Vulnerability	FOR SPECIFIC INTERVENTION PLAN (Operationalized Behaviors) ☺☺ ☺☺ ☺☺	SELECTED UCC ITEMS	CHECK ALL THAT APPLY		
			A	B	C
		#1 Has difficulty recognizing the feelings and thoughts of others (mindblindness) #4 Lacks tact or appears rude #5 Has difficulty making or keeping friends #8 Tends to be less involved in group activities #12 Expresses strong need for routine or sameness #18 Has problems handling transition and change	#41 Responds in an unusual manner to sounds #52 Displays poor problem-solving skills #53 Has poor organizational skills #60 Has attention problems #76 Is easily stressed #89 Has difficulty managing stress and/or anxiety			
  Sensory and Biological	Sensory and Biological Intervention:	• Use noise-canceling headphones while studying and soft earplugs on days when roommate has to wake early. • Make an appointment with a doctor at the student health center to discuss medications for your symptoms of anxiety and attention problems. • Try to sign up for early morning or late evening classes where class size is typically smaller. • Get involved in regular physical activities to help keep the mind/body alert prior to studying and attending lectures. • Prior to attending large lecture classes, take time to relax and prepare yourself by taking deep breaths and reminding yourself that you can handle the crowd for the duration of class. Arrive to class early and select a seat away from "traffic." If you need to, you can take a quick break.	✓		
	Underlying Characteristics Addressed:	#41 Responds in an unusual manner to sounds #60 Has attention problems #76 Is easily stressed		✓	
  Respectful Reinforcement	Reinforcement Intervention:	• Develop a self-reinforcement system. You will need to monitor your own progress on specific goals (e.g., study goals, academic goals, and social goals). For example, reward yourself with a timed game of chess on the Internet after you finish reading a chapter. • Join clubs in your area of interests such as movie club, or chess club, in order to provide yourself with rewarding social opportunities. • Tell yourself that you have done a good job after you notice a minor change in your dorm room and handle it without complaining.		✓	✓
	Underlying Characteristics Addressed:	#5 Has difficulty making or keeping friends #8 Tends to be less involved in group activities #12 Expresses strong need for routine or sameness #52 Displays poor problem-solving skills #53 Has poor organizational skills #60 Has attention problems #76 Is easily stressed			

Figure 8.4. Ziggurat worksheet for Steve's global intervention.

ZIGGURAT WORKSHEET

			✓		✓
			✓	✓	
			✓	✓	

Structure & Visual/Tactile Supports	Structure & Visual/Tactile Support Intervention:	• Purchase small handheld computer (PDA) or paper calendar. Record all assignments and tests. Schedule time to study each day. Schedule time to meet with professor or assistant before tests. Review schedule daily. *Note.* This intervention applies to multiple levels. • Schedule reinforcement time after tasks are completed. • Make written notes of questions to ask teaching assistant or professor when attending office hours. • Review list of relaxation/coping skills (provided) when feeling upset. • Place items (clothing, book bag, etc.) in the same location to avoid losing them.
	Underlying Characteristics Addressed:	#52 Displays poor problem-solving skills #53 Has poor organizational skills #76 Is easily stressed
Task Demands	Task Demand Intervention:	• Enroll in classes that have study sessions and teaching assistants. • Arrange through student support center to have professors provide you copies of their class notes to reduce the amount of writing you will do or get a copy of a peer's notes or record lecture. • Use PDA or paper calendar to record assignments and tests and schedule time to study (see Structure and Visual/Tactile Supports level for description). • Attend office hours and study sessions. • Read script (provided) how to address concern with roommate (e.g., "Could you please help me find my sweater?"). *Note.* This intervention applies to multiple levels. • Educate the RA on your floor about autism. Notify him when there is conflict between you and your roommate. When possible, have the RA mediate by helping you under-stand how your roommate feels or how your behavior may have impacted Mark.
	Underlying Characteristics Addressed:	#1 Has difficulty recognizing the feelings and thoughts of others (mindblindness) #60 Has attention problems #53 Has poor organizational skills #76 Is easily stressed
Skills to Teach	Skill Intervention:	• Categorize statements that are "rude" versus those that are "kind" on a T-chart with RA. If not certain, ask RA or Nicole for help. • Read a book written for young adults with high-functioning ASD to gain more insight and skills. • Attend college seminar on organization and study skills. • Learn relaxation and coping skills through participation in counseling. • If you fail a test, schedule an appointment with the teaching assistant or professor in order to learn the material. • If you have an argument with your roommate, meet with your RA and conduct a social au-topsy in order to better understand what happened and develop ideas to resolve problems.
	Underlying Characteristics Addressed:	#4 Lacks tact or appears rude #53 Has poor organizational skills #89 Has difficulty managing stress and/or anxiety

Figure 8.4. Ziggurat worksheet for Steve's global intervention (continued).

chapter, etc.). Now that he was in college, Steve was having a difficult time taking the initiative to ask for help and following through with activities necessary to learn the material. Nicole quickly recognized the seemingly obvious concept to be taught: that the responsibility for student success essentially shifted to his shoulders when he left the high school environment. Steve did not recognize that the role of professor and college student were defined differently than that of high school teacher and student. Nicole taught Steve this concept using a T-chart (see Figure 8.5). She emphasized that he must ask for help from his professors and teaching assistants.

Both Steve and Nicole recognized that Steve needed to develop new social skills in order to become successful in the college environment. Challenges with ToM seem to underlie most of Steve's interpersonal difficulties. Nicole suggested that Steve meet with his RA to address roommate difficulties. She plans to teach Steve's RA how to conduct a social autopsy. The process will occur after Steve and Mark argue. Based on the information gathered through the social autopsy, the RA will help create a chart listing "rude" versus "kind" words. Steve will be encouraged to add to the list based on his daily interactions. The list will include a section for Steve to write examples of statements that he is not certain how to categorize, with a reminder for him to ask his RA or Nicole to help him to understand these statements when they meet.

High School Teacher	College Professor
• Will provide students with regular reminders of upcoming assignments	• Will often only announce assignments at the beginning of a semester or simply list them on a syllabus
• May ask students to turn in homework	• Will only tell students when assignments are due or list them on a syllabus
• May tell students about missing assignments	• Will record a zero for missing assignments
• Will contact students' parents regarding declining progress in class	• May post grades but will not make individual contact with students
• Will ask to see students following a low test grade	• Will not make a personal request; however, may offer scheduled office hours or copies of the answers for students to review
• Will make an effort to avoid overlap tests on same day	• Will likely not coordinate test schedules across classes

Figure 8.5. **T-chart of differences between the responsibilities of high school teachers and college professors.**

Finally, Nicole was concerned with the increasing level of anxiety that Steve reported. She believed it contributed to his difficulties with concentration and recommended that he speak with a counselor who could assist him in learning relaxation skills to cope with his stress. Figure 8.6 shows Steve's M-CAPS.

Modified Comprehensive Autism Planning System (M-CAPS)

Child/Student: _Steve_

Activity	Skills to Teach	Task Demands & Positive Environment and Structure & Visual/Tactile Supports	Respectful Reinforcement	Sensory & Biological	Communication/ Social Skills	Data Collection	Generalization
Dorm Life	• Cooperation with roommate	• Books about autism for self and RA • Video for roommate (if interested) • Use RA as mediator • Develop a place for everything to be put	• *Star Trek* or *Halo* movie with roommate	• Noise-canceling headphones, as needed	• Conversation starters with roommate • List of kind/versus rude words (develop with RA) • Script on addressing concerns with roommate • Social autopsies for problems with roommate	• Cooperative (Y/N)	• Use kind words throughout day
Classes	• Class attendance • Relaxation • Organization	• Early-morning or late-evening classes (check for low enrollment) • Ensure that classes have a TA • Attend all study sessions • Get class notes from help center • Arrive early and sit in first row about midway from door • Laptop for notes • PDA for scheduling	• 30 min to 1 hour of leisure time before beginning homework after classes	• Deep breathing before class • Walk before and after class	• Prepare written questions for professor or RA • Meet with professor or TA 1 week before test	• Class notes (Y/N) • Assignment in PDA (Y/N) • Supplies needed (Y/N) • Relaxed (Y/N)	• Laptop and PDA as organizing tools
Extra-Curricular	• Communication and Fun	• Join chess club, science fiction, or computer club • Attend class on organization and study skills • Attend local autism adult group	• None other than activities	• Learn relaxation and self-understanding in counseling sessions	• Conversation starter cards	• Communicate with others (Y/N) • Outing with friends at least once a week (Y/N)	• Enjoy activities and remain calm throughout day
Homework (Studying)	• Assignment completion • Being prepared for test	• Use library or help center for study, when possible • Schedule at least 4 hours per day of study time	• *Star Trek* or *Halo* online after studying • 15 minutes of preferred activity after every hour of study	• Sound canceling headphones • Deep breathing every 30 minutes • Walk before and after studying	• List of polite ways to say "Be quiet"	• Grades on tests and assignments	• Deep breathing throughout day as needed

Figure 8.6. M-CAPS for Steve.

Skills to Teach Interventions – Penny

Penny's team identified deficits in the areas of social, communication, and coping skills. Because difficulties with theory of mind appear to underlie each of these areas, many interventions were designed to teach ToM skills (Figure 8.7). The speech therapist recommended that Penny learn pragmatic (social) language skills.

She will work directly with Penny on learning how to start conversations. She also recommended that Ms. Simpson help Penny survey her peers about their interests by asking them simple questions such as, "What are your three favorite TV shows?" "What do you like to do on the weekend?" and "What is your favorite sport?" Penny and Ms. Simpson will keep a list of peers' responses on separate index cards. Using the cards, Penny will practice starting conversations with her speech therapist. The cards will also help Penny to focus on topics of interest when speaking with her peers.

The speech therapist pointed out that in order for Penny to maintain conversations with others, she will need to learn to read the listener's cues. That is, she must recognize when a listener is bored, confused, or engaged. This requires theory of mind skills. Penny will be taught to tune into the listener's facial expressions, tone of voice, gestures, and comments. The speech therapist will provide Penny's parents with a detailed description of what they are working on so that they may emphasize similar skills at home.

Theory of mind skills were also important in addressing Ms. Simpson's concern about Penny's rude and disruptive comments in class (Figure 8.8). She plans to enlist the help of the speech therapist in writing a Social Story™ to address the seemingly obvious concept that things that are true are not necessarily kind. This story, coupled with cartooning, will help Penny to make connections between her behavior (i.e., rude comments) and the peers' responses (rejection).

In order to help Penny to be more successful on the playground, she will need to learn specific skills for initiating play with her peers. The team recognized the value of using discretely defined steps to teach specific skills. They used an established curriculum (see Figure 8.9).

Penny's team discussed the need for her to learn skills to cope with feelings of frustration. The psychologist pointed out that increased behavioral difficulties mostly occur during times of transition or change. Based on this tendency, he recommended that Penny be taught skills for coping during these times. First, he believed that Penny would benefit from

ZIGGURAT WORKSHEET

BEHAVIOR/AREAS OF CONCERN	FOR SPECIFIC INTERVENTION PLAN (Operationalized Behaviors)	SELECTED UCC ITEMS	A	B	C
Social, Restricted Patterns of Behavior, Communication, Motor Differences, Emotional Vulnerability	ⓐ ⓑ ⓒ	#1 Difficulty recognizing the feelings and thoughts of others (mindblindness) #4 Lacks tact or appears rude #5 Difficulty making or keeping friends #8 Tends to be less involved in group activities #14 Has eccentric or intense preoccupations/absorption in own unique interests #18 Has difficulty handling transition and change #25 Has difficulty with rules of conversation #47 Seeks activities that provide touch, pressure, or movement #66 Resists or refuses handwriting tasks #77 Appears to be depressed or sad #85 Has low frustration tolerance			
Sensory and Biological — Sensory and Biological Intervention:	• Seek consultation from the occupational therapist (OT) to assess handwriting including sensory factors and hand fatigue. • Provide Penny with a sensory diet with direction of an OT to help address anxious or agitated behaviors. • Seek medical consultation regarding possible need for pharmacotherapy.		✓		
Underlying Characteristics Addressed:		#47 Seeks activities that provide touch, pressure, or movement #66 Resists or refuses handwriting tasks #77 Appears to be depressed or sad #85 Has low frustration tolerance			
Reinforcement Intervention:	• Develop a positive behavior management plan to address social skills and work completion. Have Penny help to select items for a reinforcer menu. Reinforcers are earned both in home and school. Penny should have frequent opportunities to "cash in" by selecting reinforcers from her menu. • Reinforce Penny for being able to categorize statements as "rude" or "kind." • Provide reinforcement for initiating work on a writing assignment without negative comments. Also reinforce her for working for an increasing amount of time. • Reinforce social success by pairing social interaction with a well-established reinforcer. For example, arrange an opportunity to create and present a project on praying mantises to the third grade during their unit on insects. • Develop a token reinforcement system to address transitioning to school. Parents will provide Penny's token reinforcer system. Parents will provide Penny with a visual checklist/schedule for the morning routine and transition to school. Make the last item on the checklist a school task (e.g., put backpack away). Reinforce Penny at school for following checklist/schedule. Provide additional reinforcement for following the schedule independently. *Note.* This intervention applies to multiple levels.			✓	✓
Respectful Reinforcement — Underlying Characteristics Addressed:		#4 Lacks tact or appears rude #5 Difficulty making or keeping friends #8 Tends to be less involved in group activities #14 Has eccentric or intense preoccupations/absorption in own unique interests #25 Has difficulty with rules of conversation #77 Appears to be depressed or sad			

Figure 8.7. Ziggurat worksheet for Penny's global intervention.

ZIGGURAT WORKSHEET

			✓	✓
		✓	✓	
		✓	✓	

Structure & Visual/Tactile Supports

Structure & Visual/Tactile Support Intervention:	• Create visual chart "Rude versus kind words." Update as kind/unkind words occur and keep a copy at home and in school. • Use a Comic Strip Conversation to help illustrate the thoughts and feelings of others in the context of a problem situation. For example, teach Penny to recognize the response of others to her comments. *Note.* This intervention applies to multiple levels. • Parents will provide Penny with a visual checklist/schedule for the morning routine and transition to school (see Reinforcement level for description). • Provide Penny with a weekly schedule to increase predictability.
Underlying Characteristics Addressed:	#1 Difficulty recognizing the feelings and thoughts of others (mindblindness) #4 Lacks tact or appears rude #5 Difficulty making or keeping friends #18 Has difficulty handling transition and change #85 Has low frustration tolerance

Task Demands

Task Demand Intervention:	• The speech therapist will provide Penny with a small note card with prompts for starting a conversation with peers. Keep note cards on preferred peers and their interests. *Note.* This intervention applies to multiple levels. • Have Penny be responsible for taking the soccer ball out on the playground and give her a visual script for how to start playing the game at recess. Teach the playground soccer rules to Penny and remind her that the "playground" rules differ from "league" rules. *Note.* This intervention applies to multiple levels. • Train a peer to be Penny's "buddy" at recess. The peer will help to integrate her into ongoing play activities such as soccer.
Underlying Characteristics Addressed:	#5 Difficulty making or keeping friends #25 Has difficulty with rules of conversation #85 Has low frustration tolerance

Skills to Teach

Skill Intervention:	• Teach Penny the implied playground rules. For example, the difference between playground soccer and league soccer. • Teach her how to work with a peer buddy. • Teach Penny how to use a checklist/schedule. • Teach Penny to recognize the response of others to her comments (see Structure & Visual/Tactile Support level for description), role play and actual situations. • Teach Penny how to start a conversation with peers. • Teach Penny how to recognize and discuss the interests of others. • The speech therapist will instruct Penny on how to keep a conversation going (by asking questions on others' interests). • Teach Penny to replace negative comments about assignments with requests for help. • Teach Penny some strategies to calm when she is feeling frustrated.
Underlying Characteristics Addressed:	#1 Difficulty recognizing the feelings and thoughts of others (mindblindness) #4 Lacks tact or appears rude #5 Difficulty making or keeping friends #14 Has eccentric or intense preoccupations/absorption in own unique interests #18 Has difficulty handling transition and change #25 Has difficulty with rules of conversation #85 Has low frustration tolerance

Figure 8.7. Ziggurat worksheet for Penny's global intervention (continued).

ZIGGURAT WORKSHEET

BEHAVIOR/ AREAS OF CONCERN	FOR SPECIFIC INTERVENTION PLAN (Operationalized Behaviors)	SELECTED UCC ITEMS	CHECK ALL THAT APPLY A	B	C
Class disruption	• Says, "I don't have to do this work." • Insults peers • Does not complete writing tasks	#1 Mindblindness #4 Lacks tact #16 Unmotivated by customary rewards #18 Difficulty with transition and change #33 Gives false impression of understanding more than she actually does #63 Has difficulty understanding the connection between behavior and consequences			
Sensory and Biological	Sensory and Biological Intervention:	• Seek consultation from the occupational therapist (OT) to assess handwriting, including sensory factors and hand fatigue. • Provide Penny with a sensory diet with direction of an OT to help address anxious or agitated behaviors. • Provide a calming sensory activity prior to giving lengthy writing task. • Teach Penny to recognize body cues that indicate stress or frustration (e.g., muscle tension, heart rate, breathing pattern). • Teach Penny strategies to address her stress and frustration (e.g., engage in sensory calming strategy, ask for help, take slow, deep breaths). *Note.* This intervention applies to multiple levels.	✓	✓	
	Underlying Characteristics Addressed:	#66 Resists handwriting #85 Low frustration tolerance #88 Difficulty understanding own and others' emotions #89 Difficulty managing stress and anxiety			
	Reinforcement Intervention:	• Develop a positive behavior management plan to address social skills and work completion. Have Penny help to select items for a reinforcer menu. Reinforcers are earned both in home and school. Penny should have frequent opportunities to "cash in" by selecting reinforcers from her menu. • Reinforce Penny for being able to categorize statements as "rude" or "kind." • With the assistance of a speech therapist, develop a card that has rules for class discussion. During a class discussion, give Penny a card – one side green (with rules for appropriate class discussion; e.g., no insults, on-topic remarks) and the other side red (with a list of appropriate listening behaviors). Begin each class discussion with the green side up. Turn card to red if Penny makes an inappropriate contribution. Remove card at the end of class discussion. Reinforce Penny for following the rules on either side of the card. *Note.* This intervention applies to multiple levels. • Provide reinforcement for initiating work on a writing assignment without negative comments. Also reinforce her for working for an increasing amount of time. • Develop a token reinforcement system to address transitioning to school. Use alligator or other favorite animal stamps in Penny's token reinforcer system. Parents will provide Penny with a visual checklist/ schedule for the morning routine and transition to school. Make the last item on the checklist a school task (e.g., put backpack away). Reinforce Penny at school for following checklist/schedule. Provide additional reinforcement for following the schedule independently. *Note.* This intervention applies to multiple levels. • Provide Penny with a strong reinforcer on Mondays when she arrives to school with her completed morning home checklist.	✓	✓	✓
Respectful Reinforcement	Underlying Characteristics Addressed:	#4 Lacks tact #16 Unmotivated by customary rewards #18 Difficulty with transition and change #66 Resists handwriting #85 Low frustration tolerance			

Figure 8.8. Ziggurat worksheet for Penny's specific intervention.

ZIGGURAT WORKSHEET

Structure & Visual/Tactile Supports	Structure & Visual/Tactile Support Intervention:	• Create visual chart "Rude versus kind words." Update as kind/unkind words occur and keep a copy at home and in school. • Videotape a same-age class during discussion time. Prior to taping, remind all students of behavioral expectations. Show Penny the tape, stopping to view specific skills (raising hand, refraining from negative comments when peers answer incorrectly, etc.) and to explore facial expressions and gestures of the peer models. Practice skills with Penny and reinforce. Provide Penny with a visual reminder of class discussion rules and reinforce her for successfully following them. • Use red/green class discussion card (see Reinforcement level for description). • Create a visual chart for tracking her progress on earning rewards. For example, use a drawing of a bug. Let Penny color in a segment each time she earns a reinforcer for being on-task or making appropriate comments in class. She selects a reinforcer from the menu when the drawing is completely colored. • Use cartooning to help illustrate the thoughts and feelings of others in the context of a problem situation. For example, teach Penny to recognize the response of others to her comments. *Note.* This intervention applies to multiple levels. • Parents will provide Penny with a visual checklist/schedule for the morning routine and transition to school (see Reinforcement level for description) • Provide Penny with a weekly schedule to increase predictability.
	Underlying Characteristics Addressed:	#1 Has mindblindness #4 Lacks tact #16 Unmotivated by customary rewards #18 Difficulty with transition and change #33 Gives false impression of understanding more than she actually does #63 Has difficulty understanding the connection between behavior and consequences #88 Difficulty understanding own and others' emotions
Task Demands	Task Demand Intervention:	• Use red/green class discussion card (see Reinforcement level for description). The card explicitly lists the steps for discussion for Penny to use as a guide/reminder. • Provide Penny with list of sentence starters she can use when writing. • Teacher may shorten some lengthy writing assignments or allow Penny to type or respond orally.
	Underlying Characteristics Addressed:	#1 Has mindblindness #63 Has difficulty understanding the connection between behavior and consequences #66 Resists handwriting
Skills to Teach	Skill Intervention:	• Teach Penny strategies to address her stress and frustration (see Sensory/Biological level for description). • Use red/green class discussion card (see Reinforcement level for description). • Teach Penny to recognize the response of others to her comments using Comic Strip Conversation (see Structure & Visual/Tactile Support level for description), role play and actual situations. • With the assistance of the speech therapist, create a Social Story™ to teach Penny that some comments may not be polite even though they may be true. Additionally, the story will assist her in learning social consequences of her disruptive, disrespectful comments. • Teach Penny keyboarding skills.
	Underlying Characteristics Addressed:	#1 mindblindness #4 Lacks tact #66 Resists handwriting #85 Low frustration tolerance

Figure 8.8. Ziggurat worksheet for Penny's specific intervention (continued).

recognizing this pattern herself. He suggested that Ms. Simpson and Penny's parents point out, using a calendar, that her behavioral difficulties are more severe and frequent following weekends and holidays. Next, Penny needs to be taught some coping skills for use during these times (e.g., ask for a sensory break, ask for assistance, take deep breaths, go to safe place). Knowing that reinforcement is necessary for learning the skills, Ms. Simpson plans to provide additional reinforcement on Mondays for demonstrating coping skills. Figure 8.10 shows Penny's CAPS.

Inviting Someone to Play

To invite someone to play, you:
1. Choose someone.
2. Walk close.
3. Smile.
4. Ask.
5. If "yes," go play.
6. If "no," ask someone else.

To answer someone who wants to play with you:
1. Smile.
2. Look.
3. Answer.

From *Super Skills: A Social Skills Group Program for Children with Asperger Syndrome, High-Functioning Autism and Related Challenges* (p. 322), by J. Coucouvanis, 2005, Shawnee Mission, KS: AAPC Publishing. Reprinted with permission.

Figure 8.9. Task analysis for inviting someone to play.

Comprehensive Autism Planning System (CAPS)

Child/Student: _Penny_

Time	Activity	Skills to Teach	Task Demands & Positive Environment and Structure & Visual/Tactile Supports	Respectful Reinforcement	Sensory & Biological	Communication/ Social Skills	Data Collection	Generalization Plan
8:00	Priming	• Turn-taking • Initiating and maintaining appropriate conversation • Transitioning successfully • Emotion recognition • Self-calming	• Visual schedule • Resource room • *Mindreading* software • Visual checklist of morning routine • Train peers	• Review book on insects after priming and completed morning checklist • Verbally reinforce targeted skills	• Koosh ball • Disco seat to sit on	• Conversation starter cards • "Ask a question" card • Incredible 5-Point Scale	• *M:* Turn-taking (Y/N) • *M-F* Identification of emotion in self (correct/ incorrect) • *T, W:* Conversation skills • *M-F:* Initiates/ prompts self-calming	• Conversation starter card and Incredible 5-Point Scale for Girl Scouts and lunch
8:15	Reading	• State reading standards • Asking for help • Handing in work	• Visual checklist of assignment steps • Keyboard or dictate assignments that require extensive writing • Quiet area for tests and assignments • Home base card • Fewer problems to complete	• Token economy with reinforcer menu for achieving targeted skills • Verbally reinforce targeted skills	• Disco seat • Have Penny hand out out materials, run errands, put away materials, to provide movement • Theraband around chair legs	• Conversation starter cards • Help card • Incredible 5-Point Scale	• Mastery of reading standards • Handing in work • *T:* Asking for help • # of times to home base (resource room)	• Help card throughout the day
9:00	Math	• State math standards • Asking for help • Handing in work	• Visual checklist of assignment steps • Pair with other student • Quiet area for tests and assignments • Home base card • Fewer problems to complete	• Token economy • Verbally reinforce targeted skills	• Disco seat • Have Penny hand out materials, run errands, put away materials, to provide movement • Theraband around chair legs	• Conversation starter cards • Help card • Incredible 5-Point Scale	• Mastery of math standards • *W:* Asking for help • # of times to home base (resource room)	
9:45	Bathroom	• None	• Early release	• None	• None	• None	• None	• None
9:55	Transition to Specials	• Independence in transitioning	• Transition card from visual schedule	• Verbally reinforce transition	• None	• None	• None	• Transition to recess and lunch

Figure 8.10. CAPS for Penny.

Comprehensive Autism Planning System (CAPS)

Time	Activity	Skills to Teach	Task Demands & Positive Environment and Structure & Visual/Tactile Supports	Respectful Reinforcement	Sensory & Biological	Communication /Social Skills	Data Collection	Generalization Plan
10:00	Music (MW), Art (T), Spanish (R), Computer Technology (F)	• State standards • Asking for help	• Visual checklist of tasks • Home base card • List of kind/rude words	• Token economy • Verbally reinforce targeted skills	• Koosh ball	• Help card • Incredible 5-Point Scale	• Mastery of standards	
11:00	Social Skills	• Conversation skills • Asking for help • Talking about others' interests • Stress management • Emotion recognition in self and others • Self-calming • Working with a peer buddy	• Visual checklist of tasks • Checklist of skills • Home base card • Modeling, role play, video narration • List of kind/rude words • Self-calming social narrative	• Token economy • Verbally reinforce targeted skills	• Disco seat • Have Penny hand out materials, run errands, put away materials, to provide movement • Theraband around chair legs	• Conversation starter cards • Help card • Cartooning of social situations • Role play of actual situations • Incredible 5-Point Scale with calming instruction	*T, W:* • Conversation • Asking for help • Talking about others' interests • Stress management • Emotion recognition in self and others	• Communication skills in group academic classes • List of kind/rude words inside notebook
11:35	Cash in Tokens	• None	• None	• Reinforcement menu	• None	• None	• None	• None
11:45	Lunch (in RR with peer group) Bathroom	• Conversation skills	• Early entry into cafeteria • Resource room for lunch • Peer buddies	• Reinforcer menu to use after eating and conversation	• None at this time	• Conversation starter cards	• None	• Conversation starter cards at home
12:15	Social Studies	• State social studies standards • Asking for help	• Visual checklist of assignment steps • Keyboard or dictate assignments • Quiet area for tests and assignments • Home base card • Fewer problems to complete • Focus assignments around special interests • List of kind/rude words	• Token economy • Verbally reinforce targeted skills	• Disco seat • Have Penny hand out materials, run errands, put away materials, to provide movement • Theraband around chair legs	• Help card • Incredible 5-Point Scale	• Mastery of reading standards • Handing in work • *R:* Asking for help • # of times to home base (resource room)	• List of kind/rude words at home

Figure 8.10. CAPS for Penny (continued).

Comprehensive Autism Planning System (CAPS)

Time	Activity	Skills to Teach	Task Demands & Positive Environment and Structure & Visual/Tactile Supports	Respectful Reinforcement	Sensory & Biological	Communication/ Social Skills	Data Collection	Generalization Plan
1:00	Language Arts	• State language arts standards • Asking for help	• Visual checklist of assignment steps • Keyboard or dictate assignments • Quiet area for tests and assignments • Home base card • Fewer problems to complete • Focus assignments around special interests • List of kind/rude words	• Token economy targeted skills	• Disco seat • Have Penny hand out materials, run errands, put away materials, to provide movement • Theraband around chair legs	• Help card • Incredible 5-Point Scale	• Mastery of LA standards • Asking for help • *F*: Asking for help • # of times to home base	
1:45	Science	• State science standards • Asking for help	• Visual checklist of assignment steps • Keyboard or dictate assignments • Quiet area for tests and assignments • Home base card • Fewer problems to complete • List of kind/rude words • Focus assignments around special interests	• Reinforcer menu at end of class • Asking for help • Special interest books in classroom	• Disco seat • Have Penny hand out materials, run errands, put away materials, to provide movement • Theraband around chair legs	• Help card • Incredible 5-Point Scale	• Mastery of SS/S standards • *F*: Asking for help • Rumbling and rage • # of times to home base	
2:15	Recess	• Conversation	• Visual checklist • Structured activities with peer • Home base card • Peer buddy	• Computer time on special interest at end of period	• None at this time	• Conversation starter cards	• *T*: Appropriate conversation/ play (Y/N)	• Community social skills group
2:45	Ready for Dismissal	• Organization	• Homework planner • Priming for any schedule changes	• Cash in tokens after materials are organized	• Koosh ball	• Review of day	• Organized (independent/ prompted)	• Priming at home for changes

Figure 8.10. CAPS for Penny (continued).

SUMMARY

This chapter opened with a discussion of the importance of teaching skills, especially the "seemingly obvious" ones. While many behavior problems can be resolved using strategies on the first four levels of the Ziggurat, failure to address underlying skill deficits will likely result in the reemergence of challenging behaviors. Methods for addressing skill deficits in eight key areas were discussed, followed by application of the model to Steve and Penny. The following chapter will cover common pitfalls to intervention and how to resolve them.

CHAPTER HIGHLIGHTS

- *The concepts "seemingly obvious" and "hidden curriculum" refer to lessons that typically developing persons learn simply through living. These essential lessons must be taught explicitly to individuals on the autism spectrum as they do not pick them up on their own.*

- *Pivotal response training (PRT) is a unique approach to social skill instruction because it targets essential or "pivotal" behaviors that are believed to be central to other behaviors.*

- *It is unlikely that repetitive behaviors and obsessive interests can be completely eliminated; however, it is possible to teach how to limit such behaviors to specified times.*

- *Joint attention is the basis for early social behavior and is the precursor to language skills, play, and imitation.*

- *Symbol use underlies social problem solving and conversation skills such as shifting topics appropriately and terminating a conversation.*

- *It is important to teach those on the spectrum to recognize and manage their response to the sensory environment.*

- *In the motor area, a balance between adjusting demands and teaching skills must be found.*

- *The neurological underpinnings of ASD are believed to impair the process of making social decisions and responding appropriately.*

- *Three recommended approaches for preventing rage include instruction, interpretation, and restructuring.*

- *Cognitive behavior therapy is based on the premise that perception of an event impacts feelings and, ultimately, behavior. This approach has been shown to be effective for teaching skills to address emotional vulnerability.*

9 Pulling It All Together

*"Make everything as simple as possible
but not simpler."*

– Albert Einstein

WHY USE THE ZIGGURAT MODEL?

Any approach to intervention design that is simpler than the Ziggurat Model presented in this book is likely to be too simple. Most current interventions are designed to treat the visible behaviors. However, such a narrow, band-aid approach fails to address the true need – the underlying hidden deficits – and provide for sustained change.

No single solution is sufficient to resolve complex needs. The five tiers of the Intervention Ziggurat and three points of intervention (A-B-C) are based on an understanding of the characteristics and needs of individuals on the spectrum. Addressing the levels of the Ziggurat ensures that the stage is set and skills are taught. Furthermore, because antecedent interventions are required, every plan, by definition, is proactive. Use of the ZM (UCC, ISSI, ABC-I, and ZW) facilitates the identification of needs and provision of comprehensive treatment through an interdisciplinary approach. The Ziggurat Model is not a set of intervention techniques; rather, it is a framework for decision making. The model does not describe how to intervene; it describes how to *design* an intervention using a set of evidence-based strategies. These strategies are selected with an emphasis on maximal and effective use of reinforcement and positive behavior supports. The strengths of the Ziggurat Model are summarized below.

STRENGTHS OF THE ZIGGURAT MODEL

The Ziggurat Model:

1. Provides a process and framework for designing an intervention plan and is consistent with a PBS/PBIS approach
2. Addresses underlying characteristics of autism
3. Emphasizes and enhances evidence-based strategies
4. Facilitates comprehensive intervention design
5. Incorporates assessment
6. Emphasizes a positive approach/reinforcement
7. Facilitates the design of proactive interventions
8. Facilitates interdisciplinary interventions
9. Prevents a "band-aid" approach to intervention
10. Prevents punitive approaches

Consider the example in Figure 9.1 depicting two interventions for a 10-year-old girl, Beth, who displays severe tantrums when required to write. The top portion represents a simple "solution" to the problem; the bottom briefly describes strategies on each level of the Intervention Ziggurat. At first glance, both approaches appear to have resolved the initial concern; however, upon closer inspection, it becomes clear that the more simplistic approach results in a partial resolution that addresses only surface needs. In the simple solution, the intervention's effectiveness is limited to the setting in which it occurs. Also, there is no long-term benefit or learning that will eventually lead to independent functioning.

In contrast, the ZM provides for more global improvement as well as skill development. Specifically, sensory breaks can help Beth to remain more calm throughout the day (increasing her ability to tolerate frustration) as well as address aspects of writing impacted by sensory issues. Furthermore, the pencil grip is portable and likely to help her in multiple settings. Reinforcement strategies serve to increase desired behaviors such as coping and help-seeking skills that will be taught to eliminate the tantrums. Visual strategies, such as a timer and mini-schedule, will help provide structure and predictability. Reducing task demands by shortening the length of the task and teaching Beth coping skills will help increase success. The intervention is comprehensive because it occurs at all three points (antecedent, behavior, and consequence) and on all levels of the Ziggurat.

This chapter will help the reader avoid common intervention pitfalls and suggest ways to troubleshoot if solutions appear to fail.

GENERAL TROUBLESHOOTING

It has been said, "The whole is more than the sum of its parts" (Aristotle, 1990). Without active, ongoing communication, there are only parts. One strength of the ZM is that it facilitates the otherwise difficult task of working together. Effective intervention is a daunting process and, when possible, should not be undertaken alone. When problems arise, and they will, we recommend that those involved in implementation come together to problem solve. In the event that access to a team is limited or challenging, it is advisable to seek help from others who are knowledgeable. Parent groups, teacher networks, on-line forums, and colleagues can be valuable sources of support.

Intervention requires perseverance. Given the pervasive nature of autism, is not realistic to expect rapid improvement. In fact, we often see an increase in undesired behaviors – known as an extinction burst – prior to improvement. Ironically, this brief increase may be a sign that the intervention is working.

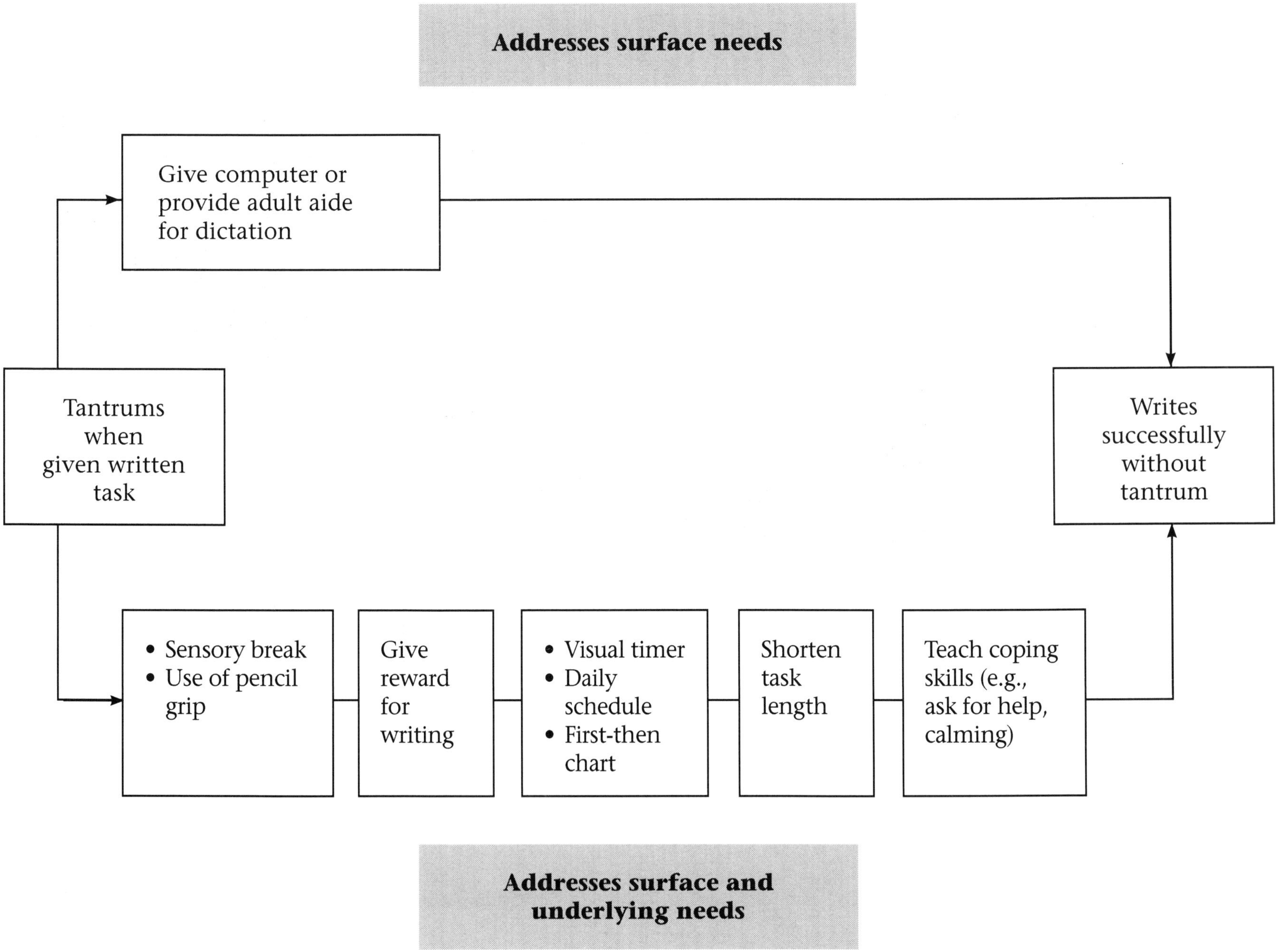

Figure 9.1. How the Ziggurat Model addresses both surface and underlying needs.

Addresses surface needs

Writes successfully without tantrum

Give computer or provide adult aide for dictation

Tantrums when given written task

Addresses surface and underlying needs

Teach coping skills (e.g., ask for help, calming)

Shorten task length

- Visual timer
- Daily schedule
- First-then chart

Give reward for writing

- Sensory break
- Use of pencil grip

The dignity of autistic individuals is paramount and should be a guiding principle in all assessment and intervention efforts. Including the individual in intervention planning is a form of empowerment. It shows respect, encourages independence, increases acceptance of the plan, and adds a valuable, direct source of information. Developmental level should be considered when deciding the extent of involvement of an individual on the spectrum. The goal is to increase participation and involvement over time, and eventually for the individual on the spectrum to be able to select interventions and monitor their progress as much as possible.

The example of Steve helps to illustrate this principle. Although his parents' phone call set the intervention in motion, Steve was responsible for following up on their recommendation, and he was the key communicator with the other team members – Nicole, his professors, RA, counselor, and physician.

ASSESSMENT

Assessment guides intervention. We find that it is helpful to reference the UCC, ISSI, and ABC-I during the development of an intervention plan to ensure that interventions are anchored to identified strengths and needs. In the event that the anticipated improvements are not attained, it may be helpful to review information previously gathered and note the areas of the UCC where many characteristics were endorsed. Review specific items to see whether they are being addressed through the current intervention plan. If not, it may be that some of these are "pivotal" skills necessary for improvement. At times, additional assessment is necessary. For example, it may be advisable to conduct another functional assessment using the ABC-I or update the UCC, drawing on additional informants to gain a broader perspective.

In order to determine when additional assessment is needed, several factors must be considered. First, individuals are "moving targets," making any assessment a snapshot of a moment in time. This is especially true for young children because they develop rapidly, outdating assessment more quickly. Next, behaviors may differ greatly from setting to setting. For example, a child may experience more difficulties at school than in the home due to the nature of demands (e.g., requirement to sit for an extended period of time and cooperate with peers). For this reason, it may be beneficial to gather information from additional informants in order to form a more complete picture. Last, given the high incidence of coexisting disorders (estimated 65% psychiatric disorders in those with AS, Ghaziuddin et al., 1998; and 6% medical conditions in those with autism, Fombonne, 2003), it is also advisable to consider the possibility that some difficulties are manifestations of additional underlying factors.

The perspective of informants, or those who complete the UCC/ISSI and ABC-I, also may need to be considered. Experience with typically developing students helps to establish criteria for expectations at any point of the lifespan. In our experience, parents reporting on only children or oldest children sometimes express concerns that they may not have a realistic picture of "normal" development. In this situation, informants who have experiences with a wide range of students, such as teachers and psychologists, may provide a more global or developmental perspective.

What is salient for the observer is what is challenging or distressing. This is another consideration when evaluating assessment results. For example, parents may report violent rages whereas teachers may emphasize attention problems and disruptive behaviors. This tendency is sometimes seen in reports of parents of children who experience both depression and ADHD. Disruptive, hyperactive, and impulsive behaviors may be noted while the emotional distress of the child goes undetected. Because overt behavioral difficulties are so prominent and tend to dominate the energies of the informant, other underlying emotional characteristics may be overlooked.

As discussed earlier, it is important to attain the perspective of the individual on the spectrum as much as possible. Additionally, it is advisable to pay close attention to factors that are more subtle and therefore less likely to be salient to informants.

Keeping in mind that the top half of the ABC-I contains the elements of a functional assessment, it may be helpful to enlist the expertise of a psychologist or behavior specialist to help review the possible function (purpose) of the behavior of concern. In order to uncover the function, it may be necessary to collect additional data regarding the patterns observed.

SENSORY AND BIOLOGICAL

Chapter 4 began with a quote by Blaise Pascal, "The last thing one knows in constructing a work is what to put first." Our understanding of the nature of autism has led us to put sensory and biological needs at the foundation of this model; therefore, interventions at this level should closely be reexamined when troubleshooting. Unmet sensory and biological needs result in changes in behavior. The following are signs that needs at this level have not been adequately addressed.

- Sensation avoidance (e.g, touch, sounds, light, movement, smells)
- Sensation seeking (e.g., jumping, touching others, rocking, lifting heavy objects, swinging, preference for tight clothes, hugging)
- Distress in response to sensory stimuli
- Difficulty concentrating in noisy environments
- Pain
- Sudden change in behavior

- Delayed actions and responses
- Failure to attend to sensory stimuli (e.g., not responding to sounds)
- Low energy level
- Anxiety and/or depression
- Irritability
- Regression in behavior

Also, be certain to include those with expertise in these areas (occupational therapists, physicians, etc.) in this process. Occupational therapists, for example, may assist in developing strategies to help calm a student and regulate sensory functioning, whereas a physician will be required to address medical factors and adjust medications. Keep in mind that needs in the biological and sensory area tend to wax and wane. It is recommended to gather information across time and settings and have ongoing communication with these professionals so that they may be responsive to changing needs.

REINFORCEMENT

A reinforcer is, by definition, something/anything that follows a behavior and increases the likelihood that the behavior will occur. Reinforcement has an impact on interventions that occur on all levels of the Ziggurat. If meaningful progress is not observed, it is necessary to review the implementation of reinforcement. The following are signs that reinforcement has not been sufficiently addressed.

- Failure to increase desired behavior
- Failure to "buy in" to the behavior plan
- Low self-esteem
- High frustration level

- Hopelessness
- Failure to frequently earn reinforcers
- Decrease in goal behaviors
- Escape behaviors

One of the most common difficulties among parents, educators, and other practitioners is an unwillingness to provide reinforcement or a sense that provision of reinforcement is impractical or even misguided. Teachers or parents may make statements such as:

- "I don't have time for this."
- "I shouldn't have to reinforce for behaviors I expect him to do at this age."
- "It is not fair to others who aren't getting reinforced."

We strongly believe that if the behaviors of concern are important enough for intervention, they are important enough to reinforce. Simply put, *if there is no reinforcement, there is no intervention*. While reinforcement usually involves a time commitment, we view this as an "up-front" investment. That is, time spent on reinforcement on the "front end" will have a far greater payoff.

Next, we find it helpful to keep a disability perspective when looking at behaviors. Given that autism is a pervasive *developmental* condition, it is not realistic to expect that all skills will be evenly developed and consistent with those of same-age peers. Therefore, reinforcing for behaviors that others readily exhibit is appropriate. Moreover, we should seek to create success experiences for individuals on the spectrum, who often encounter challenges in all aspects of their daily lives.

"There is nothing more unequal than the equal treatment of unequal [needs]" (unknown). The concept of fairness must take into account differing needs. Most typically developing individuals do not require reinforcement for initiating greetings, returning a smile, and staying on topic. Meeting needs is fair. It is also important to consider that the natural re-inforcers available in most environments (e.g., school, home, recreational activities, com-munity) may not be as meaningful to those on the spectrum. Therefore, we must construct and provide salient reinforcers in settings where behavioral expectations are held.

In troubleshooting, reevaluate the selection of reinforcers, making certain that they are rotated often enough to maintain their value and that self-selection is used to the extent possible. Over time, the value of established reinforcers may change, making it necessary to identify new reinforcers by conducting additional observation, interviews, or a rein-forcement survey as described in Chapter 5. If the expected behavior does not occur, per-haps the reinforcer is not being delivered with enough frequency.

Keep in mind that working towards long-term reinforcers may be more difficult for individuals on the spectrum. For children, setting a goal at the end of a day or week may be too long. Early in the learning process, the goal behavior should be reinforced every time and include reinforcement for prompted practice. Another problem that sometimes occurs is that a criterion is set so high that it cannot be attained. This results in "learned defeat," whereby the reinforcement system comes to be ignored because the payoff never occurs. Reinforcement is then sought through other, sometimes less constructive, behaviors. One remedy is simply changing the criterion to ensure that the goal is more easily attained.

No reinforcement system, regardless of how well designed, will be effective if negative feedback outweighs the positive. Consider the possibility that the ratio of positives to negative is out of balance. It may be helpful to collect data to gain a realistic perspective and evaluate whether this is a factor contributing to lack of progress. While a ratio between 4:1 and 10:1 is generally considered optimal, when teaching new skills, each skill should *always* be reinforced.

Negative feedback or punishment of the related target behavior (the problem behavior) should not begin until the skill has been learned. Implementing negative consequences too early essentially results in punishing an individual for something she cannot yet do. Only after the skill has been mastered and reinforced consistently is it appropriate to add consequences for failure to display the skill.

Some erroneously believe that negative consequences are an essential component of an intervention because they teach behavior. In reality, some characteristics of punishment can interfere with the effectiveness of intervention. A common error in this area occurs when parents, in an attempt to support teachers, punish for behaviors that have already been addressed at school. This essentially results in "double punishment." Double punishment may lead to anger, anxiety, preoccupation, and rumination – all of which are counter to learning. Often, teachers tell us that a student's behaviors rapidly escalate after they give a consequence because the child anticipates that there will be more negative consequences once he arrives home.

When negative feedback is necessary, it should be delivered within the ratio of positives to negatives, taking into consideration possible side effects. As long as the ratio of positives to negatives is kept in check, there will always be accomplishments to celebrate across settings.

STRUCTURE AND VISUAL/TACTILE SUPPORTS

From a troubleshooting perspective, it is important to ask if the necessary structure and visual/tactile supports are in place. Needs in this area are more intense for individuals on the spectrum than for most people, hence the inclusion of Structure and Visual/Tactile Supports as one of the five levels of the Ziggurat. Structure and visual/tactile supports are interrelated concepts. Both increase the ability of individuals on the spectrum to predict and understand their world. Signs that needs on this level are not sufficiently addressed may include the following.

- Increased behavioral difficulties around periods of change (e.g., weather, substitute teacher)
- Repetitive questioning
- Increased anxiety

- Increased behavioral difficulties during transition (e.g., from one activity to another, weekend to weekdays)
- Failure to learn (e.g., skills, routines)
- Increased anger and rages

One common pitfall is the tendency to discontinue a visual support because it is working or because the student does not appear to use it. While it may be true that a student is not routinely using a given support, during periods of increased anxiety or difficulty, having the visual support available is necessary to maintain behavioral success. Many of us keep a road map in our cars. While we do not use it daily, when lost, we rely on this visual support.

Not all individuals on the spectrum have a strength in visual processing; however, structure is critical and must be addressed. If a visual mode is not a strength, alternative approaches that rely on known strengths (e.g., auditory, kinesthetic, tactile) must be developed.

TASK DEMANDS & POSITIVE ENVIRONMENT

The level of demands placed on an individual is important. If a task is too demanding, the following will likely happen:

- Failure at a task
- Quitting before the task is completed
- Expressing feelings that the task is overwhelming

- Meltdowns
- Increased isolation
- Rejection from peers

When such difficulties persist, it is important to consider the possibility that task demands have been set too high. On the other hand, if the task is too easy, skills will not expand.

The zone of proximal development represents an optimal level for new learning. Review the three questions (see page 247) to determine if demands are excessive and keep in mind that, if the challenge level is too low, progress will be limited. It is also important to remember that antecedent events that cannot be predicted may impact the level of demand.

It may also be helpful to review the task analysis to determine if prerequisite skills or skill components were overlooked. If that is the case, it may explain a lack of progress and provide a place to intervene. For example, Buddy, a high school student on the spectrum, works at an office supply store through the vocational program. His job coach, Ann, and store manager, Susan, had observed him to be successful on projects with a coworker. When it was time to conduct inventory, they assigned Buddy to the team. However, he had great difficulty working cooperatively with others and walked out because they were not doing it "the right way."

Ann and Susan had overlooked the possibility that working in larger groups required different skills than working in pairs. After conducting another task analysis, they determined the skills Buddy was lacking and targeted them so that he would be successful in future group assignments. For the remainder of the inventory task, Ann supervised Buddy in his work with the group in order to provide the support necessary until he had mastered the identified skills.

SKILLS TO TEACH

It is possible to resolve many behavior concerns using strategies on the first four levels of the Ziggurat Model without ever teaching skills. Indeed, many improvements may be seen across areas of functioning even if this level is excluded. Comfortable with behavior gains, intervention teams may overlook teaching skills. However, such a "partial" approach to intervention will have negative long-term outcomes because it does not allow for independence or promote growth. The following are some signs that intervening at the Skills to Teach level has not adequately been accomplished:

- Lack of progress on goals

- Lack of generalization of skills

- Overdependence on assistance

- Overdependence on modifications and accommodations

- Failure to identify level of skill development and specific skill deficits

Virgie

Virgie is a fourth-grade student on the spectrum. Each year as reading comprehension tasks have become increasingly challenging, her team has agreed to exempt Virgie from the comprehension section of the language arts assessment. This decision has been based on their awareness that reading comprehension is very challenging for many students on the autism spectrum.

At the end of the fourth grade, as the team wrote goals and objectives for the fifth grade, the psychologist proposed that the team consider adding goals to address reading comprehension rather than simply continue to exempt Virgie from expectations for demonstrating this important skill. The addition of skills to teach in the area of reading comprehension was the step necessary for her eventual increased independence and long-term success.

Recognizing which skills to teach is not always as straightforward as it was for Virgie's team. Many times, we fail to teach a skill because we assume that a given concept is so obvious that it does not require instruction – deficits are essentially hidden in plain sight. If behavioral progress is not attained, it is important to reconsider whether the intervention is addressing "seemingly obvious" or skill deficits that may have been overlooked. In order to discover the seemingly obvious, it is helpful to ask, "Why are most people the same age NOT exhibiting this behavior?" The following are indicators that suggest an oversight:

- The behavior is persistent after multiple attempts to intervene
- The behavior appears "odd" or the level of response appears out of proportion to the situation

Wilda

Wilda was a sixth-grade student on the spectrum. She excelled academically and expressed a strong desire to have friends. Wilda frequently experienced a runny nose, which she usually wiped with her sleeve. She cleaned her face after a meal in a similar fashion. As a result, her face was often dirty and her classmates avoided being around her, which concerned her teacher. Her teacher tried reminding Wilda to wipe her face. She even wrote a small note that said, "Use your napkin;" however, her behavior persisted.

Over a long period of time with no improvement and fewer peers willing to play with her, Wilda's teacher enrolled Wilda in a social skill group at school. The counselor focused on skills such as how to make and keep friends. After a while her teacher still saw no improvement, so she spoke to the psychologist, who observed Wilda on the playground after lunch. The psychologist noticed food smeared on her face and saw her peers point to her saying, "That's gross." It was apparent to the psychologist that Wilda's mindblindness had prevented her from recognizing her peers' disgust and aversion to her dirty appearance. This was a concept that other sixth-graders had naturally learned many years prior and the reason why they did not display similar behaviors. This was the seemingly obvious lesson and the reason that previous interventions to teach her to use a napkin or tissue were unsuccessful. Figure 9.2 depicts the seemingly obvious concept and associated skills selected for instruction. After this simple intervention, Wilda learned the skills easily and her relationships improved.

This is a perfect example of the seemingly obvious (see Figure 9.2) being overlooked. Wilda's behavior appeared odd for a sixth-grade student and persisted in spite of reminders and even group social skills instruction. Because the notion that food and mucus on the face are considered "gross" was so obvious to everyone else, it was difficult to pinpoint this as the actual missing concept.

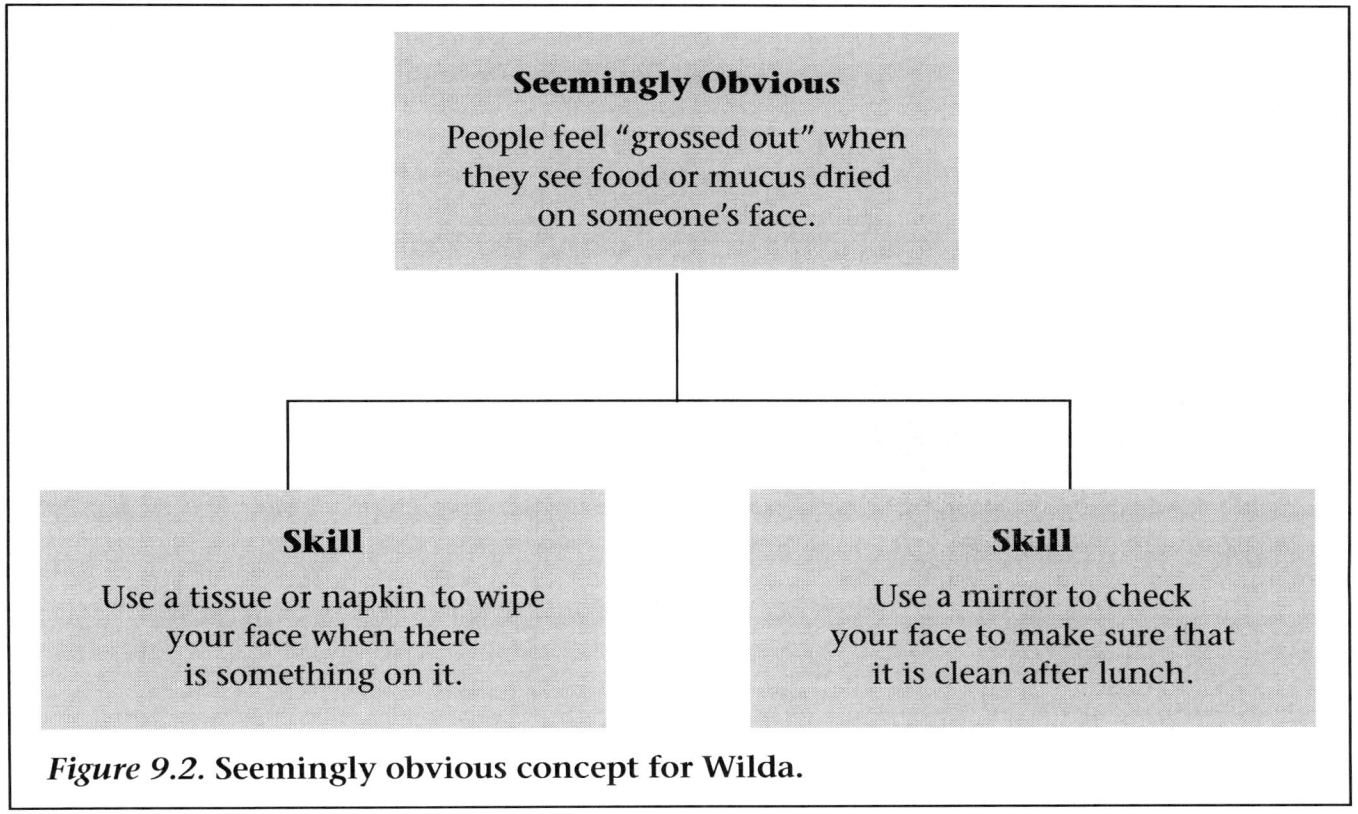

Figure 9.2. Seemingly obvious concept for Wilda.

APPLICATION

Troubleshooting Process – Steve

Nicole met with Steve periodically through the course of the semester. As is true with most interventions, some adjustments were required. Steve met with the campus physician and began taking medication to address his anxiety. Over a period of weeks, it became apparent that he was not benefiting from the medication, so another was prescribed. His anxiety eventually decreased, and Steve found that it was easier for him to focus on his studies. Noise-canceling headphones were also helpful, and Mark was pleased that he did not have to be so cautious about disturbing Steve. The self-reinforcement system worked smoothly and, over time, Nicole encouraged Steve to review his grades in each class. Because his grades in literature were borderline, they agreed that he would increase the amount of time studying for that course and receive double reinforcers each time he earned a B or higher on weekly assignments. Steve purchased an electronic calendar/organizer (PDA). After he attended the seminar that Nicole had recommended, he learned to keep "to do" lists and schedule important long-term tasks such as papers and tests.

Steve had not been able to join clubs or activities. He read about them on the Internet but rarely attended the meetings, and when he did, he did not interact with anyone there. After speaking with Steve, Nicole determined that asking him to do this independently set the task demand too high. Steve did not have the prerequisite skills to accomplish this without support. Specifically, he lacked the interpersonal skills required to maintain conversations with unfamiliar peers. She phoned the president of the clubs and recruited members to mentor Steve and facilitate his inclusion in club activities. She also encouraged Steve to work with his counselor to learn these interpersonal skills in addition to the coping and relaxation skills they were already addressing.

Steve's relationship with his roommate improved. With the assistance of the RA, Steve made progress in his ability to decipher arguments; however, he continued to be angered by Mark's "refusal to compromise" – especially over Mark's need to use an alarm clock in order to make it to his early morning class. It became apparent to the RA that, as bright as Steve was, he did not know the meaning of the word "compromise." This was the seemingly obvious that had been overlooked. Steve knew that a compromise was a good way to resolve a conflict, but he did not understand the underlying concept – that in a compromise *each* person receives a little of what he wants. He also failed to understand that some things are not subject to compromise, such as Mark's need to attend an early class. Steve's RA showed him the definition of "compromise" in the dictionary and copied it for him to reference. As simple as this was, Steve immediately held a new understanding of the concept of compromise. The RA suggested the compromise that Steve would agree to wear noise-canceling headphones to bed the night before Mark had early classes and Mark would agree not to use the snooze bar on his alarm clock. After coaching, Steve was able to propose this to Mark, and the number of disagreements declined.

While this process may appear deceptively simple, it actually describes troubleshooting at each level of the intervention. These steps of adjustment and fine-tuning are required in order for an intervention to continue to be effective.

Troubleshooting Process – Penny

Penny's intervention team met on a regular basis to review her progress. Each time they met, they worked through each level of the Ziggurat to pinpoint potential difficulties. Later in the year, it became apparent that additional assessment was warranted. The team reviewed and revised the UCC/ISSI and ABC-I. This allowed them to address new underlying factors of which they had not been aware.

Because the team did such a thorough job of identifying and addressing prerequisite and component skill deficits in addition to seemingly obvious concepts, Penny made excellent progress throughout the year. For example, because the team targeted underlying concerns, such as mindblindness, Penny learned how to tell when her statements were hurtful to others. With assistance (Task Demand intervention), she was able to repair relationships. Her speech therapist taught Penny how to start and maintain conversations. Due to Penny's mindblindness, the therapist needed to focus on Penny's ability to "read" others' faces. Penny continued to have long-winded conversations with peers. During the troubleshooting process, the speech therapist discovered that she had not fully incorporated visual supports. She decided to add interventions such as photographs and video taping Penny's peers modeling being "bored" during conversations. Sensory strategies appeared to help calm Penny, and the team concluded that the strategies were effective and should continue. Over time, the team recognized that some of the items on Penny's reinforcement menu were no longer valued by her. Based on periodic reinforcer surveys, new items were identified and added.

SUMMARY

From assessment to troubleshooting, the ZM facilitates best practices for designing interventions. Use of the ZM ensures that interventions occur at each of the five levels – Sensory/Biological; Reinforcement; Structure and Visual/Tactile Supports; Task Demands and Positive Environment; and Skills to Teach – and that the plan includes antecedent, behavior, and consequence inter-ventions (the three points of intervention).

This chapter begins with a quote by Albert Einstein – "Make everything as simple as possible but not simpler." Use of the ZM ensures that an intervention plan addresses critical areas of need and includes essential elements – that the plan is not too simple. Yet, it is our purpose to make the plan "as simple as possible" – user friendly or accessible to individuals with various roles in the life of the autistic person, including (depending on developmental and skill level) the individual on the spectrum him or herself. The ultimate purpose of the ZM is to positively impact the lives of those on the spectrum.

CHAPTER HIGHLIGHTS

- *The Ziggurat Model facilitates and encourages members of a team to work together to problem solve.*

- *The dignity of autistic individuals is paramount and should be a guiding principle in all assessment and intervention efforts.*

- *Assessment information gathered through the UCC, ISSI, and ABC-I during the development of an intervention plan should be reviewed and updated periodically in order to ensure that interventions are anchored to identified characteristics and needs.*

- *Because overt behavioral difficulties are so prominent and tend to dominate the energies of the informant, care should be given to ensure that other underlying emotional characteristics are not overlooked.*

- *It is important to attain the perspective of autistic individuals as much as possible.*

- *Unmet sensory and biological needs will necessarily result in changes in behavior; therefore, interventions at this level should closely be reexamined when troubleshooting.*

- *Reinforcement has an impact on interventions that occur on all levels of the Ziggurat.*

- *If the behaviors of concern are important enough for intervention, they are important enough to reinforce.*

- *Some characteristics of punishment interfere with the effectiveness of intervention.*

- *One common pitfall is the tendency to discontinue a visual support because it is working or because the student does not appear to use it.*

- *If behavioral progress is not attained, it is important to reconsider whether the intervention is addressing "seemingly obvious" or skill deficits that may have been overlooked.*

References

Adams, N. C., & Jarrold, C. (2011). *Effects of weak central coherence on resistance to distracter inhibition for children with autism.* Retrieved from http://imfar.confex.com/imfar/2011/webprogram/Paper7804.html

Alberto, P. A., & Troutman, A. C. (2003). *Applied behavior analysis for teachers* (6th ed.). Upper Saddle River, NJ: Merrill Prentice Hall.

Alcantara, P. R. (1994). Effects of videotape instructional package on the purchasing skills of children with autism. *Exceptional Children, 61,* 40-55.

Aldred, C., Green, J., & Adams, C. (2004). A new social communication intervention for children with autism: Pilot randomized controlled treatment study suggesting effectiveness. *Journal of Child Psychology and Psychiatry, 45,* 1420-1430.

Aman, M. G., Lam, K. S., & Collier-Crespin, A. (2003). Prevalence and patterns of use of psychoactive medicines among individuals with autism in the Autism Society of Ohio. *Journal of Autism and Developmental Disorders, 33*(5), 527-534.

American Psychiatric Association. (2013). *Diagnostic and statistical manual of mental disorders (5th ed.).* Washington, DC: Author.

American Psychiatric Association. (2000). *Diagnostic and statistical manual of mental disorders. Fourth edition, text revision.* Washington, DC: Author.

Anderson, G. M., Gutknecht, L., Cohen, D. J., Brailly-Tabard, S., Cohen, J. H., Ferrari, P., Roubertoux, P. L., & Tordjman, S. (2002). Serotonin transporter promoter variants in autism functional effects and relationship to platelet hyperserotonemia. *Molecular Psychiatry, 7*(8), 831-836.

Anderson, G. M., Horne, W. C., Chatterjee, D., & Cohen, D. J. (1990). The hyperserotonemia of autism. *Annual of the New York Academy of Sciences, 600,* 331-342.

Apple, A. L., Billingsley, F., & Schwartz, I. S. (2005). Effects of video modeling alone and with self-management on compliment-giving behaviors of children with high-functioning ASD. *Journal of Positive Behavior Interventions, 7,* 33-46.

Aristotle. (1990). Metaphysica (W. D. Ross, Trans). In *The works of Aristotle* (Vol. 1). Chicago: Encyclopedia Brittanica.

Attwood, T. (1998). *Asperger's Syndrome: A guide for parents and professionals*. London: Jessica Kingsley Publishers.

Attwood, T. (2003a). Understanding and managing circumscribed interests. In M. Prior (Ed.), *Learning and behavior problems in Asperger Syndrome* (pp. 126-147). New York: Guilford Press.

Attwood, T. (2003b). Frameworks for behavioral interventions. *Child and Adolescent Psychiatric Clinics of North America, 12*, 65-86.

Attwood, T. (2004a). *Exploring feelings: Cognitive behaviour therapy to manage anxiety*. Arlington, TX: Future Horizons.

Attwood, T. (2004b). *Exploring feelings: Cognitive behaviour therapy to manage anger*. Arlington, TX: Future Horizons.

Ayres, A. J. (1979). *Sensory integration and the child*. Los Angeles: Western Psychological Services.

Ayres, A. J. (1987). *Sensory integration and the child*. Los Angeles: Western Psychological Services.

Bachevalier, J., & Loveland, K. A. (2006). The orbitofrontal-amygdala circuit and self-regulation of social-emotional behavior in autism. *Neuroscience and Biobehavioral Reviews, 30*, 97-117.

Bainbridge, N., & Myles, B. S. (1999). The use of priming to introduce toilet training to a child with autism. *Focus on Autism and Other Developmental Disabilities, 14*(2), 106-109.

Baker, M. J. (2000). Incorporating the thematic ritualistic behaviors of children with autism into games: Increasing social play interactions with siblings. *Journal of Positive Behavior Interventions, 2*, 66-84.

Baker, M. J., Koegel, R. L., & Koegel, L. K. (1998). Increasing the social behavior of young children with autism using their obsessive behaviors. *The Journal of the Association for Persons with Severe Handicaps, 23*, 300-308.

Bandura, A. (1977). *Social learning theory*. Englewood Cliffs, NJ: Prentice Hall.

Baranek, G. T. (2002). Efficacy of sensory and motor interventions for children with autism. *Journal of Autism and Developmental Disorders, 32*(5), 397-422.

Bareket, R. (2006). *Playing it right! Social skills activities for parents and teachers of young children with autism spectrum disorders, including Asperger Syndrome and autism*. Shawnee Mission, KS: AAPC Publishing.

Baron-Cohen, S., & Belmonte, M. K. (2005). Autism: A window onto the development of the social and the analytic brain. *Annual Review of Neuroscience, 28*, 109-126.

Baron-Cohen, S., & Hammer, J. (1997). Parents of children with Asperger syndrome: What is the cognitive phenotype? *Journal of Cognitive Neuroscience, 9*, 548-554.

Baron-Cohen, S., & Swettenham, J. (1997). Theory of mind in autism: Its relationship to executive function and central coherence. In D. Cohen & F. Volkmar (Eds.), *Handbook of autism and pervasive developmental disorders* (2nd ed., pp. 880-893). Oxford, UK: John Wiley and Sons.

Barry, L. M., & Burlew, S. B. (2004). Using social stories™ to teach choice and play skills to children with autism. *Focus on Autism and Other Developmental Disabilities, 19*(1), 45-51.

Barry, T. D., Klinger, L. G., Lee, J. M., Palardy, N., Gilmore, T., & Bodin, D. (2003). Examining the effectiveness of an outpatient clinic-based social skills group for high-functioning children with autism. *Journal of Autism and Developmental Disorders, 33*(6), 685-701.

Beck, J. S. (1995). *Cognitive therapy: Basics and beyond*. New York: Guilford Press.

Beck, J. S., Lundwall, R. A., Gabrielsen, T., Cox, J. C., & South, M. (2020). Looking good but feeling bad:"Camouflaging" behaviors and mental health in women with autistic traits. *Autism, 24*(4), 809-821.

Bennetto, L., Pennington, B. F., & Rogers, S. J. (1996). Impact and impaired memory functions in autism. *Child Development, 67,* 1816-1835.

Bono, M. A., Daley, T., & Sigman, M. (2004). Relations among joint attention, amount of intervention and language gains in autism. *Journal of Autism and Developmental Disorders, 34*(5), 495-505.

Booth, R., Charlton, R., Hughes, C., & Happé, F. (2003). Disentangling weak coherence and executive dysfunction: Planning drawing in autism and attention-deficit/hyperactivity disorder. In U. Frith & E. Hill (Eds.), *Autism: Mind and brain* (pp. 211-223). New York: Oxford University Press.

Booth, R., & Happé, F. (2010). Hunting with a knife and . . . fork: Examining central coherence in autism, attention deficit/hyperactivity disorder, and typical development with a linguistic task. *Journal of Experimental Child Psychology, 107,* 377-393.

Boucher, J., & Lewis, V. (1989). Memory impairments and communication in relatively able autistic children. *Journal of Child Psychology and Psychiatry, 30,* 99-122.

Boyd, B. A. (2005). *Effects of restricted interests on the social behaviors of young children with autism spectrum disorders.* Unpublished doctoral dissertation, University of Florida.

Bregman, J. D., & Gerdtz, J. (1997). *Behavioral interventions.* In D. J. Cohen & F. R. Volkmar (Eds.), *Handbook of autism and pervasive developmental disorders* (2nd ed., pp. 606-630). New York: John Wiley and Sons.

BBC (British Broadcasting Company) (producer). (1996). *Rage for order: Autism* [Motion picture]. (Available from Films Media Group, P.O. Box 2053, Princeton, NJ 08543-2053.)

Brothers, L. (1990). The social brain: A project for integrating primate behavior and neurophysiology in a new domain. *Concepts in Neuroscience, 1,* 27-51.

Bryan, L. C. & Gast, D. L. (2000). Teaching on-task and on-schedule behaviors to high-functioning children with autism via picture activity schedules. *Journal of Autism and Developmental Disorders, 30,* 553-567.

Buck, O. D. (1995). Sertraline for reduction of violent behavior. *The American Journal of Psychiatry, 152*(6), 953.

Buitelaar, J. K., & Willemsen-Swinkels, S.H.N. (2000). Medication treatment in subjects with autistic spectrum disorders. *European Child & Adolescent Psychiatry, 9,* 185-197.

Burnette, C. P., Mundy, P. C., Myer, J. A., Sutton, S. K., Vaughan, A. E., & Charak, D. (2005). Weak central coherence and its relations to theory of mind and anxiety in autism. *Journal of Autism and Developmental Disorders, 35*(1), 63-73.

Buron, K. D., & Curtis, M. (2022). *The Incredible 5-Point Scale.* St. Paul, MN: 5 Point Scale Publishing.

Butler, A. C., Chapman, J. E., Forman, E. M., & Beck, A. T. (2006). The empirical status of cognitive behavior therapy: A review of meta-analyses. *Clinical Psychology Review, 26,* 17-31.

Camm-Crosbie, L., Bradley, L., Shaw, R., Baron-Cohen, S., & Cassidy, S. (2019). 'People like me don't get support': Autistic adults' experiences of support and treatment for mental health difficulties, self-injury and suicidality. *Autism, 23(6),* 1431-1441.

Carlson, S. M., Mandell, D. J., & Williams, L. (2004). Executive function and theory of mind: Stability and prediction from ages 2 to 3. *Developmental Psychology, 40*(6), 1105-1122.

Carlson, S. M., Moses, L. J., & Breton, C. (2001). How specific is the relation between executive function and theory of mind? Contributions of inhibitory control and working memory. *Infant and Child Development, 11,* 73-92.

Carlson, S. M., Moses, L. J., & Claxton, L. J. (2004). Individual differences in executive functioning and theory of mind: An investigation of inhibitory control and planning ability. *Journal of Experimental Child Psychology, 87*, 299-319.

Carper, R. A., Moses, P., Tigue, Z. D., & Courchesne, E. (2002). Cerebral lobes in autism: Early hyperplasia and abnormal age effects. *Neuroimage, 16*, 1038-1051.

Carr, E. G. (1994). Emerging themes in the functional analysis of problem behavior. *Journal of Applied Behavior Analysis, 27*, 393-399.

Carr, E. G., Binkoff, J. A., Kologinsky, E., & Eddy, M. (1978). Acquisition of sign language by autistic children. I: Expressive Labeling. *Journal of Applied Behavior Analysis, 11*, 489-501.

Carr, E. G., & Durand, V. M. (1985). Reducing behavior problems through functional communication training. *Journal of Applied Behavior Analysis, 18*, 111-126.

Carr, E. G., Horner, R. H., Turnbull, A. P., Marquis, J. G., Magito-McLaughlin, D., McAtee, M. L., et al. (1999). *Positive behavior support for people with developmental disabilities: A research synthesis.* Washington, DC: American Association on Mental Retardation.

Case-Smith, J., & Bryan, T. (1999). The effects of occupational therapy with sensory integration emphasis on preschool-age children with autism. *The American Journal of Occupational Therapy, 53*(5), 489-497.

Chandana, S. R., Behen, M. E., Juhasz, C., Muzik, O., Rothermel, R. D., Manger, T. J., Chakraborty,

P. K., Chugani, H. T., & Chugani, D. C. (2005). Significance of abnormalities in developmental trajectory and asymmetry of cortical serotonin synthesis in autism. *International Journal of Developmental Neuroscience, 23*, 171-182.

Charlop, M. H., & Milstein, J. P. (1989). Teaching autistic children conversational speech using video modeling. *Journal of Applied Behavior Analysis, 22*(3), 275-285.

Charlop-Christy, M. H., Carpenter, M., Le, L., LeBlanc, L. A., & Kellet, K. (2002). Using the Picture Exchange Communication System (PECS) with children with autism: Assessment of PECS acquisition, speech, social-communicative behavior, and problem behavior. *Journal of Applied Behavior Analysis, 35*, 213-231.

Charlop-Christy, M. H., & Daneshvar, S. (2003). Using video modeling to teach perspective taking to children with autism. *Journal of Positive Behavior Interventions, 5*, 12-21.

Charlop-Christy, M. H., & Haymes, L. K. (1996). Using obsessions as reinforcers with and without mild reductive procedures to decrease inappropriate behaviors of children with autism. *Journal of Autism and Developmental Disorders, 26*, 527-546.

Charlop-Christy, M. H., & Haymes, L. K. (1998). Using objects of obsession as token reinforcers for children with autism. *Journal of Autism and Developmental Disorders, 28*, 189-198.

Charlop-Christy, M. H., & Kelso, S. E. (2003). Teaching children with autism conversational speech using a cue card, written script program. *Education and Treatment of Children, 26*(2), 108-127.

Charlop-Christy, M. H., Kurtz, P. F., & Casey, F. G. (1990). Using aberrant behaviors as reinforcers for autistic children. *Journal of Applied Behavior Analysis, 23*, 163-181.

Charlop-Christy, M. H., Le, L., & Freeman, K. A. (2000). A comparison of video modeling with in vivo modeling for teaching children with autism. *Journal of Autism and Developmental Disorders, 30*(6), 537-552.

Chiang, H., & Lin, Y. (2007). Mathematical ability of students with Asperger Syndrome and high-functioning autism: A review of literature. *Autism, 11*(6), 547-556.

Chugani, D. C., Muzik, O., Behen, M., Rothermel, R., Janisse, J. J., Lee, J., & Chugani, H. T. (1999). Developmental changes in brain serotonin synthesis capacity in autistic and nonautistic children. *Annuals of Neurology, 45*(3), 287-295.

Clarke, S., Dunlap, G., & Vaughn, B. (1999). Family-centered, assessment-based intervention to improve behavior during an early morning routine. *Journal of Positive Behavior Interventions, 1,* 235-241.

Clawson, A., Krauskopf, E., Johnston, O., Crowley, M. J., South, M., & Larson, M. J. (2010). *Performance-monitoring and evaluative control in high-functioning autism.* Retrieved from http://imfar.confex.com/imfar/2010/webprogram/Paper6983.html

Cobb, S., Beardon, L., Eastgate, R., Glover, T., Kerr, S., Neale, H., Parsons, S., Benford, S., Hopkins, E., Mitchell, P., Reynard, G., & Wilson, J. (2002). Applied virtual environments to support learning of social interaction skills in users with Asperger's Syndrome. *Digital Creativity, 13*(1), 11-22.

Conroy, M. A., Asmus, J. M., Sellers, J. A., & Ladwig, C. N. (2005). The use of antecedent-based intervention to decrease stereotypic behavior in a general education classroom: A case study. *Focus on Autism and Other Developmental Disabilities, 20*(4), 223-230.

Cook, D. G. (1990). A sensory approach to the treatment and management of children with autism. *Focus on Autistic Behavior, 5*(6), 1-19.

Coucouvanis, J. (2005). *Super skills: A social skills group program for children with Asperger syndrome, high-functioning autism and related challenges.* Shawnee Mission, KS: AAPC Publishing.

Courchesne, E., & Pierce, K. (2005). Brain overgrowth in autism during a critical time in development: Implications for frontal pyramidal neuron and interneuron development and connectivity. *International Journal of Developmental Neuroscience, 23,* 153-170.

Couturier, J. L., & Nicolson, R. (2002). A retrospective assessment of citalopram in children and adolescents with pervasive developmental disorders. *Journal of Child and Adolescent Psychopharmacology, 12*(3), 243-248.

Coyne, S. M., Archer, J., & Eslea, M. (2003). Cruel intentions on television and in real life: Can viewing indirect aggression increase viewers' subsequent indirect aggression? *Journal of Experimental Child Psychology, 88,* 234-253.

Crozier, S., & Tincani, M. J. (2005). Using a modified Social Story™ to decrease disruptive behavior of a child with autism. *Focus on Autism and Other Developmental Disabilities, 20*(3), 150-157.

Culp, S. L. (2011). *A buffet of sensory interventions: Solutions for middle and high school students with autism spectrum disorders.* Shawnee Mission, KS: AAPC Publishing.

Cummins, A., Piek, J. P., & Dyck, M. J. (2005). Motor coordination, empathy, and social behavior in school-aged children. *Developmental Medicine and Child Neurology, 47,* 437-442.

D'Ateno, P., Mangiapanello, K., & Taylor, B. A. (2003). Using video modeling to teach complex play sequences to a preschooler with autism. *Journal of Positive Behavior Interventions, 5,* 5-11.

Dawson, P., & Guare, R. (2003). *Executive skills in children and adolescents: A practical guide.* New York: Guilford Press.

DeLong, G. R., Teague, L. A., & McSwain, K. M. (1998). Effects of fluoxetine treatment in young children with idiopathic autism. *Developmental Medicine and Child Neurology, 40*(8), 551-562.

Delprato, D. J. (2001). Comparisons of discrete-trial and normalized behavioral language intervention for young children with autism. *Journal of Autism and Developmental Disorders, 31,* 315-325.

Dettmer, S., Simpson, R. L., Myles, B. S., & Ganz, J. B. (2000). The use of visual supports to facilitate transitions of students with autism. *Focus on Autism and Other Developmental Disabilities, 15,* 163-169.

Dhossche, D. M., & Wachtel, L. E. (2010). Catatonia is hidden in plain sight among different pediatric disorders: a review article. Pediatric neurology, 43(5), 307-315.

Di Martino, A., Melis, G., Cianchetti, C., & Zuddas, A. (2004). Methylphenidate for pervasive developmental disorders: Safety and efficacy of acute single dose test and ongoing therapy: An open-pilot study. *Journal of Child and Adolescent Psychopharmacology, 14*(2), 207-218.

Dooley, P., Wilczenski, F. L., & Torem, C. (2001). Using an activity schedule to smooth school transitions. *Journal of Positive Behavior Interventions, 3,* 57-61.

Dunn, W. (1999). *Sensory profile.* San Antonio, TX: Psychological Corporation.

Dunn, W., Myles, B. S., & Orr, S. (2002). Sensory processing issues associated with Asperger Syndrome: A preliminary investigation. *The American Journal of Occupational Therapy, 56*(1), 97-102.

Durand, V. M., & Merges, E. (2001). Functional communication training: A contemporary behavior analytic intervention for problem behaviors. *Focus on Autism & Other Developmental Disabilities, 16,* 110-119, 136.

Edelson, S. M., Edelson, M. G., Kerr, D.C.R., & Grandin, T. (1999). Behavioral and physiological effects of deep pressure on children with autism: A pilot study evaluating the efficacy of Grandin's hug machine. *American Journal of Occupational Therapists, 53*(2), 145-152.

Ellingson, S. A., Miltenberger, R. G., Stricker, J., Galensky, T. L., & Garlinghouse, M. (2000). Functional assessment and intervention for challenging behaviors in the classroom by general classroom teachers. *Journal of Positive Behavior Interventions, 2,* 85-97.

Erickson, C. A., Stigler, K. A., Posey, D. J., & McDougle, C. J. (2005). Risperidone in pervasive developmental disorders. *Expert Review of Neurotherapeutics, 5*(6), 713-719.

Ferguson, H., Myles, B. S., & Hagiwara, T. (2005). Using a personal digital assistant to enhance the independence of an adolescent with Asperger Syndrome. *Education and Training in Developmental Disabilities, 40,* 60-67.

Ferter-Daly, D., Bedell, G., & Hinojosa, J. (2003). Effects of a weighted vest on attention to task and self-stimulatory behaviors in preschoolers with pervasive developmental disorders. In C. B. Royeen (Ed.), *Pediatric issues in occupational therapy* (pp. 215-229). Bethesda, MD: AOTA Press.

Fisher, N., & Happé, F. (2006). A training study of theory of mind and executive functions in children with autism spectrum disorder. *Journal of Autism and Developmental Disorders, 35,* 757-771.

Foley, B. E. & Staples, A. H. (2003). Developing augmentative and alternative communication (AAC) and literacy interventions in a supported employment setting. *Topics in Language Disorders, 23,* 325-343.

Fombonne, E. (1999). The epidemiology of autism: A review. *Psychological Medicine, 29,* 769-786.

Fombonne, E. (2003). Epidemiological surveys of autism and other pervasive developmental disorders: An update. *Journal of Autism and Developmental Disorders, 33,* 365-382.

Food and Drug Administration. (2004, October). *FDA Public Health Advisor. Suicidality in children and adolescents being treated with antidepressant medications.* Retrieved November 23, 2005, from http://www.fda.gov/cder/drug/antidepressants/SSRIPHA200410.htm

Foster-Johnson, L., & Dunlap, G. (1993). Using functional assessment to develop effective, individualized interventions for challenging behaviors. *Teaching Exceptional Children, 25*(3), 44-50.

Frederickson, N., & Turner, J. (2003). Utilizing the classroom peer group to address children's social needs: An evaluation of the Circle of Friends intervention approach. *The Journal of Special Education, 36(4)*, 234-245.

Frederickson, N., Warren, L., & Turner, J. (2005). "Circle of friends" – An exploration of impact over time. *Educational Psychology in Practice, 21*(3), 197-217.

Freedman, S. G. (2005, January 19). Back to the basics of a legible hand. *The New York Times*, p. B8.

Frith, C. D. (2003). What do imaging studies tell us about the neural basis of autism? In M. Rutter (Ed.), *Autism: Neural basis and treatment possibilities* (pp. 149-176). Chichester, UK: Wiley.

Frith, U. (1989). *Autism: Explaining the enigma.* Oxford, UK: Blackwell Publishing.

Frith, U. (2003). *Autism: Explaining the enigma* (2nd ed.). Oxford, UK: Blackwell Publishing.

Frith, U., & Happé, F. (1994). Autism: Beyond "theory of mind." *Cognition, 50,* 115-132.

Frost, L., & Bondy, A. (2002). *The picture exchange communication system training manual.* Newark, DE: Pyramid Educational Products.

Gadow, K. D., DeVincent, C. J., Pomeroy, J., & Azizian, A. (2004). Psychiatric symptoms in preschool children with PDD and clinic comparison samples. *Journal of Autism and Developmental Disorders, 34*(4), 379-393.

Gagnon, E. (2001). *Power Cards: Using special interests to motivate children and youth with Asperger Syndrome and autism.* Shawnee Mission, KS: AAPC Publishing.

Ganz, J. B., & Simpson, R. L. (2004). Effects on communicative requesting and speech development of the Picture Exchange Communication System in children with characteristics of autism. *Journal of Autism and Developmental Disorders, 34,* 395-409.

Geurts, H. M., Verté, S., Oosterlaan, J., Roeyers, H., & Sergeant, J. A. (2004). How specific are executive functioning deficits in attention deficit hyperactivity disorder and autism? *Journal of Child Psychology and Psychiatry, 45*(4), 836-854.

Ghaziuddin, M. (2002). Asperger syndrome: Associated psychiatric and medical conditions. *Focus on Autism and Other Developmental Disabilities, 17*(3), 138-144.

Ghaziuddin, M., & Butler, E. (1998). Clumsiness in autism and Asperger syndrome: A further report. *Journal of Intellectual Disability Research, 42*(1), 43-48.

Ghaziuddin, M., Ghaziuddin, N., & Greden, J. (2002). Depression in persons with autism: Implications for research and clinical care. *Journal of Autism and Developmental Disorders, 32*(4), 299-306.

Ghaziuddin, M., Weidmer-Mikhail, E., & Ghaziuddin, N. (1998). Comorbidity of Asperger syndrome: A preliminary report. *Journal of Intellectual Disability Research, 42*(4), 279-283.

Gill, V. (2003). Challenges faced by teachers working with students with Asperger syndrome. In M. Prior (Ed.), *Learning and behavior problems in Asperger syndrome* (pp. 194-211). New York: Guilford.

Gillberg, C. (1991). Clinical and neurobiological aspects of Asperger syndrome in six family studies. In U. Frith (Ed.), *Autism and Asperger syndrome* (pp. 122-146). Cambridge, UK: Cambridge University Press.

Gillberg, C., & Billstedt, E. (2000). Autism and Asperger syndrome: Coexistence with other clinical disorders. *Acta Psychiatrica Scandinavica, 102,* 321-330.

Glaeser, B. C., Pierson, M. R., & Fritschman, N. (2003). Comic Strip Conversations™: A positive behavioral support strategy. *Teaching Exceptional Children, 36*(2), 14-19.

Goetz, E. T., Alexander, P. A., & Ash, M. J. (1992). *Educational psychology: A classroom perspective.* New York: Macmillan Publishing Company.

Gold, D. (1994). We don't call it a 'circle': The ethos of a support group. *Disability & Society, 9*(4), 435-452.

Goldberg, E. (2001). *The executive brain: Frontal lobes and the civilized mind.* New York: Oxford.

Goldstein, H. (2002). Communication intervention for children with autism: A review of treatment efficacy. *Journal of Autism and Developmental Disorders, 32*(5), 373-396.

Goldstein, H., & Cisar, C. L. (1992). Promoting interaction during sociodramatic play: Teaching scripts to typical preschoolers and classmates with disabilities. *Journal of Applied Behavior Analysis, 25*(2), 265-280.

Goldstein, H., Kaczmarek, L., Pennington, R., & Shafer, K. (1992). Peer-mediated intervention: Attending to, commenting on, and acknowledging the behavior of preschoolers with autism. *Journal of Applied Behavior Analysis, 25,* 289-305.

Gordon, C. T., Rapoport, J. L., Hamburger, S. D., State, R. C., & Mannheim, G. B. (1992). Differential response of seven subjects with autistic disorder to clomipramine and desipramine. *American Journal of Psychiatry, 149,* 363-366.

Gordon, C. T., State, R., Nelson, J., Hamburger, S., & Rapoport, J. (1993). A double-blind comparison of clomipramine, desipramine, and placebo in the treatment of autistic disorder. *Archives of General Psychiatry, 50,* 441-447.

Graham, S., & Harris, K. R. (2005). Improving the writing performance of young struggling writers: Theoretical and programmatic research from the center on accelerating student learning. *The Journal of Special Education, 39,* 19-33.

Gray, C. A. (1994). *Comic strip conversations™: Colorful, illustrated interactions with students with autism and related disorders.* Arlington, TX: Future Horizons.

Gray, C. A. (1998). Social Stories™ and comic strip conversations™ with students with Asperger syndrome and high functioning autism. In E. Schopler, G. B. Mesibov, & L. J. Kunce (Eds.), *Asperger syndrome or high functioning autism* (pp. 167-198). New York: Plenum Press.

Gray, C. A. (2000). *The new Social Story™ book: Illustrated edition* (2nd ed.). Arlington, TX: Future Horizons.

Gray, C. A., & Garand, J. D. (1993). Social Stories™: Improving responses of students with autism with accurate social information. *Focus on Autistic Behavior, 8*(1), 1-10.

Green, I. (2003). *Red and green choices: A positive behavioral development strategy for students with autism or behavioral predispositions.* Mansfield, OH: Atlas Books.

Green, J., Gilchrist, A., Burton, D., & Cox, A. (2000). Social and psychiatric functioning in adolescents with Asperger syndrome compared with conduct disorder. *Journal of Autism and Developmental Disorders, 30*(4), 279-293.

Gresham, F. M., Watson, T. S., & Skinner, C. H. (2001). Functional behavioral assessment: Principles, procedures, and future directions. *School Psychology Review, 30*(2), 156-172.

Griffin, H. C., Griffin, L. W., Fitch, C. W., Albera, V., & Gingras, H. (2006). Educational interventions for individuals with Asperger syndrome. *Intervention in School and Clinic, 41*(3), 150-155.

Haddon, M. (2003). *The curious incident of the dog in the night-time.* New York: Vintage Books.

Hagiwara, T., & Myles, B. S. (1999). A multimedia social story intervention: Teaching skills to children with autism. *Focus on Autism and Other Developmental Disabilities, 14*, 82-95.

Handen, B. L., Johnson, C. R., & Lubetsky, M. (2000). Efficacy of methylphenidate among children with autism and symptoms of attention-deficit hyperactivity disorder. *Journal of Autism and Developmental Disorders, 30*, 245-255.

Handen, B. L., & Lubetsky, M. (2005). Pharmacotherapy in autism and related disorders. *School Psychology Quarterly, 20*(2), 155-171.

Hansen, R. S., & Hansen, K. (n.d.). *What do employers really want? Top skills and values employers seek from job-seekers.* Retrieved March 13, 2006, from http://www.quintcareers.com/job_skills_values.html

Happé, F. (1997). *Autism: Understanding the mind, fitting together the pieces.* Retrieved July 19, 2006, from http://www.mindship.org/happe.htm

Happé, F., & Frith, U. (2006). The weak coherence account: Detail-focused cognitive style in autism spectrum disorders. *Journal of Autism and Developmental Disorders, 36*, 5-25.

Hardan, A. Y., Jou, R. J., & Handen, B. L. (2005). Retrospective study of quetiapine in children and adolescents with pervasive developmental disorders. *Journal of Autism and Developmental Disorders, 35*(3), 387-391.

Haring, T., Kennedy, C., Adams, M., & Pitts-Conway, V. (1987). Teaching generalization of purchasing skills across community settings to autistic youth using videotape modeling. *Journal of Applied Behavioral Analysis, 20*, 89-96.

Harper, C. B., Symon, J.B.G., & Frea, W. D. (2008). Recess is time-in: Using peers to improve social skills of children with autism. *Journal of Autism and Developmental Disorders, 38*, 815-826.

Harrison, J., & Hare, D. J. (2004). Brief report: Assessment of sensory abnormalities in people with autistic spectrum disorders. *Journal of Autism and Developmental Disorders, 34*(6), 727-730.

Henry, S. A., & Myles, B. S. (2007). *The Comprehensive Autism Planning System (CAPS) for individuals with Asperger Syndrome, autism and related disabilities: Integrating best practices throughout the student's daily schedule.* Shawnee Mission, KS: AAPC Publishing.

Hill, E. L., & Frith, U. (2003). Understanding autism: Insights from mind and brain. In U. Frith & E. L. Hill (Eds.), *Autism: Mind and brain* (pp. 1-19). New York: Oxford University Press.

Hodgdon, L. A. (1995). *Visual strategies for improving communication: Practical supports for school and home.* Troy, MI: Quirk Roberts Publishing.

Hodgetts, S., Magill-Evans, J., & Misiaszek, J. (2011). Effects of weighted vests on classroom behavior for children with autism and cognitive impairments. *Research in Autism Spectrum Disorders, 5*(1), 495-505.

Hoekman, L. (n.d.). *Writing Social Stories™ ... Some suggestions.* Retrieved December 8, 2005, from http://www.thegraycenter.org/socialstorywriting.cfm

Hoffman, C. D., Sweeney, D. P., Gilliam, J. E., Apodaca, D. D., Lopez-Wagner, M. C., & Castillo, M. M. (2005). Sleep problems and symptomology in children with autism. *Focus on Autism and Other Developmental Disabilities, 20*(4), 194-200.

Hollander, E., Kaplan, A., Cartwright, C., & Reichman, D. (2000). Venlafaxine in children, adolescents, and young adults with autism spectrum disorders: An open retrospective clinical report. *Journal of Child Neurology, 15*(2), 132-135.

Hollander, E., Phillips, A. T., & Yeh, C. (2003). Targeted treatments for symptom domains in child and adolescent autism. *Lancet, 362*, 732-734.

Hollander, E., Phillips, A., Chaplin, W., Zagursky, K., Novotny, S., Wasserman, S., & Iyengar, R. (2005). A placebo controlled crossover trial of liquid fluoxetine on repetitive behaviors in childhood and adolescent autism. *Neuropsychopharmacology, 30*, 582-589.

Honomichl, R. D., Goodlin-Jones, B. L., Burnham, M., Gaylor, E., & Anders, T. F. (2002). Sleep patterns of children with pervasive developmental disorders. *Journal of Autism and Developmental Disabilities, 32*(6), 553-561.

Horner, R. H., & Carr, E. G. (1997). Behavioral support for students with severe disabilities: Functional assessment and comprehensive intervention. *Journal of Special Education, 31*, 84-104.

Horner, R. H., Carr, E. G., Strain, P. S., Todd, A. W., & Reed, H. K. (2002). Problem behavior interventions for young children with autism: A research synthesis. *Journal of Autism and Developmental Disorders, 32*(5), 423-446.

Howlin, P., Baron-Cohen, S., & Hadwin, J. (1999). *Teaching children with autism to mind-read: A practical guide.* New York: John Wiley & Sons.

Howlin, P., Goode, S., Hutton, J., & Rutter, M. (2010). Savant skills in autism: Psychometric approaches and parental reports. In F. Happé & U. Frith (Eds.), *Autism and talent* (pp. 13-24). Oxford, UK: University Press.

Howlin, P., & Yates, P. (1999). The potential effectiveness of social skills groups for adults with autism. *Autism, 3*(3), 299-307.

Hrdlicka, M., Komarek, V., Propper, L., Kulisek, R., Zumrova, A., Faladova, L., Havlovicova, M., Sedlacek, Z., Bloatny, M., & Urbanek, T. (2004). Not EEG abnormalities but epilepsy is associated with autistic regression and mental functioning in childhood autism. *European Child & Adolescent Psychiatry, 14*, 209-213.

Huebner, R. A. (2001). *Autism: A sensorimotor approach to management.* Gaithersburg, MD: Aspen Publishers, Inc.

Hughes, C., & Russell, J. (1993). Autistic children's difficulty with mental disengagement from an object: Its implications for theories of autism. *Developmental Psychology, 29*(3), 498-510.

Hughes, J. N., & Hasbrouck, J. E. (1996). Television violence: Implications for violence prevention. *School Psychology Review, 25*(2), 134-151.

Hull, L., Levy, L., Lai, M. C., Petrides, K. V., Baron-Cohen, S., Allison, C., Smith, P. & Mandy, W. (2021). Is social camouflaging associated with anxiety and depression in autistic adults?. *Molecular Autism, 12(1)*, 1-13.

Hume, K., & Odom, S. (in press). Effects of an individual work system on the independent functioning of students with autism. *Journal of Autism and Developmental Disorders.*

Hung, D. W. (1978). Using self-stimulation as reinforcement for autistic children. *Journal of Autism and Childhood Schizophrenia, 8*, 355-366.

Hwang, B., & Hughes, C. (2000). The effects of social interactive training on early social communicative skills of children with autism. *Journal of Autism and Developmental Disorders, 30*(4), 331-343.

Individuals with Disabilities Education Act. (2004). *The Individuals with Disabilities Education Act Amendments of 2004.*

Jaffe, A. V., & Gardner, L. (2006). *My book full of feelings: How to control and react to the size of your emotions.* Shawnee Mission, KS: AAPC Publishing.

Jahr, E., Eldevik, S., & Eikeseth, S. (2000). Teaching children with autism to initiate and sustain cooperative play. *Research in Developmental Disabilities, 21*, 151-169.

Jarrold, C., Butler, D. W., Cottington, E. M., & Jiminez, F. (2000). Linking theory of mind and central coherence bias in autism and in the general population. *Developmental Psychology, 36*, 126-138.

Jones, E. A., & Carr, E. G. (2004). Joint attention in children with autism: Theory and intervention. *Focus on Autism and Other Developmental Disabilities, 19*, 13-26.

Jordan, R. (2003). School-based intervention for children with specific learning difficulties. In M. Prior (Ed.), *Learning and behavior problems in Asperger Syndrome* (pp. 35-54). New York: Guilford Press.

Joseph, R. M., & Tager-Flusberg, H. (2004). The relationship of theory of mind and executive functions to symptom type and severity with autism. *Development and Psychopathology, 16*, 137-155.

Kadesjo, B., & Gillberg, C. (2000). Tourette's disorder: Epidemiology and comorbidity in primary school children. *Journal of the American Academy of Child and Adolescent Psychiatry, 39*, 548-555.

Kahne, D., Tudorica, A., Borella, A., Shapiro, L., Johnstone, F., Huang, W., & Whitaker-Azmitiam, P. M. (2002). Behavioral and magnetic resonance spectroscopic studies in the rat hyperserotonemic model of autism. *Physiology and Behavior, 75*(3), 403-410.

Kalyva, E., & Avramidis, E. (2005). Improving communication between children with autism and their peers through the 'circle of friends': A small-scale intervention study. *Journal of Applied Research in Intellectual Disabilities,18*, 253-261.

Kamps, D. M., Dugan, E., Potucek, J., & Collins, A. (1999). Effects of cross-age peer tutoring networks among students with autism and general education students. *Journal of Behavioral Education, 9*(2), 97-115.

Kamps, D. M., Leonard, B. R., Vernon, S., Dugan, E. P., Delquadri, J. C., Gershon, B., Wade, L., & Folk, L. (1992). Teaching social skills to students with autism to increase peer interactions in an integrated first-grade classroom. *Journal of Applied Behavior Analysis, 25*, 281-288.

Kamps, D. M., Potucek, J., Lopez, A., Kravits, T., & Kemmerer, K. (1997). The use of peer networks across multiple settings to improve social interaction for students with autism. *Journal of Behavioral Education, 7*(3), 335-357.

Kaplan, H., Hemmes, N. S., & Motz, P. (1996). Self-reinforcement and persons with developmental disabilities. *Psychological Record, 46*, 161-178.

Kasari, C., Gulsrud, A. C., Wong, C., Kwon, S., & Locke, J. (2010). Randomized controlled caregivers mediated joint engagement intervention for toddlers with autism. *Journal of Autism and Developmental Disorders, 40*, 1045-1056.

Keeling, K., Myles, B. S., Gagnon, E., & Simpson, R. L. (2003). Using the Power Card Strategy to teach sportsmanship skills to a child with autism. *Focus on Autism and Other Developmental Disabilities, 18*, 105-111.

Kemner, C., Willemsen-Swinkels, S.H.N., DeJonge, M., Tuynman-Qua, H., & Van Engerland, H. (2002). Open-label study of olanzapine in children with pervasive developmental disorder. *Journal of Clinical Psychopharmacology, 22*, 455-460.

Kerr, S., & Durkin, K. (2004). Understanding of thought bubbles as mental representations in children with autism: Implications for theory of mind. *Journal of Autism and Developmental Disorders, 34*(6), 637-648.

Kiernan, C. (1983). The use of nonvocal communication techniques with autistic individuals. *Journal of Child Psychology and Psychiatry, 24*, 339-375.

Kim, J. A., Szatmari, P., Bryson, S. E., Streiner, D. L., & Wilson, F. J. (2000). The prevalence of anxiety and mood problems among children with autism and Asperger syndrome. *Autism, 4*, 117-132.

Kinney, E. M., Vedora, J., & Stromer, R. (2003). Computer-presented video models to teach generative spelling to a child with an autism spectrum disorder. *Journal of Positive Behavior Interventions, 5*, 22-29.

Klin, A., Jones, W., Schultz, R., Volkmar, F., & Cohen, D. (2002). Designing and quantifying the social phenotype in autism. *American Journal of Psychiatry, 159*, 895-908.

Klin, A., Sparrow, S. S., Marans, W. D., Carter, A., & Volkmar, F. R. (2000). Assessment issues in children and adolescents with Asperger syndrome. In A. Klin, F. R. Volkmar, & S. S. Sparrow (Eds.), *Asperger Syndrome* (pp. 309-339). New York: Guilford Press.

Klin, A., & Volkmar, F. R. (1997). Asperger's syndrome. In D. J. Cohen & F. R. Volkmar (Eds.), *Handbook of autism and pervasive developmental disorders* (pp. 94-122). New York: Wiley.

Klintwall, L., Holm, A., Eriksson, M., Carlsson, L. H., Olsson, M. B., & Hedvall, A., et al. (2011). Sensory abnormalities in autism: A brief report. *Research in Developmental Disabilities, 32*, 795-800.

Koegel, L. K., & Koegel, R. L. (1990). Extended reductions in stereotypic behavior of students with autism through a self-management treatment package. *Journal of Applied Behavioral Analysis, 24*, 119-127.

Koegel, R. L., Carter, C. M., & Koegel, L. K. (1998). Setting events to improve parent-teacher coordination and motivation for children with autism. In J. K. Luiselli & M. J. Cameron (Eds.), *Antecedent control: Innovative approaches to behavioral support* (pp. 167-186). Baltimore: Paul H. Brookes Publishing Company.

Koegel, R. L., Frea, W. D., & Surratt, A. V. (1994). Self-management of problematic social behavior. In E. Schopler & G. B. Mesibov (Eds.), *Behavioral issues in autism* (pp. 81-97). New York: Plenum Press.

Koegel, R. L., & Koegel, L. K. (2006). *Pivotal response treatments for autism: Communication, social, & academic development.* Baltimore: Paul H. Brookes Publishing Company.

Koegel, L. K., Koegel, R. L., Frea, W., & Green-Hopkins, I. (2003). Priming as a method of coordinating educational services for students with autism. *Language, Speech, and Hearing Services in the Schools, 34*, 228-235.

Koegel, L. K., Koegel, R. L., Harrower, J. K., & Carter, C. M. (1999). Pivotal response intervention I: Overview of approach. *Journal of the Association for Persons with Severe Handicaps, 24*(3), 174-185.

Koegel, R. L., Werner, G. A., Vismara, L. A., & Koegel, L. K. (2005). The effectiveness of contextually supported play date interactions between children with autism and typically developing peers. *Research & Practice for Persons with Severe Disabilities, 30*(2), 93-102.

Krantz, P. J., MacDuff, M. T., & McClannahan, L. E. (1993). Programming participation in family activities for children with autism: Parents' use of photographic activity schedules. *Journal of Applied Behavior Analysis, 26*, 137-138.

Krantz, P. J., & McClannahan, L. E. (1993). Teaching children with autism to initiate to peers: Effects of a script-fading procedure. *Journal of Applied Behavior Analysis, 26*, 121-132.

Krantz, P. J., & McClannahan, L. E. (1998). Social interaction skills for children with autism: A script-fading procedure for beginning readers. *Journal of Applied Behavior Analysis, 31*, 191-202.

Lai, M. C., Kassee, C., Besney, R., Bonato, S., Hull, L., Mandy, W., Szatmari, P., & Ameis, S. H. (2019). Prevalence of co-occurring mental health diagnoses in the autism population: a systematic review and meta-analysis. *The Lancet Psychiatry, 6(10)*, 819-829.

Lainhart, J. (1999). Psychiatric problems in individuals with autism, their parents and siblings. *International Review of Psychiatry, 11*, 278-298.

Lainhart, J. E., Piven, J., Wzorek, M., Landa, R., Santangelo, S. L., Coon, H., & Folstein, S. E. (1997). Macrocephaly in children and adults with autism. *Journal of the American Academy of Child and Adolescent Psychiatry, 36*, 282-290.

Lane, A. E., Young, R. L., Baker, A.E.Z., & Angley, M. T. (2010). Sensory processing subtypes in autism: Association with adaptive behavior. *Journal of Autism and Developmental Disorders, 40*, 112-122.

Lasater, M. W., & Brady, M. P. (1995). Effects of video self-modeling and feedback on task fluency: A home-based intervention. *Education and Treatment of Children, 18*(4), 389-408.

Laushey, K. M., & Heflin, L. J. (2000). Enhancing social skills of kindergarten children with autism through the training of multiple peers as tutors. *Journal of Autism and Developmental Disorders, 30*(3), 183-193.

Lewis, V., & Boucher, J. (1995). Generativity in the play of young people with autism. *Journal of Autism and Developmental Disorders, 25*, 105-121.

Lifter, K., Sulzer-Azaroff, B., Anderson, S., & Cowdery, G. E. (1993). Teaching play activities to pre-school children with disabilities: The importance of developmental considerations. *Journal of Early Intervention, 17*(2), 139-159.

Lorimer, P. A., Simpson, R. L., Myles, B. S., & Ganz, J. B. (2002). The use of Social Stories™ as a preventative behavioral intervention in a home setting with a child with autism. *Journal of Positive Behavior Interventions, 4*(1), 53-60.

Lynn, G. (2007). *The Asperger plus child: How to identify and help children with Asperger Syndrome and seven common co-existing conditions.* Shawnee Mission, KS: AAPC Publishing.

MacDuff, G. S., Krantz, P. J., & McClannahan, L. E. (1993). Teaching children with autism to use photographic activity schedules: Maintenance and generalizations of complex response chains. *Journal of Applied Behavior Analysis, 26*, 89-97.

Madras, B. K., Miller, G. M., & Fischman, A. J. (2005). The dopamine transporter and attention-deficit/hyperactivity disorder. *Biological Psychiatry, 57*(11), 1397-1409.

Magiati, I., & Howlin, P. (2003). A pilot evaluation study of the picture exchange communication system for children with autism spectrum disorders. *Autism, 7*, 297-320.

Maher, B. S., Marazita, M. L., Ferrell, R. E., & Vanyukov, M. M. (2002). Dopamine system genes and attention deficit hyperactivity disorder: A meta-analysis. *Psychiatric Genetics, 12*, 207-215.

Manasco, H. (2006). *The way to A: Empowering children with autism spectrum and other neurological disorders to monitor and replace aggression and tantrum behavior.* Shawnee Mission, KS: AAPC Publishing.

Marcus, L. M., Lansing, M., Andrews, C. E., & Schopler, E. (1978). Improvement of teaching effectiveness in parents of autistic children. *Journal of the American Academy of Child Psychiatry, 17*, 625-639.

Mares, M., & Woodard, E. (2005). Positive effects of television on children's social interactions: A meta-analysis. *Media Psychology, 7*(3), 301-322.

Mari, M., Marks, D., Marraffa, C., Prior, M., & Castiello, U. (2003). Autism and movement disturbance. In U. Frith & E. Hill (Eds.), *Autism: Mind and brain* (pp. 226-246). New York: Oxford University Press.

Masiello, T. (2007). Effectiveness of pivotal response training as a behavioral intervention for young children with autism spectrum disorders. *Winterberry Research Syntheses, 1*, 14.

Massey, N. G., & Wheeler, J. J. (2000). Acquisition and generalization of activity schedules and their effects on task engagement in a young child with autism in an inclusive pre-school classroom. *Education and Training in Mental Retardation and Developmental Disabilities, 35*, 326-335.

Mayes, S. D., & Calhoun, S. L. (2003). Relationship between Asperger syndrome and high-functioning autism. In M. Prior (Ed.), *Learning and behavior problems in Asperger Syndrome* (pp. 15-34). New York: Guilford Press.

McAffee, J. (2002). *Navigating the social world.* Arlington, TX: Future Horizons.

McClure, M. K., & Holtz-Yotz, M. (1991). Case report – The effects of sensory stimulatory treatment on an autistic child. *American Journal of Occupational Therapy, 45,* 1138-1142.

McDougall, D. (1998). Research on self-management techniques used by students with disabilities in general education settings: A descriptive review. *Remedial and Special Education, 19,* 310-321.

McDougle, C. J., Brodkin, E. S., Naylor, S. T., Carlson, D. C., Cohen, D. J., & Price, L. H. (1998). Sertraline in adults with pervasive developmental disorders: A prospective open-label investigation. *Journal of Clinical Psychopharmacology, 18,* 62-66.

McDougle, C. J., Holmes, J. P., Carlson, D. C., Pelton, G. H., Cohen, D. J., & Price, L. H. (1998). A double-blind, placebo-controlled study of risperidone in adults with autistic disorder and other pervasive developmental disorders. *Archives of General Psychiatry, 55,* 633-641.

McDougle, C. J., Kresch, L. E., & Posey, D. J. (2000). Repetitive thoughts and behavior in pervasive developmental disorders: Treatment with serotonin reuptake inhibitors. *Journal of Autism and Developmental Disorders, 30*(5), 427-435.

McDougle, C. J., Naylor, S. T., Cohen, D. J., Aghajanian, G. K., Heninger, G. R., & Price, L. H. (1996). Effects of tryptophan depletion in drug-free adults with autistic disorder. *Archives of General Psychiatry, 53*(11), 993-1000.

McDougle, C. J., Naylor, S. T., Cohen, D. J., Volkmar, F. R., Heninger, G. R., & Price, L. H. (1996). A double-blind, placebo-controlled study of fluvoxamine in adults with autistic disorder. *Archives of General Psychiatry, 53,* 1001-1008.

McDougle, C. J., Price, L. H., Volkmar, F. R., Goodman, W. K., Ward-O'Brien, D., Nielsen, J., Bergman, J., & Cohen, D. J. (1992). Clomipramine in autism: Preliminary evidence of efficacy (case study). *Journal of the American Academy of Child and Adolescent Psychiatry, 31,* 746-750.

McDougle, C. J., Scahill, L., Aman, M. G., McCracken, J. T., Tierney, E., Davies, M., et al. (2005). Risperidone for the core symptom domains of autism: Results from the study by the autism network of the research units on pediatric psychopharmacology. *American Journal of Psychiatry, 162*(6), 1142-1148.

McPheeter, M., Davis, M., Navarre, J., & Scott, T. (2011). Family report of ASD concomitant with depression or anxiety among U.S. children. *Journal of Autism and Developmental Disorders, 41*(5), 646-653.

Mesibov, G. B. (1984) Social skills training with verbal autistic adolescents and adults: A program model, *Journal of Autism and Developmental Disorders 14,* 395-404.

Mesibov, G. B., Browder, D. M., & Kirkland, C. (2002). Using individualized schedules as a component of positive behavioral support for students with developmental disabilities. *Journal of Positive Behavioral Interventions, 4,* 73-79.

Mesibov, G. B., Shea, V., & Schopler, E. (2004). *The TEACCH approach to autism spectrum disorders.* New York: Springer Science +Business Media, Inc.

Mesibov, G. B., & Shea, V. (2006). *Evidence-based practice, autism and the TEACCH program.* Manuscript in preparation.

Miller, M. C., Cooke, N. L., Test, D. W., & White, R. (2003). Effects of friendship circles on the social interactions of elementary age students with mild disabilities. *Journal of Behavioral Education, 12*(3), 167-184.

Miller, P. (1993). *Theories of developmental psychology* (3rd ed.). New York: W. H. Freeman and Company.

Moore, D., Cheng, Y., McGrath, P., & Powell, N. J. (2005). Collaborative virtual environment technology for people with autism. *Focus on Autism and Other Developmental Disabilities, 20,* 231-243.

Morales, M., Mundy, P., Delgado, C.E.F., Yale, M., Messinger, D., Neal, R., et al. (2000). Responding to joint attention across the 6- through 24-month age period and early language acquisition. *Journal of Applied Developmental Psychology, 21*(3), 283-298.

Morgan, B., Maybery, M., & Durkin, K. (2003). Weak central coherence, poor joint attention, and low verbal IQ: Independent deficits in early autism. *Developmental Psychology, 39*, 646-656.

Morgan, C. N., Roy, M., Nasr, A., Chance, P., Hand, M., Mlele, T., & Roy, A. (2002). A community survey establishing the prevalence rate of autistic disorder in adults with learning disability. *Psychiatric Bulletin, 26*, 127-130.

Morrison, R. S., Sainato, D. M., Benchaaban, D., & Endo, S. (2005). Increasing play skills of children with autism using activity schedules and correspondence training. *Journal of Early Intervention, 25*, 58-72.

Moses, L. J. (2001). Executive accounts of theory-of-mind development. *Child Development, 72*, 688-690.

Mouridsen, S. E., Rich, B., & Isager, T. (2011). A longitudinal study of epilepsy and other central nervous systems diseases in individuals with and without a history of infantile autism. *Brain and Development, 33*, 361-366.

Myles, B. S., & Adreon, D. (2001). *Asperger Syndrome and adolescence: Practical solutions for school success.* Shawnee Mission, KS: AAPC Publishing.

Myles, B. S., Cook, K. T., Miller, N. E., Rinner, L., & Robbins, L. (2000). *Asperger Syndrome and sensory issues: Practical solutions for making sense of the world.* Shawnee Mission, KS: AAPC Publishing.

Myles, B. S., Hagiwara, T., Dunn, W., Rinner, L., Reese, M., Huggins, A., & Becker, S. (2004). Sensory issues in children with Asperger Syndrome and autism. *Education and Training in Developmental Disabilities, 3*(4), 283-290.

Myles, B. S., & Henry, S. (2008, February). *Educational supports for school-aged children that foster social skills and understanding of the hidden curriculum.* Presentation at Alabama Autism Conference, Tuscaloosa, AL.

Myles, B. S., & Simpson, R. L. (2001). Understanding the hidden curriculum: An essential social skill for children and youth with Asperger Syndrome. *Intervention in School and Clinic, 38*(5), 279-286.

Myles, B. S., Simpson, R. L., Carlson, J., Laurant, M., Gentry, A., Cook, K. T., & Earles-Vollrath, T. L. (2004). Examining the effects of the use of weighted vests for addressing behaviors of children with autism spectrum disorders. *Journal of the International Association of Special Educators, 5*(1), 47-62.

Myles, B. S., & Southwick, J. (2005). *Asperger Syndrome and difficult moments: Practical solutions for tantrums, rage, and meltdowns* (expanded and revised ed.). Shawnee Mission, KS: AAPC Publishing.

Myles, B. S., Trautman, M. L., & Schelvan, R. L. (2004). *The hidden curriculum: Practical solutions for understanding unstated rules in social situations.* Shawnee Mission, KS: AAPC Publishing.

Namerow, L. B., Thomas, P., Bostic, J., Prince, J., & Monuteaux, M. (2003). Use of citalopram in pervasive developmental disorders. *Developmental and Behavioral Pediatrics, 24*, 104-108.

National Public Radio. (May 5, 2004). *Dr. Fred Volkmar on Asperger's Syndrome.* Retrieved Janurary 21, 2005, from http://www.npr.org/templates/story/story.php?storyId=1872620

National Research Council. (2001). *Educating children with autism.* Washington, DC: National Academy Press.

Nayate, A., Bradshaw, J. L., & Rinehart, N. J. (2005). Autism and Asperger's disorder: Are they movement disorders involving the cerebellum and/or basal ganglia? *Brain Research Bulletin, 67*, 327-334.

Nicolson, R., & Szatmari, P. (2003). Genetic and neurodevelopmental influences in autistic disorder. *Canadian Journal of Psychiatry, 48*(8), 526-537.

Nikopoulos, C. K., & Keenan, M. (2003). Promoting social initiation in children with autism using video modeling. *Behavior Interventions, 18*, 87-108.

Nikopoulos, C. K., & Keenan, M. (2004). Effects of video modeling on social initiations by children with autism. *Journal of Applied Behavior Analysis, 37*, 93-96.

Norbury, C., & Nation, K. (2011). Understanding variability in reading comprehension in adolescents with autism spectrum disorders: Interactions with language status and decoding skills. *Studies of Reading, 15*, 191-210.

Ogletree, B. T., & Fischer, M. A. (1995). An innovative language treatment for a child with high-functioning autism. *Focus on Autistic Behavior, 10*, 1-10.

Ohta, M., Kano, Y., & Nagai, Y. (2006). Catatonia in individuals with autism spectrum disorders in adolescence and early adulthood: a long-term prospective study. *International Review of Neurobiology, 72*, 41-54.

O'Loughlin, C., & Thagard, P. (2000). Autism and coherence: A computational model. *Mind & Language, 15*(4), 375-392.

O'Neill, R. E., Horner, R. H., Albin, R. W., Sprague, J. K., Storey, K., & Newton, J. S. (1997). *Functional assessment and program development for problem behavior: A practical handbook* (2nd ed.). Pacific Grove, CA: Brooks/Cole.

Ozbayrak, K. (1997). Sertraline in PDD. *Journal of the American Academy of Child & Adolescent Psychiatry, 36*, 7-8.

Ozonoff, S. (1997). Components of executive function in autism and other disorders. In J. Russell (Ed.), *Autism as an executive disorder* (pp. 179-211). Oxford, UK: Oxford University Press.

Ozonoff, S., & Cathcart, K. (1998). Effectiveness of a home program intervention for young children with autism. *Journal of Autism and Developmental Disorders, 28*, 25-32.

Ozonoff, S., & Miller, J. N. (1995). Teaching theory of mind: A new approach to social skills training for individuals with autism. *Journal of Autism and Developmental Disorders, 25*(4), 415-433.

Ozonoff, S., & Strayer, D. L. (1997). Inhibitory function in nonretarded children with autism. *Journal of Autism and Developmental Disorders, 27*, 59-77.

Ozonoff, S., Strayer, D. L., McMahon, W. M., & Filloux, F. (1994). Executive function abilities in autism and Tourette syndrome: An information processing approach. *Journal of Child Psychology and Psychiatry, 35*, 1015-1032.

Page, J., & Boucher, J. (1998). Motor impairments in children with autistic disorder. *Child Language Teaching & Therapy, 14*(3), 233-259.

Panerai, S., Ferrante, L., & Zingale, M. (2002). Benefits of the treatment and education of autistic and communication handicapped children (TEACCH) programme as compared with a non-specific approach. *Journal of Intellectual Disability Research, 46*, 318-327.

Parsons, S., & Mitchell, P. (2002). The potential of virtual reality in social skills training for people with autistic spectrum disorders. *Journal of Intellectual Disability Research, 46*(5), 430-443.

Parsons, S., Mitchell, P., & Leonard, A. (2004). The use and understanding of virtual environments by adolescents with autistic spectrum disorders. *Journal of Autism and Developmental Disorders, 34*(4), 449-466.

Paul, R. (2003). Promoting social communication in high functioning individuals with autistic spectrum disorders. *Child and Adolescent Psychiatric Clinics, 12*, 87-106.

Pellicano, E. (2010). Individual differences in executive function and central coherence predict later theory of mind in autism. *Developmental Psychology, 46*, 530-544.

Pellicano, E., Maybery, M., & Durkin, K. (2005). Central coherence in typically developing pre-schoolers: Does it cohere and does it related to mindreading and executive control? *Journal of Child Psychology and Psychiaäry, 46*(5), 533-547.

Pelphrey, K. A., Sasson, N. J., Reznick, J. S., Paul, G., Goldman, B. D., & Piven, J. (2002). Visual scanning of faces in autism. *Journal of Autism and Developmental Disorders, 32*(4), 249-261.

Pennington, B. F., & Ozonoff, S. (1996). Executive functions and developmental psychopathology. *Journal of Child Psychology and Psychiatry, 37*, 51-87.

Perel, M., Margarita, A., & Inmaculada, G. (1999). Fluoxetine in children with autism. *Journal of the American Academy of Child & Adolescent Psychiatry, 38*(12), 1472-1473.

Pfeiffer, B., & Kinnealey, M. (2003). Treatment of sensory defensiveness in adults. *Occupational Therapy International, 10*(3), 175-184.

Pfeiffer, B., Kinnealey, M., Reed, C., & Herzberg, G. (2005). Sensory modulation and affective disorders in children and adolescents with Asperger's disorder. *The American Journal of Occupational Therapy, 59*(3), 335-345.

Pierce, K., & Schreibman, L. (1995). Increasing complex social behaviors in children with autism: Effects of peer-implemented pivotal response training. *Journal of Applied Behavior Analysis, 28*(3), 285-295

Pierce, K. L., & Schreibman, L. (1994). Teaching daily living skills to children with autism in unsupervised settings through pictorial self-management. *Journal of Applied Behavior Analysis, 27*, 471-481.

Pierson, M. R., & Glaeser, B. C. (2005). Extension of research on social skills training using comic strip conversations™ to students without autism. *Education and Training in Developmental Disabilities, 40*(3), 279-284.

Plaisted, K., Saksida, L., Alcántara, J., & Weisblatt, E. (2003). Towards an understanding of the mechanisms of weak central coherence effects: Experiments in visual configural learning and auditory perception. In U. Frith & E. Hill (Eds.), *Autism: Mind and brain* (pp. 187-210). New York: Oxford University Press.

Polemini, M. A., Richdale, A. L., & Francis, A.J.P. (2005). A survey of sleep problems in autism, Asperger's disorder, and typically developing children. *Journal of Intellectual Disability Research, 49*(4), 260-268.

Posey, D. I., Litwiller, M., Koburn, A., & McDougle, C. J. (1999). Paroxetine in autism. *Journal of the American Academy of Child and Adolescent Psychiatry, 38*(11), 111-112.

Posey, D. I., & McDougle, C. J. (2000). The pharmacotherapy of target symptoms associated with autistic disorder and other pervasive developmental disorders. *Harvard Review of Psychiatry, 8*(2), 45-63.

Raja, M. (2014). Suicide risk in adults with Asperger's syndrome. *The Lancet Psychiatry, 1(2)*, 99-101.

Rapin, I. (1996). Neurological examination. In I. Rapin (Ed.), *Preschool children with inadequate communication* (pp. 98-122). Cambridge, UK: Cambridge University Press for MacKeith Press.

Rast, J.E., Garfield, T., Roux, A.M., Koffer Miller, K.H., Hund, L.M., Tao, S., Kerns, C.M., Rosenau, K.A., Hotez, E., Anderson, K.A., Shattuck, P.T., and Shea, L.L. *National Autism Indicators Report: Mental Health. Philadelphia, PA: Life Course Outcomes Program*, A.J. Drexel Autism Institute, Drexel University, August 2021.

Redcay, E., & Courchesne, E. (2005). When is the brain enlarged in autism? A meta-analysis of all brain size reports. *Biological Psychiatry, 58*, 1-9.

Reese, R. M., Richman, D. M., Zarcone, J., & Zarcone, T. (2003). Individualizing functional assessments for children with autism: The contribution of perseverative behavior and sensory disturbances to disruptive behavior. *Focus on Autism and Other Developmental Disabilities, 18*(2), 87-92.

Reeve, C. E., & Carr, E. G. (2000). Prevention of severe behavior problems in children with developmental disorders. *Journal of Positive Behavior Interventions, 2*(3), 144-160.

Reitzel, J., & Szatmari, P. (2003). Cognitive and academic problems. In M. Prior (Ed.), *Learning and behavior problems in Asperger Syndrome* (pp. 35-54). New York: Guilford Press.

Research Units on Pediatric Psychopharmacology (RUPP) Autism Network. (2002). Risperidone in children with autism and serious behavioral problems. *New England Journal of Medicine, 347*(5), 314-321.

Rinehart, N. J., Bradshaw, J. L., Brereton, A. V., & Tonge, B. J. (2002). A clinical and neurobehavioral review of high-functioning autism and Asperger's disorder. *Australian and New Zealand Journal of Psychiatry, 36*, 762-770.

Rinehart, N. J., Bradshaw, J. L., Moss, S. A., Brereton, A. V., & Tonge, B. J. (2000). Atypical interference of local detail on global processing in high-functioning autism and Asperger's disorder. *Journal of Child Psychology and Psychiatry, 41*, 769-778.

Robbins, L., & Miller, N. (2007). *Sensation station.* Shawnee Mission, KS: AAPC Publishing.

Roberts, R. J., & Pennington, B. F. (1996). An interactive framework for examining prefrontal cognitive processes. *Developmental Neuropsychology, 12*, 105-126.

Rogers, M. F., & Myles, B. S. (2001). Using social stories and comic strip conversations™ to interpret social situations for an adolescent with Asperger Syndrome. *Intervention in School and Clinic, 36*, 310-313.

Rubin, E., & Laurent, A. C. (1994). Implementing a curriculum-based assessment to prioritize learning objectives in Asperger Syndrome and high-functioning autism. *Topics in Language Disorders, 24*(4), 298-315.

Rubin, E., & Lennon, L. (2004). Challenges in social communication in Asperger Syndrome and high-functioning autism. *Topics in Language Disorders, 24*(4), 271-285.

Russell, E., & Sofronoff, K. (2005). Anxiety and social worries in children with Asperger syndrome. *Australian and New Zealand Journal of Psychiatry, 39*, 633-638.

Russo, R., Flanagan, T., Iarocci, G., Berringer, D., Zelazo, P. D., & Burack, J. A. (2007). Deconstructing executive deficits among persons with autism: Implications for cognitive neuroscience. *Brain and Cognition, 65*, 77-86.

Rutter, M. (2000). Genetic studies of autism: From the 1970s into the millennium. *Journal of Abnormal Child Psychology, 28*, 3-14.

Rutter, M., & Bartak, L. (1973). Special educational treatment of autistic children: A comparative study- II. Follow-up findings and implications for services. *Journal of Child Psychology and Psychiatry, 14*, 241-270.

Rutter, M. L. (2011). Progress in understanding autism: 2007-2010. *Journal of Autism and Developmental Disorders, 41*, 395-404.

Sakai, K. (2005). *Finding our way: Practical solutions for creating a supportive home and community for the Asperger Syndrome family.* Shawnee Mission, KS: AAPC Publishing.

Sanosti, F. J., Powell-Smith. K. A., & Kincaid, D. (2004). A research synthesis of social story™ interventions for children with autism spectrum disorders. *Focus on Autism and Other Developmental Disabilities, 19*(4), 194-204.

Santangelo, S. L., & Tsatsanis, K. (2005). What is known about autism: Genes, brain, and behavior. *American Journal of Pharmacogenomics, 5*(2), 71-92.

Sarokoff, R. A., Taylor, B. A., & Poulson, C. L. (2001). Teaching children with autism to engage in conversational exchanges: Script fading with embedded textual stimuli. *Journal of Applied Behavior Analysis, 34*, 81-84.

Scattone, D., Wilczynski, S. M., Edwards, R. P., & Rabian B. (2002). Decreasing disruptive behaviors of children with autism using social stories™. *Journal of Autism and Developmental Disorders, 32*(6), 535-543.

Schain, R. J., & Freedman, D. X. (1961). Studies on 5-hydroxyindole metabolism in autistic and other mental retarded children. *Journal of Pediatrics, 58*, 315-320.

Scheuermann, B., & Webber, J. (2002). *Autism: Teaching does make a difference.* Belmont, CA: Wadsworth/Thomson Learning.

Schilling, L. S., & Schwartz, I. S. (2004). Alternative seating for young children with autism spectrum disorders: Effects on classroom behavior. *Journal of Autism and Developmental Disorders, 34*(4), 423-432.

Schmit, J., Alper, S., Raschke, D., & Ryndak, D. (2000). Effects of using a photographic cueing package during routine school transitions with a child who has autism. *Mental Retardation, 38,* 131-137.

Schopler, E. (1994). Behavioral priorities for autism and related developmental disorders. In E. Schopler & G. B. Mesibov (Eds.), *Behavioral issues in autism* (pp. 55-75). New York: Plenum Press.

Schopler, E., Brehm, S. S., Kinsbourne, M., & Reichler, R. J. (1971). Effect of treatment structure on development in autistic children. *Archives of General Psychiatry, 24*, 415-421.

Schreck, K. A., Mulick, J. A., & Smith, A. F. (2004). Sleep problems as possible predictors of intensified symptoms of autism. *Research in Developmental Disabilities, 25*, 57-66.

Schreibman, L., & Ingersoll, B. (2005). Behavioral interventions to promote learning in individuals with autism. In F. R. Volkmar, R. Paul, A. Klin, & D. Cohen (Eds.), *Handbook of autism and pervasive developmental disorders: Volume two: Assessment, interventions, and policy* (3rd ed., pp. 882-896). Hoboken, NJ: John Wiley & Sons.

Schreibman, L., Whalen, C., & Stahmer, A. C. (2000). The use of video priming to reduce disruptive transition behavior in children with autism. *Journal of Positive Behavior Interventions, 2*, 3-11.

Schultz, R. (2005). Developmental deficits in social perception in autism: The role of the amygdala and fusiform face area. *International Journal of Developmental Neuroscience, 23*, 125-141.

Schwartz, I. S., Garfinkle, A. N., & Bauer, J. (1998). The Picture Exchange Communication System: Communicative outcomes for young children with disabilities. *Topics in Early Childhood Special Education, 18*, 144-159.

Shah, A. (2019). *Catatonia, shutdown and breakdown in autism: A psycho-ecological approach.* Jessica Kingsley Publishers.

Shah, A., & Wing, L. (2006). Psychological approaches to chronic catatonia-like deterioration in autism spectrum disorders. In R. J. Bradley, R. A. Harris, & P. Jenner (Series Ed.), & D. M. Dhossche, L. Wing, M. Ohta, & K. Neumärker (Vol. Eds.), *International Review of Neurobiology: Vol. 72. Catatonia in autism spectrum disorders* (pp. 246-263). New York: Academic Press.

Sherer, M., Pierce, K. L., Paredes, S., Kisacky, K. L., Intersoll, B., & Schreibman, L. (2001). Enhancing conversational skills in children with autism via video technology: Which is better, "self" or "other" as a model? *Behavior Modification, 25*, 140-148.

Sherry, J. L. (2001). The effects of violent video games on aggression: A meta-analysis. *HumanCommunicationResearch,27*(3), 409-431.

Shic, F., Bradshaw, J., Klin, A., Scassellati, B., & Chawarska, S. (2011). Limited activity monitoring in toddlers with autism spectrum disorder. *Brain Research, 1380,* 246-254.

Short, A. B. (1984). Short-term treatment outcome using parents as co-therapists for their own autistic children. *Journal of Child Psychology and Psychiatry, 25,* 443-458.

Siegel, B. (2003). *Helping children with autism learn: Treatment approaches for parents and professionals.* New York: Oxford University Press.

Simonoff, E., Pickles, A., Charman, T., Chandler, S., Loucas, T., & Baird, G. (2008). Psychiatric disorders in children with autism spectrum disorders: Prevalence, comorbidity, and associated factors in a population-derived sample. *Journal American Academy Children Adolescent Psychiatry, 47*(8), 921-929.

Simpson, A., Langone, J., & Ayres, K. M. (2004). Embedded video and computer based instruction to improve social skills for students with autism. *Education and Training in Developmental Disabilities, 39*(3), 240-252.

Simpson, R. L., deBoer-Ott, S. R., Griswold, D. E., Myles, B. S., Byrd, S. E., Ganz, J. B., et al. (2005). *Autism spectrum disorders: Interventions and treatments for children and youth.* Thousand Oaks, CA: Corwin Press.

Snead, B. W., Boon, F., & Presberg, J. (1994). Paroxetine for self-injurious behavior. *Journal of the American Academy of Child and Adolescent Psychiatry, 33,* 909-910.

Sofronoff, K., Attwood, T., & Hinton, S. (2005). A randomised controlled trial of a CBT intervention for anxiety in children with Asperger syndrome. *Journal of Child Psychology and Psychiatry, 46*(11), 1152-1160.

South, M., Ozonoff, S., & McMahon, W. M. (2005). Repetitive behavior profiles in Asperger Syndrome and high functioning autism. *Journal of Autism and Developmental Disorders, 35*(2), 145-158.

Stackhouse, T. M., Graham, N. S., & Laschober, J. S. (2002). Occupational therapy intervention and autism. In R. L. Gabriels & D. E. Hill (Eds.), *Autism – From research to individualized practice* (pp. 155-177). Philadelphia: Jessica Kingsley Publishers.

Stahmer, A. C., Intersoll, B., & Carter, C. (2003). Behavioral approaches to promoting play. *Autism, 7*(4), 401-413.

Stahmer, A. C., & Schreibman, L. (1992). Teaching children with autism appropriate play in unsupervised environments using a self-management treatment package. *Journal of Applied Behavioral Analysis, 25,* 447-459.

Staller, J. (2003). Aripiprazole in an adult with Asperger disorder. *Annals of Pharmacotherapy, 37,* 1628-1631.

Staple, K. L., & Reid, G. (2010). Fundamental movement skills and autism spectrum disorders. *Journal of Autism and Developmental Disorders, 40,* 209-217.

Stevenson, L. S., Krantz, P. J., & McClannahan, L. E. (2000). Social interaction skills for children with autism: A script-fading procedure for nonreaders. *Behavioral Interventions, 15,* 1-20.

Stigler, K. A., Desmond, L. A., Posey, D. J., Wiegand, R. E., & McDougle, C. J. (2004). A naturalistic retrospective analysis of psychostimulants in pervasive developmental disorders. *Journal of Child and Adolescent Psychopharmacology, 14,* 49-56.

Stigler, K. A., Posey, D. J., & McDougle, C. J. (2004). Aripiprazole for maladaptive behavior in pervasive developmental disorders. *Journal of Child and Adolescent Psychopharmacology, 14*(3), 455-463.

Stromer, R., Kimball, J. W., Kinney, E. M., & Taylor, B. A. (2006). Activity schedules, computer technology, and teaching children with autism spectrum disorders. *Focus on Autism and Other Developmental Disabilities, 21,* 14-24.

Sturm, H., Fernell, E., & Gillberg, C. (2004). Autism spectrum disorders in children with normal intellectual levels: Associated impairments and subgroups. *Developmental Medicine & Child Neurology, 46,* 444-447.

Sugai, G., & White, W. J. (1986). Effects of using object self-stimulation as a reinforcer on the prevocational work rates of an autistic child. *Journal of Autism and Developmental Disorders, 16,* 459-471.

Sundberg, M. (2005, September). *Teaching language to children with autism and other developmental disabilities.* Paper presented at the Families for Effective Autism Treatment, North Texas Workshop, Dallas, TX.

Tantum, D. (2003). Assessment and treatment of comorbid emotional and behavior problems. In M. Prior (Ed.), *Learning and behavior problems in Asperger Syndrome* (pp. 148-174). New York: Guilford Press.

Tarascon Pocket Pharmacopeia Deluxe. (2005). http://www.tarascon.com/index.php

Taylor, B. A., Levin, L., & Jasper, S. (1999). Increasing play-related statements in children with autism toward their siblings: Effects of video modeling. *Journal of Developmental and Physical Disabilities, 11*(3), 253-264.

Terpstra, J. E., Higgins, K., & Pierce, T. (2002). Can I play? Classroom-based interventions for teaching play skills to children with autism. *Focus on Autism and Other Developmental Disabilities, 17*(2), 119-126.

Thiemann, K. S., & Goldstein, H. (2001). Social stories, written text cues, and video feedback: Effects on social communication of children with autism. *Journal of Applied Behavior Analysis, 34,* 425-446.

Thieman, K. S., & Goldstein, H. (2004). Effects of peer training and written text cueing on social communication of school-age children with pervasive developmental disorder. *Journal of Speech Language and Hearing Research, 47,* 126-144.

Thomas, N., & Smith, C. (2004). Developing play skills in children with autistic spectrum disorders. *Educational Psychology in Practice, 20*(3), 195-206.

Thorp, D. M., Stahmer, A. C., & Schreibman, L. (1995). Effects of sociodramatic play training on children with autism. *Journal of Autism and Developmental Disorders, 25*(3), 265-282.

Tjus, T., Heimann, M., & Nelson, K. E. (1998). Gains in literacy through the use of a specially designed multimedia computer strategy: Positive findings from thirteen children with autism. *Autism: The International Journal of Research and Practice, 2,* 139-154.

Tjus, T., Heimann, M., & Nelson, K. (2004). Reading acquisition by implementing a multimedia intervention strategy for fifty children with autism or other learning and communication disabilities. *Journal of Cognitive and Behavioral Psychotherapies, 4*(2), 203-221.

Towbin, K. (2003). Strategies for pharmacologic treatment of high functioning autism and Asperger syndrome. *Child and Adolescent Psychiatric Clinics of North America, 12,* 23-45.

Troost, P. W., et al. (2005). Long-term effects of risperidone in children with autism spectrum disorders: A placebo discontinuation study. *Journal of the American Academy of Child & Adolescent Psychiatry, 44*(11), 1137-1144.

Van Bourgondien, M. E., Reichle, N. C., & Schopler, E. (2003). Effects of a model treatment approach on adults with autism. *Journal of Autism and Developmental Disorders, 33,* 131-140.

Vandenberg, N. L. (2001). The use of a weighted vest to increase on-task behavior in children with attention difficulties. *The American Journal of Occupational Therapy, 55,* 621-628.

Volkmar, F. R., Cohen, D., & Paul, R. (1986). An evaluation of DSM-III criteria for infantile autism. *Journal of the American Academy of Child and Adolescent Psychiatry, 25,* 190-197.

Webb, B. J., Miller, S. P., Pierce, T. B., Strawser, S., & Jones, W. P. (2004). Effects of social skill instruction with autism spectrum disorders. *Focus on Autism and Other Developmental Disabilities, 19,* 53-62.

Wellman, H. M., Baron-Cohen, S., Caswell, R., Gomez, J. C., Swettenham, J., Toye, E., & Lagattuta, K. (2002). Thought-bubbles help children with autism acquire an alternative to a theory of mind. *Autism, 6,* 343-363.

Wert, B. Y., & Neisworth, J. T. (2003). Effects of video self-modeling on spontaneous requesting in children with autism. *Journal of Positive Behavior Interventions, 5,* 30-34.

Whalen, C. M., & Schreibman, L. (2003). Joint attention training for children with autism using behavior modification procedures. *Journal of Child Psychology and Psychiatry, 44,* 456-468.

Whitaker-Azmitia, P. M. (2005). Behavioral and cellular consequences of increasing serotonergic activity during brain development: A role in autism? *International Journal of Developmental Neuroscience, 23,* 75-83.

White, S. W., Oswald, D., Ollendick, T., & Scahill, L. (2009). Anxiety in children and adolescents with autism spectrum disorders. *Clinical Psychology Review, 29*(3), 216-229.

Williams, K. (2001). Understanding the student with Asperger syndrome: Guidelines for teachers. *Intervention in School and Clinic, 36*(5), 287-292.

Williams, M. W., & Shellenberger, S. (1996). *How does your engine run? A leader's guide to the Alert Program for Self-Regulation.* Albuquerque, NM: Therapy Works.

Wimmer, H., & Perner, J. (1983). Beliefs about beliefs: Representation and constraining function of wrong beliefs in young children's understanding of deception. *Cognition, 13*(1), 103-128.

Wing, L. (1981). Asperger's syndrome: A clinical account. *Psychological Medicine, 11,* 115-129.

Wing, L., & Shah, A. (2006). A systematic examination of catatonia-like clinical pictures in autism spectrum disorders. In R. J. Bradley, R. A. Harris, & P. Jenner (Series Ed.), & D. M. Dhossche, L. Wing, M. Ohta, & K. Neumärker (Vol. Eds.), *International Review of Neurobiology: Vol. 72. Catatonia in autism spectrum disorders* (pp. 21-39). New York: Academic Press.

Wolfberg, P. J. (2003). *Peer play and the autism spectrum: The art of guiding children's socialization and imagination.* Shawnee Mission, KS: AAPC Publishing.

Wolfberg, P., & Schuler, A. L. (1993). Integrated play groups: A model for promoting the social and cognitive dimensions of play in children with autism. *Journal of Autism and Developmental Disorders, 23*(3), 467-489.

Wolfberg, P., & Schuler, A. L. (1999). Fostering peer interaction, imaginative play and spontaneous language in children with autism. *Child Language Teaching and Therapy, 15,* 41-52.

Wolery, M., Kirk, K., & Gast, D. L. (1985). Stereotypic behavior as a reinforcer: Effects and side effects. *Journal of Autism and Developmental Disorders, 15,* 149-161.

Zanolli, K., Daggett, J., & Adams, T. (1996). Teaching preschool age autistic children to make spontaneous initiations to peers using priming. *Journal of Autism and Developmental Disorders, 26*(4), 407-422.

Zerbo, O., Massolo, M. L., Qian, Y., & Croen, L. A. (2015). A study of physician knowledge and experience with autism in adults in a large integrated healthcare system. *Journal of Autism and Developmental Disorders, 45(12)*, 4002-4014.

Zhang, J., & Wheeler, J. J. (2011). A meta-analysis of peer-mediated interventions for young children with autism spectrum disorders. *Education and Training in Autism and Developmental Disabilities, 46*(1), 62-77.

Zissermann, L. (1992). Case report – The effects of deep pressure on self-stimulating behaviors in a child with autism and other disabilities. *American Journal of Occupational Therapy, 46*, 547-551.

Appendix A

INTERVENTION ZIGGURAT

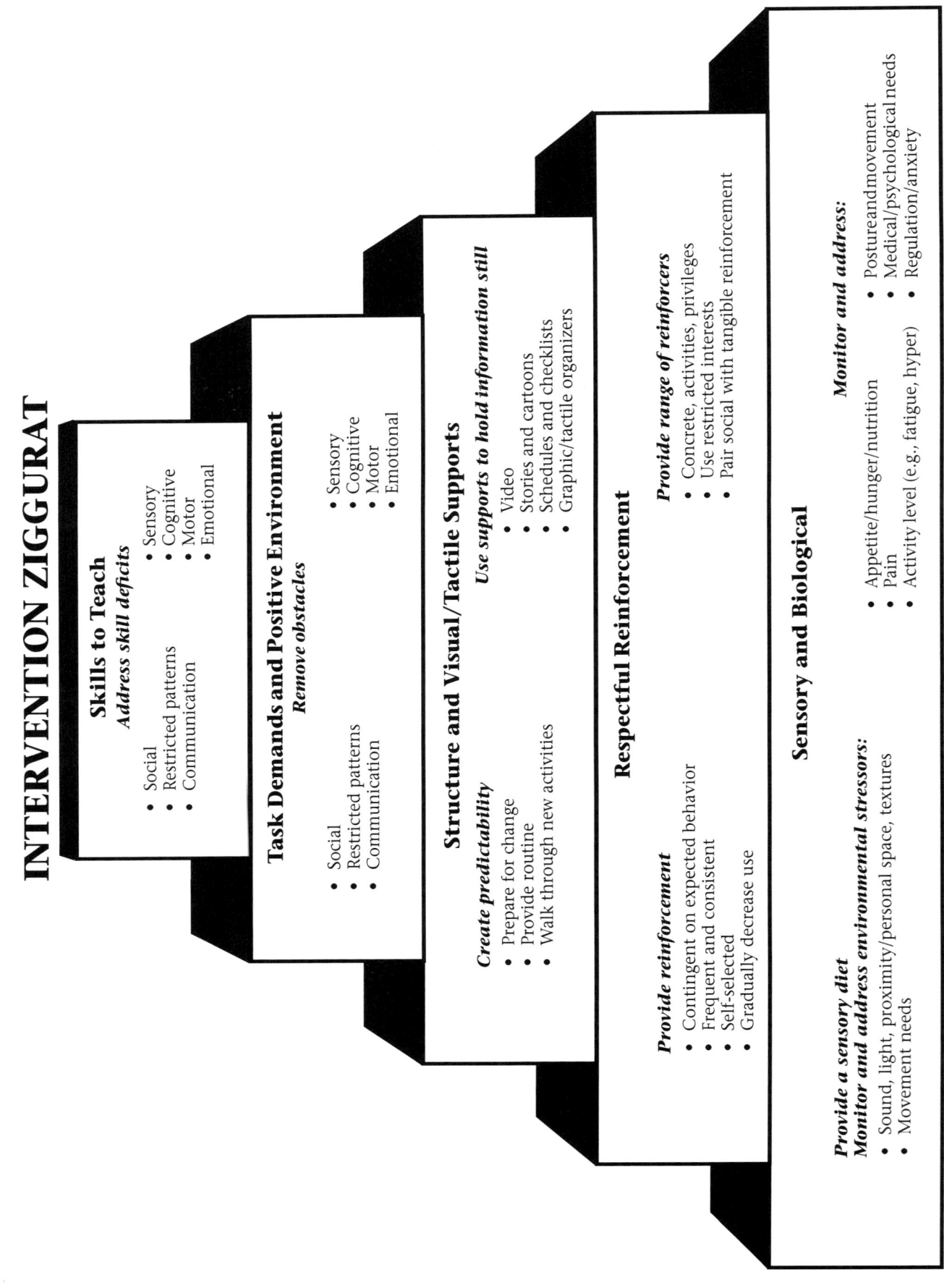

INTERVENTION ZIGGURAT

Skills to Teach
Address skill deficits

- Social
- Restricted patterns
- Communication
- Sensory
- Cognitive
- Motor
- Emotional

Task Demands and Positive Environment
Remove obstacles

- Social
- Restricted patterns
- Communication
- Sensory
- Cognitive
- Motor
- Emotional

Structure and Visual/Tactile Supports

Create predictability

- Prepare for change
- Provide routine
- Walk through new activities

Use supports to hold information still

- Video
- Stories and cartoons
- Schedules and checklists
- Graphic/tactile organizers

Respectful Reinforcement

Provide reinforcement

- Contingent on expected behavior
- Frequent and consistent
- Self-selected
- Gradually decrease use

Provide range of reinforcers

- Concrete, activities, privileges
- Use restricted interests
- Pair social with tangible reinforcement

Sensory and Biological

Provide a sensory diet
Monitor and address environmental stressors:

- Sound, light, proximity/personal space, textures
- Movement needs

Monitor and address:

- Appetite/hunger/nutrition
- Pain
- Activity level (e.g., fatigue, hyper)
- Posture and movement
- Medical/psychological needs
- Regulation/anxiety

From Aspy, R., & Grossman, B. G. (2022). *The Ziggurat Model*. Dallas, TX: The Ziggurat Group www.zigguratgroup.com; used with permission.

Appendix B

INDIVIDUAL STRENGTHS AND SKILLS INVENTORY (ISSI)

Individual Strengths and Skills Inventory

Ruth Aspy, Ph.D., and Barry G. Grossman, Ph.D.

When designing an effective intervention plan, it is important to consider individual strengths. Please describe strengths in the following areas:

Social

Behavior, Interests, and Activities

Communication

Sensory

Cognitive

Motor

Emotional

Biological

Appendix C

GLOBAL INTERVENTION PLAN:
GUIDE TO ESTABLISHING PRIORITIES

Global Intervention Plan: Guide to Establishing Priorities

Ruth Aspy, Ph.D., and Barry G. Grossman, Ph.D.

Directions: Following completion of the UCC and ISSI, the next step is to identify UCC **areas** and **items** that will result in a *meaningful* Global Intervention Plan. Consideration of priorities and strengths for an individual facilitates selection of UCC areas and items. The following questions are provided as a guide.

Selecting UCC Areas

Vision
"Begin with the end in mind" – Stephen R. Covey

- What is the long- and short-term vision of/for the individual?
  Note that "long-term" and "short-term" may be defined differently in order to be meaningful.

⊙ Which UCC **areas** would have the greatest impact on achieving this vision?

Settings

- In what settings does the individual participate?

⊙ Which UCC **areas** have the greatest impact on the individual's ability to function in multiple settings?

Quality of Life

- What is most important to the individual? What provides a sense of well-being?
  Consider independence, relationships, play/leisure activities, safety, health, etc.

⊙ Which UCC **areas** have the greatest impact on the individual's quality of life?

Key UCC Areas

Based on your answers to the questions above, place an X next to the key UCC **areas**.

*Transfer to the **Areas of Concern** section of the Ziggurat Worksheet.*

☐ Social
☐ Restricted Patterns of Behavior Interests, and Activities
☐ Communication
☐ Sensory Differences

☐ Cognitive Differences
☐ Motor Differences
☐ Emotional Vulnerability
☐ Known Medical or Other Biological Factors

Selecting UCC Items

Key UCC Items

Select key UCC **items** for *each* of the UCC **areas** listed above. Choose items that are essential (necessary for progress) and developmentally appropriate. Emphasize items that are pivotal (building blocks for additional skills). Avoid selecting redundant items.

Write key item numbers and descriptions below. These items will be used to develop interventions, keeping strengths and skills (identified on the ISSI) in mind.

*Transfer items to the **Selected UCC Item** section of the Ziggurat Worksheet and develop interventions.*

\#

\#

\#

\#

\#

\#

\#

\#

Appendix D

SPECIFIC INTERVENTION PLAN:
GUIDE TO ESTABLISHING PRIORITIES

Specific Intervention Plan: Guide to Establishing Priorities

Ruth Aspy, Ph.D., and Barry G. Grossman, Ph.D.

INSTRUCTIONS: Use the ABC-I when designing an intervention to address specific behavioral concerns. Complete the questionnaire below. Transfer the information to the ABC-I form (using the numbers as a guide) and to the Ziggurat Worksheet as indicated. Once the information has been transferred to the Ziggurat Worksheet, develop interventions for each level of the Ziggurat and ensure that the intervention is complete (5 levels, 3 points, addresses underlying needs).

Behavior

What specific behavior is of greatest concern? _____

Transfer behavior to the top of the ABC-I ❶ and to the upper-left corner of the Ziggurat Worksheet.

Next to the 👁 icon, describe the behavior in observable, measurable terms.

👁   👁
👁   👁
👁   👁

Place observable, measurable behavior descriptions next to the 👁 icon on the ABC-I ❷ and on the Ziggurat Worksheet.

Antecedents

When and where does the behavior occur? List what is happening at the time or just before.

•   •   •

•   •   •

Transfer to the antecedents column of the ABC-I ❸

Consequences

List what usually happens after the behavior occurs.

•   •   •

•   •   •

Transfer to the consequences column of the ABC-I ❹

Underlying Characteristics

Review **ALL** the checked UCC items. Identify underlying characteristics that may be associated with the behaviors described on the ABC-I. *List the UCC item numbers and a brief description of the item on the bottom of the ABC-I ❺ and next to the # icons in the "Selected UCC Items" section on the Ziggurat Worksheet.*

Function

Behavior serves a purpose. Common functions include:
- Escape/avoidance
- Sensory stimulation
- Adult/peer attention
- Access to preferred activity
- Tangible items
- Other

What is the hypothesized function of the behavior? _____

ABC-I

Ruth Aspy, Ph.D., and Barry G. Grossman, Ph.D.

Antecedent(s) ⟶ **Behavior** ⟶ **Consequence(s)**

Specific Behaviors

Underlying Characteristics

From Aspy, R., & Grossman, B. G. (2022). The Ziggurat Model. Dallas, TX: The Ziggurat Group www.zigguratgroup.com; used with permission.

Appendix E

ZIGGURAT WORKSHEET

Ziggurat Worksheet

BEHAVIOR/AREAS OF CONCERN	FOR SPECIFIC INTERVENTION PLAN (Operationalized Behaviors) ② ② ②	SELECTED UCC ITEMS # # # # # # # #	CHECK ALL THAT APPLY		
			A	B	C
Sensory and Biological	Sensory and Biological Intervention:				
	Underlying Characteristics Addressed:				
Respectful Reinforcement	Reinforcement Intervention:				
	Underlying Characteristics Addressed:				
Structure & Visual/ Tactile Supports	Structure & Visual/Tactile Support Intervention:				
	Underlying Characteristics Addressed:				
Task Demands	Task Demand Intervention:				
	Underlying Characteristics Addressed:				
Skills to Teach	Skill Intervention:				
	Underlying Characteristics Addressed:				

From Aspy, R., & Grossman, B. G. (2022). The Ziggurat Model. Dallas, TX: The Ziggurat Group www.zigguratgroup.com; used with permission.

Appendix F

COMPREHENSIVE AUTISM PLANNING SYSTEM

Comprehensive Autism Planning System (CAPS)

Child/Student: _____

Time	Activity	Skills to Teach	Task Demands & Positive Environment and Structure & Visual/Tactile Supports	Repectful Reinforcement	Sensory & Biological	Communication/ Social Skills	Data Collection	Generalization Plan

From Henry, S. A., & Myles, B. S. (2007). *The Comprehensive Autism Planning System (CAPS) for Individuals with Asperger Syndrome, Autism, and Related Disabilities.* Shawnee Mission, KS: AAPC Publishing. Adapted and used with permission.

Appendix G

MODIFIED COMPREHENSIVE AUTISM PLANNING SYSTEM (M-CAPS)

Modified Comprehensive Autism Planning System (M-CAPS)

Child/Student: _____

Activity	Skills to Teach	Task Demands & Positive Environment and Structure & Visual/Tactile Supports	Respectful Reinforcement	Sensory & Biological	Communication/ Social Skills	Data Collection	Generalization
Independent Work							
Group Work							
Tests							
Lectures							
Homework							

From Henry, S. A., & Myles, B. S. (2007). *The Comprehensive Autism Planning System (CAPS) for Individuals with Asperger Syndrome, Autism, and Related Disabilities.* Shawnee Mission, KS: AAPC Publishing. Adapted and used with permission.

Appendix H

VOCATIONAL COMPREHENSIVE AUTISM PLANNING SYSTEM (V-CAPS)

Vocational Comprehensive Autism Planning System (V-CAPS)

Name: _____

Activity	Skills to Teach	Task Demands & Positive Environment and Structure & Visual/ Tactile Supports	Respectful Reinforcement	Sensory & Biological	Communication/ Social Skills	Data Collection	Generalization
Arrival at Work							
Work Activity							
Break							
Meetings							
Lunch							
Departure from Work							

From Myles, B. S., & Henry, S. A. (2008). Adapted and used with permission.

The Ziggurat Group

www.zigguratgroup.com